Civics *for* Today

Participation and Citizenship

Steven C. Wolfson

ASSISTANT PRINCIPAL
Supervision Social Studies (Retired)
Fort Hamilton High School
Brooklyn, New York

Second Revision

AMSCO SCHOOL PUBLICATIONS, INC.
315 Hudson Street
New York, N.Y. 10013

DEDICATION

To the most important people in my life, whose love and support make it all worthwhile: my wife, Raymonde; our children, Laurie and David, Lisa and Aryeh; and our grandchildren, Helene, Robert, Rebecca, Julia, and those yet to arrive.

REVIEWERS

Richard L. Caner
Monroe Middle School
Columbus, Ohio

Ivan Jeffrey Corbin
Social Studies Department Chair
South High School Urban Academy, Columbus, Ohio

Michelle Uzelac
Social Studies teacher in junior high schools
in Maryland and Florida

Cover/Text Design:
Delgado and Company, Inc.

Maps, Charts, Graphs, Cartoons:
Hadel Studio

Composition:
Northeastern Graphic, Inc.

Photo Research:
Photo Affairs, Inc.

Please visit our Web site at: *www.amscopub.com*

When ordering this book, please specify:
either **R 0380 P** *or* CIVICS FOR TODAY: PARTICIPATION AND CITIZENSHIP

ISBN: 978-1-56765-685-5 / NYC Item: 56765-685-4

CONTENTS

★ POWER OF ONE FEATURES

★ REALITY CHECK FEATURES

PREFACE

Being a citizen is easy and hard. One only needs to be born in a country to be a citizen of it. Or one can go through the naturalization process to become a citizen. But to be an active, concerned citizen requires participation in public life. "Participation" is a key word in the title of this text—*Civics for Today: Participation and Citizenship*—and in the narrative.

The content and organization of *Civics for Today* follows the guidelines set forth in *Civitas: A Framework for Civic Education* developed by the Center for Civic Education in collaboration with the Council for the Advancement of Citizenship and the National Council for the Social Studies.

The 16 chapters of *Civics for Today* are divided into four units. The narrative clearly explains why laws are necessary in a society, the philosophical background of the Constitution, how the political system operates, how the three branches of government at each level interact, why the Constitution is a living document, how Supreme Court decisions affect us all, how the free-enterprise system works, why taxes are necessary, how to be a wise participant in the economy, the role of business and labor in the economy, the rights and responsibilities of citizens, how active citizens affect public policy, and what goes into the making of foreign policy. Throughout, emphasis is placed on the importance of citizen involvement in public life. Voting and volunteering are stressed, and guidelines for how to do both are laid out.

The easy-to-read narrative explains concepts with examples familiar to today's students. The "Reality Check" features expand on key points in the narrative through real situations that organizations and individuals face on all levels.

The "Power of One" features introduce students to real individuals of the past and present who have made a difference in the nation or their communities by taking steps to address a need or problem.

Concepts are clarified and amplified by the original drawings, political cartoons, photos, charts, tables, diagrams, and maps. Key terms are shown in boldface and defined in context. They are also included in the Glossary at the end of the text. Other terms with which students might be unfamiliar are in italic.

The varied question program ensures that students will understand the concepts and ideas in the narrative and be able to apply their knowledge to real-life situations. The "Let's Think" section-end questions help students recall basic information and facts. The "Chapter Review" questions include "Matching, Multiple-Choice, Essay, A Challenge for You" (projects and extended activities), and a "Document-Based Question."

The "Chapter Focus" at the beginning of each chapter provides (in question form) the key concepts presented in the narrative. The "Chapter Summary" reviews these concepts.

In addition to the Glossary, the end-of-text material includes the Declaration of Independence, the Constitution, and a full Index.

All in all, *Civics for Today: Participation and Citizenship* is designed to help students develop an understanding of the operation of our government and the responsibilities of public life so that they can make decisions necessary to lead this nation throughout the 21st century and to keep our democracy strong.

STEVEN C. WOLFSON

UNIT 1

Life in Society

CHAPTER 1

The Nature of Law

★ CHAPTER FOCUS

 1. What purpose do laws serve in society?
 2. How did early civilizations contribute to the development of laws in the United States?
 3. Why is there a need for different types of laws?

Do you ever think about how many laws affect you each day? Just consider the period from the moment you wake up in the morning until you get to school. During even this short time span, hundreds of laws touch your life.

Your clock radio wakes you up in the morning. Did you realize that the time of day is set by law? (Laws determine when Daylight Saving Time starts and ends and where time zones begin and end.) The radio station you listen to is regulated by laws. Radio and television stations are granted licenses by the federal government. The procedure is established by law.

As you walk to school, you stop at a red light and cross at the crosswalk. Why? One obvious reason why you wait at the red light is that you are protecting yourself from being hit by a car. Laws regulate the traffic flow on city streets. As you wait for the light to change, you notice a litter basket on the corner. In most communities, it is illegal to litter the streets. A flashy, late-model car passes by. You dream about driving a car like that. Once again, there are laws! Laws tell us the age we must reach before we are allowed to drive. They also establish the test we must take before

we can get a driver's license. New cars have safety features such as seat belts and air bags. Laws call for putting these devices into vehicles.

As you continue your walk to school, you think about why you are going there. Of course, you need an education. You have friends there, but there is also a state law that requires you to go to school. When you enter the classroom, you meet your teacher. In most school districts, teachers, by law, must be licensed to teach. Look at how many laws have touched your life, and you have only just arrived at school!

Rules and regulations affect all parts of our lives. Some laws may seem to be annoying or unnecessary. But laws are needed because we live in a society with other people. Laws help us live our lives in a way that we can enjoy without interfering with the lives of others.

What Are Laws?

Laws are a set of rules made and enforced by society. They guide the way we behave. They rein-

3

Laws affect almost every part of your life.

force the difference between right and wrong by rewarding or punishing us. Laws also protect us from harm and organize our lives. They provide us with a uniform system of enforcing what society believes to be good behavior.

How Do Laws Guide Us?

When we are young, we learn the difference between right and wrong. Our families, our teachers, and our religious leaders show us the proper way to conduct ourselves. Respecting others and telling the truth are right behaviors. We are rewarded for these behaviors by being respected in turn and by feeling good about ourselves.

Lying and stealing are wrong behaviors. Lying can hurt others and get them or ourselves into trouble. If we steal, we are breaking a law. We are hurting someone else, and we are likely to be caught by authorities. Punishment for stealing is called a "formal" punishment. The legal system provides guidelines for what must be done to a person who is convicted of stealing.

When you break family rules, you are punished in an "informal" way. The rules and punishments are not part of the legal system. For example, one day you come home very late from a school function. Your parents wanted you to be home at five o'clock, and you walk into the house at seven. Your mother is angry, and you know you will be punished even though you feel you have a good excuse. Your parents punish you by not allowing you to attend the next school dance. You feel bad because you disobeyed a family rule

and, as a result, cannot do something you want to do. Your parents are underlining the importance of being punctual and informing them of your whereabouts. They care and you care.

Informal punishments can go a long way toward encouraging people to follow rules. Even a simple verbal reprimand or a sharp statement from a teacher or a friend can reinforce good behavior.

There are both formal and informal rewards for obeying the rules or conforming to society's expectations. Working hard and passing all your courses in high school leads to the formal ceremony of graduation and the granting of a diploma. The Stanley Cup in the professional hockey playoffs is a formal reward for winning a championship. Getting a raise from your employer is another example of formal recognition. Your boss is letting you know that you are doing a good job and following the rules of the company.

Informal rewards take many forms. One might be getting a "high five" from your teammates for sinking the winning points in a ball game. Another might be a hug from a parent for cleaning your room without being asked. In all of the examples mentioned, society has found a way to encourage us to follow rules, which help guide our behavior.

How Do Laws Organize Society?

Take a look at the nearly 200 nations in the world today. We see countries with very large populations and very small populations. We see a wide variety of cultures and governmental systems. At first glance, we might not notice much that they have in common. But, in actuality, all of the countries of the world have one basic thing in common: They have a system of laws to organize society.

Laws give shape to governments and help people function in a society in an orderly way. Because laws organize, they preserve those things that society considers to be important. Primarily, laws safeguard our rights. Americans consider the legal protection of their freedoms to be a major function of the body of laws we live under.

Laws provide us with specific services such as hospitals, police, education, and transportation. They also set up systems to protect people in case of an emergency. New York City immediately implemented its disaster plan when terrorists destroyed the World Trade Center on September 11, 2001. Read "Reality Check: Government Response to Hurricane Katrina" below to see how governments at the local, state, and national levels responded to a catastrophic emergency.

◀REALITY CHECK▶

Government Response to Hurricane Katrina

In late August 2005, Hurricane Katrina developed into a massive storm that threatened the Gulf Coast of the United States. New Orleans was in the most danger because much of it lies below sea level. On August 29, Katrina made landfall near New Orleans with winds reaching 140 miles per hour. Eighty percent of the city was flooded. More than 1,500 people in Louisiana lost their lives. Across the region, the property damage caused by the storm came to at least $125 billion. And about a million people lost their homes and had to move away.

Governments in the United States at the local, state, and national levels are responsible for dealing with human-made and natural disasters. Protecting people and property is a major function of government. Sometimes, though, the best of plans and the best of intentions do not work out. Authorities cannot cope with such an emergency. The challenge of the aftermath of Katrina caused a breakdown in both communication and coordination among various agencies at all levels of government.

State Level. On August 26, as the storm approached, Governor Kathleen Blanco of Louisiana declared a state of emergency. This action mobilized many state and local agencies in an effort to protect life and property from the damage the storm might inflict. The

governor claimed control of the National Guard's efforts in the emergency, but the federal government overruled her. The National Guard would serve under federal control.

Local Level. Taking extraordinary action, Mayor Ray Nagin of New Orleans ordered the mandatory evacuation of the entire city. Tens of thousands of people fled, mostly by automobile. Unfortunately, the city did not have the means to move everybody. The public transportation system was disabled by the storm. Gas stations ran out of fuel. To shelter the thousands left behind, the huge sports Superdome and Convention Center was opened up. Some nursing home residents could not be moved. A large number of people ignored the evacuation order or were unable to leave. They stayed in or on top of their homes to ride out the storm. In some cases, they died as the floodwaters rose. Looting broke out. Police officers were not always able to keep law and order, and some quit in frustration.

Federal Level. The National Hurricane Center and the National Weather Service had provided accurate forecasts of the path of the storm several days before it reached New Orleans. Over the years, the Army Corps of Engineers had built an intricate system of levees to prevent flooding in the city. Unfortunately, the design of the levee system had flaws. As a result, water came pouring over the walls in more than 50 places.

The Coast Guard responded to the emergency quickly and efficiently. It helped rescue more than 33,000 of the 60,000 people who were stranded in New Orleans. Some 58,000 National Guard members from all 50 states were sent to the Gulf Coast to help.

The Department of Homeland Security took over coordination of rescue and relief for the federal government. Under it, the Federal Emergency Management Agency (FEMA) provided housing assistance to tens of thousands of evacuees. Some 12,000 people were put up in hotels in the region. This was meant to be for a short period, but for some the stay lasted many months. The federal government also provided house trailers for evacuees. Many of the trailers, though, were found to contain chemicals that emitted toxic fumes. Food and water were not made available in a timely way. FEMA's mishandling of the crisis came under such harsh criticism that its administrator, Michael Brown, eventually resigned.

Nongovernmental Help. All sorts of charities and religious organizations responded to pleas for help. The largest group, the Red Cross, appealed to the American public for funds. It set up shelters for evacuees to stay in. It provided comfort kits and cleanup kits. And it served meals to both victims and rescue workers. Volunteers from across the country came to the region to help the various nongovernmental groups give out supplies, provide counseling, and rebuild homes.

1. Which level or levels of government, if any, do you think should be responsible for dealing with emergencies? Explain your answer.
2. What problems did the people of New Orleans encounter during and after the time Hurricane Katrina hit the city in 2005?
3. Which problem or problems could have been avoided? Explain your answer.
4. Write a letter to a newspaper describing what you think should be done to avoid problems in your community if a natural or human-made disaster occurs.

Laws organize society as well as protect people. It would not be possible to choose a mayor, governor, or president without procedures established by law. If we did not have laws, how could we be sure that the planes we fly are safe? How could we pave our roads, build bridges, or create parks? Laws organize society to provide people with important services and safeguards that they as individuals cannot provide for themselves. We form governments to carry out the functions that benefit communities, states, and the nation as a whole. The organization of society is one of the important functions of government.

Laws Protect Civil Liberties

Laws protect us in yet another way. They safeguard our rights. The national government, through the Constitution, is prevented from denying us our rights. The Bill of Rights, in particular, spells out the rights the government cannot take away. We can speak freely and practice our religions without having to fear government interference. Newspapers can print articles that are critical of government officials. These are just a few of the rights protected by law. Americans consider the protection of their rights to be a major function of the body of laws they live under.

Let's Think

1. Define the term "law" and explain its importance.
2. What are the major functions of law?
3. How do laws affect the way we live our daily lives?

Sources of Laws

Where do laws come from? The moment individuals decided to live with other people, laws came into play. Think about this for a minute. If you are a person living alone, you can do almost anything you want. Your actions do not affect others. However, we are social beings. We like to talk to each other, share our experiences, and work with one another. As long as humans have existed, they have chosen to live in groups. We call these groups **society**.

Developing Rules

Groups developed rules and regulations to help guide the behavior of the group members. One reason was to protect people, to keep them from harm. For instance, it is against the law to drive your automobile down a sidewalk because you might injure someone walking there.

Another reason that groups have rules is to make sure that people can enjoy life within reasonable boundaries. When you live in a society, you agree to limit some of your freedoms. If you live all by yourself away from other humans and decide to play your favorite CD at top volume at 2 A.M., you can do it. However, once you live near people in a community, you would be prevented from blasting it. Other people would be unable to sleep. You would be disturbing the peace and could be arrested.

We are lucky here in the United States. We are usually free to do whatever we want as long as we do not cause harm to another person or to another person's property.

Social Contract

The idea that people are willing to give up some of their freedoms in exchange for living in society was outlined by a man named Jean-Jacques Rousseau. He lived in France in the 1700s. Rousseau declared that when people live alone in a state of nature, they are free to do whatever they want. There are no restrictions. But when people decide to live with others, they give up their right to do anything they want. They now must show consideration for other people.

Rousseau said that when people decide to live together, they enter into an agreement. This agreement is with society (the people they live with). It states that in exchange for giving up total freedom to do whatever they want, society will help them and give them protection. The agreement Rousseau wrote about is called the **social contract**.

This social contract is not an agreement between government and the people. Rousseau thought of it, instead, as an agreement among people. People by their nature, he believed, are basically good and considerate. This philosophy can best be understood by a simple question he often asked, "What wisdom can you find that is greater than kindness?"

This kindness would allow people to agree that they abide by what he called the **general will**. We might think of the general will as those rules that people agree to live by. Rousseau goes

Living in a community involves some restrictions on extreme behavior.

on to explain that if a person does not wish to submit to the general will, that person must be forced to do so. Therefore, society's will prevails.

Many people of his time saw Rousseau's ideas as being extreme. But those who came to believe in democratic ideas found much to admire in Rousseau's writings. Particularly inspiring is the idea that people must respect one another in order to be able to live together in society.

Let's Think

1. Define the term "society."
2. Give two major reasons for developing rules.
3. Briefly explain what Rousseau meant by "social contract" and "general will."

How Do Written Laws Ensure Fairness?

If laws are to be effective, they must be applied with regularity and equality in all parts of a nation and to all levels of society. Laws must be understandable to all and have the same meaning for all.

To ensure that these goals are achieved, it is necessary to create a body of written laws. Some of the early sets of written laws that have influenced our laws came from the Babylonian Empire, the Roman Empire, and England.

The Influence of Religion

Laws are derived from custom and usage. Many laws that have evolved in the United States are based on ideas from religions such as Judaism and Christianity. Religious teachings provide us with moral standards. Laws generally develop from an understanding of what is right and wrong. One source of many laws is the Ten Commandments, which come from the Torah, or Old Testament of the Bible. As you may know, they include such important ideas as not taking another person's life and not stealing or lying.

Another section of the Old Testament also re-

inforces the idea of justice: "You shall do no injustice in judgment, you shall not be partial to the poor or defer to the great, but in righteousness shall you judge your neighbor." This passage emphasizes the importance of judging everyone equally. Whether a person on trial is rich and famous or poor and unknown should not matter. Each person should be judged by the merits of the case against him or her.

Additional ideas of what is right and wrong are found in the New Testament of the Bible. In the Book of Matthew, we read, "Blessed are the merciful, for they shall obtain mercy." This statement urges us to believe that mercy is important and that special circumstances should be considered before judging the actions of a person.

Religious teachings provide us with standards of proper behavior. The development of laws in the United States has been strongly influenced by Judaism and Christianity. But many similar principles of proper behavior can be found in other religions, such as Islam and Buddhism.

Hammurabi's Code

Hammurabi ruled the Babylonian Empire from 1792 to 1750 B.C. During this time, he compiled one of the earliest *legal codes*, collections of written laws. Previously, officials had kept laws in their memories. Each person might remember the law a little differently. The Code of Hammurabi was unique because it was written. As a result, the Babylonian government could apply the same laws throughout the empire. Anyone who could read could know what the laws were.

Many of the laws seem harsh to us today. Scholars say that the laws followed the philosophy of "An Eye for an Eye and a Tooth for a Tooth." (If you do something to someone, that same thing can be done to you in return as punishment.)

Here are some ideas set forth in this ancient code of laws:

If a man commits a robbery and is captured, he will be put to death.

If a son strikes his father, his hands shall be hewn off.

Carving on an ancient pillar of black stone showing Hammurabi (on the right) and the sun god. Hammurabi's Code of laws is written in cuneiform below the figures.

If a man destroys the eye of another man, they shall destroy his eye.

If a man destroys the eye of a freeman or breaks the bone of a man's slave, he shall pay one mina of silver. (Thought to be about $100 in U.S. currency today.)

If a man strikes another man . . . he shall pay one mina of silver.

If a man would put away his wife who has not borne him children, he shall give her money to the amount of her marriage settlement and he shall make good to her the dowry which she brought from her father's house, and then he may put her away.

As you can see, most of the punishments are physical. They call for parts of the body to be cut off or for a person to be put to death. The severity of the punishment depended on the social class to which a person belonged. For example, if a slave committed an assault, he or she would be put to death, while a free person might only lose a limb. The laws were strictly enforced by judges.

Public officials took their duties seriously. They were expected to arrest thieves and other lawbreakers. If they failed in their duties, these officials were personally obligated to replace any missing property. If murderers were not caught, the responsible official paid a fine to the relatives of the victim.

Even though these early laws were harsh, they were applied to everyone throughout the empire. People knew what the consequences of their actions would be if they broke the law.

Roman Law

A later civilization, the Roman, is credited with giving the Western world many ideas about laws. These ideas came from the sets of laws called the Twelve Tables and the Justinian Code.

The Twelve Tables

The Twelve Tables were put together in 451 and 450 B.C. Laws were carved onto 12 stone tablets and set up in the Forum in Rome, the empire's capital city. (The Forum was the central part of the city where many important government buildings were located.) Anyone could read them. Schoolboys had to memorize the laws. (Girls didn't go to school.) The Twelve Tables set forth legal procedures; regulations concerning property ownership, building codes, and marriage; and punishments for crimes.

Although penalties could be harsh, they were not as severe as in Hammurabi's Code. A person's private property was carefully protected. In fact, some crimes against a person's property were considered to be more serious than crimes of violence! The Twelve Tables stressed two principles. They are the protection of society—maintaining order—and the right of a person to protect his or her property.

The death penalty was called for in only a limited number of situations. The laws in the Twelve Tables strictly separated the rights of the various social and economic classes. But, like Hammurabi's Code, the Twelve Tables tried to protect all citizens from being unjustly punished.

The Justinian Code

In A.D. 528, Emperor Justinian of the Byzantine (Eastern Roman) Empire ordered officials to gather together all evidence of Roman law that they could find. This action preserved much of the great Roman legal heritage and made it possible for people who lived later to learn from it. The collection of laws that Justinian ordered to be created has come to be known as the "Justinian Code."

The word "justice" comes from the Latin term *jus*. It stands for what is correct and fair. *Justice* means that a person who is convicted of a crime will receive a proper punishment. One way of expressing this idea is to say, "let the punishment fit the crime." Sometimes when a person commits a crime, there are special circumstances surrounding the act. If so, the law may soften the punishment. When the law can be reasonable and flexible in dealing with people who are convicted of crimes, the public generally accepts the idea that the law is fair and, therefore, just. The Justinian Code reflects these ideas.

The following are several provisions of the Justinian Code:

Any privilege that is not given to the defendant [accused person] should not be given to the plaintiff [person bringing a lawsuit]. . . .

No one must suffer a penalty for what he thinks.

When a court decides that a man must pay a fine as a penalty, it should not take away all of his possessions. It should be careful that the convicted man is not reduced to complete poverty and want. . . .

[It is] better for the crime of a guilty person to go unpunished than for an innocent person to be convicted. . . .

In the case of a major offense, it makes a difference if the crime was committed accidentally or on purpose. Those who accidentally commit a crime should be moderately punished. Those who purposely commit a crime should be dealt with more severely.

A son should not be blamed for the actions of his father. Everyone must be judged for his own actions.

When a punishment is given by the court, the age and inexperience of the guilty party must be taken into account.

The person who accuses someone must prove that his charge is true.

The ideas in these laws are almost 1,500 years old. Yet they are still very much alive. The justice system in the United States today contains many ideas that come from the Justinian Code.

Let's Think

1. What was the importance of Hammurabi's Code, the Twelve Tables, and the Justinian Code?
2. What do you think is meant by the expression "an eye for an eye and a tooth for a tooth"?
3. Many people believe that the penalties outlined by Hammurabi's Code were too harsh. How do they compare with the punishments in the Justinian Code and in U.S. law?
4. Justinian uses *jus* as the idea of what is good and fair. How does this apply to our idea of justice?

The Influence of English Law

The influence of these earlier civilizations played an important role in the development of laws in other societies. The idea of having written codes of law spread throughout Europe as nations developed.

One nation that borrowed ideas from these early civilizations and that had a major impact on the development of laws in the United States was England. The United States was a colony of England and has been greatly influenced by English ideas about government and law.

Common Law

A major part of our legal system is the **common law**. This is the body of law based on common practices in a community and on past decisions by judges. Common law originated in England. It dates back at least to the Norman Conquest of England in 1066. King Henry II, who ruled England from 1154 to 1189, firmly established the practice of common law.

At that time, judges traveled throughout England to administer justice. Sometimes the judges found that there were few if any regulations or written laws to help them decide specific problems. As a result, they made rulings that might be considered unique. Yet, the decisions were generally based on local practices and past cases. Eventually, the decisions were written down and served as guides, or precedents, for future cases. These rulings became part of the body of laws accepted by the government and the people—the common law.

Common law has been characterized as law based on common sense and logic. Sir Edward Coke, an English legal scholar, in describing common law, wrote in 1628, "Reason is the life of law; nay, the common law is nothing else but reason."

Statutory law is different from common law. Statutory law is written law that is often put together in codes, such as Hammurabi's Code and the Justinian Code. Today, statutory laws are usually passed by a legislature, or lawmaking body. Common law is judge-made law—written decisions of cases that judges have decided. These decisions often carry the same importance as statutory laws. In the United States, we have both common law and statutory law.

Written Laws in England

English laws have greatly influenced the legal system of the United States. One of the most influential is the *Magna Carta* (Great Charter) signed in 1215. This document set forth several major legal ideas. A key one was the right to a jury trial—to be judged in court by a group of one's peers, or equals. It also established the idea that the ruler is not above the law and must take into consideration the wishes of the people.

Another English law established the principle that a person who is accused of a crime must be formally charged. At times in England, people were arrested and imprisoned without being formally charged before a judge. Occasionally, a

A drawing of King John reluctantly signing the Magna Carta, watched by nobles and members of the clergy.

trial was not held, and the person stayed in jail indefinitely. This practice ended with the passage of the **Habeas Corpus** Act in 1679. *Habeas corpus* is a Latin phrase meaning "you have the body." The term refers to the "body," or person, who is in jail. A judge can order the jailer to bring the person before the court immediately. The accused is then charged or let go.

A third major English contribution to law was the *English Bill of Rights* of 1689. Many provisions of this document promoted democratic ideas in England. It limited the power of the monarch and extended important **civil liberties** to the people. Civil liberties are individual rights such as the right to vote, freedom of speech, and freedom of the press.

The English Bill of Rights states: "That the election of members of Parliament [lawmaking body of England] ought to be free; That freedom of speech and debates or proceedings in Parliament ought not be . . . questioned in any court or place out of Parliament; That excessive bail ought not to be required, nor excessive fines imposed nor cruel and unusual punishment inflicted." Each of these ideas protects some aspect of what people consider to be important freedoms. Similar protections eventually became part of our own Bill of Rights.

In the United States, we enjoy many freedoms based on ideas from England. As you recall, most of the earliest settlers of what became the United States were from England. They brought their ideas about law, government, and the proper way of life with them. Their feelings about English ways influenced the way of life they created here.

Let's Think

1. What are common law and statutory law? Explain the differences between the two.
2. How did common law develop in England?
3. How did each of the following play an important role in the development of law in both England and the United States: Magna Carta, Habeas Corpus Act, English Bill of Rights?
4. What is meant by the term "civil liberties"? Why are they important?

Types of Law

Laws are commonly grouped into two categories. The first is **civil law**. It concerns disputes between individuals and between individuals and the government. This category makes up the largest body of laws in the United States. The second category is **criminal law**. This set of laws relates to offenses against public order. It mainly provides for punishments for specific actions.

Civil Law

Civil laws help us resolve problems that may exist among people. When people live together, disputes occur. These disputes are sometimes difficult to settle. To resolve the issue, the two parties in a dispute may find it necessary to seek the assistance of the legal community. Often this means relying on the court system to provide a solution.

Civil law is the group of laws that affects many different parts of daily life. Business agreements between different parties, contract law, is part of civil law. If a person is wronged or injured by another, civil law helps decide how to correct

the problem. Even if people are covered by insurance policies, civil law regulates the settlements given to the parties in the dispute.

You purchase a state-of-the-art computer that comes with a 60-day limited warranty against defects in parts. The machine performs well and meets your expectations. Then, after you have had it for 80 days, it breaks down. You take it to the store where you bought it. The manager says that he can't do anything because the warranty period is over. The store is not responsible. He suggests that you call the manufacturer. The manufacturer also tells you that it cannot do anything because the warranty period is over. You will have to pay $750 for the needed repairs. You argue that computers should last years and that parts certainly should not break down after being used for only 80 days. The manufacturer still refuses to do anything for you. You believe that you have been wronged.

Under these circumstances, you have a right to go to court and file a *lawsuit* against the manufacturer. If the case goes to trial, a jury will hear the evidence and make a decision. The decision will attempt to resolve the problem. A law has not been broken, but there is a genuine difference of opinion. This is the kind of case that comes under civil law. The state government provides civil courts to referee such disputes.

If people go to court, the decision of the court is binding on both parties. If you lose a dispute, generally you must accept the outcome and move on. The procedure used to settle these issues is the trial.

Criminal Law

When someone commits a crime, criminal law comes into play. The police will investigate and arrest the person who is suspected of committing the crime. That person is advised by the police of his or her rights.

The accused will move through the criminal justice system. To better understand this, let us take the case of Joe. Joe is arrested for robbing a local convenience store. At the time of the arrest, the police follow the law and inform him of his rights. Among these rights is the right to an attorney to give the accused advice. The authorities

P O W E R *of* ★ N E

King Henry II of England

From going to the movies or watching television, you may be familiar with Richard I, the Lion Hearted, and his brother John. Both were kings of England—first Richard and then John. But few people have the name of their father at the tip of the tongue.

Their father, King Henry II, is considered to be one of England's greatest kings. He ruled from 1154 until his death in 1189. When Henry came to the throne, he found the English legal system in a state of disrepair. The administration of justice was left in the hands of local authorities and was far from uniform throughout the nation. In reality, there were three different courts in existence at the same time. These courts sometimes claimed authority over the same legal disputes or criminal issues, which caused confusion.

Being a wise individual, Henry saw as one of his major tasks the unification of this system. He wanted it to be administered more efficiently. In 1166, in the Assize (edict) of Clarendon, Henry set forth the fundamental parts of what was to become the new legal system of the nation.

One of the provisions promoted the use of a jury in trials. The assize called for justices to travel around the countryside to get reports from the local sheriffs and try cases. The local courts continued to decide local matters. When the royal justices came to a community to do their work, the king ordered members of the clergy, the local lords, and others to be in attendance. In addition to changing the court system, the new policy helped to unify all the people under one king and one central authority.

Eventually, Henry saw the need to create three distinct courts. Each would have the authority to handle certain types of cases. The first court was Common Pleas. It tried civil cases. The second court was called the Exchequer. It handled tax problems. The third court, the King's Bench, was in charge of handling criminal cases.

A centerpiece of Henry's reforms was the introduction of a jury system. Although different from ours, it did pave the way for our own. It all started with the grand jury, which pointed out cases that should be tried by a king's justice. This jury protected the person who was the probable victim. Sometimes the victim could be frightened into remaining quiet and not bringing charges against the accused wrongdoer. The 12 men on a grand jury decided if the accused should be held for trial.

Before the jury system became common, the innocence or guilt of an accused person was determined by an ordeal. For instance, the person might be thrown into a body of water. If he or she floated, guilt would be indicated. If the person sank, he or she would be declared innocent. The jury system was a far kinder and fairer way of judging.

An important contribution of Henry's reign was the development of common law. As judges traveled from area to area, they based their decisions on decisions by other judges in previous cases. This is called the case system. Eventually, the cases were gathered into books that other judges could use as references.

Through governmental and legal reforms, Henry II left England a better, more organized nation than it was before. His justice system continues to influence our courts today.

1. What reforms did Henry make in the legal system of England?
2. How did the reforms affect the monarchy?
3. What was the role of the traveling justices?
4. What role did the grand jury have in the time of Henry II?

TYPES OF LAW

Civil Law	Criminal Law
Sets procedures to conduct business	Sets procedures of arrest
Settles disputes	Sets procedures for criminal trials
Establishes court procedure to settle disputes	Sets procedure for punishing lawbreakers

fingerprint Joe. Within a short period of time, he faces a judge with his lawyer and is informed of the charge against him. He enters a plea. If Joe pleads innocent, the judge will set a trial date and possibly the amount of bail required.

Bail is an amount of money that a person who is accused of a crime may present to the court. If the bail is given to the court, Joe is allowed to go home. If he fails to appear for any hearings before trial or for the trial itself, he will forfeit, give up, the bail. He will then be arrested again and held in jail until after the trial. Bail is designed to guarantee that a person accused of a crime will appear for trial.

Eventually, the accused will go to trial. In the trial, the innocence or guilt of the person is determined, usually by a jury. If the person is convicted, he or she may be punished by being sent to prison. Most criminal courts are created and regulated by the states. Some cases are tried in federal courts.

Let's Think

1. What is criminal law? Civil law?
2. What role does the court play in a civil trial?
3. What role does the court play in a criminal trial?

Chapter Summary

Laws are rules made and enforced by society. People accept them as a way to organize their lives and their associations with others. Laws serve several functions. They guide the way we behave and remind us of what is right and wrong. They reinforce what society believes is proper conduct.

Laws also organize society so that people can live together without "stepping on each other's toes." The chief organizer of this function is government.

Protection is another function of law. Laws make sure our freedoms are not taken away from us.

Major ideas about how people should live with each other in society were outlined by Jean-Jacques Rousseau, a French writer of the 1700s. He believed that people were basically good and could learn to live with one another in harmony. In exchange for total freedom, they entered into a social contract to gain help and protection from society. He also stated that when people decided to live together, they had to obey what he called the "general will" of the people.

Sources of fundamental law in the Western world are the teachings of Judaism and Christianity, the Code of Hammurabi, the Roman Twelve Tables, and the Justinian Code. These codes, in particular, tried to establish a standard system of fair punishment.

Besides written law, which we call statutory law, there is a large body of laws known as common law. Common law is judge-made law. It is based on cases that judges have decided over the years. Judges read the decisions in these earlier cases and use them to make decisions in similar cases.

Common law came to us from England, as did a number of other legal ideas. The Magna Carta helped establish the right to a trial by jury and the idea that a ruler is not above the law. The Habeas Corpus Act put forth the idea that a person must be told of the charges against him or her within a reasonable amount of time after being arrested. The English Bill of Rights limited the power of the monarch and protected certain civil liberties.

Laws are normally grouped into two categories: civil and criminal. Civil law concerns property rights and contract agreements. Criminal law concerns wrongdoing against another person, such as robbery or murder.

★ CHAPTER REVIEW ★

A. Matching
Match each term in Column A with the correct definition in Column B.

Column A
1. *habeas corpus*
2. Henry II
3. Hammurabi
4. Rousseau
5. Justinian
6. *jus*
7. statutory law
8. bail
9. common law
10. general will

Column B
a. written law, often in codes
b. a sum of money to ensure a person's appearance at a trial
c. judge-made law
d. ruler who reformed England's legal system
e. person who developed the idea of the social contract
f. ruler who developed one of the earliest written sets of laws
g. a Latin term meaning what is correct and fair
h. Roman emperor who established a uniform system of laws
i. rules people agree to live by
j. Latin for "you have the body"

B. Multiple Choice
Select the statement or word that most correctly answers the question or completes the statement.

1. The rules of society that regulate the way we behave are called (a) punishments (b) laws (c) plans (d) commandments.

2. One of the earliest collections of written laws is (a) Hammurabi's Code (b) Common Law (c) English Bill of Rights (d) Habeas Corpus Act.

3. The early civilization that gave the Western world many ideas about laws is (a) the English (b) the United States (c) the Roman Empire (d) the French.

4. Disputes of a non-criminal nature are often settled with the help of (a) criminal law (b) social contract (c) civil law (d) Magna Carta.

5. Two parties make a business arrangement and sign a written agreement. This is called (a) civil law (b) contract law (c) criminal law (d) trial law.

6. The idea that laws must be fair comes from the word (a) justice (b) penalty (c) bail (d) contract.

7. The idea that people agree to behave in a certain way when they decide to live with other people comes from the (a) Magna Carta (b) Bill of Rights (c) Justinian Code (d) social contract.

8. Which of the following is NOT a function of law? (a) provide protection (b) guide behavior (c) organize society (d) give knowledge.

9. One source of the civil liberties the United States adapted from another society is (a) Rousseau's social contract (b) the English Bill of Rights (c) Hammurabi's Code (d) the Justinian Code.

10. An early English document that contributed to the development of the jury trial was the (a) Twelve Tables (b) Ten Commandments (c) Habeas Corpus Act (d) Magna Carta.

C. Essay
Write a paragraph about *one* of the following:

1. The difference between criminal and civil law.

2. Why laws are important to people living in society.

3. The contributions of early codes of law to American law.

4. How laws touch our everyday life.

D. A Challenge for You

1. Interview the manager of a fast-food restaurant, a pizza parlor, the manager of any other business, or the principal of your school to find out what laws affect the operation of the business or school. Create a series of questions before the interview to help you to conduct the interview in an organized way. Report back to the class or write an article about the interview for publication in your school newspaper.

2. The chapter explains that we in the United States derive our laws from many sources. Select one of the sources. Write a letter to your best friend explaining why you believe the one you selected is the one that has contributed the most to our system of laws.

3. Interview your parents or other adults to find out whether they think the legal system works for the average person. Before the interview, make a list of five important questions you want to ask them about this topic. Report your findings to the class.

4. Draw a cartoon or a series of cartoons to explain the differences between civil and criminal law. Give the cartoon a title. Ask the teacher to post the best ones on the bulletin board. Or submit the best ones to the school newspaper for publication.

5. Create a newspaper that will tell the story of the contributions other societies have made to the development of the U.S. system of laws. In the paper, you could have news articles, opinion pieces, cartoons, charts, and graphs. Explore Internet sources to find background information to put into your articles.

Document-Based Question

State the main idea expressed in *each* of the following documents. Then use information in the documents and your own knowledge to write an essay explaining how these documents contributed to the ideas about law and justice in the United States.

The Magna Carta, 1215

12. No scutage [military tax] or aid [feudal tax on nobles] shall be imposed in our kingdom unless by common counsel [consent of nobles] of our kingdom. . . .

21. Earls and barons shall not be amerced [fined] except by their peers [equals], and only according to the degree of the offense.

38. No bailiff shall in future . . . put anyone to trial upon his own bare word, without reliable witnesses produced for this purpose.

The Habeas Corpus Act, 1679

[W]hereas . . . many of the king's subjects have been long detained in prison in such cases where by law they are bailable [could be released pending trial] . . . be it enacted that whenever any person shall bring any habeas corpus . . . unto any sheriff . . . jailor, minister, or other person . . . the said officer . . . shall within three days . . . bring or cause to [be] brought the body of the party so committed or restrained . . . before the lord chancellor . . . or the judges or barons . . . and shall . . . then certify the true causes of the imprisonment. . . .
And if any person or persons committed as aforesaid . . . shall not be indicted [charged with a crime] . . . the judges . . . are hereby required upon motion in open court . . . to set at liberty the prisoner upon bail. . . . And if any person shall not be indicted . . . after his commitment . . . he shall be discharged from his imprisonment.

The Many Forms of Government

 1. What are the major unlimited and limited forms of government?

 2. What are the important principles of a democratic government?

 3. How do the U.S. Constitution and federalism support democratic principles?

People in communities all over the United States have many ideas about how to make their neighborhoods nice places in which to live. Some might like a new park. Some might believe that their community is growing so fast that it will need a new high school in a few years. Perhaps a local bridge is old and needs replacement. We do not expect the local grocery store owner to build a high school. Nor do we think that the owner of a local automobile dealership should have to build a new bridge. People look to governments to do those things that they cannot do for themselves and to provide a variety of services. Fighting fires, policing the streets, and making sure that restaurants maintain health standards are services governments perform.

How are governments organized to accomplish what is expected of them? Who makes the decisions in a government? Are the people allowed to have a say in something like planning a new park or paying for a new bridge? The answers to these questions show that there are many different kinds of governments.

Unlimited Governments

Some countries have governments that do not follow any law that places limits on the behavior of the rulers. When this situation exists in a country, it is said to have an **unlimited government**. There is no one or no mechanism in place in the country to say "Stop! This is wrong!" The government's power is limitless. Such governments include dictatorships as well as some forms of monarchies. Such governments are also known as **authoritarian governments**.

Since they are unlimited in their authority, authoritarian governments do not consider the needs of the people. They follow their own desires without worrying about violating the freedoms of the individual or protecting civil liberties.

Monarchies

A **monarchy** is a government headed by one person—the king or queen (the monarch). This person is thought to be of royal birth and is the ruler for all of his or her life. The authority of the ruling monarch is generally inherited. It is handed down from father to son or to the nearest living relative. (Only in rare cases did daughters inherit the throne.) The pharaohs of Ancient Egypt are an example of an early form of monarchy. China, which has one of the oldest continuous civilizations in the world, was dominated by monarchs, called emperors, until 1912.

In the Western world, the notion that the king was an all-powerful ruler lasted until the 1700s. **Absolute monarchs** controlled European nations such as France, Spain, England, and Russia in the 1500s and 1600s.

The absolute monarchies were highly centralized and did not pay attention to the wishes or ideas of their subjects. Monarchs ruled by decree, creating laws by their verbal or written commands. They acted as unlimited governments because there was no one to check their powers. Through their trusted assistants, monarchs controlled law enforcement, tax collection, local laws, and foreign policy. Those who benefited from supporting the king enforced the monarch's policies. For their loyalty, they were given special privileges, large amounts of land, and royal titles.

Many monarchs claimed that they were given their authority to rule by God. This justification of a monarch's authority was known as the **divine right theory**. Those who accepted this theory rejected any claim by the people that they had the right to remove monarchs who were bad rulers. Declaring that a ruler's power came from a divine source had a long tradition. The Chinese emperors claimed their authority from what was known by them as the "mandate from heaven." Indeed, some emperors of the Roman Empire even had themselves declared gods.

Dictatorships

Another type of one-person rule is a **dictatorship**. It is an unlimited government because there are no curbs to prevent it from taking any action it desires. Dictators rule by edict—personal commands that ignore any action by elected officials.

The power modern dictators exercise is called **totalitarian,** or absolute. A dictator attempts to control all aspects of the lives of the people. The press and the educational system are heavily regulated. People are not free to criticize the government. Those who oppose government policies are arrested, are usually imprisoned, and may be killed. This system uses terror as a way to maintain its power. Dictators destroy human freedom by using secret police to spy on their citizens. The philosophy of a dictatorship is that the people exist to serve the state. The state does not exist to serve the people.

Dictatorships seldom provide for an orderly way to transfer power when the leader dies. Usually, the leadership is changed when the leader is killed (assassinated) or when the people revolt.

During the 1920s and 1930s, dictatorships emerged in Italy, Germany, and the Soviet Union. As a result of World War I, hard economic times had come to these nations, and the people looked for strong leadership to turn things around. History has shown that they looked to the wrong people for help. Two of the worst dictators ever to exist were Joseph Stalin in the Soviet Union and Adolf Hitler in Germany.

Stalin ruled the Soviet Union from 1924 until 1953. He eliminated all opposition within his own Communist Party. Millions of people who opposed his economic and agricultural policies were killed, and many others were sent to prison. Stalin indoctrinated people with the idea that they owed allegiance only to him. Loyalty to the leader was the same as loyalty to their country, the Soviet Union. Stalin alone, his followers believed, could make the Soviet Union great.

Hitler came to power in 1933 as a Nazi (National Socialist). Besides starting aggression that led to World War II, he initiated a policy known as the Holocaust. It called for the extermination of Jews in particular and others he deemed unworthy of living in the German Empire. Tens of millions of people died as a result of his actions.

In 2003, we saw the end of another dictatorship when Saddam Hussein of Iraq was removed by a coalition of forces led by the United States.

Oligarchy

Still another form of unlimited government is the **oligarchy**. An oligarchy is a government in

Who Makes the Decisions?

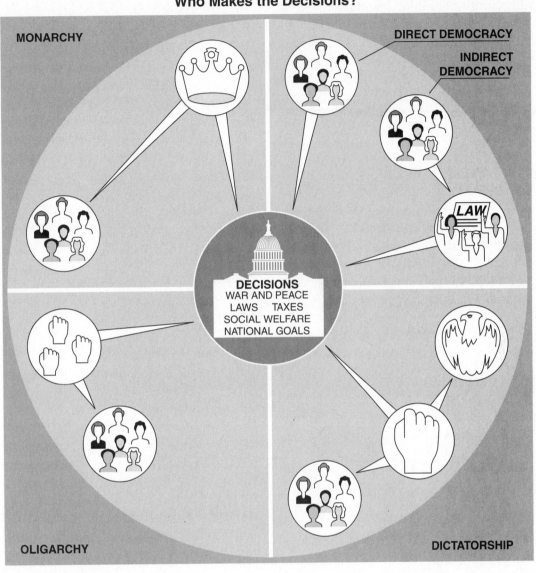

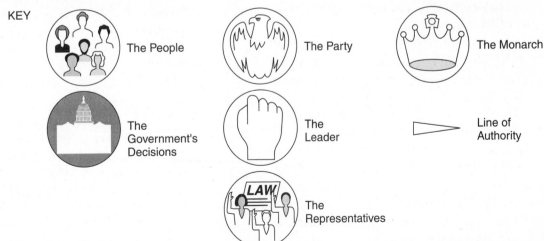

which a small group of people make the decisions and control the nation. The makeup of an oligarchy varies. In some places, the rulers are a small group of military officers. In other places, the rulers could be a group of wealthy citizens. From the late 1940s until the 1990s, the nations of Eastern Europe were each ruled by a small group of leaders from the Communist Party. These governments were oligarchies.

Let's Think

1. What is unlimited government?
2. How does an absolute monarchy operate?
3. How does a totalitarian dictatorship operate?
4. What is an oligarchy? How is an oligarchy different from a dictatorship?

Limited Governments

In contrast to unlimited governments, **limited governments** protect individual rights and abide by the laws of the land. They agree to follow the plan of government established by the people and to work to benefit the public good. Gaining power is not the principal aim (as it is in unlimited governments).

Under limited government systems, such as that in the United States, the rules and plan of government are generally stated in a **constitution**. This document is considered to be the highest law of the land. No one, not even a high government official, is permitted to ignore the rules established by the constitution. As U.S. Supreme Court Justice Louis Brandeis wrote in 1928, "Decency, security and liberty alike demand that government officials shall be subjected to the same rules of conduct that are commands to the citizen. In a government of laws, existence of the government will be imperiled if it fails to observe the law scrupulously."

The British system is somewhat different and is not based on a single, written constitution. Instead, it operates under what is called an **unwritten constitution**. This means that it is based on deep-rooted customs and practices as well as written documents. There is no one document that can be consulted. The written documents include parliamentary laws, common law, and the written decisions of judges. The English Bill of Rights is considered to be part of the British constitution. One example of a long-established practice is the custom that the monarch may never attend a cabinet meeting. All the components together provide the British with a source of democratic authority.

Unitary System

Some nations with limited governments have created highly centralized, or **unitary**, governmental systems. Major services such as police, education, and health care are directed from a central authority. Local governments or communities have little control over the things they may want to do. It is the role of local officials to carry out the policies and directives of the central government. France is an example of a nation that uses a unitary system to administer government. Local officials are appointed by the national government and are expected to carry out the policies and programs developed by the national government. Local officials have only limited authority to act independently.

Although the unitary system is one in which the central government makes most of the decisions, it can be a democratic system. For example, the president of France is directly elected by the people as are the members of the French lawmaking body. The people's rights are protected by the government and the constitution. The governments of the states of the United States are classified as unitary.

Federal System

In a **federal system**, authority is divided between states, or other political divisions, and a national government. The central government exercises power over the important national and international issues. Examples are the power to wage war or the power to regulate trade among the states. Many activities in a federal system are the concern only of the state governments. Examples are laws regulating marriage and divorce, decisions about where to build schools,

Where Power Is Located in Three Forms of Government

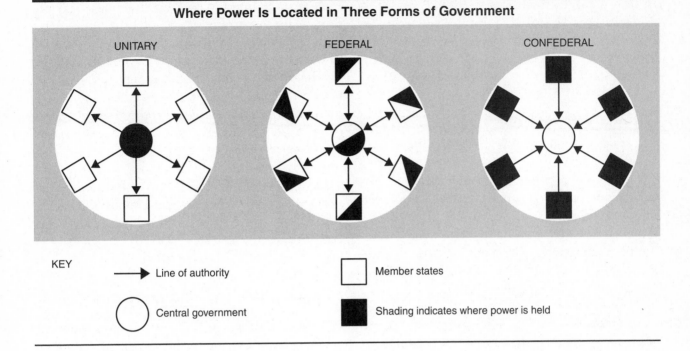

UNITARY   FEDERAL   CONFEDERAL

KEY

→ Line of authority

◯ Central government

☐ Member states

■ Shading indicates where power is held

and traffic regulations. You will learn more about the federal system in the United States later in the chapter.

Confederal System

Still another type of government is a **confederal system**. In this system, the states delegate authority to a central government. The purpose is to give the central government the power to do only those things that the states might not be able to do efficiently for themselves. An example might be the creation of an army. It might be easier for a central government to develop an army than for each state to put together its own defense system.

Generally, a confederal system is characterized by a weak central government. The states keep most of the power for themselves. The first government organized in the United States employed a confederal model. Its frame of government was called the Articles of Confederation. Our present Constitution replaced the Articles.

Let's Think

1. What is limited government?

2. How is a constitution used in a limited government?

3. Describe each of the following types of government: unitary, federal, confederal.

4. What are the advantages and disadvantages of each?

The Meaning of Democracy

We live in a democratic society. Have you ever thought about what this means? We can travel easily from place to place, engage in discussions of all kinds, and freely complain about government officials. We can read any book we want about any topic. There is no fear that we will be punished for any of these actions. Because these freedoms are a fundamental part of our way of life, we tend to take them for granted.

Democracy means rule by the people. This idea sets up an important distinction between democracies and all other governments. Remember that in a dictatorship and other forms of unlimited government, it is believed that the people of a nation exist to serve the state. The opposite is true in a democracy, a limited government.

Under this system, the government exists to serve the people. Democratic societies are dedicated to the idea of improving the way of life of their people.

Types of Democracies

One type of democracy is **direct democracy**. In such a democracy, all citizens are expected to participate in making governmental decisions and to vote on laws. Athens, in ancient Greece, practiced this type of democracy. In the New England states of the United States, some communities still practice direct democracy. The public makes a variety of governmental decisions in the annual town meetings.

It is difficult to make direct democracy work in communities or nations that have large populations. You can imagine what it might be like for several million voters to come to one location to debate and vote on the great issues of the day. (Electronic computer linkups or interactive television could make direct democracy possible in the future.)

Nations with large populations developed another form of democracy called **representative democracy**. In a representative democracy, citizens elect people to speak for them in the government. These representatives are given the power to vote on laws and develop important programs for a community or state or nation. A trust is placed in the hands of the representatives to act in the best interests of all of the people. Periodically, the representatives have to face their public through the election process. If the citizens are unhappy with their representatives, they can vote the representatives out of office.

Any government in which the citizens delegate power to representatives is called a **democratic republic**. Therefore, the United States can be thought of as a democratic republic.

Another form of representative government is the **parliamentary system**. In a parliamentary system, the people vote for representatives to the parliament, the lawmaking body. The leader of the political party that wins a majority of the seats in parliament becomes the prime minister, the chief executive. This person is also a member of parliament. A group of advisers, called a "cab-

inet," is appointed to conduct the day-to-day affairs of the government.

If a majority in the parliament votes down an important piece of legislation favored by the ruling party, the prime minister may dissolve the government and call for new elections. A vote by members of parliament of "no confidence" in the cabinet will also trigger new elections. These unplanned elections can occur even before the next regularly scheduled elections.

A number of nations follow the parliamentary system. Among them are the United Kingdom, Israel, Japan, and most of the countries in Western Europe.

Democracy Protects Freedoms

How does a democracy strive to better the lives of its citizens? During the 1600s, the philosopher John Locke of England questioned the authority of the monarchies. He developed theories about the role of government in society.

In 1690, Locke wrote *Two Treatises of Government*. In this work, he argued that people have the right to live freely and expect certain things from their government. Locke believed that individuals should think of themselves as having been born in a state of nature. In this natural state, they are totally free to make decisions, speak freely, and enjoy life. He also believed that people agree to form governments in order to protect themselves. Therefore, it becomes the responsibility of the government to protect the basic rights of the people.

Locke called the rights that all people should enjoy the **natural rights of man**. What are these natural rights that are so important? He explained them in general terms as life, liberty, and ownership of property. Governments exist, he said, to protect these rights, not to give them.

Locke believed that people should be able to reject any government that violates the faith the people place in it. Government must be fair and just. If a government undermines that trust through greed or corruption, Locke thought that people have the right to eliminate the government and replace it.

Locke's words and ideas greatly influenced Thomas Jefferson as he wrote the Declaration of

Independence. Locke's ideas about freedom and the rights of people are preserved in modern democracies and, indeed, in our own structure of government.

Roots of Democracy

American ideas about democracy and rights and freedoms have been gathered from many sources. One is the English Bill of Rights of 1689. This document, as you recall from Chapter 1, took a major step toward limiting the authority of the monarch and protecting the rights of the people. During the Glorious Revolution of 1689, the people of England removed their king. Through their Parliament, the lawmaking body, the people invited a new king and queen (William and Mary) to assume the throne of England. The royal couple had to agree to support the Bill of Rights before they were allowed to become England's reigning monarchs. The new rulers of England were asked by the people to rule. No longer could they claim they were ruling because God gave them that right.

An early colonial document planted a seed for democracy in the American colonies long before they won their independence from England. This document is known as the *Mayflower Compact*. When the Pilgrims arrived in Massachusetts Bay in 1620, they created the compact, an agreement among the men on the ship *Mayflower*. The men agreed to form a government that would rule with the consent of the people who were being governed. The document was not a constitution as we understand it, but a statement of ideas. So strong were the ideas expressed in the Mayflower Compact that they became the basis of future democratic practices.

The Mayflower Compact

IN THE NAME OF GOD, AMEN.

We whose names are underwritten, the loyal subjects of our dread Sovereign Lord King James, by the Grace of God of Great Britain, France and Ireland, King, Defender of the Faith, etc.

Having undertaken, for the Glory of God and advancement of the Christian Faith and Honour of our King and Country, a Voyage to plant the First Colony in the Northern Parts of Virginia, do by these presents solemnly and mutually in the pres-

ence of God and one of another, Covenant and Combine ourselves together into a Civil Body Politic, for our better ordering and preservation and furtherance of the ends aforesaid; and by virtue hereof to enact, constitute and frame such just and equal Laws, Ordinances, Acts, Constitutions and Offices from time to time, as shall be thought most meet and convenient for the general good of the Colony, unto which we promise all due submission and obedience. In witness whereof we have hereunder subscribed our names at Cape Cod, the 11th November, in the year of the reign of our Sovereign Lord King James, of England, France and Ireland the eighteenth, and of Scotland the fifty-fourth. Anno Domini 1620.

The idea of a representative government responsible to the people who are governed was furthered by the creation of the *Fundamental Orders of Connecticut* in 1639. As the first written constitution in America, it laid the foundation of government in the colony of Connecticut. Several provisions from this document are quoted below.

The Fundamental Orders included several ideas that are still considered important. It provided for an assembly called the Court of Election that would represent the people in selecting officials of the colony, including the governor.

Fundamental Orders of Connecticut

1. It is ordered, sentenced, and decreed that there shall be yearly two general assemblies or courts; . . . The first shall be the Court of Election. Wherein shall be yearly chosen . . . so many magistrates and other public officers as shall be found requisite [necessary], . . . one to be chosen governor for the year ensuing [following] and until another be chosen, and . . . there be six chosen besides the governor; . . . shall have power to administer justice according to the laws here established. . . .

4. It is ordered . . . that no person be chosen governor above once in two years, and that the governor be always a member of some approved congregation. . . .

11. It is ordered . . . that when any general court . . . has agreed upon any . . . sums of money to be levied upon the several towns within this jurisdiction . . . a committee be chosen to set out . . . the proportion of every town to pay of the said levy, provided the committees be made up of an equal number out of each town.

The document limited the governor's term of office. It also required the governor to be a member of the approved religious group, "congregation," of the colony. This was a Christian Protestant group. Such a requirement was common at the time.

Among the most significant provisions is number 11. It sets forth how taxes will be levied and who should approve the amounts. Throughout British history the issue of how taxes should be levied had been a major area of disagreement between the people and the monarch. The issue became increasingly important in the mid-1700s, just before the American Revolution started. Taxes are still a controversial subject in the United States.

Democracy and Majority Rule

What makes people accept a law, program, or policy passed by their government? In a democratic society, people accept, or at least obey, government actions that are decided by the majority of lawmakers. **Majority rule**, decisions made by more than half of those involved, is democratic because it considers the will of most of the people in a community. Majority rule does not satisfy all people, but it does attempt to satisfy the demands of most of the people.

Majority rule is an important principle of a democracy. If the majority of people in a democracy want to move society in a certain direction, this direction will be taken. We have seen how monarchs and dictators do not concern themselves with the will of the majority. Democratic thinking maintains that the destiny of a nation lies in the power of the people and reflects the will of most of the people. People in a democratic society believe that majority rule works better than placing power in the hands of a few decision makers.

Democracy Protects the Minority

Although the majority rules in a democracy, we care about preserving the rights of everyone, even those who disagree with the majority. Therefore, democracy must protect the rights of the minority. Everyone's opinion must be respected. It is possible that over time, minority views may become accepted by the majority. If criticism is blunted, the democratic process is hurt.

An example of a majority-supported policy that hurt a smaller group in society happened in the United States. Our government and the majority of the population once tolerated slavery. Slavery was abolished in 1865 by the 13th Amendment to the Constitution. Within a few years, many states passed laws that discriminated against African Americans. Some laws prevented them from participating in the voting process. Other laws forced African Americans to use separate public facilities such as schools, lunch counters, and public bathrooms. Through a slow process, these laws were overturned by a change in public attitudes and by court decisions. Although the work to maintain equality continues, the rights of the African-American minority are now more fully recognized and accepted by the majority.

Let's Think

1. Define the following terms: democracy, direct democracy, representative democracy, democratic republic.
2. According to John Locke, if a government violates the people's trust, what do the people have a right to do?
3. How did such documents as the English Bill of Rights, the Mayflower Compact, and the Fundamental Orders of Connecticut contribute to the development of America's ideas about democratic government?
4. How does a democracy work to protect the rights and ideas of the majority and the minorities in a society?

The United States Constitution

Law codes, such as Hammurabi's and the Twelve Tables, were created so that everyone in a nation or empire could know what the laws were. For

P O W E R *of* ★ NE

Thomas Jefferson

Throughout his life, Thomas Jefferson demonstrated the "Power of One." He helped shape the great American experiment in democracy.

Jefferson was born in Shadwell, Virginia, on April 13, 1743, one of ten children. His parents owned a large plantation and many slaves. At age 16, Jefferson entered the College of William and Mary in Williamsburg. He studied philosophy and the law and was admitted to the bar in 1767.

Two years later, Jefferson began his public life by becoming a member of the Virginia House of Burgesses. Jefferson served as a delegate to the Second Continental Congress in 1775 and 1776. Those around Jefferson knew of his great intellect and his ability to write well. So, at the age of only 33, he was asked to serve on the committee that would create the Declaration of Independence. Jefferson became the major writer of this now cherished American document.

The Declaration of Independence set forth the many grievances the people of the American colonies had against the British government. It also formally declared our independence from Great Britain. But its main focus for us centers on individual rights and what citizens should expect from their government. These concepts echo the philosophy of Locke and Rousseau.

The ideas contained in the following section of this document serve as a guiding philosophy for our nation to this day. They have also inspired other revolutionaries throughout the world as they struggled to rid themselves of oppressive rulers.

"We hold these truths to be self-evident, that all men are created equal, that they are endowed by their Creator with certain unalienable Rights, that among these are Life, Liberty and the pursuit of Happiness. That to secure these rights, Governments are instituted among Men, deriving their just powers from the consent of the governed; That whenever any Form of Government becomes destructive of these ends it is the Right of the People to alter or to abolish it, and to institute new Government, . . ."

After the young United States gained its independence from Great Britain, Jefferson served as ambassador to France; as the first secretary of state in President George Washington's Cabinet; as vice president under John Adams, the second president; and as the nation's third president (1801–1809).

When Jefferson was elected president in 1800, it was the first time that the leadership of the nation passed from one political group to another—from the Federalists to the Democratic-Republicans. Partly because of Jefferson's actions the change was peaceful and without anger. Jefferson's group did not take revenge on the old group. In his inaugural address, Jefferson stated, "We are all Republicans, we are all Federalists. If there be any among us who would wish to dissolve this Union or change its . . . form, let them stand undisturbed as monuments of the safety with which error of opinion may be tolerated where reason is left free to combat it." He made clear that the party one supported did not matter; all were Americans. The right to disagree should be protected.

Thomas Jefferson died on July 4, 1826, the day that marked the 50th anniversary of the signing of the Declaration of Independence.

1. What ideas of Locke did Jefferson incorporate into the Declaration of Independence?
2. What was important about the election of 1800 that made Jefferson our third president?
3. Of all of Jefferson's contributions mentioned here, which do you think are the most important? Why?

the same reason, nations have created written constitutions. A constitution is a system of laws and legal principles that establish the way a government is constructed. A constitution also sets limits on the power of a government and defines the rights of the people. It is a public document that anyone can read to find out how the government works.

The U.S. Constitution sets forth the way our government is organized. It also specifies what the national government is permitted to do and what it is not allowed to do. If the government acts illegally or in a way that will be harmful to the public, the Constitution serves as the final authority that protects the rights of the people. As President Calvin Coolidge said in 1924, "The Constitution is the sole source and guarantee of national freedom."

The Function of the Constitution

Created in 1787 and ratified in 1788, the U.S. Constitution is considered to be the supreme law in the United States. No person, whether a private citizen or a government official, may legally violate this document. At the same time, no state or local government may pass a law that would violate the principles and regulations written into the Constitution.

Article VI, Section 2, of the document states, "This Constitution, and the laws of the United States which shall be made in pursuance thereof, and all treaties made, or which shall be made, under the authority of the United States, shall be the supreme law of the land, and the judges in every State shall be bound thereby, anything in the constitution or laws of any State to the contrary notwithstanding." The **Supremacy Clause**, as this section is called, establishes the U.S. Constitution as the highest law in the nation.

A major function of the Constitution was to organize the national government. It established three branches of government. The first is the **legislative** branch, called the Congress. It is primarily responsible for creating laws. A second is the **executive**, headed by the president. The president is responsible for carrying out the nation's laws and watching over the day-to-day operation of the national government. The third branch is the **judicial**. It consists of the federal court system and is responsible for interpreting laws and punishing lawbreakers. The Supreme Court heads this branch. The Constitution outlines the responsibilities of each of the three branches of government.

The Constitution contains seven sections, or articles. The articles outline the shape of the government, list the responsibilities of each branch, and in general, describe how the parts will operate. Provision is made for adding ideas to the Constitution. These additions are called **amendments**. Currently, there are 27. The first ten amendments became part of the Constitution in 1791 and the last in 1992. Because the Constitution can be amended, it can be adjusted to meet the needs of a changing nation.

Separation of Powers

There is a very important reason why the Framers of the Constitution decided to create three branches of government. After the experience of being ruled by the king of England, the Framers wanted to make sure that no one part of the government could become more powerful than any other part. They were influenced by the ideas of John Locke, Jean-Jacques Rousseau, and Montesquieu.

Montesquieu, of France, wrote about concepts of government in the early 1700s. Montesquieu believed that if democracy was to survive, the people must avoid giving any one person or any one branch of government too much power. If the head of a government or a legislature became too powerful, the principles that democracy stands for would be violated.

By dividing the government into three branches, the Constitution prevents any one part from becoming too strong. Each branch has specific powers that are different from those exercised by the other two. This principle is called **separation of powers**. Separation of powers is an important pillar of our system.

Checks and Balances

The branches of government were not only given separate powers, they were also given the responsibility of watching over each other. They have the ability to curb one another's power.

The Separation of Powers

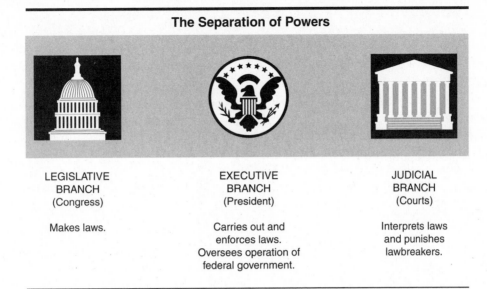

LEGISLATIVE BRANCH (Congress)	EXECUTIVE BRANCH (President)	JUDICIAL BRANCH (Courts)
Makes laws.	Carries out and enforces laws. Oversees operation of federal government.	Interprets laws and punishes lawbreakers.

This system of having each branch act as a watchdog over the other two is called **checks and balances**.

One way the president checks the authority of the Congress is in the lawmaking process. Although the Constitution gives Congress the main authority to create laws, it also includes the president in the lawmaking process. After Congress passes a bill (proposal for a law), the bill does not become a law until the president signs it. If the president refuses to sign it, the bill, in most instances, will not become law. This refusal of the president to sign a bill is called a **veto**. It is a check by the executive branch on the legislative branch. Under special circumstances, Congress can override a veto by the president. (See Chapter 5.) This, too, is a check—on the president.

The third branch, the judiciary, can check the other two branches. Over time, the Supreme Court has acquired the power to declare unconstitutional laws passed by Congress and signed by the president. **Judicial review**, as it is called, is a way of checking the other branches and preventing laws that are contrary to the Constitution from continuing in force. The Court can also review actions of the president and declare them legal or illegal.

Let's Think

1. What is a constitution? Why is it important to a nation?

2. What are the specific jobs of each of the three branches of government: executive, legislative, and judicial?

3. Why is the idea of separation of powers considered to be a democratic idea?

4. Do you think it is important for a government to have a system of checks and balances? Explain your answer.

Federalism

We are a nation consisting of 50 states. We identify with our states, yet we see ourselves as Americans, loyal to our nation. The Constitution recognizes that people have a strong identity with their home states. The Framers of the Constitution were concerned about keeping that identity. They therefore divided the power of government between the national government and the state governments. We call the system of dividing the power between the national and state governments **federalism**.

Reasons for Federalism

The shared-powers system accomplishes an important purpose. The federal system helps to avoid giving too much power to any one person or group. This is a major safeguard of the democratic process.

◄REALITY CHECK►

United States v. Nixon (1974)

What happens if there is a conflict between different branches of the federal government? During the early 1970s, a dispute developed between the U.S. courts and President Richard M. Nixon. The Constitution, through its provisions for separation of powers and checks and balances, provides for the resolution of this type of conflict.

The court case grew out of the Watergate Scandal of 1972. During the presidential campaign that year, a break-in occurred at the Democratic Party's National Committee offices in the Watergate Building in Washington, D.C. Some employees of a Republican Party committee to re-elect President Nixon were trying to get information there that could be used against the Democratic candidate, George McGovern. The burglars were caught, arrested, and (in 1973) convicted of various charges. By then, rumors existed that individuals close to Nixon had attempted to block the investigation into the burglary. A Senate committee held hearings to look into the matter.

Because of public pressure, President Nixon was forced to appoint a special federal prosecutor, Archibald Cox, to look into the charges. He would work independently of the Justice Department, which is under the authority of the president. Cox asked the White House for newly revealed audiotapes of conversations between the President and his aides recorded in his office. Some believed that there was evidence on the tapes that would implicate seven close aides. The President refused to turn over the tapes to Cox.

Nixon claimed **executive privilege**. It is a long-standing principle that there are times when a president must be able to speak freely and in secrecy with advisers, when discussing diplomatic or military strategies, for example. Although the idea of executive privilege is not included in the Constitution, it falls under the constitutional umbrella of separation of powers. When Nixon refused to re-linquish the audiotapes, Cox got a subpoena (court order) forcing him to turn over the tapes. Mr. Nixon, in turn, fired Cox. The President claimed that the special prosecutor had gone too far. A new prosecutor, Leon Jaworski, was then appointed by the President. Despite Nixon's wishes, however, Mr. Jaworski continued the quest for the tapes.

The conflict was stalled until the case *United States v. Nixon* came before the United States Supreme Court. In July 1974, in a unanimous decision, the Court ruled that the President must turn the tapes over to the special prosecutor. The idea that the President had unlimited executive privileges on all matters was denied. According to the Court, there was no evidence that revealing any of the taped conversations would hurt the country's security. In its decision, the Court ruled: "We conclude that when the ground for asserting privilege as to subpoenaed materials sought for use in a criminal trial is based only on the generalized interest in confidentiality, it cannot prevail over the fundamental demands of due process of law in the fair administration of criminal justice. The . . . assertion of privilege must yield to the demonstrated, specific need for evidence in a pending criminal trial. . . ."

Shortly after the Court made this ruling, Nixon resigned as president. It had become apparent to him that he would be **impeached** (charged by the House of Representatives and tried by the U.S. Senate) for obstruction of justice.

1. What were the important facts in the case *United States v. Nixon*?
2. How did separation of powers play a role in this case?
3. What legal arguments did President Nixon make to keep the audiotapes secret?
4. How did the Supreme Court rule in this case?

Checks and Balances in American Government

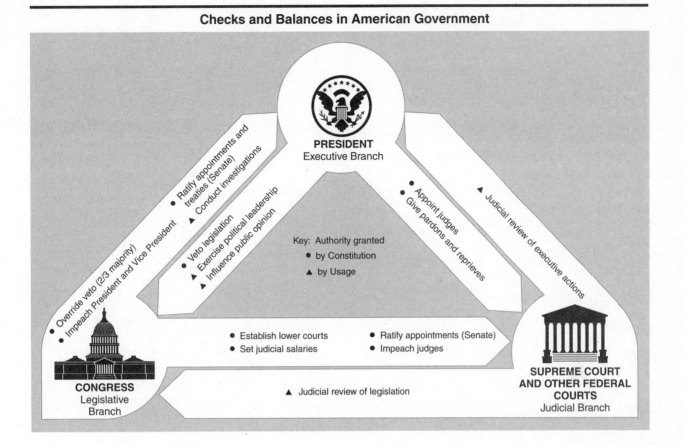

After they declared their independence from Great Britain in 1776, the leaders of the new United States decided that a central government had to be created. The former colonies, now states, each had its own government. Some form of national government had to be created to help hold the country together and to show the rest of the world that the revolutionaries could govern themselves. The leaders of the American Revolution also wanted to create a government that would eliminate the abuses they had lived under when King George III ruled them from England. In response to this experience, they created a government framework called the Articles of Confederation. This system was in place from 1781 to 1789.

The Articles of Confederation set up a confederal system. In this type of system, the states retain the major portion of power in a nation and give limited power to a central government. The national government of the United States in the 1780s was very weak. Most of the power of governing was held by the states. There was no elected national leader, or executive, to direct the policies of the new nation. The lawmaking body, Congress, had very little authority. If taxes were needed, Congress had to ask the individual states for approval to collect the money. If military action was necessary, Congress had to rely on the individual states to provide armed forces. Even the regulation of commerce between the states was not within the powers of Congress. You can imagine that there was some confusion.

Although the confederation government managed to survive for eight years, people realized that the central authority needed strengthening. A Constitutional Convention was called in 1787 to amend the Articles of Confederation. As the meetings in Philadelphia proceeded, it became apparent that major changes were needed. Soon the delegates agreed that a whole new system of government had to be created. What resulted was the U.S. Constitution. It still serves us today.

The major problem the Framers of the Constitution faced was how to distribute power in the government without making the central government too powerful. If the central government was given all the power, then the local govern-

Division of Powers Between the Federal Government and the States

FEDERAL GOVERNMENT POWERS (Delegated Powers)	POWERS SHARED by Federal and State Governments (Concurrent Powers)	STATE GOVERNMENT POWERS (Reserved Powers)
Regulate interstate and international commerce	Levy and collect taxes	Regulate trade within the state
Establish rules of naturalization	Establish courts	Establish local governments
Establish rules of bankruptcy	Enforce laws	Conduct elections
Coin money	Borrow money	Determine qualifications of voters
Provide for the punishment of counterfeiting	Build roads	Establish and support public schools
Establish post offices and post roads		Incorporate business firms
Establish rules for patents and copyrights		Make marriage and divorce laws
Establish federal courts lower than the Supreme Court		License professional workers
Establish punishment for piracy on the high seas		Keep all powers not granted to the federal government nor prohibited to the states
Declare war		
Raise and support armies and a navy		
Call state militia into service to carry out the laws of the nation		
Govern the District of Columbia		
Make all laws "necessary and proper" to carry out its powers as listed in the Constitution		

ments would have little control over policies that directly affect the lives of their citizens. A balance had to be created. What resulted was federalism.

Division of Powers

The Constitution divides power three ways. The powers given exclusively to the federal government are called **delegated**, or **enumerated, powers**. The powers to be exercised only by the states are called **reserved powers**. The third group of powers are those exercised by both the federal government and the state governments. They are called **concurrent powers**.

Delegated Powers

Look at the headlines (right). Suppose this were true. What problems do you think this would create for the nation? Think about what would hap-

State of Michigan to Print Own Money: "Michigan Nuggets"

All doing business in state must change to new currency

Credit cards to be banned

Dollars no longer accepted

pen if you were traveling in the United States and part of your trip took you through Michigan. If you wanted to stay in a hotel, you would find your dollars unacceptable when you went to pay the bill. You might have to go to a local bank to exchange your dollars for nuggets. Filling up your car with gasoline in Michigan would create problems as well. You would have to use nuggets instead of dollars. After you left Michigan, you would find it difficult to spend your leftover nuggets. No other state recognizes them as legal currency.

Imagine what would happen if every state decided to create its own individual currency. Conducting business among the different states would be difficult, confusing, and disorganized. It would be as though 50 different countries existed, giving you 50 different currencies to work with.

This type of situation is a major reason why the Framers of the Constitution decided that certain powers must be exercised only by the national government. The powers that the states gave up so that the national government could make the nation operate smoothly are called delegated powers. Delegated powers are detailed in Article I, Section 8, of the Constitution.

Powers Delegated to Congress

- Regulate interstate and international commerce
- Establish rules of naturalization
- Establish rules of bankruptcy
- Coin money
- Provide for the punishment of counterfeiting
- Establish post offices and post roads
- Establish rules for patents and copyrights
- Establish federal courts lower than the Supreme Court
- Establish punishment for piracy on the high seas
- Declare war
- Raise and support armies and a navy
- Call state militia into service to carry out the laws of the nation
- Govern the District of Columbia
- Make all laws "necessary and proper" to carry out its powers as listed in the Constitution

The listed powers are to be exercised only by the national government. By keeping these powers for Congress alone, the Framers hoped to avoid the confusion and possible chaos that might result if each state could also carry out these responsibilities. Imagine the problems that would develop if a state could declare war on a country or another state! We have already seen what difficulties people and businesses would have if each state coined its own money.

Concurrent Powers

The Framers also realized that some powers must be shared by both the state and national governments. They are called concurrent powers. Some are listed below:

Concurrent Powers

- Levy and collect taxes
- Establish courts
- Enforce laws
- Borrow money
- Build roads

Reserved Powers

When the Constitutional Convention decided to create a federal system, some delegates feared that the authority the states had had under the Articles of Confederation would be greatly diminished. This fear was strongly expressed during the debates in the states over the ratification (approval) of the Constitution. To win over the states' rights group, the supporters of the Constitution agreed to add an amendment to the document. This amendment, the Tenth, gives the states all powers not specifically delegated to the national government. Passed in 1791, the Tenth Amendment states: "The powers not delegated to the United States, by the Constitution, nor prohibited by it to the States, are reserved to the States respectively, or to the people."

Adding this amendment to the Constitution quieted the states' rights argument for a time. It did gather strength in the 1800s and contributed to the outbreak of the Civil War in 1861. Even today, people continue to discuss the question of the proper balance of power between the federal and state governments.

Powers Denied

When the Constitution was created, the Framers decided to deny some powers to both the national and state governments. Article I, Section 9, Clause 3, states: "No bill of attainder or ex post facto law shall be passed." A **bill of attainder** is a law that convicts a person of a crime, sets the punishment, and denies the person a trial by jury.

Ex post facto means "after the fact." An **ex post facto law** provides for punishing a person for an act that was legal before the new law was passed. To illustrate this idea, let us suppose that your community has no law against making a U-turn on Independence Avenue, a very busy street. On October 3, Josh makes a U-turn on Independence Avenue. The mayor sees what Josh did. On November 1, the City Council passes a law making a U-turn on the avenue illegal. Now that there is a law on the books to enforce, the police go to Josh's house and arrest him for making the U-turn on the previous October 3. This action is prohibited by the Constitution. When Josh made the U-turn, he did not violate any law. At the time, there was no law prohibiting the action. Local, state, and national governments cannot pass a law that makes illegal an action that took place before the law went into effect.

Let's Think

1. What is meant by the term "federalism"?
2. What purpose does this system of government serve in a democratic nation?
3. What are the differences between the following powers: delegated, reserved, and concurrent?
4. Why did the Constitution ban passage of bills of attainder and ex post facto laws?

Chapter Summary

There are many types of governments. An unlimited government exercises complete control over a country. Seldom do such governments regard the rights of their citizens as an important issue. There are several different types of unlimited governments: absolute monarchies, dictatorships, and oligarchies.

The power of other types of governments is limited, usually by a constitution. Such governments are bound by the law of the nation. They protect the rights of their citizens. Democracies are limited governments.

How governmental powers are distributed in a nation is important. Some national governments make most of the decisions for the entire nation, even deciding local issues. This type of system is a unitary system. France is an example of a unitary government.

Democracy means rule by the people. The United States is a democracy. Athens in ancient Greece had all its male citizens participate in the passage of laws and other government decisions. It had what is called a direct democracy. Nations that elect representatives to pass laws and help the government operate are known as representative democracies. When people delegate their power to representatives, they have what is known as a democratic republic. The United States is one example of this type of democracy.

A major contributor to the concept of democracy was John Locke. He believed that if a government is corrupt or does not work to protect the rights of the individual, then the people have the right to replace this government.

The roots of American democracy can be found in several sources; among them are: the English Bill of Rights of 1689, the Mayflower Compact of 1620, and the Fundamental Orders of Connecticut of 1639. Each document established the idea of voting and the right of those who are governed to have a say in the government.

An important idea in a democracy is majority rule. Under this principle, the opinion of the majority prevails when there is disagreement.

Another important element of democracy is the protection of those in the minority. The rights of all people must be respected if a nation is to consider itself a democracy.

The early leaders of the United States created a constitution in 1787. The U.S. Constitution is a written document that outlines the structure of our government and what it can and cannot do.

A major principle contained in the Constitution is the idea that no one person or group should have too much power. To prevent this, the Constitution provides for a separation of powers. Each branch of the government—legislative, executive, and judicial—has specific powers different from the other two. In addition, each branch has the ability to watch over the other two branches. In this way, no one branch can become too powerful. We call this a checks-and-balances system. The Framers of the Constitution also made it possible to alter, or amend, the document as new conditions arise.

The Constitution set up a system called federalism. In it the national government shares power with the state governments. Three divisions of power were created: delegated, those given only to the national government; reserved, those given only to the states; and concurrent, those shared by both the state and federal governments.

★ CHAPTER REVIEW ★

A. Matching
Match each term in Column A with its correct definition in Column B.

Column A
1. oligarchy
2. monarchy
3. Joseph Stalin
4. dictatorship
5. democracy
6. John Locke
7. Mayflower Compact
8. federalism
9. delegated power
10. amendment

Column B
a. system of dividing powers between state and national governments
b. one-person rule in an unlimited government
c. promoted the idea of the natural rights of man
d. colonial contribution to the idea of democratic government
e. government headed by king or queen
f. expressed responsibility given to the national government
g. rule by the people
h. addition to the original U.S. Constitution
i. rule by a small group in an unlimited government
j. dictator of the Soviet Union, 1924–1953

B. Multiple Choice
Select the statement or word that most correctly answers the question or completes the statement.

1. Which form of government does not provide for an orderly transition of leaders? **(a)** monarchy **(b)** democracy **(c)** dictatorship **(d)** republic.

2. The idea of separation of powers among three branches of government was first set forth by the writer **(a)** Montesquieu **(b)** Locke **(c)** Rousseau **(d)** Jefferson.

3. The following form of government is limited: **(a)** dictatorship **(b)** absolute monarchy **(c)** democracy **(d)** totalitarian.

4. A justification for the American Revolution can be found in the following historical document: **(a)** Mayflower Compact **(b)** Fundamental Orders of Connecticut **(c)** Constitution **(d)** Declaration of Independence.

5. This person put forth the idea that in a natural state, individuals are free to make decisions, speak freely, and enjoy life: **(a)** Montesquieu **(b)** Locke **(c)** Jefferson **(d)** Rousseau.

6. The event that put an end to the idea of "Divine Right of Kings" in England was the **(a)** Glorious Revolution **(b)** American Revolution **(c)** rise of Hitler **(d)** signing of the Mayflower Compact.

7. The right of the U.S. Congress to declare war is an example of a **(a)** delegated power **(b)** concurrent power **(c)** reserved power **(d)** dictatorial power.

8. The United States is an example of a **(a)** dictatorship **(b)** monarchy **(c)** direct democracy **(d)** representative democracy.

9. The system in which one branch of government "watches over" another branch is called **(a)** separation of powers **(b)** checks and balances **(c)** division of power **(d)** civil liberties.

10. The U.S. Constitution **(a)** sets the limits within which our government may operate **(b)** grants

its citizens freedom (c) provides for a limited monarchy (d) can never be changed.

C. Essay

Write a paragraph about *one* of the following:

1. John Locke's ideas about the role of government.
2. How power must be distributed if democracy is to be preserved.
3. How dictatorships and absolute monarchies deny people their basic rights.
4. The differences between a unitary government and a federal system.

D. A Challenge for You

1. Write an editorial for your student newspaper explaining why it is necessary to protect the rights of the minority as well as of the majority in a democracy.
2. Make a scrapbook or bulletin board display of articles selected from newspapers, magazines, or Web sites that demonstrate the federal system in action. Summarize the major points in each and explain how the action shows the operation of federalism.
3. Prepare *two* speeches for a debate. One should give the arguments for representative democracy, while the other should argue in favor of direct democracy.
4. Create a cartoon strip that demonstrates how our Constitution limits the role of government in American life.
5. You are president of a community organization that believes it is important to give more power to the state government. You are asked to write a position paper to present arguments in favor of taking away responsibilities from the federal government in order to give more authority to the states. This position paper will be sent to the president and your two U.S. senators. You might want to consult sources on the Internet to get background information. Possibly, you could send the fin-ished paper to the president and your senators by e-mail.
6. Do research to find out the names of three dictators who rule countries today. Select *one* and write an essay explaining how the person governs his or her country. You might want to use the Internet to help you find current information.

Document-Based Question

State the main idea expressed in each document. Then use information in the documents and your own knowledge to write an essay explaining the different views about the new form of government that was proposed in 1787.

Patrick Henry Warns of the Possibility of Monarchy, 1788

The constitution is said to have beautiful features; but when I come to examine these features, sir, they appear horribly frightful: among other deformities, it has an awful squinting; it squints towards monarchy. . . . Your president may easily become king: your senate is so imperfectly constructed that your dearest rights may be sacrificed by what may be a small minority. . . .

If your American chief be a man of ambition and abilities, how easy it is for him to render himself absolute. . . . Away with your president, we shall have a king: the army will salute him monarch; your militia will leave you and assist in making him king, and fight against you. . . .

Alexander Hamilton Supports a Strong Central Government, 1788

The principal purposes to be answered by union are these: The common defence of the members; the preservation of the public peace, as well against internal convulsion as external attacks; the regulation of commerce with other nations, and between the states. . . .

The authorities essential to the care of the common defence are these: To raise armies; to build and equip fleets; to prescribe rules for the government of both; to direct their operations; to provide for their support. . . .

CHAPTER 3

People and Their Community

 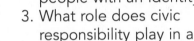
★ CHAPTER FOCUS

1. What are the forces that unite a people?
2. How do communities provide people with an identity?
3. What role does civic responsibility play in a democratic society?

When you say the words "the United States of America," what do you see in your mind? If you see the American flag, a bald eagle, the Liberty Bell, or the Statue of Liberty, you are thinking of a **symbol**, a visible sign that represents the nation. These objects are designed to give the people of the United States positive feelings about our country. The symbols remind us of the ideals the United States stands for.

We feel a surge of patriotism when we catch sight of the stars and stripes of the flag waving over a public building or when we sing the national anthem. Our love for our country is deepened. The strength and freedom represented by the bald eagle, our national bird, and the seal of the president also give us a sense of pride in being part of such a great nation. This sense of pride in our nation is called **nationalism**. Loyalty to our nation and support for its interests bind us together as a people. Pride, loyalty, devotion to the ideals of our country help to make us Americans.

The American Way of Life

The people of America share a common way of life. Most of us speak or understand the same language—English. We follow similar ways of conducting our personal and business lives. We believe in the democratic form of government and the free enterprise economic system. In other words, we share the same American culture—the way of life that is special to the United States. **Culture** is the shared ideas, beliefs, and values of a particular group of people. It also includes art, technology, and governmental and economic systems created by the group.

Customs Shape Our Culture

Through customs and traditions, we pass our culture from generation to generation. **Customs** are the ways things are done over a long period of time. It is customary for people to stand when they sing our national anthem. When we greet people or are introduced to someone, our custom

◀ THE AMERICAN FLAG ▶

A History

Americans express their pride in and loyalty to their country by flying the U.S. flag at home and in public places. You probably see the flag every day. Have you thought about how the flag came into existence?

In 1776, during the American Revolution, General George Washington had the flag of the Continental Army displayed near Boston. He believed that there needed to be a symbol for his soldiers to rally around. This first flag had 13 stripes alternating between white and red. In the corner was the British Union Jack. That flag was soon replaced because the British Union Jack on it was seen by many as a sign of surrender to Great Britain.

The Continental Congress passed the first Flag Act on June 14, 1777: "Resolved, That the flag of the United States be made of thirteen stripes, alternate red and white;

that the union be thirteen stars, white in a blue field, representing a new Constellation."

Over the years, the design of the flag has varied. But one constant was the stars and stripes; another was the red, white, and blue colors. A 1794 act stated that the flag should have 15 stars and 15 stripes. In 1818, President James Monroe signed an act that set the design for the flag. It would contain 13 stripes and 1 star for each state. Thus, for example, the flag in 1820 had 23 stars.

Today's flag was designed in 1959. It consists of seven red stripes, six white stripes, and one star for each of the 50 states. Each color has its own importance. Red represents hardness and valor; white represents purity; and blue symbolizes vigilance, perseverance, and justice.

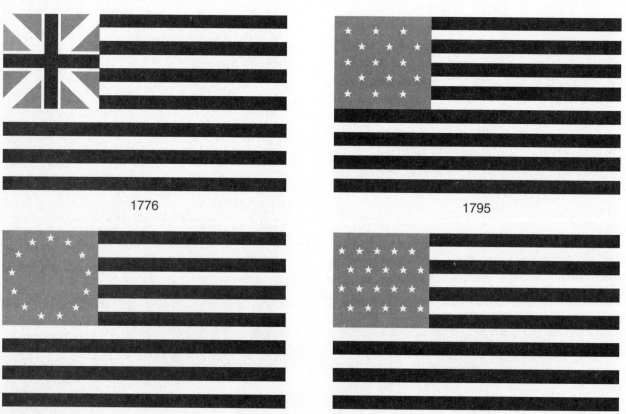

1776

1795

1777

1818

is to shake hands. People in other countries have different ways of greeting each other. In Japan, for example, people bow to one another as a sign of respect when they meet.

Traditions are usual patterns of behavior or ways of doing things. Traditions link us to our past and help us establish our identity. They affect the way we celebrate special events and holidays. Fireworks shows are one tradition of Fourth of July celebrations. Eating a large meal and giving thanks for our blessings are traditions of Thanksgiving Day get-togethers.

Everyone in the United States looks forward to our national holiday—the Fourth of July. It is a great celebration that marks the declaration of the independence of the American colonies from Great Britain. In effect, it is the birthday of the United States of America. On July 4, 1776, the Second Continental Congress adopted the document called the Declaration of Independence. In Philadelphia, then the seat of the government, a celebration took place on July 8, the following Monday. Not until 1777 was the first "Independence Day" celebration observed on July 4th. The day was "celebrated . . . with ringing bells, bonfires, and fireworks. Ships in the harbor fired thirteen-gun salutes, and houses in the city were illuminated with candles in the windows."

July 4th became a national celebration because it honored an important moment in the history of our nation. All people living here can identify with the spirit of the holiday because it stands as a symbol of freedom. When a national event is important to a large number of people, they usually find a way to recognize that event. This recognition unites us and helps us come together as one people.

Values and Their Importance in Our Lives

What do you want to be when you are an adult? This is a question you undoubtedly hear often. Part of your decision will be based on what you learn from society, the community as a whole. A person's goals are influenced by society as well as by those close to us. Custom and tradition also play a part. Some people want a high-paying career. Others think of dedicating their lives to helping people. Still others will decide to enter into government service and run for elective office. We are influenced by what our society considers to be important, good, and desirable. These ideas are known as **values**.

One value that society holds as being important is success. To some, success is achieved by gaining wealth and power. Others might see it as reaching a position in life in which you are respected by others. Another form of success is leading a quiet life of doing good for others. Some might even say you are a success if you fulfill your daily obligations with dignity and devotion to good moral principles.

A second value American society considers important is equality. Ideally, the United States stands for equal opportunity and equal treatment. This value, however, is a national goal that has not yet been totally achieved. But most Americans believe that we should strive to achieve equality for all.

The value Americans most likely hold closest to their hearts is freedom. Our country came into

A motor home on a bridge near Denali National Park in Alaska. Americans cherish their right to travel freely throughout the United States.

being because the early colonists wanted to be free from persecution, from harsh rule. Even today, people want to be free to do what they want with their lives without government interference.

Success, equality, and freedom are values because people in our society consider them to be important. The vast majority of people support the concepts these values represent. Since they are shared by so many people, they help form the rules and customs and traditions we live by.

Norms Guide Behavior

The rules we live by are known as **norms**. They are shared guidelines of behavior that society accepts. Norms determine the way we act in school and with our friends, how we play, and how we develop relationships with others. They help to form the rules of behavior that guide us through life. People follow norms because they believe in these rules. Sometimes norms are so important that society decides they must be written down. When norms are written and approved by government bodies, they become laws.

Let's Think

1. What is nationalism?
2. How can nationalism bring people together?
3. Define the following terms: customs, traditions, values, and norms.
4. How do customs and traditions create a common bond for people?
5. Describe what brings Americans together as a nation.

Community, What It Means

There are many small towns and cities across the United States. They have certain features that are easily described, such as a specific geographic location, a pattern of streets, and special buildings. Residents identify with their surroundings and feel a sense of loyalty to the spirit of a specific

place—their community. A **community** is a place where people feel a sense of belonging.

Most people who live in a community share many things. The children go to local schools and may belong to the Little League. Almost everyone attends the neighborhood houses of worship. The community joins together in celebrating holidays.

Citizens of a community also share many common concerns. These concerns include the environment, safety, and education. Community members are interested in maintaining and improving the quality of life. That spirit of community often translates into a desire to take action to solve problems that arise. People want to feel connected to the place where they live.

Types of Communities

There are several types of communities. One is the *urban community*—a city. It is usually densely populated. An urban setting provides people with a wide range of work opportunities and living choices. There are also a variety of entertainment facilities, from movies to plays to museums to concerts. Cities are lively, energetic places that are home to many different types of people.

Another type of community is the *suburban community*. This type of community is near a city. Many people find they prefer to live in the suburbs and commute to the city for their work. Transportation to the city by train, bus, or car is reasonably easy. Traditionally, the suburbs, which grew in numbers during the post-World War II period of the 1950s, are thought of as being "bedroom communities." They are primarily residential with many single-family homes. Suburban life is usually quiet and safe.

A third type of community is the *rural community*. These communities are more sparsely populated than the urban or suburban centers. Rural communities are generally a distance from urban centers and are often near agricultural areas. They have the lowest **population density** of any of the three types of communities. This means that rural communities have the fewest number of people living on each square mile of land that the communities occupy.

Each of these types of communities is unique and yet has many similarities. There are also many differences among them. They are all similar in that people live and work in each and identify themselves as community members. The local culture is shared by those who live there. Communities are different when we compare the size of the populations and the area each occupies. Suburban and rural communities are defined by their closeness to major urban communities. Each community has its own set of concerns, but they all have many problems in common, such as pollution, crime, waste disposal, and traffic control.

The Neighborhood Community

Cities and towns are made up of neighborhoods. Your neighborhood can also be thought of as a community. It is a distinct place with a particular identity. Here, you have your friends, the places where you like to shop and eat, and your favorite places for entertainment. People in a neighborhood know each other and help each other. They send their children to the same school. The neighborhood community gives us an identity, and we are loyal to it. Our experiences here help to make us who we are.

The Global Community

With the maturing of the electronic age and the ease of communication and travel today, the world seems to be shrinking. Because we hear about events in other parts of the world so rapidly, we feel connected to places that once seemed exotic and remote. Today you might have exchanged e-mail with a person located halfway around the world! This connectedness makes us think of the world as a community. In fact, we often hear the expression "the global community."

Let's Think

1. What is a community?
2. What are the differences between urban, suburban, and rural communities?
3. Why do people think of a neighborhood as an important place?

4. How has the electronic age helped to create the image of the global community?

Civic Responsibility

As members of a community, we have certain responsibilities. One is to behave in an accepted way. Citizens of a community are expected to obey laws and respect other citizens. We pay taxes so that the government of our community can provide us with needed services such as hospitals, police, firefighters, and schools.

Many of us do more than pay taxes. We join volunteer fire departments, emergency medical teams, and neighborhood watches. Some volunteer to deliver lunches to the elderly or help the homeless. Others decide to devote their careers to public life and seek government jobs. Some choose to run for office and participate in the policy-making decisions of communities. Taking part in public affairs is called the **civic life**. This is the part of our life that is responsible to the community, city, state, and national governments.

Cooperation

Of major importance to a community is the ability of people to cooperate with each other to accomplish tasks that achieve a common goal. There may be special projects that members of the community decide to carry out. They might build a park, clear vacant lots of debris, or raise funds for a new youth recreation center.

One way people focus their energies on a particular cause is to join community organizations. These organizations might be business associations, local charities, community planning councils, youth organizations, or local volunteer programs. The goal of each group is to improve the quality of life in the community. The one very important ingredient needed by each organization is people committed to their community. Such people are willing to participate actively in their civic life.

Besides cooperation, people build a sense of community by understanding each other. A major aspect of developing a strong sense of

Volunteers with the organization Habitat for Humanity building a house for a poor family in Houston, Texas.

community is the need for people to learn to live peacefully with each other. Remember Rousseau. (See Chapter 1.) He talked about the social contract. When individuals live in society, they agree to respect one another's rights in exchange for the privilege of living with other people. We agree to exercise our rights responsibly in order to protect the safety and security of everyone.

Communication

How can we learn to cooperate, work together, and respect one another? These goals can be reached mainly through *interaction*, the exchange of ideas. We exchange ideas by communicating. Communication is accomplished through spoken and written language, symbols, and body language. We learn from newspapers, books, and magazines. We create and read information on the computer screen. We watch television. We talk with one another and watch how others react to what we say. All of these forms of communication and interaction help us learn from each other.

Common Experiences

We all have friends. What makes another person your friend? Probably you just feel comfortable with certain individuals. Common interests (such as liking the same kinds of sports, music, or movies) may draw you together. You enjoy talking with each other. Over the years, you become close to your friends because you understand each other and share common experiences. Similarly, people in society learn to get along with each other. They share common experiences, strive for common goals, and respect each other's differences.

Ever since the United States began as a nation, it has attracted people from all over the world who have wanted to become part of American life. The United States is a **pluralistic society**. Such a society is one in which people of many different ethnic backgrounds live. Even though the citizens of the United States think of themselves as Americans, they still consider their personal heritage to be very important. Many Americans keep the customs of their parents and grandparents who came from other countries. Therefore, many people see themselves as Italian Americans, Arab Americans, Mexican Americans, African Americans, Chinese Americans, and so on.

Often, there has been friction among different groups in the United States. As each new wave of immigrants swept into this country, it was greeted with suspicion and disrespect by many people who had come before. In time, as people had the opportunity to learn more about

POWER of ★ ONE

Fernando Mateo

Today, many people feel "lost in the crowd." Why, they ask, should I do community work? I can't make a difference. The following story is about a man who not only believed he could make a difference but who did!

Fernando Mateo was born in the Dominican Republic and grew up in New York City. He

learned the linoleum and carpet trades and opened his own carpet business. After almost losing the business, he convinced others to help him keep it going. He also prayed for success and health. He followed an old Dominican custom called "la promesa." Mateo promised God that if his prayers were answered, he would make some sacrifice. In this case, he promised to help his community.

Fernando Mateo kept that promise by creating a program in a New York City prison that taught inmates skills such as carpet laying and plumbing. The program became known as the Mateo Institute of Training.

In the 1990s, his 14-year-old son, Fernando Mateo, Jr., suggested that his father create a different kind of program. Mateo, Jr., wanted to get guns off the streets. Why not encourage people to turn in their guns to the authorities and receive gift certificates to be exchanged for toys during the Christmas season?

The senior Mateo decided to try out the idea with $5,000 of his own money. This money was spent in one day! The program was an amazing success. It grew so large that Mateo had to seek the help of other businesses in order to get more money. The New York City Police Department was astounded by the response to what became known as the "Toys for Guns" program. Other cities throughout the country set up similar programs.

Mateo knew that not every gun in private hands would be turned in. But he also knew that every gun turned in meant one fewer available for committing murders or holdups or shootings. A 14-year-old boy's idea and his father's willingness to act on it created a positive program that improved their city. Civic life is very important to Mateo. He truly believes that one person can make a difference.

Today, Mateo is the president of the New York State Federation of Taxi Drivers.

1. How did Mateo turn his private life experiences into action in his civic life?
2. Even though Mateo was not successful in getting all guns "off the streets," do you think his program was worth the effort? Why or why not?

---

one another, much of this friction died down. People discovered that regardless of one's background, everyone considered many of the same ideas about life to be important. They all wanted respect, freedom, a decent job, a safe environment, and a good education for their children. Slowly, people learned that, in spite of what ethnic or religious group they belong to, they have more in common with other groups than they have differences about the important things in life.

Causes of Conflicts

What brings about conflicts between individuals or between groups of people? There are many reasons. Among them is the inability of some to accept others as individuals like themselves. They prejudge others in a negative way. In other words, they show **prejudice** against anyone who is different.

People who make such judgments often form sweeping generalizations about others. They

The United States: A Multi-Ethnic Nation

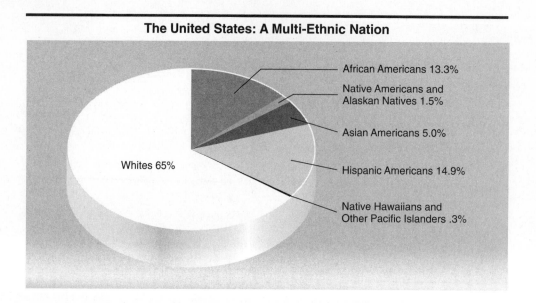

African Americans 13.3%

Native Americans and Alaskan Natives 1.5%

Asian Americans 5.0%

Whites 65%

Hispanic Americans 14.9%

Native Hawaiians and Other Pacific Islanders .3%

might say such things as "all old people are sickly," "women are too emotional," or "everyone who lives there is a hillbilly." Such sweeping generalizations, which are usually based on little or no factual information, are called **stereotypes**. Stereotyping is often used to justify prejudice against a group of people. It may lead to acts of **discrimination**. Discrimination is treating an individual or group in a way that denies them their basic rights as human beings. For instance, until the 1960s, African Americans had to cope with many open forms of discrimination, such as not being allowed to eat in most restaurants or stay in most hotels.

Another idea that causes friction among different groups is **ethnocentrism**. Ethnocentrism is thinking that your culture or your group is superior to another. This bias leads you to judge another culture by the standards of your culture. Instead of respecting a custom of another society and understanding that it is their practice, some people think a practice that is different from their own is inferior. Ethnocentrism can create hatred and bitterness among people. Witness recent wars in Sudan and Chad. People were killed or persecuted just because they were born into a particular religious or ethnic group.

A major concern for a nation that is as diverse as ours is how to bring people of so many different backgrounds together. One way is to respect each other for who we are. Another is to honor our common bonds. All Americans are protected by the Constitution. We share in the joy of our national holidays. We respect our patriotic symbols.

In this land of many different cultures, national holidays bring people together in celebration. Holidays remind us of happy times and times of sacrifice and courage. They help us remember what our flag and our patriotic songs and symbols stand for. Holidays give us common experiences that reinforce our loyalty to one another and our nation.

Let's Think

1. Explain the difference between a civic life and a private life.
2. Make a list of the many ways a person can fulfill his or her responsibilities in civic life.
3. Explain how communication and common experiences help people cooperate with one another.
4. Give one or more examples of how to overcome friction in relations among different groups of people that is caused by prejudice, discrimination, and ethnocentrism.

Solving Problems

In a community, many complicated issues may arise that can create friction among people. Is-

◄REALITY CHECK►
Zoning Laws

Most cities and towns have divided up the community into areas called **zones**. Zoning laws designate certain parts of a city for houses, other parts for stores and office buildings, and still others for factories. The reasons for zoning are many. A special industrial zone will keep smelly, noisy factories away from places where people live. A special business zone will keep traffic and crowds away from residences.

The coastal town of Castine, Maine, has a separate institutional zone for the Maine Maritime Academy. This public college has about 800 students pursuing a variety of majors having to do with ships, shipping, and marine life. Castine's special zone for the Maritime Academy was designed to prevent other uses within the zone. The zoning law was also designed to prevent the expansion of the Academy farther into the town. A controversy arose in 2007 when the Academy bought a residence just outside its zone for the use of its president. The large house and its six acres of grounds are in a residential zone.

Many of the people who live near the Maritime Academy are upset. They say that more traffic will come to their neighborhood when the president of the Academy hosts official functions. They fear that the Academy will want to build dormitories, parking lots, and other school projects on the grounds. One Castine native, Harold Hatch, said, ". . . I fear that the peninsula [which both the town and the school now both share] will become a future campus instead of the historic town it is."

School officials, however, feel they were justified in buying the property across the street from its campus. They say that the use of the property will remain the same—as a residence for the president of the Maine Maritime Academy. The current president, Leonard Tyler, has said, "The rationale behind [the purchase] is that the current president's residence is not at all private and activity at that location (children playing and dogs barking) is occasionally disruptive to those working or studying in the classrooms in Quick Hall." Regarding the new residence, he said, "We respect the integrity and historical value of the structure and will not do anything to diminish it. There are no current or long-term plans for using the additional land surrounding the [president's house] for any purpose."

Town officials will have to decide whether to change the zoning laws to allow the Academy to expand or to leave the current zoning laws in place.

1. What steps should the town government and the college take to resolve the controversy?
2. Write a statement from the point of view of the residents of Castine who do not wish to see changes in the zoning of their town. Write another statement that takes the point of view of the Maine Maritime Academy.
3. What are the differences in the points of view of the two sides? What areas of agreement are there? What creative compromises can you think of?
4. Assume that you are the governor of Maine. What could you do to help resolve the controversy? (The Maine Maritime Academy was founded by the state of Maine, which has jurisdiction over it.)

sues often become very emotional. Where should a shelter for the homeless be placed? Should a major highway be built near an elementary school? Somehow, people must find ways of resolving these issues.

By calmly exchanging ideas and proposing solutions, people who don't agree on controversial issues learn about each other's point of view. They offer ideas for change and propose compromises. This is the peaceful way for people to solve problems among friends, neighbors, or community interests.

Let's Think

1. Think of a problem you've had with a friend or someone else recently that involved poor communication. Write a diary entry that describes how you resolved the conflict.
2. Write a letter to your mayor describing how you think your community should go about solving a local problem.
3. Do a personal reaction assessment: When you first meet, how do you view someone from another community, someone who has a different color skin from yours, someone who practices a different religion? Do you stereotype any of these individuals? Do you show prejudice until you get to know the person better?

Chapter Summary

Symbols such as the American flag give people positive attitudes about our pluralistic country and encourage feelings of nationalism and patriotism. Customs and traditions also bring people together. Shared ways of celebrating holidays such as the Fourth of July and Thanksgiving contribute to a common culture that characterizes the American way of life.

Values are the ideas that a group of people, a society, considers to be important. Major American values are success, equality, and freedom. Norms guide a people's behavior and shape a society. Written norms that have been approved by governments are laws.

Communities create a sense of belonging for people. Different types of communities include urban, suburban, and rural. Communities are different in size and population. They are similar in that people live and work in each. All have individual concerns and problems in common, such as pollution and crime. One community we all identify with is the neighborhood community. It is the immediate area where we live.

Because of the rapid changes in transportation and communication, people from all over the world are able to be in contact with each other almost instantly. This connectedness makes us think of the world as a "global community."

When we live in a community, we have civic responsibilities to that community. This responsibility means paying our taxes, obeying laws, respecting one another, and taking part in public affairs. Part of our civic responsibility includes cooperating with one another and learning to communicate with others.

The United States is a pluralistic society. This means that many different types of people live here. Most of these groups immigrated here at one time in our history. Many met with intolerance. Some became the objects of discrimination and prejudice. One cause of this is ethnocentrism.

Communities face problems all the time. Solving these problems is not always easy. People often disagree on what the best course of action should be. Therefore, it is important for people with different opinions to talk to each other to develop the most satisfactory solutions.

★ CHAPTER REVIEW ★

A. Matching
Match each term in Column A with its definition in Column B.

Column A	Column B
1. nationalism	a. referring to a society of people of different cultural backgrounds
2. community	b. what society considers to be important, good, and desirable
3. value	
4. norms	
5. custom	c. guidelines of behavior
6. stereotype	d. the way something has been done over a long period of time.
7. rural	
8. urban	e. an area of low population density
9. interaction	f. the process of exchanging ideas
10. pluralistic	g. an untrue generalization about a group of people
	h. a densely populated area
	i. a sense of pride in one's nation
	j. a place where people feel a sense of belonging

B. Multiple Choice
Select the statement or word that most correctly answers the question or completes the statement.

1. The saluting of the flag and the singing of the national anthem tend to give people this feeling about their nation: **(a)** anger **(b)** nationalism **(c)** fear **(d)** inadequacy.

2. The national bird of the United States is the **(a)** pelican **(b)** falcon **(c)** bald eagle **(d)** wild turkey.

3. Success, equality, freedom are concepts important to the American people. They are also known as **(a)** norms **(b)** culture **(c)** community **(d)** values.

4. Which is an example of a custom? **(a)** a group of people meet to go to the movies **(b)** a 16-year-old girl has a traditional sweet sixteen party **(c)** attending school each day **(d)** filing income tax forms each year.

5. A person from the United States goes to Japan and thinks that bowing when people meet is a funny custom. This is an example of **(a)** ethnocentrism **(b)** discrimination **(c)** racism **(d)** ridicule.

6. The immediate area within which you live is called a **(a)** country **(b)** neighborhood **(c)** rural center **(d)** suburban center.

7. One reason for the development of the idea of a "global community" is that **(a)** wars have been fought throughout the world **(b)** there has been a decrease in the ability of people to communicate quickly **(c)** there has been an increase in the ability of people to communicate quickly **(d)** the United Nations headquarters moves to a new city every five years.

8. Which of the following is an acceptable way to reduce friction among people of different backgrounds who live together in the United States? **(a)** increase communication among the groups **(b)** decrease communication among groups **(c)** encourage people to write negative things about each other **(d)** force people to give up their beliefs.

9. Judging another culture by standards established by one's own culture is **(a)** prejudice **(b)** discrimination **(c)** stereotyping **(d)** ethnocentrism.

10. Which of the following is an example of participating in civic life? **(a)** opening a store **(b)** working with the volunteer fire department **(c)** investing in the stock market **(d)** going on vacation.

C. Essay
Write a paragraph about *one* of the following:

1. The exchange of ideas among people of different cultural and ethnic backgrounds can reduce distrust among groups.

2. The type of community you would most like to live in—rural, urban, or suburban.

3. National symbols contribute to a spirit of patriotism.

4. Every citizen has the responsibility to participate in the public life of a society.

5. Values that should be important in our society.

D. A Challenge for You

1. Write a letter to your school principal or to the school newspaper explaining how you think students can learn to get along better with one another.

2. Keep a diary for a week. In it enter as many examples of American culture as you notice each day.

3. Draw a series of cartoons showing differences and similarities among urban, rural, and suburban communities.

4. Create a poster that promotes a value that is important in American society.

5. The leaders of a new nation want to bring its people closer together. They hope to strengthen the feeling of national pride and create an atmosphere that will encourage the people to "pull together" to solve the nation's problems. Which of the following steps would you take to accomplish these goals? Give reasons for your choices.

   a. Create a new flag that will serve as the symbol of the nation.

   b. Write a song that praises the accomplishments of the nation.

   c. Publicize the greatness of the people and their culture.

   d. Film a video about the beauty of the land and its people to encourage tourism.

Document-Based Question

State the main idea expressed in each document. Then use information in the documents and your own knowledge to write an essay explaining how each leader appealed to the nationalistic feelings of Americans.

"The New Nationalism" by Theodore Roosevelt, August 31, 1910

We come here today to commemorate one of the epoch-making events . . . [in] the long struggle for the rights of man, the long struggle for the uplift of humanity. Our country—this great republic—means nothing unless it means the triumph of a real democracy, the triumph of popular government, . . . That is why the history of America is now the central feature of the history of the world; for the world has set its face hopefully toward our democracy; and, oh, my fellow citizens, each one of you carries on your shoulders not only the burden of doing well for the sake of your own country, but the burden of doing well and seeing that this nation does well for the sake of mankind.

Inaugural Address by President John F. Kennedy, January 20, 1961

Let every nation know, whether it wishes us well or ill, that we shall pay any price, bear any burden, meet any hardship, support any friend, oppose any foe to assure the survival and the success of liberty. . . .

In your hands, my fellow citizens, more than mine, will rest the final success or failure of our course. Since this country was founded, each generation of Americans has been summoned to give testimony to its national loyalty. The graves of young Americans who answered the call to service surround the globe.

Now the trumpet summons us again—not as a call to bear arms, though arms we need—not as a call to battle, though embattled we are—but a call to bear the burden of a long twilight struggle, year in and year out, "rejoicing in hope, patient in tribulation"—a struggle against the common enemies of man: tyranny, poverty, disease, and war itself.

UNIT 2

The Nature of Our Government

CHAPTER 4

The Political Process

★ CHAPTER FOCUS

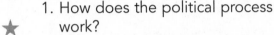
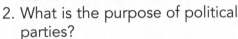
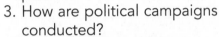
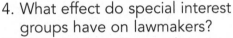

★ 1. How does the political process work?

2. What is the purpose of political parties?

★ 3. How are political campaigns conducted?

★ 4. What effect do special interest groups have on lawmakers?

5. How do the mass media influence our opinions?

6. What role do public opinion polls play in the governmental process?

How do you and your friends decide what movie to see on Saturday night? Sometimes everyone agrees on going to the latest popular release. Other times there may be a controversy, a dispute, about the choice. You want to stay in the neighborhood and pick a film showing locally. A few want to go across town to the new multiplex for the opening of an action film. One or two prefer to go to a movie based on the life of a famous general. How do you settle the controversy? Do you vote? Do you go along with the choice of the person with the loudest voice? Or do you decide to do something entirely different—such as going to a basketball game? The final decision may not be enthusiastically supported by everyone. But everyone goes along with it in order to have fun with the group.

What Is the Political Process?

Making decisions is something every person and every group has to do. Individuals, families, clubs, and governments all have to make decisions about large and small issues every day. Sometimes, the decisions are easy because almost everyone agrees on what to do. At other times, reaching an agreement is difficult because each member of a group has a different point of view, or opinion, about a situation or question.

What Affects Decisions?

Some issues, such as the location of a new sports stadium in your community, the placement of a traffic light near your school, or the decision to send U.S. troops to a foreign country, are likely to be more important to you than others. What influences how you feel about an issue? Obviously, how much money you have—your economic circumstances—will color your attitude toward money matters. Where you live—in a private house or an apartment, in the country, in a small town, or in a city—may make a difference. Your ethnic background and religious preference also contribute to your view of an issue. Customs, traditions, and values all shape your opinions.

Controversies arise because each person looks at an issue from a different point of view. People disagree about which point of view is right or wrong.

"A big surprise!"

Making Decisions

How can we learn to resolve disputes without making enemies of those who disagree with us? First of all, we can respect another's point of view even though we may strongly disagree with it. We can find out the facts about a problem or question and try not to be swayed by emotional reactions. Sometimes this can be difficult because people feel very deeply about issues. For example, what would you as a junior in high school say if only entering freshmen were given special privileges such as being allowed to select their teachers? How would you react if the state decided to raise the minimum legal driving age from 16 to 20? Is it reasonable for the federal government to commit billions of dollars to build a permanent space station when health care program budgets are being reduced?

Most issues concerning society are complicated. People have many different opinions about them. Those of us who are interested in reaching a solution that is fair for the largest group of people will examine all sides of an issue before making a decision. Will it satisfy everyone? Probably not! Issues are usually resolved through **compromise**, a "give-and-take" process. Each side gives up something in order to reach an agreement all can live with. Once the decision is agreed upon, it is followed by the group. Political decisions made by government bodies are binding on the public. These decisions usually take the form of laws.

In a democratic society, the procedure followed to resolve important issues that concern a large number of people is known as the **political process**. We act through elected government representatives to work out solutions to problems. We let our public officials know what we think. They gather information and debate the issue. A variety of points of view are considered. Solutions are suggested. Compromises are made. A law or policy is developed, and a vote is taken. Once the majority has made a decision for or against an issue, the public accepts the decision. Of course, groups that disagree can work to change the decision in the future.

Establishing Public Policy

Through the workings of politics, public goals are established at every level of government. The community in which you live might decide to give small businesses special help in getting started. On the state level, a goal might be increasing aid to education. A national goal might be to provide medical insurance for everyone under the age of ten. Goals are translated into plans of action to benefit the greater good. The resulting product, these plans of action, is known as **public policy**.

Let's Think

1. Explain what influences the way people feel about an issue.
2. Make a list of steps that people should take in making controversial decisions.
3. Explain the meaning of the following terms: compromise, political process.
4. Study your local newspaper for a few days or a week. Make a list of the important issues featured on the front page. Which, in your opinion, would be of greatest concern to you and your family? Why?

Political Parties

Public policies are constantly being formed and re-formed. Views change about how to solve problems facing any level of government. Various groups try to influence government officials as they try to decide on public policy.

People who have similar ideas about the direction of public policy join together in **political parties**. These are organizations created to win elections. Their goal is to control government and help construct public policy. Parties name candidates to run for office at all levels of govern-ment—local, state, and national. Parties are most visible at election time. This is especially true during presidential election years.

We find political parties in all democracies. Some nations have many political parties competing with one another to control the government. Other nations, such as the United States, have a two-party system. The two major political parties in the United States are the Democratic Party and the Republican Party. At times, additional parties have been created to compete with the two major parties.

The Constitution and Political Parties

When the Framers wrote the United States Constitution in 1787, they did not provide for political parties. Many feared that political parties would tend to tear the country apart. They argued that such organizations would create a great deal of friction, cause disunity among people, and lead to an unstable government.

Others did not believe that this would be the case. Among them was James Madison. (He played a leading role in the creation of the U.S. Constitution and later became our fourth president.) Madison joined with Alexander Hamilton and John Jay to write a series of essays in support of the new Constitution. These essays are known as the *Federalist* or the *Federalist Papers*.

In *Federalist*, Number 10, Madison explained that factions were bound to develop in a free society. (**Factions** are groups of people who hold

What Do We Do When We Volunteer or Work for a Political Party?

1. Canvass by telephone—make phone calls that solicit opinions on issues and money contributions or urge people to vote for your candidate.
2. Do clerical work—assist the party or candidate in keeping records, schedules, etc.
3. Hand out leaflets—information flyers about the candidate and the party are given to people in public areas such as train stations and busy street corners.
4. Help plan meetings—some local candidates like to meet with small groups in private homes and speak to groups of people in individual neighborhoods. Someone is needed to arrange these events.

Political Parties Winning the Presidency Since 1796

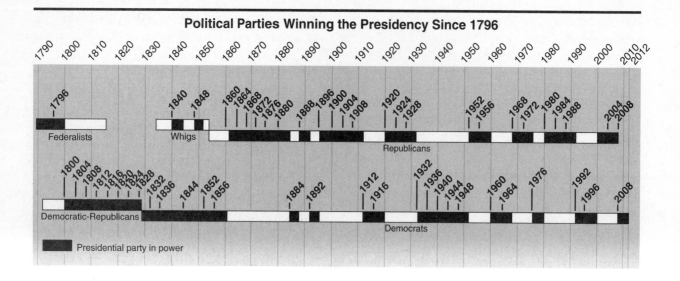

similar ideas. Sometimes they form political parties or interest groups.) We are, Madison wrote, many people with many ideas and opinions. Therefore, people will naturally choose sides when deciding how to approach issues. Madison went on to predict that because there are many different opinions, no one faction will gain so much control that it will destroy representative government. The variety of opinions will create a system in which factions will counter, or balance, the power and policies of each other. Madison believed that this condition ensured that representative government would be supported and not destroyed by the development of political parties.

The History of U.S. Political Parties

Many different political parties have been created in the United States since the 1790s. But for most of our history, the nation has had only two major parties at any one time. Both have had control of the government at different periods. Occasionally, there have been more than two parties on the American political scene.

Political parties in the United States can be traced back to the presidential administration of George Washington (1789–1797). Two of President Washington's advisers, Alexander Hamilton and Thomas Jefferson, disagreed about what the proper role of the national government should be. Jefferson believed that much of the

power of government should be given to the states. Hamilton believed in a strong central government.

Each of these men represented a different part of early American society. Hamilton was considered to be a champion of the wealthy property owners. He once wrote, "All communities divide themselves into the few and the many. The first are the rich and wellborn, the other the mass of the people. . . . The people are turbulent and changing; they seldom judge or determine right. Give therefore to the first class a distinct, permanent share in the government. They will check the unsteadiness of the second, . . ." Hamilton believed that the common person could not be trusted to make wise decisions for the nation. The well-to-do property holders and businesspeople were better suited to make decisions for all.

Jefferson was seen to be the supporter of the "common" person, the farmers and laborers. His first inaugural address in 1801 reflects that view. "Equal and exact justice to all men, of whatever state or persuasion, religious or political, . . ." In referring to "state," he means the social status of the individual. He is assuring the American people that the government is for all people.

Two political parties formed around these philosophies. The *Federalist Party* was Hamilton's party. Jefferson's party became known as the *Democratic-Republican Party*. By 1830, the name had changed to just *Democratic Party*. In the early 1800s, the Federalist Party disbanded, and in the

1830s, the *Whig Party* was created. The controversy over slavery in the mid-1800s led to the birth of the *Republican Party*. In 1860, the Republicans succeeded in electing their second presidential candidate, Abraham Lincoln, to office. The Democrats and the Republicans are the major national parties that dominate American politics today.

Third Parties

Throughout American history, groups with ideas different from those of the Democrats and Republicans have formed new political parties. Called **third parties**, they have nominated candidates to run for office. Often a third party focuses on one or two issues of particular importance to its members.

One of the strongest third parties developed during the late 1800s. In the South and West, many farmers with small farms found themselves losing money because the prices for their crops kept falling. They had to take out bank loans. But they had a hard time paying back the loans. Many lost their farms. The farmers believed that both of the major parties were not addressing their problems at any level of government. They moved away from the Republicans and Democrats to form a new political party. Known as the *Populist Party*, its program aimed at addressing the needs of the farmers.

One idea called for the unlimited coinage of silver to increase the amount of money in circulation and make it easier for farmers to repay their debts. Populists wanted an income tax that would require the wealthier people to pay more taxes. They also supported government ownership of railroads and an eight-hour workday.

The Populists nominated James B. Weaver to run against the Republican and Democratic nominees in the presidential election of 1892. Grover Cleveland, the Democratic nominee, won the election, but Weaver took 8 percent of the popular vote and 22 electoral votes. The income tax and the eight-hour workday did eventually become law.

Having a third-party candidate on the ballot has sometimes changed the outcome of elections. For instance, in the 1912 presidential election, Theodore Roosevelt, running as a Progressive (Bull Moose) candidate, took votes away from the Republican candidate, William Howard Taft. This allowed Democrat Woodrow Wilson to win the election. Roosevelt had been a popular Republican president (1901–1909).

Third-party movements have not lasted long for a variety of reasons. Sometimes the issue they promoted became less urgent. Usually, though, it was taken from them by one of the major parties. Once the third party's central issue was made into law, the party no longer had a reason to exist. Today, we might call some of the minority parties

Third Parties Winning Electoral Votes in Presidential Elections Since 1832

Year	Party and Candidate	Electoral Votes
1832	Anti-Masonic, William Wirt	7
1856	Whig, Millard Fillmore	8
1860	Constitutional, John Bell Southern Democrat, John Breckinridge	39 72
1892	Populist, James B. Weaver	22
1912	Progressive (Bull Moose), Theodore Roosevelt	88
1924	Progressive, Robert M. LaFollette	16
1948	States' Rights (Dixiecrat), Strom Thurmond	39
1960	Socialist-Labor, Eric Hass	15
1968	American Independent, George C. Wallace	46

of the past "single-issue" parties. Such groups, now fairly common, focus on one major idea that may have a limited appeal for the majority of voters over time.

Voters in recent elections have seen a number of "third" parties listed on their ballots. The Libertarian Party, founded in 1971, calls for less government interference in the private lives of citizens and the elimination of most taxes. The Green Party surfaced in 1996. Its first presidential nominee was the consumer advocate Ralph Nader. He campaigned against increasing corporate influence in America. The abortion issue has led to the development of Right to Life parties in many states. None of these parties has gained widespread support for its candidates.

The Purpose of Political Parties

Political parties serve several important functions in the United States. Foremost on their agenda is to elect party members to public office. The hope is to elect enough people to gain control of the government at any level—local, state, national. When it is out of power, a political party "keeps an eye" on how its opponent is running the government. The "out" party makes sure that the voters hear about the errors it believes the opposition is making.

Political parties also identify issues they believe are important to American voters. Parties conduct opinion polls and telephone surveys and send out questionnaires to see what kinds of issues people care about. Parties use this information to offer solutions to major problems.

You might hear candidates explaining their party's policy toward taxes, health care, Social Security, the homeless, and foreign affairs. The policies a party names and supports during an election year are put together in a **platform**. The platform tells the voters what the party stands for. The party's nominees support the platform throughout the campaign. Each party hopes its platform will appeal to more voters than the platform of the rival party.

When a party gets into power, it tries to put its policies into action. If the policies work, voters will be happy. At the next election, they will return the party and its candidates to office. If the policies fail or become unpopular, the voters might turn to a different party. They will elect its candidates and give it a chance to run the government. An example of this reaction was the 2008 election to fill seats in Congress. The voters expressed their dissatisfaction with the way the Republicans were running the government and chose Democrats in most races. The Democratic Party gained control of both houses of Congress, the Senate and the House of Representatives, and the presidency.

It costs a great deal of money to run a campaign. Political parties help raise funds for the campaigns of individuals and for party functions. They hold fund-raising dinners and other events and request donations through the mail and e-mail.

Getting out the vote is another important party function. On election day, party workers call voters to urge them to go to the polls. Child care and transportation may be arranged for those who need it.

Let's Think

1. What is a political party?
2. What did James Madison say about the formation of political parties (factions)?
3. How did the ideas of Thomas Jefferson differ from those of Alexander Hamilton?
4. What role have third parties played in American political life?
5. List the functions political parties serve. Which do you think is the most important? Why?

The Structure of Political Parties

The structure of both the Republican and Democratic political parties is similar. Each has national, state, and local levels. The levels are only loosely connected. The national organization has no real authority over the state and local levels.

Organization of a Political Party

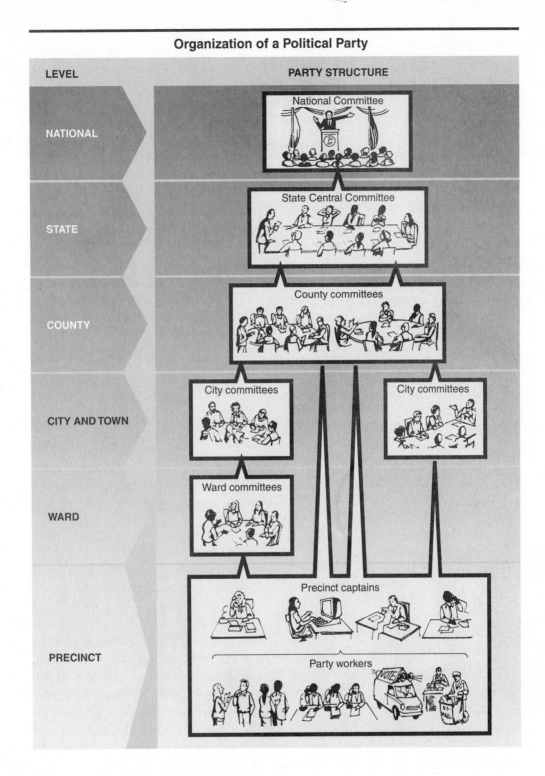

LEVEL	PARTY STRUCTURE
NATIONAL	National Committee
STATE	State Central Committee
COUNTY	County committees
CITY AND TOWN	City committees / City committees
WARD	Ward committees
PRECINCT	Precinct captains / Party workers

National Committee

We hear about national parties mainly during presidential election years. Headquartered in Washington, D.C., the national committees consist of representatives from each state, the District of Columbia, and each U.S. territory. The chairperson of the party is chosen by the presidential candidate at the end of the national convention.

One of the key responsibilities of a national committee is to organize and run the national party convention. The convention brings together the party leaders and representatives every four years. They conduct party business and nominate candidates for president and vice president. The convention delegates, through committees, prepare and vote on the party platform that the candidates will run on.

Another major function of the national committee is to raise money to carry out the election campaign. Some money is also used to pay the expenses of the day-to-day operation of the party.

State Central Committees

Each major party is represented in each of the 50 states by a state central committee. Members of the committee are chosen at party primaries or at the annual state party convention. The leader, who is the official party head in the state, is chosen by the committee. Often, major political figures in the state recommend a candidate.

The state committee coordinates the work of the county organizations, organizes the party convention, raises money for campaigns, and helps select candidates. It also publicizes party positions and activities. In addition, the committee has a say in passing out party patronage. This means that it helps determine who should get government jobs, contracts, and other favors. Obviously, party supporters receive preference.

County Committees

The county party leader is selected by a convention or a primary. This person works closely with the state committee. The county committee takes care of political activities in the area, selects candidates, and works to make elections go smoothly. It also tries to influence local policies on such matters as the location of buildings and business development.

Precinct Level

The political organization closest to the average person is the precinct committee. Every city and town is divided into voting districts called precincts. The leader is called a captain. This person takes care of voters' problems when possible, gets petitions signed, helps people get to the polls, and recommends possible candidates. The captain is chosen by the local committee.

Let's Think

1. What are the major functions of the national committee of a political party?
2. How are the state and county committee responsibilities similar and different?
3. What is the importance of the precinct to a political party?

Conducting a Political Campaign

How does one run for president? First, a potential candidate has to become known to the American people and to his or her own party leaders. Many who seek the presidency started out in local and state offices and then moved on to the national stage in the Senate or House of Representatives. Others might have a business background or have been a high-ranking officer in the military. Each has to have drive, stamina, and an acceptable personal background.

Early Stages

A year or more before the presidential election, a potential candidate may travel around the country making speeches and trying to get as much media coverage as possible. He or she talks about public policy issues and how his or her plans would help the country. The person tests his or her ability to raise money to fund a serious campaign. To be successful, a candidate must have the support of influential public and political officials. Having an appealing personality isn't always enough. The person's ideas must attract favorable attention and be acceptable to the voters.

One of the earliest tasks a candidate must undertake is putting together a campaign staff. It consists of professional campaigners as well as volunteers who believe in the candidate and want to take part in the process of electing a public official. One of the most important staff people is the *campaign manager*. He or she is charged with the huge task of planning strategy and coordinating campaign activities.

Speechwriters are also vital in getting the candidate's message across.

Winning Primaries

To test public and party support, a potential candidate files petitions and takes the proper steps to get his or her name put on the ballot in a number of **primary** elections. During the early months of a presidential election year, primaries are held in many states. These elections help the state parties select delegates to the national conventions. The winning slate of delegates is pledged to support a particular candidate.

To get support and votes, the candidate travels about the country. He or she speaks at rallies, attends fund-raising dinners, and contacts local, state, and national organizations. The candidate will greet people at factories, in shopping malls, on street corners, and at commuter train stations. As time goes on, the candidate will appear on local and national television and radio shows. In some states, debates among the candidates will be held.

National Convention

In the middle of the summer of a presidential election year, thousands of party delegates from all over the country take part in a great political spectacle called the national convention. Delegates to the convention are selected in three ways. The first is by the state committee, the second is by a statewide vote, and the third is by a state convention.

In recent years, the national conventions have become less important in the process of selecting a presidential candidate. By the time the convention is held, one person has usually triumphed over rivals in the primaries. So, the convention delegates normally do not choose the candidate at the convention. They vote for the person they are already committed to.

Conventions do give parties exposure on national television. But network television now covers only the highlights of the conventions. Conventions also allow the party faithful to band together and show their enthusiasm for the party's platform and candidate. Differences in political philosophy are put aside in order to rally behind the chosen candidate. Conventions also provide an opportunity to showcase up-and-coming political figures.

Before or during the convention, the leading presidential nominee names his or her choice for vice president. The delegates confirm the choice. On the last day of the convention, the presidential and vice presidential nominees address the delegates and, through the media, the nation. The candidates sound the challenge to the opposing party and lay out the major themes of the campaign. A joyous and noisy celebration breaks out—one arranged by the convention planners.

Final Stages

After the political conventions, the candidates fine-tune their campaign strategies. Then they set off on their travels around the country. They normally concentrate on the states with the most electoral votes and those that may swing to one party or the other with extra attention.

The candidates' aim is to put forth a message and a personality that will appeal to as many voters as possible. Advertisements are prepared for broadcast on television and radio. Web pages are created. Focus groups are held, and polls are taken to see how the voters are perceiving the message and to find out what should be changed or emphasized. Spouses and children also make appearances. A great deal of time and energy is spent on raising funds to pay for the travel and advertisements. Usually, the major presidential candidates hold two or three nationally televised debates in September and October. The vice presidential candidates also debate at least once.

The long, hard, exhausting campaign ends on election day in November (the first Tuesday after the first Monday). After they vote, the candidates go to their election headquarters to await the decision of the voters.

Let's Think

1. What is the purpose of a primary?
2. What function does the national convention serve?

3. Why is fund-raising such an important job for the candidates?

Special Interest Groups

Lawmakers are not the only people who have a hand in creating laws and public policy. Organizations that are not officially part of government also influence its actions. These organizations are called **lobbies**, **special interest groups**, or **pressure groups**.

What Does a Lobby Do?

The purpose of a lobby is to persuade lawmakers to pass laws that will be in the best interest of the group the lobby represents. The individuals who act on behalf of the lobbies are called **lobbyists**.

Most lobbyists are professionals who spend all their working hours trying to influence lawmakers. Their goal is to get the lawmakers to shape laws and vote in ways that benefit the people who hire the lobby. To accomplish this goal, lobbyists furnish information to lawmakers. For example, during consideration of Farm Subsidy Bill of 2008, all kinds of lobbyists pressured Congress. They represented corn growers, cattle ranchers, salmon fishers, school lunch operators, environmentalists, and others.

Lobbyists make personal phone calls to legislators and their staffs. They give social receptions and dinners to influence lawmakers to have a favorable opinion about the aims of the lobby.

When lawmakers consider a bill, a proposed law, they often hold hearings to learn about the opinions of experts in the field. Lobbyists may also testify at such hearings.

Who Participates in a Lobby?

Lobbyists represent all kinds of people, organizations, and businesses who are interested in influencing our laws. Interest groups speak for

INTEREST GROUP	PEOPLE REPRESENTED
American Medical Association (AMA)	doctors
American Federation of Labor and Congress of Industrial Organizations (AFL-CIO)	unionized workers in a variety of industries
National Rifle Association of America (NRA)	gun owners, hunters, gun industry, and those who oppose restricting the right to own guns
Common Cause	people who want to bring about political and social reform to make the government more responsive to the needs of all citizens, not just special interests
National Association for the Advancement of Colored People (NAACP)	African Americans and others interested in reducing prejudice and promoting civil rights
AARP (American Association of Retired People)	people 50 years of age or older
Sierra Club	people interested in preserving wilderness areas and protecting the environment
League of Women Voters	people who are interested in good government, one that is responsible to all citizens

<REALITY CHECK>

Reduction in the Importance of Presidential Nominating Conventions

Late in the summer every four years, a great American drama occurs. Delegates of the major political parties gather to nominate presidential and vice-presidential candidates and adopt a platform (set of principles) on which the candidates will base their campaigns. With the popularity of television in the second half of the 20th century, the national party conventions became "happenings." Millions of Americans tuned in to find out who would capture the nominations. In the late 1960s and early 1970s, the Democrats and Republicans adopted a primary system to sort out the contenders for national office. They thought that this system would help avoid controversy at the nominating conventions and make each party look as unified as possible to the American public. Primaries would also give more voters an opportunity to support the candidates they preferred. The primary system helped weed out the weaker or less popular candidates.

Over the years, the primaries have greatly diminished the drama of the national conventions. Now Americans know who the nominee of each party will be before the candidates are formally selected by the conventions. Let us look at the 2008 primary season to see why this is the case.

As 2008 began, it became apparent that history was about to be made. In the Republican Party, one candidate for president who was given almost no chance to win became the nominee. The Democratic Party soon had two history-making front-runners. One was a woman, and the other was an African-American man.

Many of the candidates from each party had announced their candidacies before the "primary season" began. On the Republican side, Senator John McCain of Arizona declared his candidacy 16 months prior to the first primary. Former Governor of Massachusetts Mitt Romney declared 18 months before it. Leading Democratic candidates also announced early. Senator Hillary Rodham Clinton of New York and Senator Barack Obama of Illinois declared almost a year before. Former Senator John Edwards of North Carolina announced almost two years before.

On January 3, 2008, eight months before the party conventions, the race for each party's nomination to run for president of the United States formally began with the Iowa caucuses. In caucus states, party loyalists meet, debate, and vote for the candidate of their choice. The field of candidates was crowded. At this stage of the primary season, more than 20 candidates in both parties hoped to win the support of voters. The results of the first caucus produced a win for Democrat Barack Obama, an African American, and for former Arkansas Governor Mike Huckabee on the Republican side.

Just five days later, both parties held primaries in New Hampshire. There, Democrat Hillary Clinton and Republican "dark horse" candidate John McCain won. Only five months earlier, a poll of New Hampshire Republicans had shown that McCain had just 15 percent support, while front-runner Mitt Romney had support from 35 percent of the voters. It was a very important come-from-behind victory for McCain.

After winning all four Republican primaries on March 4, McCain reached the magic number needed for the Republican nomination—more than 1,191 pledged delegates. He could now head to the Republican convention in September as the presumptive nominee of his party.

On June 3, history was made on the Democratic side when Barack Obama gathered enough pledged delegates to become the presumptive nominee of the Democrats. He received more than the 2,118 pledged delegates needed. A reluctant Hillary Clinton suspended her bid for the nomination. Obama was the first African American to become the official nominee of a major political party for president of the United States.

The Democrats held their convention in Denver, Colorado, from August 25 to 28, while the Republicans held theirs in St. Paul, Minnesota, from September 1 to 4. There was very little drama or suspense in the proceedings because everyone already knew who the presidential nominees would be. But the conventions do bring party members together to officially confirm the nominees and reaffirm their loyalty to party principles. Conventions provide an opportunity to showcase prominent party members and introduce up-and-coming party leaders.

1. Why do individuals enter presidential primary elections?
2. How do primary victories lead to increased support for a candidate?
3. Why were the results of the 2008 primary season historic for the country?
4. Give arguments for or against holding party national nominating conventions.

farmers, doctors, lawyers, members of labor unions, retired people, automobile owners, youth groups, educators, and many others. The table on page 58 lists a few interest groups and the types of people each represents.

Political Action Committees

A special kind of interest group is called a **political action committee (PAC)**. They were created by unions, business associations, and professional groups to raise money to influence elections. The organizations that created the PACs are not allowed to give money directly to candidates. A PAC gives money to the political candidates it believes will promote the PAC's best interests.

Many believe that political action committees exert too much influence on elections because they spend so much. Lawmakers may find it difficult to vote against the interests of groups that helped elect them to office. Various federal laws try to regulate the activities and spending of PACs.

Pros and Cons of Lobbies

A newsmagazine columnist in the 1990s had this to say about lobbies: "[W]hile lobbyists have become every politician's favorite whipping boy, virtually every American now depends on them in some way to petition the government and make democracy work: backpackers and snack makers, publishers and professors, churches and

chain stores. Says Mark Helmke, a Washington public-relations strategist: 'All people attack special interest groups—but 90 percent belong to one.'"

Lobbyists use a variety of techniques to gain support for their positions. In addition to meeting directly with lawmakers, they try to reach the public at large in order to sway people's opinions. Lobbyists hope that if public opinion supports their positions, people will influence the way lawmakers vote. To get their message out to the public, lobbying groups take out advertisements on television and in magazines and newspapers.

Lobbyists in a corridor of the Connecticut State Capitol in Hartford. They had been working hard to influence legislation to deregulate the electricity industry in the state.

P O W E R *of* ★ N E

Candy Lightner

Why do people become involved in public affairs? Some have a special desire to follow a career of public service. Others enjoy the give and take of politics. Still others have a passion for a single cause that they believe is not being a addressed by the government and society at large.

Such a person is Candy Lightner, the founder of Mothers Against Drunk Driving (MADD), a special interest group dedicated to protecting people from the tragedies caused by drunk driving. One Saturday in 1980, Lightner and her family suffered a terrible tragedy. Her 13-year-old daughter Cari was killed by a drunken hit-and-run driver as she walked to a nearby church carnival. The person who drove the car had been convicted of drunk driving three times in four years, but had never been put in jail.

From this tragedy came Lightner's commitment to do something about the penalties for drunk driving in the state of California, where she lived. She believed they were too lenient. Lightner decided to form what became a major national organization. Early in the development of MADD, Lightner tried to see then California Governor Jerry Brown to get his support for a commission to investigate drunk-driving laws. At first, Lightner found it difficult to see the governor. Newspapers publicized her plight, and the governor finally met with her. He agreed to create a commission to deal with issues related to drunk driving and make Lightner a member.

One of the earliest campaigns that Lightner and her organization started was to pressure individual states to raise the legal drinking age from 18 to 21. Statistics showed that many accidents occurred among drunk drivers under the age of 21. As time went on, chapters of MADD spread throughout the nation. Currently, there are chapters in all 50 states and related groups in other nations.

During the eight years that Lightner headed MADD, she campaigned for a national law to raise the drinking age to 21. This was difficult to achieve because such authority is actually in the hands of state legislators. MADD chapters pressured legislators in the states, but Lightner believed Congress and the president also had to take a stand. The liquor and beer lobbies worked to undermine her efforts.

In December 1983, a presidential commission recommended federal penalties for states that did not enact a minimum drinking age of 21. Lightner personally lobbied senators and representatives in an effort to get their support for a bill to turn this recommendation into a law. Although the law could not require the states to raise the legal age for drinking, it did threaten to cut off federal highway funds to those states that did not comply. Since then, every state has made 21 the legal drinking age.

Schools throughout the nation have created chapters of Students Against Drunk Driving (SADD). These groups educate students about the dangers of drunk driving. Both MADD and SADD urge people who are going to "party" to choose one person to be the designated driver and refrain from drinking.

Now residing in Dallas, Texas, Lightner spends much of her time traveling around the nation on speaking tours and writing articles about issues related to drunk driving. Her work over the years has been credited with saving hundreds of lives.

1. Why did Candy Lightner get involved in an effort to raise the drinking age around the nation?
2. What is Mothers Against Drunk Driving?
3. What kind of legislation was Lightner instrumental in passing?
4. How is MADD an example of a special interest group?

They send mail directly to voters' homes in the form of position papers and flyers. In return, the groups urge voters to write or call their government representatives to support or oppose a position.

Critics of lobbies believe that they exert too much influence on government officials. Lobbyists set up permanent offices near the seat of government. They spend a great deal of money to publicize their positions and to help legislators gather information and prepare laws. Some lobbyists try to gain access to decision makers by giving gifts and doing favors. In most cases, these actions are legal. But the question may be asked: Do lawmakers feel a special obligation to promote the lobbyist's cause as the result of accepting favors?

Many lobbies offer to assist lawmakers in their election campaigns by giving money and expert advice. Laws have been passed to limit the amount of money that can be given to candidates. Critics believe that more restrictions should be placed on lobbyists' activities in political campaigns.

A variety of groups represent what is considered to be the interest of the general public. They take up causes such as consumer rights, maintaining a clean and safe environment, preserving our natural resources, and protecting the health of Americans. As a result of the work of public interest groups, many people see the role of lobbyists as positive.

New Regulations

In 1946, a law regulating lobbyists who try to influence federal government officials was passed. The Federal Regulation of Lobbying Act was designed to identify professional lobbyists. Lobbyists who receive money for representing special interests are required to register with Congress.

In 1995, the first reform bill since 1946 to regulate lobbyists' activities became law. It defines a lobbyist as a person who spends at least 20 percent of his or her time lobbying members of Congress, their staffs, or executive branch officials. This requirement increases the number of people who must openly declare themselves lobbyists. Lobbyists must also register with the Clerk of the

House of Representatives and the Secretary of the Senate and report their clients and issues and the agencies or legislators they lobbied. They must also estimate the amount they were paid. If a lobbyist violates these rules, he or she may be punished with a fine of up to $50,000.

Also in 1995, the House of Representatives and the Senate approved rules that limit the gifts members can accept from lobbyists. These new rules are designed to curb the amount of personal influence that lobbyists exert on members of Congress. A law passed in 2007 put further restrictions on members of Congress and the executive branch. For example, senators now have to wait two years after retiring before they can become lobbyists.

Adding Your Voice

At one time or another, most of us would like to influence government decisions. We may contact our representatives in the local, state, or national government. But we're not sure that one letter, phone call, or e-mail message will have an impact on the representative's decision. But over and over again, officials say that individual voices do matter. In fact, they pay particular attention to personal letters.

Another way to influence decisions is to become part of a lobby or special interest group. Many organizations that people belong to or donate to try to influence government policy. For example, you or your family may have given money to an organization like the Sierra Club, which works to protect the environment. This organization lobbies governments on all levels. Your money aids the group's work. It adds your voice in with the voices of many others to give the organization greater strength in its lobbying efforts.

Let's Think

1. What is a special interest group or lobby?
2. List and explain the functions of a special interest group.
3. How is a PAC (political action committee) different from a lobby?

4. Why do some people feel that lobbies and PACs have too much influence?

Mass Media Influence Our Opinions

Mass media are the forms of communication that transmit information to great numbers of people. Millions can be reached at the same time. For instance, through the medium of television, fans all over the world could watch the 2008 Summer Olympics from Beijing, China. One of the most significant developments has been the ability of people to communicate ideas to others throughout the world within minutes.

Print Media

We read newspapers and magazines to be entertained and to gather information. You may look in the daily newspaper to find out the score of last night's baseball, hockey, or basketball game. But newspapers give you even more information about current happenings in your community and state, in the nation, and around the world. Some newspapers provide more serious coverage of events than others. Most news articles written by responsible journalists report events in a factual way and do not offer opinions. However, all newspapers include *editorials*. Editorials are essays that give the opinion of the paper about important issues of the day. They are designed to influence public opinion. Many newspapers have what is known as an *op-ed* page (op = opposite; ed = editorial), which contains features and commentary about a variety of topics, serious or lighthearted.

Newspapers have become less influential because their readership has declined. A variety of factors have brought this about: young people tend not to read newspapers; there are more all-news television channels; access to the Internet has expanded; people claim they do not have time to read.

A wide variety of magazines is available at any newsstand. Some entertain us with stories describing our favorite movie star's home. Others tell us about the best equipment to use in caving expeditions. A few publications give us in-depth opinion pieces about public policy issues. A great many focus on single interests. For instance, there are magazines that deal with news coverage, hunting and the outdoors, investing and the economy, business, or music and the entertainment industry.

Radio

What do people do when they want to find out what's happening right now? Possibly, they turn to an all-news radio station or television channel or go online. Portable radios keep us in touch with events no matter where we are. Call-in talk shows allow us to express our opinions on the topic of the day. The ordinary person's ideas are listened to by as many people as listen to the host's views.

Television

In 2008, in the United States, 113.1 million households owned at least one television set. Television programs provide a primary source of news and entertainment. How events and people are presented on the television screen influences our opinions about these images and individuals.

News Programs

Television focuses on the most dramatic, unusual, or entertaining aspect of an event. TV producers like action scenes. Seldom does a program linger on an issue or event for more than a few minutes. Short, catchy quotes—sound bites—are featured. Lengthy, thoughtful discussions about hard questions do not appeal to large numbers of people.

News anchors become more familiar to us than many of our friends and relatives. We have come to trust our favorite newscaster's presentation of information about an event. We forget that this person is usually reading a script prepared by someone else. Seldom does the newscaster have personal, on-site knowledge of an

"Is this too much information?"

event. The person may not even be a trained news gatherer.

A few longer news shows are presented in prime time. The Public Broadcasting System (PBS), for example, has several programs that provide us with in-depth coverage of important issues—from politics to the environment; from elections to health care.

Effect on Elections

Candidates for political office must make appearances on television. If they don't, they are generally not taken seriously. If they do not make a positive appearance on television, because of physical appearance or personality, the viewer/voter may react negatively. During the 1960 campaign for president, Richard Nixon and John F. Kennedy conducted the first live presidential debates on television. It was generally agreed that the television camera was kinder to Kennedy than to Nixon. Nixon had a dark beard that tended to show under the camera lights, and he looked unshaven and tired. In contrast, the handsome Kennedy looked well-groomed and energetic.

President Ronald Reagan (1981–1989) was considered to be a master of television. As a former actor, he had spent a major portion of his life in front of the camera and knew how to talk to people through television. It helped make him one of the more popular presidents of the 20th century.

Benefits and Dangers

Television is powerful. We have to be aware of its dangers as well as its benefits. Learning to evaluate television coverage of any event is important. We should ask ourselves a variety of questions about the scenes in front of us. What is happening outside of the camera shot? Who is directing the shots? When were they taken? Are people acting naturally, or are they performing for the camera? Is one part of an event getting more attention than another part? Why?

Television has the wonderful capacity to draw us together in the face of celebration and tragedy. The whole nation focused on New York City in September 2001. Americans watched with concern as rescue workers looked for survivors of the attack on the World Trade Center. We cheered the bravery and dedication of the rescuers and sympathized with the victims' families. Through television, we felt connected to the people of New York City as they struggled to cope with the tragedy.

The Internet

More and more government officials and departments are going "online." As a result, information about them is becoming readily available to people who have an Internet connection. Many schools and public libraries provide access to the Internet. Senators and representatives have e-mail addresses and may have "pages" on the World Wide Web. Constituents can communicate through e-mail to give their opinions to government officials and to find out information from officials. The Internet also makes it possible for people to easily research laws, voting records of officials, and background information on issues in such sources as the Library of Congress. Access on the Internet to up-to-date and accurate information about public issues can help individuals be better informed about a question. Through blogs, people can share their political opinions.

The Media Monitor Officials

In addition to providing information about events and issues, reporters for the media write and talk about the conduct of public officials. Reporters ask questions to find out why officials made the decisions they did. Sometimes, officials' actions follow a path different from the one their public statements indicate. Reporters try to find out why, so that the general public can understand the officials' motives.

The continual effort to get the "real story" behind the public statements and actions may be irritating. Sensitive public figures may feel harassed by the relentless questioning.

The Media Provide Feedback

Decision makers pay attention to what is printed in newspapers and magazines, what is shown on television, and what people discuss in the chat rooms on the Internet. They want to know which issues and events are being highlighted. Issues emphasized by the media will be the ones the public becomes concerned about. Lawmakers like to know what people are thinking. This information guides the lawmakers' views on issues under consideration and helps them create public policies to meet constituents' needs.

Let's Think

1. Name the different forms of mass media.
2. How does the media help shape public opinion?
3. How has television influenced the public perception of candidates?
4. How can we keep from being overly influenced by the media?

Public Opinion Polls

Public leaders have to make policy about complex issues. How do they find out what the general public feels about an issue? A candidate running for political office wants to know what the voters think about his or her latest advertisement. What does he or she do? A major daily newspaper wants to find out what problems the public is most worried about. How does the paper gather this information?

How Polls Are Conducted

One tool that is used to find out what people think is the **public opinion poll**. This is a survey to determine what people's views are on particular issues. Through a scientific method, *pollsters* decide how many people from different walks of life should be included in a survey to make it representative of the population as a whole. The pollsters ask every member of the pool of people the same questions. The results of the poll are analyzed, summarized, and then published. Professionally conducted polls are considered to be accurate within a small margin for error.

Pollsters make projections based on a sampling of the answers people give to survey questions. For instance, pollsters hired by candidates or political parties try to predict which candidates may be ahead in a race for elected office. Every four years, the media is full of polls telling the American public which presidential candidate is most likely to be elected. These polls tell you why the voting public might favor a candidate and how voters feel about the issues raised by the candidate.

On election day, reporters and pollsters interview voters as they leave the polls after they vote. These exit polls include questions on who the voter voted for and why. The information collected may show how the election is going—who is winning and why. News commentators use the information to project winners soon after the polls close. Candidates analyze the information to see what was effective or ineffective in their campaigns.

Pros and Cons of Polls

Critics say that polls have a way of changing people's opinions. People, they say, see how others think about issues and decide to go along with the majority. Politicians often use polls to help them decide how to vote on important laws. Elected officials take many things into consideration when they vote. Among the influences is the way the people the officials represents think about issues. To find out the district's views, the official may use a public opinion poll.

If an official's votes are guided mainly by poll results, the person is said to be following public opinion. Critics think that decision making based on polls is not always in the best interest of the district or the nation. Elected representatives need to lead and shape public views, not just follow poll results.

Poll results may not always show a true picture of public opinion. How questions are phrased and the personality of the pollsters can influence the kinds of answers people give. People may also give what they feel are the "right" answers rather than reveal what they really think.

If an officeholder can accurately gauge public opinion in his or her district, the officeholder can better serve the district. The official can focus on problems that are important to the people he or she represents. Time, energy, and money aren't wasted on promoting policies that will not be supported.

Let's Think

1. What is a public opinion poll?
2. What functions do public opinion polls serve?
3. Why should the results of public opinion polls be examined carefully by both public officials and ordinary citizens?

Chapter Summary

Controversy is a dispute about choices that people have to make. The political process is the resolution of controversies about public policy. It is important to understand what influences the way people think. A person's background, income, living conditions, and religious beliefs all play a role in forming his or her opinions. The process of deciding issues that have more than one solution involves considering many points of view. Ultimately, the decision makers arrive at a compromise solution that they hope will satisfy the greatest number of people. Minority rights and opinions are protected in the process. Solutions may be rethought if they turn out to be unacceptable in the long run.

Political parties have been a natural development in the American political system. Because people have a variety of opinions and express them freely, it is logical to assume that there will be differences in the way people think the government should operate. The first parties were the Federalists, led by Alexander Hamilton, and the Democratic-Republicans, led by Thomas Jefferson. Over the years, these parties gave way to others. By the Civil War period (1861–1865), the two major political parties were the Democratic and Republican.

At times, "third parties" have sprung up. These are often single-issue groups that believe

Polls can reflect public opinion about an issue or affect how people view an issue. Politicians are often criticized for basing public policy on poll results.

the major parties are not addressing a particular need of the nation. Most third parties died out because the issue they promoted was resolved or the major parties adopted the issue.

Political parties serve several functions. First, they exist to elect candidates to government positions in order to gain control of the government. This is the case on all levels of government. They help choose candidates for office, select issues that are to be addressed, and raise funds for political campaigns.

Each political party has national, state, and local organizations. The main function of the national committee is to plan for and run the national party convention. It is held every four years to nominate presidential and vice-presidential candidates and to set forth the party platform. A party chairperson is selected by the presidential nominee to tend to the party's business between conventions. Each state party or-

ganization has a state committee. The committee chooses a state leader who coordinates activities with the national committee. There are county committees and leaders, and at the city and town level, precinct captains. The precinct captain is instrumental in developing support for party candidates on a local level and getting out the vote on election day. He or she also helps voters solve problems.

Running for the presidency is a complicated and prolonged process. Candidates usually declare their desire to run long before the actual election. This helps them gain the early support of voters in the party primaries. Essential to a well-run campaign is the candidate's choice for campaign manager. Speechwriters and other members of the planning staff also provide support to the candidate. A key element in the successful campaign is the ability to raise funds to pay for advertisements and travel expenses.

Primaries in the states are held early in the election year. They determine who the delegates to each party's national convention will be and what candidates the delegation will support.

Private citizens, corporations, charities, public-service-minded groups, and others all want to influence government policy. As a result, professional lobby organizations and special interest groups exist. They represent specific points of view and try to influence members of the government to support their position. These groups have sometimes been criticized as having too much influence on elected officials. Consequently, the government passed a lobby reform act in 1995. This was the first time regulations had been changed since 1946.

Political action committees (PACs) are organizations that make contributions to the campaign funds of those running for office. PACs have been formed by business organizations, public service groups, and unions. PACs have also been criticized as having too much influence on candidates.

Another influence on our government is the media. Print media, television, and radio have a great impact on the way Americans think. They bring issues to the surface and present different points of view. Television is the primary source of information about public affairs for most people.

It is important for public officials to know what American voters think about the issues of the day. Therefore, the media and political parties conduct many surveys or polls. Through the use of a scientific sampling method, the poll results usually accurately reflect the ideas of most people. Poll results can be affected by the wording of questions and by the personality of the pollster.

★ CHAPTER REVIEW ★

A. Matching
Match each term in Column A with its definition in Column B.

Column A
1. controversy
2. political process
3. Federalist Papers
4. public policy
5. political party
6. Federalist
7. Populist Party
8. Republican Party
9. lobby
10. mass media

Column B
a. group representing a special interest that tries to influence laws
b. essays written in support of the U.S. Constitution
c. magazines, newspapers, television, radio, Internet
d. plans of action created by a government
e. procedure followed to resolve important issues
f. organization that tries to elect candidates to public office
g. example of a third party
h. member of one of the first political parties
i. political organization that chose Abraham Lincoln as its second presidential candidate
j. disputes about an issue

B. Multiple Choice
Select the statement or word that most correctly answers the question or completes the statement.

1. Reaching a compromise involves (a) sticking to all of your demands throughout the discussion (b) using the media to put down others' points of view (c) giving in on some demands and keeping others (d) refusing to enter discussions.

2. The major aim of a political party is to (a) run elections (b) win elections (c) create new forms of government (d) create changes in the Constitution.

3. The person who wrote the Federalist Paper explaining the role of factions in the United

States was **(a)** James Madison **(b)** George Washington **(c)** Alexander Hamilton **(d)** Thomas Jefferson.

4. The programs a political party supports during an election are called its **(a)** public policy **(b)** platform **(c)** compromise **(d)** third party.

5. A major value of third parties has been to **(a)** elect good governors **(b)** support the two major parties **(c)** raise funds for candidates **(d)** identify issues that many people are concerned about.

6. One way a lobby or special interest group influences legislation is to **(a)** run elections **(b)** provide information to legislators **(c)** run for office **(d)** boycott elections.

7. Groups representing special interests that donate funds to a candidate's campaign fund are known as **(a)** political action committees **(b)** lobbies **(c)** political parties **(d)** campaign managers.

8. Which statement represents a frequent criticism of lobbies? **(a)** They exert too much influence on lawmakers. **(b)** Some help the consumer. **(c)** They form new governments. **(d)** They are weak and do little to influence the passage of laws.

9. An advantage of mass media is that it **(a)** reaches only people living in cities **(b)** is always accurate **(c)** can reach millions of people in a relatively short period of time **(d)** is boring and lacks drama.

10. Public opinion polls **(a)** are not usually accurate **(b)** are useful only during election campaigns **(c)** often help candidates improve their campaign appeals **(d)** show only what a small portion of the population thinks.

C. Essay

Write a paragraph about *one* of the following:

1. Political parties are an important part of our political system.
2. How presidential campaigns can be made shorter and less expensive.
3. Lobbies provide legislators with a valuable service.
4. Mass media have a greater role in shaping public opinion about controversial issues than any other force.

5. Public opinion polls are solid foundations on which to build public policy.

D. A Challenge for You

1. You decide to run for office. Make a list of ten issues that you think are important to the people in your community, state, or nation. Select five and develop a platform that you believe will win the support of the voters. Give reasons for your choices.

2. Go to the Internet to locate the Web sites of the two major political parties: Democratic and Republican. For each party, look for the views and other pertinent information found on the Web site. Then use this information to create a chart that compares and contrasts the two parties. Under the chart, write why you think the political parties maintain Web sites. Also, recommend how each Web site could be improved.

3. Analyze appeals from three different groups asking for help, donations, or support for a cause: one that comes in the mail, an ad in print media, and an ad on television. Make a portfolio that includes answers to the following questions: What point of view does each represent? Is it exaggerated? What pictures does each use? Do they use the names of individuals who support their cause? Who are these people? Why would you respect their opinions? Are you moved to support the appeal?

4. Draw a series of cartoons to present your reaction to public opinion polls.

5. According to what you have read, most people watch a lot of television. Write a letter to the editor of a newspaper describing your feelings about the influence of television on American citizens.

Document-Based Question

State the main idea in each document. Then, use information in the documents and your own knowledge to write an essay explaining how public opinion and lawmaking are influenced in the United States.

The Lobbyist's Image

The image of the lobbyist as fixer—patrolling the halls and twisting arms—is somewhat out-of-date. Many of the most successful lobbyists now concentrate on grassroots campaigning, stirring public sentiment on an issue and showering their targets with letters, visits, editorials and talk show calls. And this trend gives more weight to widely based forces—from small business and consumer groups to women, veterans and senior citizens—that can elicit public backing for their positions. Says former Reagan [adviser] Michael Deaver: "Successful lobbying efforts are ones where policy makers get information from all kinds of sources."

From "Clinton and the Lobbyists' Curse" by Steven V. Roberts. Copyright December 7, 1992, *U.S. News and World Report.*

Journalism and Politics

The relationship between journalism and politics is a two-way street: though politicians take advantage as best they can of the media of communication available to them, these media in turn attempt to use politics and politicians as a way of both entertaining and informing their audiences. The mass media, whatever their disclaimers [denials], are not simply a mirror held up to reality or a messenger that carries the news. There is inevitably a process of selection, of editing, and of emphasis, and this process reflects, to some degree, the way in which the media are organized, the kinds of audiences they seek to serve, and the preferences and opinions of the members of the media.

From *American Government* by James Q. Wilson, page 173. Copyright 1989 by D.C. Heath and Company.

CHAPTER 5

The United States Congress

★ CHAPTER FOCUS

1. What is the function of Congress?
2. How is Congress organized?

3. What powers does Congress have?
4. How does a bill become a law?

5. How does the committee system work?

The cartoon on page 72 illustrates that the lawmaking process is a combined effort by Congress and the president. But the Constitution created rules that give Congress perhaps the "lion's share" of the lawmaking process. Although many people try to influence the process, it is Congress that gives proposed laws their direction and wording.

The Role of Congress

Congress is the lawmaking, or legislative, body of our national government. It meets in the Capitol Building in Washington, D.C., to debate issues and vote on possible laws. It is in the chambers of this building that the short- and long-range programs of the national government are decided.

The Constitution Established Two Houses

The U.S. Congress is divided into two parts called houses. One house is the **Senate**; the other is the **House of Representatives**. There are 100 senators—two from each state in the United States. There are 435 members of the House of Representatives. The number of representatives each state has depends on the population of the state. But each state is entitled to at least one representative.

To better understand how the number of people in Congress is determined, it is important to look back in history. The delegates to the Constitutional Convention in 1787 debated for a long time about how to structure the lawmaking body.

Some of the states with large populations at the time, such as Virginia and Massachusetts, favored a plan that would create a two-house legislature. Membership in both houses would be

The lawmaking process involves both Congress and the president.

based on population. This was known as the *Virginia Plan*. States with small populations, such as Delaware and New Hampshire, balked at the proposal. These states believed that their power in the legislature would become weaker because there would be so many more representatives from the larger states.

An alternative plan was offered. The *New Jersey Plan* called for a one-house Congress. (A one-house legislature is known as a **unicameral legislature**.) There would be an equal number of representatives from each state. This meant that Delaware (population close to 50,000), for example, would have as many representatives as Virginia (population about 600,000). The large states were not happy with this proposal.

After heated debate and negotiation, the Framers of the Constitution compromised. They created a legislature with two houses. Membership in one house, the House of Representatives, would be based on population. The other house, the Senate, would have an equal number of members from each state, regardless of its population. This decision became known as the **Great Compromise**.

As a result of the Great Compromise, we have a **bicameral legislature**. Bicameral means a two-house body. There are several advantages to having this type of a legislature. The Senate preserves the concept that all states are equal and gives a loud voice to those states with smaller populations. As a result, small-state concerns cannot be ignored. The more populated states have a greater voice in the House of Representatives. We will see that in our lawmaking process, both houses must pass the same proposed legislation. If they disagree about a proposed law, they must discuss the differences, work them out, and reach agreement. In this way, each house can check the other's power. In addition, laws cannot be pushed through in too hasty a manner.

Who Can Be a Member of Congress?

The Constitution clearly outlines the qualifications a person needs in order to run for election to the House of Representatives and the Senate. You may think that members would be lawyers, since their primary responsibility is to create laws. This is not the case. You may think that the Constitution would indicate the educational and work background members of Congress should have. It doesn't. Article I, Section 2, Clause 2, states: "No person shall be a representative who shall not have attained to the age of twenty-five years, and been seven years a citizen of the United States, and who shall not, when elected, be an inhabitant of that state in which he shall be chosen."

Qualifications for members of the Senate are a bit different. Article I, Section 3, Clause 3, states: "No person shall be a senator who shall not have attained the age of thirty years, and been nine years a citizen of the United States, and who shall not, when elected, be an inhabitant of that state for which he shall be chosen."

The Constitution uses the pronoun "he." At the time the document was written, only white males could run for office. Now, of course, anyone, including females, can run if he or she meets the age and citizenship qualifications.

Terms of Office

Each member of the House is elected for a two-year term. This means that the entire House of Representatives runs for election at the same time. Some say that electing a new House of Representatives every two years is wasteful in terms of energy and money. Barely does a representative get to Washington after being elected before he or she has to start raising money for the next campaign. A campaign to win election to a House seat cost more than $1 million in 2008. Fund-raising efforts take time and attention away from legislative responsibilities.

On the other hand, many experts believe that frequent elections are a good idea. If a member of the House of Representatives has to run for office every two years, they say, the person will most likely try to be responsive to the needs of his or her constituency.

Senators are elected for six-year terms. Unlike the House of Representatives, the entire Senate does not run for election at the same time. A decision was made in the Constitutional Convention that the Senate should always have some senators who are experienced. Therefore, a staggered election system was created. One-third of the Senate runs for election every two years. A typical campaign for election to the Senate cost more than $10 million in 2008.

When the Constitution was written, senators were not elected by the people directly. They were appointed by the state legislatures. This system changed in 1913 with the passage of the 17th Amendment. It provided for the direct election of senators by the voting citizens.

The Importance of the Census

As our nation increased in population, the number of members of the House of Representatives increased. Eventually, it became clear that the size of the House of Representatives would grow too large. Therefore, in 1929, Congress decided to set the maximum number of representatives at 435.

In order to determine how many representatives each state should have, a count of people living in the country is made every ten years—in the year ending in 0. The first counting, or **census**, took place in 1790. The last was in 2000. The next will be in 2010.

When the new government under the Constitution began in 1789, each member of the House of Representatives represented about 30,000 people. No matter how small the population of a state was, it was guaranteed at least one member in the House of Representatives. In 1790, the population of the United States numbered 3,929,000. There were 65 members of the House and 26 senators from 13 states. By 2009, the population of the United States had increased to 305,900,000 people in 50 states. If we divide the total number of people by 435, we see that each member of the House then represented about 706,000 people.

In addition to telling us what the total population of the country is, the census also tells us where the people live. People move. Communities and states gain and lose residents. In recent years, many people from the Northeast and Midwest have moved to the South and Southwest, areas known as the "Sunbelt." The population of Arizona, Florida, and Texas has increased in recent years, partly due to migration from other states. If there were no census, we would not know which areas had lost population and which had gained.

States such as New York and Pennsylvania that have lost population are not entitled to as many members of the House of Representatives as they had in the past. California, Texas, and

Florida have gained residents. They are entitled to more representatives. So, every ten years, after the census is taken, the number of congressional districts in a state may change. After the 2000 census, for example, New York lost two representatives (dropping from 31 to 29), and Florida gained two (going from 23 to 25).

The process of redrawing districts every ten years to make them approximately equal in population is called **apportionment**. It ensures that the voice each citizen has in the House of Representatives will be nearly equal to another person's voice in another district.

Drawing District Lines

Drawing new district lines is complex. Usually a state legislature forms a committee to redraw the lines. This method has been criticized because the party in power in the legislature usually tries to draw the lines to favor it. Party officials know where those voters who are registered in their party live and try to put a majority of them into as many districts as possible. This maneuvering of district lines is known as **gerrymandering**.

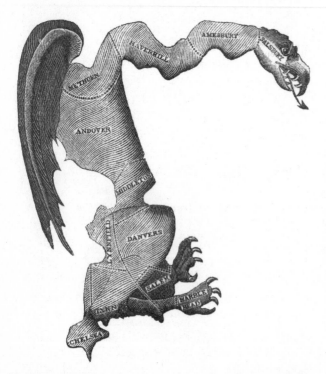

The original gerrymander cartoon. In 1812, Elbridge Gerry, a Massachusetts public official, redrew the boundaries of state election districts to favor his political party. An artist poked fun at the odd shapes by adding a head, wings, and claws to one district. Thus was created the gerrymander.

When gerrymandering occurs, district lines are drawn in weird shapes. A neighborhood may be part of two different districts. You might walk up a block, find houses on half the block in one district, then a couple of houses in a second district, and the rest of the block in the first district. Why place the two houses in a second district? The people who live in them are not registered voters in the party in power. Although this is an extreme example of line drawing, it could happen. Such decisions are made in order to benefit the party in power.

Serving the Home District

Members of Congress spend much of their time in Washington representing their home districts or states. They frequently, often weekly, commute back to their home districts to stay in touch with constituents. Senators and representatives also like to maintain contact with local officials and other leaders in their communities.

From their district and Washington offices, members of Congress and their staffs help local people solve problems and provide information. What kinds of problems might they help with? You may, for instance, have a problem relating to your passport. Perhaps it has expired, and you need a new one immediately to take a trip. Your congressperson or a staff member may be able to speed up the process. Often, a phone call from the congressperson's office is just what is needed. Or you may need information about a federal law that might affect your business. In that case, you can ask your congressperson to help you find out about the law so that you can obey it.

The congressperson often works with the local government to coordinate issues related to the district. This might involve obtaining federal funds for a new senior citizen center or a new safety program. Members of Congress and their staffs are our link to the services and power of the federal government.

Let's Think

1. Why did the delegates to the Constitutional Convention adopt the Great Compromise?

2. List the constitutional qualifications for both a member of the House of Representatives and a member of the Senate.

3. What is the meaning and the importance of the following terms: bicameral legislature, census, gerrymandering?

4. Explain why a person would want to become a member of Congress.

5. How can a member of Congress be of service to his or her constituents?

How Congress Is Organized

Both houses of Congress have officers who help the business of the legislative branch move along smoothly. Each house is organized in a slightly different way.

Organization of the House of Representatives

The leader, or presiding officer, of the House of Representatives is the **Speaker of the House**. The speaker is almost always the leader of the majority party (the one that holds the most seats). The speaker of the House of Representatives is in line to assume the presidency if the president and vice president die or are unable to fulfill their official duties at the same time.

The speaker controls the debate on the floor of the House partly by the ability to determine who will talk next. He or she is responsible for gathering support for the bills seen as important to the majority party. The speaker also decides which committee will consider proposed bills and steers bills through the legislative process.

All members of the House of Representatives serve on at least two committees and several subcommittees. It is the speaker who makes the committee assignments. Because the speaker is one of the most powerful people in the majority party, he or she is seen as a party leader and a major spokesperson for the party. In this capacity, the speaker is often interviewed by print and television reporters.

Other members of the House also have important roles. The **majority leader** is another spokesperson for the majority party. The majority leader's main responsibilities are to work to advance the policies of the party and gather support for legislation that the party considers important.

The minority party also has a leader, and that person is called the **minority leader**. An important responsibility of this person is to see that the minority party stays together and stands in opposition to the majority party. The minority leader is a major spokesperson for the minority party.

In addition, there are "whips" for both the majority and minority parties. The whip is the person who circulates on the floor and keeps his or her party members committed to voting along party lines.

Organization of the Senate

As in the House of Representatives, there is one person who presides over the Senate. The Constitution gave the vice president of the United States the duty of being the presiding officer. The title of the position is **President of the Senate**. The president of the Senate directs the debate but only votes on bills or other matters if there is a tie in the voting. In other words, this official casts a vote to break the tie.

Like the House, the Senate has several other leaders: majority and minority leaders and whips. One Senate office that has no parallel in the House is the **President Pro Tempore**. The term means temporary president. This person is usually the most senior member of the majority party. His or her major responsibility is to sit in as president of the Senate when the vice president is absent. The president pro tempore is a senator and can vote on questions.

Support Agencies

Several agencies support Congress and help it function more efficiently. One is the *Library of Congress*. It was established in 1800 to help Congress conduct its business. More than 80 million books are catalogued in the Library of

Organization of the Congress of the United States

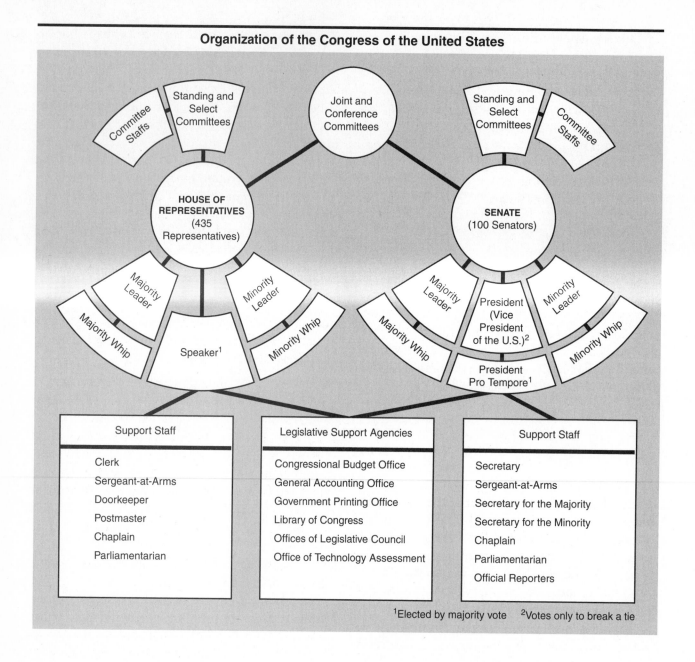

¹Elected by majority vote   ²Votes only to break a tie

Congress. Here you can find almost anything that has ever been written. The library has a large research staff that provides information to all branches of the government as well as to the general public.

The *Congressional Budget Office (CBO)* was established in 1974 to assist Congress in overseeing the budget-making process. The CBO analyzes programs in the budget and estimates the cost of proposed projects. It provides Congress with its own set of financial information. In the past, the Office of Management and Budget in the executive branch was the primary source of such data.

Congressional Staffs

In the background are many individuals who support the work that senators and members of the House do. These individuals are hired to handle routine office matters, such as answering mail from constituents, lobbyists, and others. They keep track of schedules and appointments and research information that the member needs for writing bills or holding committee hearings. Some prepare the written statements and speeches the senator or representative must make. Senior staff members may help the representative or senator make policy and draw up bills.

Let's Think

1. Which member of the House of Representatives is the most powerful? Why?
2. Explain the importance of the majority and minority leaders and majority and minority whips in each house of Congress.
3. If you had to choose an office in Congress that you would like to hold, which would you select? Why?

Powers Given to Congress

The Constitution sets forth in detail the responsibilities of Congress as a whole. Some powers are given only to the House, and some can be exercised only by the Senate. The main job of Congress is to create and pass laws.

Powers of the House

Almost any bill (potential law) can be introduced into either the House of Representatives or the Senate. The Constitution, however, specifically states that bills relating to revenue (money, taxes) must be introduced first in the House of Representatives. The Framers wanted the general public to have some control over the people who determine how tax money is to be spent. All seats in the House are up for election every two years. (Remember, until 1913, senators were chosen by state legislators, not by popular vote.) The Framers wanted to give control of money bills to the house of Congress closer to the people.

The Constitution provides that only the House of Representatives may initiate an **impeachment** proceeding against the president, federal judges, or other federal officials. Impeachment means to bring charges against—the first step in removing an official from office. The House investigates possible wrongdoing by an official. It decides whether there is enough evidence to charge an official with having committed, as the Constitution states, "high crimes and misdemeanors."

If the House passes the bill of impeachment by a majority vote, a trial will be held in the Senate. The Chief Justice of the United States, who is the head of the Supreme Court, presides over the trial if it involves the president. In cases involving other officials, the vice president, as the president of the Senate, presides over the trial. The Senate acts as a jury at the trial. In order to remove an official from office, the Senate must vote guilty by a two-thirds majority of the whole Senate. Therefore, 67 senators must vote guilty.

Only a few federal judges have been impeached, convicted, and removed from office. President Andrew Johnson was impeached in 1868 and President Bill Clinton in 1998, but the Senate did not convict them. They both finished their terms of office.

Powers of the Senate

Foreign policy is an area in which the Senate has a special power that is not shared by the House of Representatives. The president has the sole authority to enter into agreements with foreign countries in the form of treaties. The Senate, however, has the sole constitutional authority to **ratify** (approve) these agreements. The Constitution states in Article II, Section 2, Clause 2: "He [the president] shall have the power, by and with the advice and consent of the Senate, to make treaties, provided two-thirds of the senators present concur; . . ."

Another power the Senate has that the House does not is the right to confirm appointments of certain federal officials nominated by the president. The same section of the Constitution quoted above continues: "[the president] . . . with the advice and consent of the Senate, shall appoint ambassadors, other public ministers and consuls, judges of the Supreme Court, and all other officers of the United States, whose appointments are not herein otherwise provided for. . . ."

Power of the Purse

A major congressional power is to raise revenue for the government. This means that Congress decides the amount of federal taxes we will pay. Congress also works with the president to create and pass a budget. The budget is a spending plan for the government. Congress determines how to spend the government's money, deciding which programs will be given funds and in what amounts. Even if the president wants to spend money on a program, the approval must come from Congress. This we call the **power of the purse**. Congress can use the power of the purse as leverage to get the president and government agencies to agree to conditions and ideas before it sets aside funds for the desired programs.

Let's Think

1. What specific powers are given only to the House of Representatives?
2. What specific powers are given only to the Senate?
3. Why is the "power of the purse" considered to be important?

The Committee System

In order to work more efficiently, each house of Congress divides itself into committees. Just think what would happen if the entire membership of each house had to screen bills, hold hearings, write and rewrite all proposed bills, and debate the issues. Passing a law is a long and often tedious process. If all 100 members of the Senate and all 435 members of the House of Representatives had to shape every bill, Congress would never finish its work.

Standing Committees

Committees and subcommittees specialize in bills relating to certain aspects of the operations of the government. Some committees are permanent and are called **standing committees**. Standing committees exist in both the House and the Senate. On page 79 is a table of the standing committees of Congress. Standing committees are permanent because they are involved regularly with the carrying out of government operations and the lawmaking process.

The permanent committees divide into subcommittees in order to accomplish more work. Some committees are made up of members from both the House of Representatives and the Senate. These are known as **joint committees**. They are established when Congress thinks it will be more efficient if both houses handle certain matters simultaneously. Current joint committees are Taxation and Economic. Another type is a **conference committee**, which is formed when both houses pass different versions of the same bill. It is up to the conference committee to resolve the differences so that both houses can pass the same version of the bill.

The number of members who serve on the standing committees varies. Since there are two major parties in Congress (the Democratic and the Republican), members of each party sit on all committees. Each house determines the ratio of members from each party, and the committee membership reflects that ratio. For instance, if there are twice as many Republicans as Democrats, the Republicans will have a two-to-one majority in the makeup of the committees. The majority party in each house will have the majority of seats on each committee.

Temporary Committees

From time to time, as issues and circumstances arise, there is a need for a special committee. Then Congress creates such committees. They are known as **select committees**. Once the work of a select committee is finished, the committee dissolves. Select committees may last for several congresses and then disband. Select committees in the House of Representatives are Intelligence and Energy Independence and Global Warming. Select committees of the Senate are Ethics and Intelligence.

Leadership of Committees

Leadership of the committees in either house is determined by the majority party. In the 111th Congress (2009–2011), all chairpersons of the committees in both the Senate and the House of

STANDING COMMITTEES OF CONGRESS

RANKED BY GROUPS IN RELATIVE ORDER OF IMPORTANCE

House of Representatives	Senate
Rules Appropriations Ways and Means	Appropriations Foreign Relations Finance
Armed Services Judiciary Agriculture Energy and Commerce Foreign Affairs Oversight and Government Reform Homeland Security	Armed Services Judiciary Agriculture, Nutrition, and Forestry Commerce, Science, and Transportation

Financial Services
Budget
Education and Labor
Natural Resources
Science and Technology
Transportation and Infrastructure
	Banking, Housing, and Urban
	   Affairs
	Budget
	Health, Education, Labor and
	   Pensions
	Energy and Natural Resources
	Environment and Public Works

Veterans' Affairs Small Business	Homeland Security and Governmental Affairs Veterans' Affairs Rules and Administration
House Administration Standards of Official Conduct	Small Business and Entrepreneurship Indian Affairs

Representatives were members of the Democratic Party. This party held a majority of the seats in Congress during this period.

Like all committees, those in Congress need leaders. Traditionally, the most common method of selecting a committee chairperson has been through the **seniority system**. Under this system, the person on the committee who has been in Congress the longest and who is a member of the majority party is named chairperson.

Many criticize the seniority system, yet others support it. Those who support it say that the person with the most experience in the legislative process should lead the committee. Such a person knows the "ins and outs" of the workings of Congress and how to steer a bill through the system. These senior members of the House and the Senate are usually respected individuals who are seen as leaders of less senior legislators.

On the other hand, this system does not guarantee that the most qualified person will become the chairperson. Nor does seniority guarantee ability or knowledge.

In recent years, the system of choosing committee leaders has undergone several changes. Although seniority is still a factor, it isn't the most important ingredient influencing the selection of committee chairpersons or committee members. Leaders of the majority party come together to decide who will be placed on what committee and who will be the chairperson. The minority party also chooses its own members who will sit on committees. It designates a minority party leader for each committee. This person is known as the *ranking member*.

The speaker of the House plays a major role in determining committee assignments. This gives him or her power over House members. If they receive the committee assignments they request, they may feel obligated to vote as the speaker wishes.

One of the major concerns of a senator or representative is to be assigned to a committee that will be of importance to him or her. Through committee work, a congressperson may be able to fulfill some of his or her campaign promises or

POWER *of* ★ NE

Senator Daniel Ken Inouye

What makes one individual stand out above others? Some might say leadership ability, others say personality, while still others would name desire for public service. One who combines all three is Daniel K. Inouye, the first Japanese-American citizen elected to the United States Congress.

Born in Honolulu, Hawaii, in 1924, Inouye early on decided to become a doctor. He entered the University of Hawaii in 1942 as a pre-med major. A year later, he dropped out to fight in World War II, joining the newly formed U.S. Army's 442nd Regimental Combat Team. It was the first all-Japanese-American combat group. Many young Japanese Americans at that time had asked to be allowed to fight in order to prove their loyalty to the United States. (The 442nd won more military honors than any other regiment in the history of the U.S. Army.) While fighting in Europe, Lt. Inouye was severely wounded and lost his right arm. The Army presented Inouye with the highest combat medals that can be awarded, the Medal of Honor and the Distinguished Service Cross.

After the war, Inouye returned to the University of Hawaii. Instead of medicine, he decided to study government and economics. In 1952, he received his law degree from George Washington University Law School in Washington, D.C. While in law school, he worked for the Democratic National Committee.

When Inouye returned to Hawaii, it was still a U.S. territory. He decided to help it win statehood. In 1953, he was appointed public prosecutor of Honolulu. Within a year, he was elected to the territorial House of Representatives and served as the majority leader. Then in 1958, Inouye began his service in the territorial Senate. During this time, he worked to build a strong Democratic Party in the Hawaiian Islands.

On August 21, 1959, the territory of Hawaii was admitted to the Union as the 50th state. Inouye was elected Hawaii's first member of the U.S. House of Representatives. He was the first Japanese American to serve in the House of Representatives. While in the House, he supported civil rights legislation and policies that helped his home state's sugar and pineapple industries.

In 1962, he successfully ran for the U.S. Senate and began to get more involved in foreign policy issues. Inouye proved to his colleagues that he was a skilled negotiator and conciliator. As a result, he became majority whip. His popularity grew among the voters in Hawaii. He has been reelected with large majorities to the Senate ever since 1962.

An early supporter of the Vietnam War, Inouye eventually changed his view and opposed increasing American involvement in that war. To this end, he co-sponsored the War Powers Act of 1973 (see page 98 in Chapter 6). It limited the power of the president to commit American troops to foreign conflicts without the approval of Congress.

In 1973, Inouye was appointed to the Senate Watergate Committee (officially known as the Senate Select Committee on Presidential Campaign Activities). It investigated the involvement of White House personnel in covering up a burglary of the Democratic National Committee offices in 1972. The Senate committee also looked into presidential campaign finance irregularities by the Republicans in their successful effort to reelect President Richard Nixon. As a result of the findings, a number of the White House staff went to jail. The work of the Watergate Committee received constant press and television coverage. Inouye's method of questioning witnesses brought him public recognition and admiration.

Later, Inouye was appointed the first chairperson of what is now the Select Committee on Intelligence. Under his leadership, reforms helped correct scandals in the government intelligence agencies. Evidence had been uncovered that the CIA and FBI had been engaging in illegal operations.

On the domestic scene, Inouye has been a supporter of consumer rights. He backed the creation of the Consumer Protection Agency and supported antitrust legislation and laws favorable to organized labor.

In 1987, Inouye chaired the Senate committee that investigated the Iran-Contra Affair. It involved the selling of arms to Iran to win the release of hostages being held by extremist groups. Some money from the arms sales was given to Contra rebels in Nicaragua. They were fighting the Communist government of that country. This illegal transfer of funds was secretly authorized by the National Security

Council. The committee report criticized President Ronald Reagan for not knowing what his advisers were doing. A number of presidential advisers were put on trial, and some went to jail. The televised hearings once again put Inouye into the national spotlight.

Inouye is chairman of the Appropriations Committee and the subcommittee on defense. He is also on the Commerce, Science, and Transportation Committee. Inouye works hard to make government work for all people.

1. How did Daniel K. Inouye prepare himself for public service?
2. What were Inouye's interests in the House of Representatives?
3. Describe *three* of his major accomplishments in the Senate.
4. In what ways has Inouye made government work for all people?

---

gain a national reputation. For instance, if a person represents a farming community, he or she may want to be assigned to the Agriculture or Natural Resources committee.

The Work of Committees

Bills are assigned to committees based on their content. For instance, if a bill were proposed to regulate the fees charged by banks for use of automated teller machines (ATMs), it would be sent to either the House Financial Services Committee or the Senate Banking, Housing, and Urban Affairs Committee. A bill regulating the railroads would be assigned to either the House Transportation and Infrastructure Committee or the Senate Commerce, Science, and Transportation Committee.

When bills are being considered, it is important to gather as much information as possible about the form of the proposed law. Congress wants to know what the impact of the proposed law would be and how it should be enforced if

passed. Therefore, hearings are held. Experts testify before the committee. Citizens with a deep interest in the passage of the bill testify. Public officials, lobbyists, and members of special interest groups present their views. The members of the committee listen and decide how the bill might be modified, if at all.

Even before hearings are held, committee members do research on the subject the bill covers. Staff people who work directly for the committee help with the research and in setting up and carrying out the committee hearings.

Another function of committees is to investigate major controversial issues. Over the years, investigative committees have looked into possible corruption in labor unions and the influence of organized crime syndicates on certain businesses. In 1997, committees in the House and Senate held hearings about the possibility of political parties using illegal methods of raising funds for the presidential campaigns in 1996.

In 1998, the House Judiciary Committee listened to testimony regarding charges against

President Bill Clinton. He was accused of lying under oath, obstructing justice, and misusing the powers of his office to cover up details of a relationship with an employee on the White House staff. In December, the House voted to impeach Clinton on two counts: perjury and obstruction of justice. The trial in the Senate took place in February 1999. The President was found not guilty and served out his term of office.

Let's Think

1. What are the jobs of committees in both houses of Congress?
2. Why are committees important to both houses of Congress?
3. What is the difference between these types of committees: standing, select, joint?
4. Why are members of Congress concerned about their committee assignments?

How a Bill Becomes a Law

The process by which a bill becomes a law is determined by the Constitution, laws passed by our government, and tradition. The cartoon on page 72 demonstrates the importance of teamwork within our government. Two branches of government must work together in order to bring a law into existence.

Proposing a Law

Before we begin to discuss this procedure, it will be helpful to define certain terms. They are *bill*, *act*, and *law*. A **bill** is a draft of a proposed law. A **law** is a bill that has gone through the lawmaking process, been approved, and set forth as a "rule for the nation." **Act** is another word for law.

Generally, a bill does not become law until it is passed by both houses of Congress and signed by the president. The road to the passage of a law or act begins with the introduction of a proposed bill in either the Senate or the House of Representatives. The exception is that a bill to raise revenue must be first introduced in the House of Representatives. The process of lawmaking is similar in both houses.

Let us suppose that the bill is first introduced into the House of Representatives. The idea for a law can be suggested by almost anyone—a member of Congress, the president, a private citizen, a person representing a special interest group. The actual official introduction of the bill must be by a member of Congress, who is the bill's sponsor. Once the bill is written in the proper legal language, its sponsor places it in the "hopper." The hopper is a box on the desk of the clerk of the House. After the bill has been assigned an identifying number, it is sent to the proper committee for action. In the House of Representatives, a bill is given a designation that begins with the letters "H.R." and then a number, for example H.R. 125. In the Senate, the bill will be given the letter designation "S" and a number.

The Role of Committees

The committee to which the bill has been assigned examines it and decides whether the idea is one that should go through the legislative process and become a law. Many proposed bills are set aside and not acted on. When this happens, the bill is said to be **pigeonholed**. There are several reasons why a bill may be pigeonholed. For instance, if a bill goes against the stated platform of the majority party, the chairperson may wish to set it aside. An example might be a bill to add a new Cabinet department. If the majority party promised that the number of Cabinet departments would decrease, the committee might pigeonhole a bill to add a department. Sometimes a bill might affect a member's district negatively. That member will push the committee to kill the bill. If the member has enough support on the committee, the bill will be pigeonholed.

Once the committee decides to consider a bill, hearings are held. At these hearings, people testify in support of the bill or against it. Some may suggest that changes be made in the bill. The testimony that the committee members hear helps them make certain decisions. The first is how the bill might affect society if it becomes law.

◀ REALITY CHECK ▶

Congress Holds Hearings on Baseball

One way that Congress can bring about change is to hold hearings about an issue or an organization. Congress has used standing and select committees to conduct such investigations. Congress can also pass laws that reform situations that need to be changed.

Professional baseball, long considered the national pastime, came under congressional examination in 2005. The U.S. House of Representatives decided to hold hearings to investigate the use of performance-enhancing drugs by baseball players. Part of the reason for the hearings was the widespread concern that Major League Baseball officials and the players' union had not done a very good job of setting and enforcing drug-use policies. Using anabolic steroids and growth hormones without a prescription is against federal law. Their use is also dangerous.

Several big-name players were called to testify before the House committee. One was José Canseco, a former professional baseball player. He had written a book that named players he claimed had used and were using performance-enhancing drugs. Players said that the drugs helped them perform at much higher levels than they did without the drugs. High-level performance records can put players in a position to sign rich contracts or receive bonuses.

Other professional sports have implemented drug policies that randomly test players and penalize those who test positive for use. The National Football League, for example, has had such a policy for years. Major League Baseball was slower to adopt strict drug policies. Many believe that the increased number of record-breaking home run performances in the late 1990s and early 2000s resulted from the use of steroids. Most of the named players denied using the illegal drugs.

After the hearing, former Senator George Mitchell of Maine was asked by Major League Baseball to investigate the issue further. After Mitchell presented his report, additional congressional hearings were held in 2008. Several well-known players named in the report were called to testify before the House Oversight and Government Reform Committee. When the hearings ended, professional baseball adopted a stricter drug-testing policy for major league and minor league players. Nevertheless, the publicity surrounding the drug issue tarnished the image of Major League Baseball and the image of many players who had been considered heroes by fans.

Some Americans believe that Congress should not have gotten involved in the inner workings of professional baseball. People question why Congress would bother to spend money and time investigating baseball when the funds and time could have been used for more important things. Others believe that it was appropriate for Congress to conduct such investigations because the issue involved the use of banned substances. There is also a fear that young athletes aspiring to be professionals will take the chance of using harmful drugs. The long-term effects on individuals, particularly teenagers, can be devastating.

1. What issue caused Congress to investigate Major League Baseball?
2. Why are steroids and growth hormones banned in major league sports?
3. What reasons were given to support a congressional investigation of professional baseball?
4. What arguments were made against the congressional hearings?

Another is whether the bill should be changed before it is voted on by the committee. The third is whether the bill should be sent out of committee for consideration by the entire House or not acted on at all.

If a bill is not reported (sent) out of the committee, it is usually dead. In some rare instances, the entire House may require a bill that was killed by a committee to be reported out. The House as a whole would then decide the bill's fate.

The Rules Committee

The House of Representatives has one committee that is unique and quite powerful. It is called the Rules Committee. This committee decides when a bill that has been reported out of committee will be considered by the entire House for a vote. It decides how long a debate will be allowed and sets the amount of time each member will have to speak during debate. The Rules Committee can make or break a bill by allowing rapid consideration by the House or by delaying its consideration.

The Senate does not have such a committee. Once a committee reports out a bill for Senate floor consideration, the order in which it is considered is decided by the Senate majority.

The time that bills take from proposal to signature by the president varies. Some may take weeks, others, months.

Coming to a Vote

If the bill is reported out, it is placed on a *calendar*. This sets the order in which bills will be considered by the entire House. The representatives will now have the opportunity to debate the merits of the bill. The rules of debate are different for each house.

In the Senate, there is unlimited debate. This means that a senator can discuss a bill for as long as he or she wants. Sometimes one or more senators decide that they are against a bill that they fear will be passed. In an effort to kill the bill, the group engages in what is known as a **filibuster**. They will talk without giving up their right to speak to anyone else. This stalls the business of

the entire Senate. The filibuster can go on for hours or days. Even though it is annoying, the tactic can also be seen as a device to protect minority rights.

During the 104th Congress (1995–1997), there were a number of filibusters in the Senate. One involved the bill to raise the minimum wage from $4.25 to $5.15. Democrats did not like changes that Republicans were making in the bill and organized a filibuster. The bill was finally passed with changes. Another filibuster was organized to defeat the passage of the proposed constitutional amendment to limit the number of terms in office of a senator or member of the House. When a vote to stop debate was taken, it fell two votes short. The proposed constitutional amendment was withdrawn from consideration. In 2003, during the 108th Congress, Miguel Estrada asked President Bush to withdraw his nomination to a judgeship in the Federal Court. This was mainly due to a filibuster organized by the Senate Democrats to block Estrada's nomination.

There is a way that senators can stop a filibuster. It is called **cloture**. In order for cloture to be passed, 16 senators must sponsor the bill to limit debate. The vote then takes place two days later. However, the vote must be passed by three-fifths of the Senate, or 60 senators. Once cloture is agreed to, debate on the original bill is limited to one hour per senator, or a maximum of 100 hours. Then this bill must be voted on. As you can see, stopping a filibuster can be very difficult. Senators don't like to vote to close off debate because they might want to use the filibuster themselves at some future time.

In the House of Representatives, debate is limited. How limited is usually determined by the Rules Committee. It decides how long each representative will be allowed to speak for or against the bill.

During the debate on the floor of the House or the Senate, speeches are made in support of the bill, against the bill, or to offer changes to the bill. The changes are called amendments. These changes are voted on separately. Once the whole bill with all of its modifications is ready, it will be voted on by all the members of the House.

The vote on a bill is held in public and recorded. The vote may be by voice—all in favor

The Journey of a Bill Through Congress

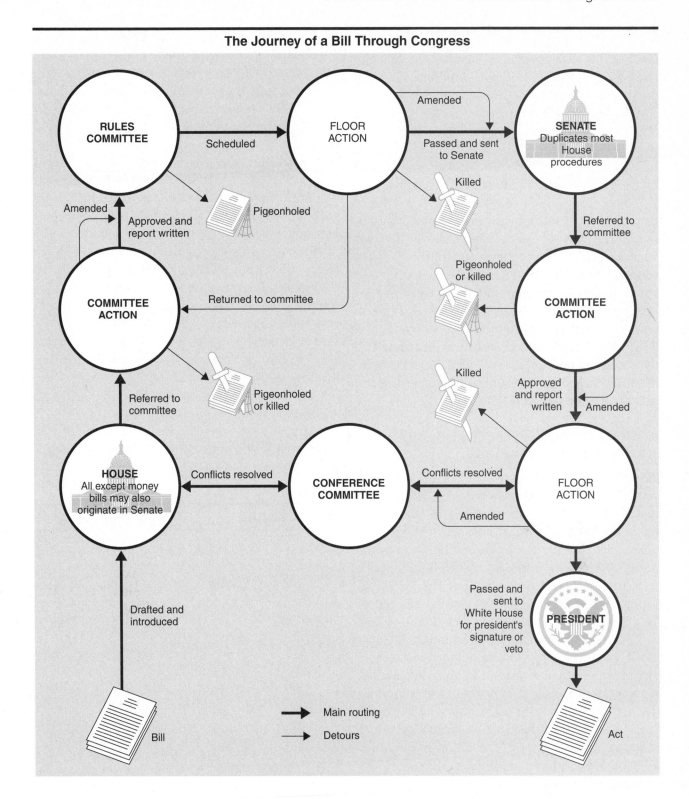

call out "aye," all opposed say "no." If the sound for the two sides is too close to judge the results, a standing vote might be taken. Those in favor stand up and are counted, and then those opposed. A third way, the roll call, is more exact. Each member is called on to state his or her de-

cision individually. (In the House, each member uses an electronic device to record his or her vote.) This allows constituents to see how their representative voted on each issue. They can then decide if the person is representing their interests.

Repeating the Process

Even if the House votes in favor of the bill, the road to passage is still not complete. The bill must undergo a similar process in the Senate. The Senate does not have to wait for the House of Representatives to pass a bill in order to consider it. Very often, similar bills are introduced in both houses at the same time. But similar bills passed by each house are usually not "identical twins."

Before Congress can send a bill to the president for approval, both houses must pass exactly the same bill. To resolve any differences in the two versions of a bill, a conference committee made up of senators and representatives is created to look at the two bills. It works out compromises that will be acceptable to the members of both houses. Once the conference committee has accomplished this task, the Senate and the House of Representatives vote on the compromise bill. After a majority in both houses approves this bill, it is sent to the president to be signed.

Action by the President

Once the president signs a bill, it officially becomes law. Sometimes the president decides to reject a bill. He exercises a veto. This means that the bill is returned to Congress with an explanation of the president's objections. The veto is one of the checks built into the Constitution. It is one way that the president can limit the power of Congress. If the president does not sign a bill or veto it within ten days, it usually becomes a law.

Congress may send the president a bill just ten days before it is about to adjourn its session. The president then may elect to exercise a **pocket veto**. If the president does not sign the bill within the ten-day period, the bill is killed. The pocket veto is used by a president to avoid explaining why the bill was vetoed. The bill might concern a sensitive issue that the president does not want to become involved in. Congress cannot reconsider the bill that is vetoed in this way because it has adjourned. A veto from one session cannot be overridden in another session of Congress.

Overriding a Veto

If Congress wants to pass the bill over the president's veto, it takes another vote. Both houses must now pass the bill by a two-thirds vote. This is different from the original vote, which requires a simple majority in both houses. Overriding a presidential veto can be difficult. Often the members of Congress cannot get enough votes to override. If this happens, the bill is dead.

Overriding a veto is another of the checks built into the Constitution. In this case, Congress can limit the authority of the president. If it can gather enough votes, it can still pass a piece of legislation over the president's objection.

Sometimes Congress decides to reconsider a bill and incorporate the president's suggestions. Then the bill is rewritten, voted on, and sent to the president for his or her signature just as any new bill would be.

The process of passing a bill into law is complex. It can be long and tough. Sometimes the process seems too slow. It does, however, allow for careful consideration of how the law will work and how it will affect the country. It is a thoughtful and careful process even with the flaws people see in it.

Let's Think

1. What is the meaning and importance of each of the following terms: pigeonholed, filibuster, veto, pocket veto?
2. What role does the Rules Committee play in the process of considering a bill in the House of Representatives?
3. What is the process by which Congress can override a president's veto?
4. Many believe that the process of passing a bill into law is too slow. Write an editorial that explains your view of this idea.

Chapter Summary

Congress is the branch of the federal government that is responsible for making laws for the nation. It is divided into two parts called houses. Membership in the House of Representatives is based on the population of each state. Membership in the Senate is composed of two senators from each state. The Great Compromise at the Constitutional Convention of 1787 created a two-house, or bicameral, legislature.

To run for office, a candidate for the House must be 25 years old, a citizen for seven years, and a resident of the state he or she wants to represent. A candidate for the Senate must be 30 years old, a citizen for nine years, and a resident of the state he or she wants to represent. Members of the House serve a two-year term, while senators are elected for six years.

Every ten years, in a year ending in zero, the nation is required to take a census. This is a "head count" of the population. The purpose is to decide how the election districts should be redrawn, or reapportioned, so that people are equally represented in Congress. People move from one location to another. Some districts lose population, while others gain. The redrawing of district lines can result in gerrymandering. This creates oddly shaped areas that usually favor the party in power.

Each house of Congress organizes itself so that it can do its job effectively. Each house has a presiding officer. In the House of Representatives, it is the speaker. In the Senate, it is the president, who is actually the vice president of the United States. When the president of the Senate is unavailable, the president pro tempore serves in his or her stead. Other leaders of each house are the majority and minority party leaders and the majority and minority whips.

Two nonlegislative agencies help Congress function more efficiently: the Library of Congress and the Congressional Budget Office. Supporting the work members of Congress do are their staffs.

In addition to the legislative powers given to Congress, each house has specific powers that the other does not. All bills related to raising revenue must begin in the House of Representatives.

Only the House can initiate impeachment proceedings against the president and other federal officials.

The Senate has the power to ratify treaties made by the president and confirm presidential appointments. Once the House of Representatives votes a bill of impeachment, it is up to the Senate to conduct a trial to determine guilt or innocence.

Congress could not function effectively without a system of committees. They work on pending bills, hold hearings, and conduct investigations. There are standing committees, select committees, and joint committees. The leadership and membership of committees are determined by several factors: seniority, interest, and knowledge.

A bill becomes a law when it is passed by both houses of Congress by a simple majority vote and signed by the president. After a bill is introduced, it is assigned a number and sent to a committee for consideration. At this point, hearings are held and votes are taken. Once it is reported out of committee favorably, a bill is considered by the entire house (Senate or House of Representatives). After the identical bill is approved by both the Senate and the House of Representatives, it is sent to the president for signing.

If the president does not want to sign the bill, he or she vetoes it. A vetoed bill goes back to Congress with a message explaining the president's objections. If a bill is sent to the president within ten days before the end of a congressional session, the president may refuse to sign the bill before Congress adjourns. This pocket veto kills the bill. If the president does not sign or veto a bill while Congress is in session, it automatically becomes law after ten days.

A veto can be overridden by Congress. The bill must get a two-thirds vote in both houses. Then the bill becomes law.

★ CHAPTER REVIEW ★

A. Matching
Match each term in Column A with its definition in Column B.

Column A
1. bicameral
2. apportionment
3. census
4. filibuster
5. standing committee
6. impeachment
7. legislature
8. speaker of the House
9. conference committee
10. cloture

Column B
a. the process of changing election district lines to account for gains or losses in population
b. unlimited debate in the Senate to kill a bill
c. permanent committee of Congress
d. the leader of the House of Representatives
e. a vote to cut off debate in the Senate
f. the process of removing a president from office
g. where different versions of the same bill are combined into one
h. the lawmaking body of a government
i. a population count of the nation
j. two-house legislature

B. Multiple Choice
Select the statement or word that most correctly answers the question or completes the statement.

1. At the Constitutional Convention, small states wanted representation in Congress to be based on (a) population (b) equality for all states (c) appointments by the president (d) appointments by the governor of each state.
2. The Great Compromise established a (a) unicameral Congress (b) legislature appointed by the president (c) bicameral Congress (d) Congress based only on equal representation from each state.
3. The organization created to assist Congress in overseeing the budget-making process is the (a) Congressional Budget Office (b) Treasury Department (c) Federal Reserve Board (d) Conference Committee.
4. This vote is needed for a bill to pass in Congress: (a) two-thirds (b) three-fifths (c) unanimous (d) majority.
5. The final step in the process of lawmaking in the United States is usually (a) a vote by both houses of Congress (b) debate on the floor of each house (c) the signing of the bill by the president (d) the vetoing of the bill by the president.
6. The most powerful committee in the House of Representatives that is involved in the lawmaking process is (a) Foreign Affairs (b) Rules (c) Judiciary (d) Armed Services.
7. The person who holds this position is third in line of succession to the presidency: (a) president of the Senate (b) majority leader of the House (c) speaker of the House (d) Senate majority whip.
8. A power given the Senate that is not given to the House of Representatives is (a) confirming presidential appointments to high government positions (b) enacting laws without presidential approval (c) introducing revenue bills (d) amending the Constitution.
9. Members of the House of Representatives serve a term of this length: (a) eight years (b) six years (c) four years (d) two years.
10. In the past, the chairperson of a committee was chosen by this system: (a) seniority (b) alphabetical order by state (c) interviews with leaders of each house (d) geographic region the person is from.

C. Essay
Write a paragraph about *one* of the following:
1. How Congress balances and checks the power of the president.
2. The role the committees of Congress play in the lawmaking process.
3. The party that controls Congress has a great deal of power.
4. The speaker of the House of Representative is one of the most powerful people in the national government.

D. A Challenge for You

1. Examine the constitutional qualifications for members of the Senate and the House of Representatives. Write an essay explaining what qualifications you think a member of Congress should have in the 21st century.

2. Find newspaper and magazine articles or download pages from the Internet that tell the story of the legislative history of a bill in Congress. Summarize each article and place the summaries into a journal. Your summaries might make a good article for the school newspaper or a bulletin board display.

3. Write a letter to your senators explaining how you would like them to represent you. Name specific issues if you can. Consider sending the letter by e-mail.

4. Create a poster that shows how a bill becomes a law. Consider using the bill you researched in question 2.

5. Some people think that changing Congress into a unicameral body would be a good idea. Write a letter to a friend explaining your position on this issue. Or explore the idea in a chat session on the Internet and report on the responses you get.

Document-Based Question

State the main idea expressed in each document. Then use information in the documents and your own knowledge to write an essay explaining the pros and cons of being a member of Congress.

The Problems of Representing People in Congress

From the standpoint of capturing voters, the congressman's lawmaking activities differ in two important respects from his pork-barrel and casework activities. First, programmatic actions are inherently [naturally] controversial. Unless his district is homogeneous [uniform], a congressman will find his district divided on many major issues. Thus when he casts a vote, introduces a piece of nontrivial legislation, or makes a speech with policy content he will displease some elements of his district. Some constituents may applaud the congressman's civil rights record, but others believe integration is going too fast. Some support foreign aid, while others believe it's money poured down a rathole. Some advocate economic quality, others stew over welfare cheaters. On such policy matters the congressman can expect to make friends as well as enemies. Presumably he will behave so as to maximize the excess of the former [friends] over the latter [enemies], but nevertheless a policy stand will generally make some enemies.

In contrast, the pork barrel [legislation for local federal projects that favor a locality] and casework [helping constituents] are relatively less controversial. New federal projects bring jobs, shiny new facilities, and general economic prosperity, or so people believe. Snipping ribbons at the dedication of a new post office or dam is a much more pleasant pursuit than disposing of a constitutional amendment on abortion. . . .

Casework is even less controversial. Some poor, aggrieved constituent becomes enmeshed in the tentacles of an evil bureaucracy and calls upon [a] Congressman . . . to do battle with the dragon. . . .

In sum, when considering the benefits of his programmatic activities, the congressman must tote up gains and losses to arrive at a net profit. Pork barreling and casework, however, are basically pure profit. . . .

From "The Rise of the Washington Establishment" by Morris P. Fiorina in *American Goverment: Readings and Cases*, 12th Ed., by Peter Woll, pages 369–370. Copyright 1996 by Peter Woll. Originally published by HarperCollins College Publishers.

The Art of Getting Reelected

Whether they are safe or marginal, cautious or audacious, congressmen must constantly engage in activities related to reelection. There will be differences in emphasis, but all members share the root need to do things—indeed, to do things day in and day out during their terms. The next step here is to present . . . a short list of the kinds of activities congressmen find it electorally useful to engage in. The case will be that there are three basic kinds of activities. . . .

One activity is advertising, defined here as any effort to disseminate [distribute] one's name among constituents in such a fashion as to create a favorable image but in messages having little or no issue content. A successful congressman builds what amounts to a brand name, which may have a generalized electoral value for other politicians in the same family. The personal qualities to emphasize are experience, knowledge, responsiveness, concern, sincerity, independence, and the like. Just getting one's name across is difficult enough; only about half the electorate, if asked, can supply their House members' names. . . .

A second activity may be called credit claiming, defined here as acting so as to generate a belief in a relevant political actor (or actors) [voters] that one is personally responsible for causing the government, or some unit thereof, to do something that the actor (actors) considers desirable. The political logic for this, from the congressman's point of view, is that an actor who believes that a member can make pleasing things happen will no doubt wish to keep him in office so that he can make pleasing things happen in the future. The emphasis here is on the individual accomplishment . . . and on the congressman as doer. . . . Credit claiming is highly important to congressmen, with the consequence that much of congressional life is a relentless search for opportunities to engage in it. . . .

The third activity congressmen engage in may be called position taking, defined here as the public enunciation [announcement] of a . . . statement on anything likely to be of interest to political actors. The statement may take the form of a roll call vote. . . .

There can be no doubt that congressmen believe positions make a difference. An important consequence of this belief is their custom of watching each other's elections to try to figure out what positions are salable. Nothing is more important in Capitol Hill politics than the shared conviction [belief] that election returns have proven a point. . . .

From "Congress: The Electoral Connection" by David Mayhew in *American Government: Readings and Cases*, 12th Ed., by Peter Woll, pages 414–418. Copyright 1996 by Peter Woll. Originally published by HarperCollins College Publishers.

CHAPTER 6

The Presidency

★ 1. What qualifications does a
person need to be president?
2. What roles is the president
★ expected to play in the
government?
3. How is a president elected?

Who Can Be President?

WANTED: President of the United
States. Must be elected to office.
No experience required.
Good benefits.

Would you apply for a job like the one described
in the advertisement? Have you thought about
some of the benefits of the job? You live in a big,
beautiful house in Washington, D.C. You have a
helicopter for short trips and a custom-designed
jet plane to whisk you to any part of the world.
You are driven in a special limousine with the
very latest communication devices. There are
many people surrounding you to offer assistance. They are there to give advice, carry out
your orders, help you decide what to wear for
certain occasions, and make sure you get to your
destinations on time. Your salary is $400,000 a
year. You are also given $50,000 a year to pay for
any expenses that develop while you carry out
your responsibilities. There is a $100,000 account
for traveling and $19,000 for entertaining.

Being the president of the United States carries awesome responsibility. As the leader of the
most powerful nation in the world, he or she
must make decisions that will affect millions of
people at home and abroad. The president then
stands alone and takes the blame or praise for the
outcome of those decisions.

Because the president is so closely watched by
the media, there is very little privacy. All activities of the "First Family" are monitored and
written about. Books are written, not only about
the job the president is doing or has done, but
also about his or her life. The media may focus on
such ordinary topics as the price of a haircut, the
clothing worn at a public function, or where the
children will go to school. A person who wants to
be president must be willing to accept both public honor and public scrutiny.

As President Harry Truman wrote in his me-
moirs: "No one who has not had the responsibility can really understand what it is like to be
President, not even his closest aides or members
of his immediate family. There is no end to the
chain of responsibility that binds him, and he is
never allowed to forget that he is President."

Qualifications

On inauguration day (January 20), the nation
watches the new president take the oath of office

After being sworn in as the nation's 44th president, Barack Obama gave his Inaugural Address in front of the U.S. Capitol on January 20, 2009.

in front of the Capitol in Washington, D.C. At 12 noon, the president-elect raises his or her right hand while placing the left on a Bible. The Chief Justice of the United States asks the person to repeat the following words: "I do solemnly swear (or affirm) that I will faithfully execute the office of President of the United States, and will, to the best of my ability, preserve, protect, and defend the Constitution of the United States." With these words from Article II, Section 1, of the Constitution, the president takes office. The oath tells us little about the person except that by the time he or she has reached this point, the people have spoken and believe that this person possesses the qualities to be a good president.

Now that you are thinking seriously about this job, you must be wondering if you are qualified. The qualifications for the presidency can be found in the Constitution. Article II, Section 1, states: "No person except a natural-born citizen, . . . shall be eligible to the office of President; neither shall any person be eligible to that office who shall not have attained to the age of thirty-five years and been fourteen years a resident

within the United States." (Natural born means that the person must have been born in the United States, its territories, or, if born abroad, to U.S. citizens.) This is all the Constitution says about the qualifications for president. However, the American public demands much more than an age, citizenship, and residency requirement.

What personal qualities should a president have? If you were to ask different people, they would very likely offer different suggestions. The vast majority of Americans most likely believe a president should be educated and experienced. But experienced in what field? Many have held previous elected office, such as governor or senator. Others have held positions of leadership in the armed forces.

On a personal level, the president must be able to make difficult decisions. The president must constantly weigh the benefits and liabilities of almost every decision made and every action taken. The president is expected to lead, be forceful, and make the tough decisions. This brings a sense of well-being to people who see the president as the center of the government.

The president now more than ever must be a skilled communicator. He or she must be able to explain programs and ideas clearly and forcefully. The person must appear to be comfortable dealing with the media. Several presidents, including Bill Clinton, George W. Bush, and Barack Obama, have given weekly radio talks to present their thoughts about issues.

In times of national crisis, the president must be able to demonstrate that the government is in control and to provide comfort to the people of the nation. He or she may personally visit the sites of disasters and meet with the people involved. For example, in New York City in September 2001, President George W. Bush visited the site of the destroyed World Trade Center and conferred with state, city, and national leaders to decide how to deal with this terrorist attack.

The office demands that the president possess the ability to deal with people on many different levels. On any given day, the president may meet with private citizens and world leaders. The president must, therefore, be knowledgeable about what is happening in our own country and about world affairs.

Even though the Constitution does not set

forth many qualifications for the president, the nature of the job and the public do. Therefore, if a person wants to be elected president, he or she must be well prepared to seek the office and once in office to demonstrate that he or she can lead as promised.

Term of Office

The president is elected for a four-year term. He or she may run for reelection. The president is allowed to serve a maximum of two full terms. This was not always the case. When the Constitution was first written, a specific limit on the total number of terms a president may serve was not included. Through custom, beginning with George Washington, presidents never served more than two terms until the presidency of Franklin Delano Roosevelt. He was elected four separate times: in 1932, 1936, 1940, and 1944. These years were an unusual time in the history of our nation. Roosevelt not only presided over the nation during the Great Depression, a time of severe economic decline in the 1930s, but also led it through most of World War II (1941–1945). The people of the nation trusted his leadership and did not want to put an untested person in office during such troubled times.

After Roosevelt, many feared that the office of president might become too powerful if one person could serve an unlimited number of terms. In 1951, the people of the nation approved the 22nd Amendment to the Constitution. It stated: "No person shall be elected to the office of the President more than twice, and no person who has held the office of President, or acted as President, for more than two years of a term to which some other person was elected President shall be elected to the office of the President more than once."

In the wording of the amendment, reference was also made to individuals who might be completing a term to which someone else had been elected. The purpose was to limit the amount of time a vice president could serve if he or she had to complete an unexpired term of a president. The total amount of time a person can serve as president, then, is limited to ten years.

Vice President

The vice president of the United States is the person who is first in line of succession to the presidency in case the president fails to complete his or her term of office. The Constitution outlines two specific responsibilities for the vice president. The first is to assume the role of president in case something happens to that person. The second is to preside as president of the Senate. Constitutionally, the vice president must have the same qualifications for office as the president.

If a president dies while in office or is unable to perform his or her duties, the vice president must be ready to step in at a moment's notice. William Henry Harrison died within one month after taking office in 1841. His vice president, John Tyler, then took over and served out the term. When John F. Kennedy was assassinated on a campaign trip to Texas in 1963, Vice President Lyndon Johnson, who was also on the trip, took the presidential oath on the plane as he headed back to Washington.

Some see the office of vice president as a dead end because of its limited responsibility. John Adams described it as "the most insignificant office that ever the invention of man contrived or his imagination conceived." Daniel Webster

A vice president can be called upon by the president to perform many tasks. Here U.S. Vice President Joseph Biden spoke while attending a NATO conference in Brussels, Belgium He met with many European leaders at this event in March 2009.

rejected a vice presidential nomination in 1848 with the phrase, "I do not choose to be buried until I am really dead."

In recent years, the office has taken on new meaning. Presidents now give vice presidents many important assignments. Some have headed up commissions to create new programs or reform existing ones. At times, the vice president is sent on diplomatic missions to other countries or to represent the president at ceremonial gatherings. How much the vice president does is in large part a decision made by the president.

Succession to the Presidency

Other questions about succession to the presidency have come up over the years. What happens if a president becomes unable to perform his or her duties? Who steps in to take over and for how long? After a vice president succeeds to the presidency, the office of the vice president is vacant. Who would take over if the new president died? Passed in 1967, the 25th Amendment attempted to answer these questions. The following is a summary of its provisions.

- If the president is removed from office or dies, the vice president would become president.
- If there is a vacancy created in the office of vice president, the president is to nominate the vice president with approval by a majority vote of both houses of Congress.
- If the president cannot carry out the duties of the office, he or she informs the president pro tempore of the Senate and the speaker of the House of Representatives in writing. When that occurs, the vice president will become the acting president. The president will resume his or her responsibilities after informing Congress in writing that he or she is able to do so.
- The amendment also provides for a procedure to allow the vice president to assume the role of president if government officials believe the president can no longer carry out the duties of the office. Congress is given the responsibility of deciding if this is the case.

Let's Think

1. What are the constitutional qualifications for president and vice president?
2. What responsibilities does the Constitution give to the vice president?
3. The job of the vice president is shaped by the president. What does this statement mean?
4. What are the major provisions of the 25th Amendment? Why do you think the nation thought it was important to pass an amendment dealing with the incapacity of the president?

The Many Roles of the President

We can make a more informed judgment about who should be president if we understand the many responsibilities of the job. The person who holds the presidency has a variety of roles to fulfill—all at the same time.

To fill all of the roles demanded of the president, a person must be intelligent, knowledgeable about government, versatile, and able to win the trust of the people. The person must be a leader the people are willing to follow.

Chief Executive

The president is the **chief executive** of the nation. If we think of an executive as someone who runs a company, we would be correct. In this case, the U.S. government is the "company." The president, as the chief executive, sees to it that the national government runs smoothly and that the laws of the land are carried out.

The Cabinet

The president must depend on many people to help carry out the responsibilities of the office. When George Washington became the first president of the United States, in 1789, he realized that he could not do the job alone. There was no provision in the new Constitution for assistants to help him. But he knew that the Constitution gave him the power to appoint various people to positions in government with the "advice and consent" of the Senate. So he proceeded to create what is known as the **Cabinet**. The Cabinet is made up of the heads of executive departments and other officials who have been given Cabinet rank by the president. These people also give the chief executive advice about public policy.

President Washington appointed four people to the first Cabinet. As the nation grew, so did the complexity of the government. In 2009, President Barack Obama presided over a Cabinet of 15 members.

Director of Foreign Policy

Keeping good relations with other nations is another of the president's responsibilities. As "director of foreign policy," the president makes many decisions that affect how we get along with countries in the rest of the world. Some of these decisions include how to react to foreign trade policies that might hurt the United States, whether or not to send money to help a poor nation, and how to persuade warring groups in a country to make peace.

In this role, the president also directs the negotiation of **treaties**. Treaties are formal agreements between two or more nations. These agreements concern issues such as disarmament, trade, and fishing rights.

When making foreign policy decisions, the president must consider many factors. For instance, some governments we want to trade with do not have a good record on human rights. Does that mean we should not deal with them? For example, the People's Republic of China has a very large population and is a good market for many products produced in the United States. It is a dictatorship. Should we give China preferential treatment in foreign trade if it continues to violate the rights of its citizens? Many questioned President George W. Bush's decision to attend the opening ceremonies of the 2008 Summer Olympic Games held in Beijing, China. Critics believed that the Chinese government should not have been so honored. Others believed that staying connected with China would help bring change in the area of human rights in that country.

Another question is, what effect will our actions or policies have on our friends, our traditional allies? In 1996, President Clinton signed into law an antiterrorist bill that punished companies that invested in the oil industry in Libya and Iran. These two countries were accused of supporting terrorist activities. Several allies of the United States disagreed with this action because they felt it interfered in their internal affairs. In this case, how does the president balance the need to have good relations with traditional allies and the need to take strong steps to stop terrorist activities?

Sometimes the United States tries to bring about peace between disputing peoples in various regions of the world. In such cases, the president uses the power of the United States and the prestige of the office to bring warring sides together. This occurred in the Middle East in the late 1970s. President Jimmy Carter brought the leaders of Israel and Egypt together to work out a peace agreement. These countries had been enemies for many years.

In 2003, President George W. Bush attempted to bring the people of Israel and Palestine together. In the wake of much terrorist activity by radical Palestinians combined with the military reaction to those acts by the Israeli government, President Bush created a timetable for peace. In 2005, Israel withdrew its settlements from the Gaza Strip. A Palestinian state has not yet been achieved.

Then there is the issue of providing foreign aid to developing nations around the world. Again, many violate human rights, so people at home believe that we should not help them unless they change. A number of people in the United States would rather see the money used to solve problems within the nation. Once again, the president must balance the issues of helping countries overseas to improve their economies and keeping the American public on his or her side.

Treaty Ratification

Even though a president may succeed in negotiating a treaty, the agreement does not automatically go into effect. The Senate is charged with the constitutional authority to approve the treaty.

Cabinet Departments

Secretary of State

Director of State Dept., created 1789. Helps president develop and carry out foreign policy.

Secretary of the Treasury

Director of Treasury Dept., created in 1789. Assists president in developing and carrying out economic policies; in charge of Secret Service.

Secretary of Defense

Director of Dept. of Defense, created in 1949. Oversees all aspects of the uniformed military services.

Attorney General

Director of Dept. of Justice, created in 1870. Enforces federal laws; oversees FBI, immigration and naturalization, and drug enforcement.

Secretary of the Interior

Director of Dept. of the Interior, created in 1849. Responsible for protecting and supervising natural resources and public lands; oversees Indian affairs.

Secretary of Agriculture

Director of Dept. of Agriculture, created in 1889. Responsible for national farm and agricultural marketing policies and safeguarding quality of food products.

Secretary of Commerce

Director of Dept. of Commerce, created in 1913. Responsible for policies to promote economic growth and international trade; oversees the taking of the census.

Secretary of Labor

Director of Dept. of Labor, created in 1913. Enforces federal labor laws; oversees job training programs.

Secretary of Housing and Urban Development

Director of Dept. of Housing and Urban Development, created in 1965. Responsible for carrying out policies relating to housing and problems in cities.

Secretary of Transportation

Director of Dept. of Transportation, created in 1966. Responsible for carrying out policies concerning mass transit, railroads, airlines, highways, and transportation safety.

Secretary of Energy

Director of Dept. of Energy, created in 1977. Responsible for carrying out policies concerning energy technology, use of natural resources such as petroleum, energy conservation, and nuclear power.

Secretary of Health and Human Services

Director of Dept. of Health and Human Services, created in 1979. Helps president formulate and carry out health and welfare policies.

Secretary of Education

Director of Dept. of Education, created in 1979. Administers federal education policies.

Secretary of Veterans' Affairs

Director of Dept. of Veterans' Affairs, created in 1989. Administers benefit programs of veterans of the armed services.

Secretary of Homeland Security

Director of Homeland Security, created in 2003, works to prevent terrorist attacks on the United States, reduce the vulnerability of the United States to terrorism, and minimize the damage and assist in recovery from terrorist attacks that do occur.

This process of approval is known as the **ratification process**. The Constitution, in Article II, Section 2, tells us: "He [the president] shall have power, by and with the advice and consent of the Senate, to make treaties, provided two-thirds of the senators present concur; . . ." This means that the Senate must approve treaties by a two-thirds majority vote. A new law may be passed by a simple majority, or 51 votes. Treaties require 67 votes to be approved. Occasionally, a treaty is rejected by the Senate.

Another way the Senate can check the treaty-making authority of the president is by changing the agreement. If such changes are made, the

The Seven "Hats" of the President

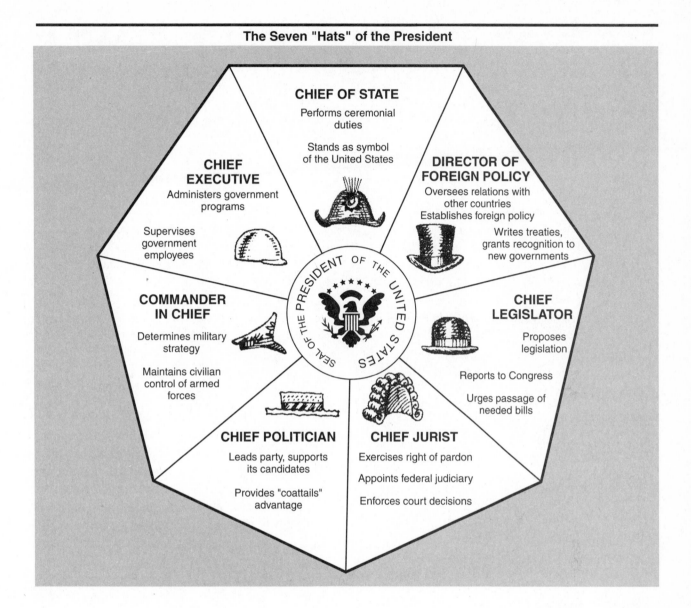

CHIEF OF STATE
Performs ceremonial duties
Stands as symbol of the United States

DIRECTOR OF FOREIGN POLICY
Oversees relations with other countries
Establishes foreign policy
Writes treaties, grants recognition to new governments

CHIEF EXECUTIVE
Administers government programs
Supervises government employees

CHIEF LEGISLATOR
Proposes legislation
Reports to Congress
Urges passage of needed bills

COMMANDER IN CHIEF
Determines military strategy
Maintains civilian control of armed forces

SEAL OF THE PRESIDENT OF THE UNITED STATES

CHIEF JURIST
Exercises right of pardon
Appoints federal judiciary
Enforces court decisions

CHIEF POLITICIAN
Leads party, supports its candidates
Provides "coattails" advantage

other nations involved must also agree to them, thus slowing down the approval process. Congress may also refuse to provide funds for carrying out the terms of the treaty.

Commander in Chief

One of the most important roles of the president is that of **commander in chief** of the nation's armed forces. The Constitution states in Article II, Section 2: "The President shall be Commander in Chief of the army and navy of the United States, and of the militia of the several States, when called into the actual service of the United States; . . ." The president is responsible for the defense and security of the United States. He or she decides where and when to use our military power. Such decisions may bring about the injury or death of military personnel.

Deciding how the budget of the armed forces will be spent, how large the military forces should be, and what kind of equipment should be purchased also lies with the president. Congress, of course, influences these decisions. This is achieved through the budget-making process and the authorization of funds for various weapons systems.

There is an interesting twist to this military power. The office of president of the United States is a civilian position. In fact, every president who had previously been a career officer in the armed forces resigned his military position before taking the presidential oath of office. Some presidents with a military background were George Washington, Andrew Jackson, and Dwight Eisenhower. They each left the army and became civilian presidents. Having a civilian leader of the military is an important characteristic of our system.

Some governments in different parts of the world have given too much power to the military. The leaders of these nations do not have ultimate control over the military. This creates a military that can act independently of the elected leader. In such nations, if the military refuses to support the leader, the leader will have little authority and is often replaced. As a result, the military may dictate who the leader should be. The Framers of our government wanted to avoid this type of unstable rule and ensure that the military will protect, not dictate to, the people of the United States. Thus, they created the civilian commander in chief.

Limit on Military Power

Although the president is the commander in chief, he or she does not have the authority to declare war. Only Congress has that power. When Congress declares war, the president as commander in chief will order the troops into battle.

Another check has been placed on the ability of the president to send troops to foreign nations without the approval of Congress. At times, the president has found it necessary to deploy troops. In the late 1960s and early 1970s, that power came under challenge because of the Vietnam War. This was not an official war because Congress never passed a declaration of war. American troops were sent to South Vietnam to keep Communist North Vietnam from taking it over. From 1964 until 1973, thousands of American troops fought and died in the conflict. People at home questioned whether the United States should be involved in this war.

The reaction of Congress was to limit the power of the president to send troops to other nations in an emergency. It passed the War Powers Act in 1973. The act limited the president's ability to send troops to foreign countries without a declaration of war. Under this law, the president is required to notify Congress within 48 hours of

sending troops overseas. There is a limit of 60 days to the commitment unless Congress extends it. Since the passage of the act, troops have been sent to nations such as Panama, Haiti, Somalia, Bosnia-Herzegovina, Afghanistan, and Iraq. The law does not stop the president from committing troops abroad, but it does require that Congress be informed and, in some cases, approve the action.

The balance of power between Congress and the president is a delicate one. Indeed, each branch guards its own power carefully. As a result, there is a continual attempt to keep any one branch from assuming more power than it should. In passing the War Powers Act, Congress reacted to protect its constitutional authority to declare war without taking away the president's constitutional role as commander in chief of the armed forces.

Ceremonial Chief of State

Frequently, we learn from the news that a head of a foreign government is visiting the United States to meet with the president. During the visit, the president will usually host a state dinner at the White House. Dignitaries in and out of government take part in the festivities. This familiar scene is played out several times a year. In this role, the president is acting as the *ceremonial chief of state*. He is the symbol of the power and strength of the United States and its policies. Other ceremonial occasions involve congratulating sports teams that win special titles, honoring individuals for their achievements, and opening a fund-raising campaign for a worthy organization.

Leader of the Political Party

The president is traditionally considered to be the leader of his or her political party. This means that the president is the person the party looks to for decisions regarding the course the party should follow during his or her term of office. The president appoints the party's chairperson. This person helps set the policies of the party and helps carry them out.

During the time the president is in office, he

The president's spouse often has unofficial duties. First Lady Michelle Obama is interested in education, health, and other social issues. She read to children when she visited a community health center in Washington, D.C., in February 2009.

or she is expected to fulfill the promises made by the party during the campaign. Party officials count on the president to be their spokesperson. In addition, almost everything the president does while in office directly affects the image of the party.

As the party leader, the president helps it raise funds. These funds are used to pay off campaign debts and fill the treasury for future campaigns. To raise money, the president attends functions where major contributors donate money to hear him or her speak. In recent years, the amount of time and energy the president devotes to fundraising activities has been criticized.

Molder of Public Opinion

The office of president holds a distinct advantage over any other office in government. When people think of the leader of the nation, they naturally look to the president. Many other government officials may enjoy national popularity and have some power to shape the direction of government. But the office of president is the one that is seen as having the greatest influence on the American people. Depending on the president's personality and ability to communicate with people, he or she can exert a great deal

of influence over what the public thinks about issues. As President Theodore Roosevelt said, ". . . most of us enjoy preaching, and I've got such a bully pulpit!"

Modern presidents often appeal directly to American voters to gain support for programs. Presidents believe that if the people of the nation understand policies, they, in turn, will exert pressure on their representatives and senators to support a program. Mass media are used to publicize ideas and shape public opinion. Hardly a day goes by without something about the president's activities or policies being mentioned in news reports.

State of the Union Address

Constitutionally, the president is required to give a report to Congress on the "state of the union." Article II, Section 3, states: "He shall from time to time give to the Congress information of the state of the Union, and recommend to their consideration such measures as he shall judge necessary and expedient; . . ."

Each year, in January, the president goes to the chamber in the Capitol where the House of Representatives meets. There both houses of Congress gather, along with other government officials and invited guests. National television networks telecast live the president's speech on the "State of the Union."

The president uses this opportunity to outline the successes and possibly the unfinished business of his or her administration. In addition, the president usually describes programs that he or she plans to propose to Congress in the coming year. The State of the Union address has become a major event through which the president talks to the entire Congress and the entire nation at one time.

Legislative Leader

The lawmaking process involves both Congress and the president. Although he or she does not make or vote on laws, the president proposes laws that Congress will be asked to pass. In this capacity as a proposer of laws, the president is a legislative leader. The laws a president sends to Congress promote his or her vision of the course the nation should take. The president consults with members of Congress to make sure that the laws he or she wants are passed. In order to get backing for the proposals, the president can do favors for members of Congress. For example, he or she can help with fund-raising or support a program a congressperson wants. The president may also punish those who work against his or her ideas. This can be done, for instance, by not accepting people recommended by a congressperson for appointment to government jobs.

The President and the Supreme Court

Members of the U.S. Supreme Court are nominated by the president. The president appoints justices who are highly qualified judges or professors of law. These individuals are recommended by the president's legal advisers. The president also seeks candidates who support his or her social and legal philosophy. This is one way the president may exert influence over the Court. After a nomination is made, the Senate is charged with confirming the appointment.

Let's Think

1. Make a list of the different roles of the president. Which role do you think is most important? Why?
2. What is the Cabinet? Why is the Cabinet important to the office of the president?
3. What were the provisions of the War Powers Act? Many people see it as a check on the president's power. Why?

How the President Is Elected

After learning about the many roles the president must fill, do you still want to run for the office? A person who wants to run for the highest office in the land has to be totally committed to the election campaign. (See Chapter 4 for a description of the campaign process.) This effort starts long before election day and involves long hours of traveling and meeting with voters and persuading people to contribute money to the campaign. Rivals and the media look into every part of the life of the candidate and his or her family. Negative information may be given out. Everything the candidate does and says is interpreted and reinterpreted. Energy, money, and intelligent, committed advisers are essential in a winning race.

To get votes, a candidate makes appearances in person at many different types of events. He or she also appears on television talk shows and interview programs. Another way for a candidate to bring his or her views before the public is in a debate with other candidates. In the weeks before election day, the major party candidates usually participate in several nationally televised debates.

Indirect Choice

Many think that when we cast a vote for a presidential candidate we are voting directly for the person named on the ballot. This is not the case. A lively argument developed when the Framers of the Constitution tried to decide how to elect a

◄REALITY CHECK►

The President Goes to the Olympics

We may sometimes wonder what "hat" a president is wearing when making overseas trips. Think about what "hat" or "hats" President George W. Bush "wore" on his trip to the opening ceremonies of the 2008 Summer Olympic Games held in Beijing, the capital of the People's Republic of China.

Bush, an avid sports fan, stated that he wanted to spend some time rooting for the American athletes at the competition. But the President had many roles to fill. If he had gone just to attend the opening ceremonies, he would have been attending as the chief of state and ceremonial leader of the United States. But as was expected, he also played other roles on this trip.

The games opened on August 8, 2008, but Mr. Bush left the United States earlier in order to make some stops along the way. One was in Seoul, the capital of South Korea, and the other was in Bangkok, the capital of Thailand. At those stops, he met with the leaders of each nation, acting in his role as director of foreign policy. It is very important for the United States to have good relations with nations around the world. The president plays a key role in maintaining these relations. During the visits to South Korea and Thailand, President Bush discussed trade and security issues with the two countries' leaders.

Going to Beijing was controversial. Many in the United States thought the President should not visit a nation that had such a poor human rights record. In March 2008, China used its army to crack down on groups protesting Chinese policies in Tibet. Once an independent nation, Tibet had come under Chinese rule. Western nations had long criticized China's policy in Tibet. Others believed that the trip to China would provide a good opportunity for Bush to talk with Chinese leaders about Tibet and the Chinese government's suppression of dissent.

Another issue was the Chinese government's support of the government of Sudan. This African country has its own human-rights issues concerning the slaughter of people in the Darfur region by government-sanctioned groups. Sudan is one of China's important trading partners. Many nations condemn China's unwillingness to criticize Sudan's treatment of its own people.

As the Olympics opening ceremonies began, a military clash between the nations of Russia and Georgia took place. Russia sent troops into neighboring Georgia in support of a province that wanted to separate from Georgia. Once again, President Bush found it necessary to put on his foreign policy "hat." Seated near Russian Prime Minister Vladimir Putin, Bush expressed the concern of the United States about the Russian invasion of Georgia.

A U.S. president must always be on the alert and switch the "hats" that are worn as circumstances demand. The United States relies on its leaders to conduct themselves in a proper manner while representing the country abroad and to make wise decisions about foreign relations and domestic policies.

1. Why did President George W. Bush decide to attend the Summer Olympic Games in Beijing?
2. Make a list of the different "hats" "worn" by the President during this trip to Asia.
3. Why did the President wear different "hats" at different times?
4. In your opinion, which role was the most important? Give reasons to support your choice.

POWER *of* ★ ONE

Franklin Delano Roosevelt

Franklin Delano Roosevelt (FDR) was born on January 30, 1882, in Hyde Park, New York. His father was a wealthy railroad executive. Roosevelt graduated from Harvard University in 1904 and then attended Columbia University Law School. He decided early on that he would dedicate his life to public service. After serving a few years in the New York State Senate, he was appointed secretary of the Navy in 1913. In 1920, he was nominated for the vice presidency on the Democratic ticket. The country voted Republican. Roosevelt then entered private business.

Just a year later, Roosevelt contracted polio, which crippled his legs. He could never again walk without leg braces and help. Nevertheless, he remained active in politics, winning the governorship of New York State in 1928.

In 1932, the Democratic Party nominated him to run for president. It was a trying time for the nation. Some 25 percent of the labor force was out of work. Businesses and banks had failed. The economy of the United States had declined so severely that history now refers to this period as the Great Depression.

During his 1932 campaign, Roosevelt promised what he termed a "New Deal" for all Americans. This New Deal called for government to create programs that would put people back to work, provide insurance for the elderly, give unemployment insurance to those who lost their jobs. Roosevelt won the election. The New Deal promised relief, recovery, and reform. During the first 100 days of the Roosevelt administration, Congress swiftly passed a large number of laws to create programs to pull the nation out of the Great Depression.

Through his speeches, his policies, and his upbeat personality, Roosevelt became very popular with the American people. He gave them hope and calmed their fears. As he told

president. Some believed that the president should be elected directly by the people. Others felt that it would be better if the president was chosen by Congress, the representatives of the people. Once again, a compromise was reached. The president would be elected by people called **electors**.

Each state would have a certain number of electors based on population but equal to the total number of representatives and senators from the state. The Framers left it to the states to determine how the electors would be chosen. Article II, Section 1, of the Constitution states: "Each state shall appoint, in such manner as the Legislature thereof may direct, a number of Electors equal to the whole number of Senators and Representatives to which the State may be entitled in the Congress, but no Senator or Representative, or person holding an office of trust or profit

under the United States, shall be appointed an elector." The electors as a group are called the **Electoral College**.

When people go to their voting booths in November of a presidential election year, they are actually voting for a group of electors pledged to a particular candidate. Electors meet in their state capitals in December to cast their votes. The results are sent in early January to Washington. Congress then counts the electoral ballots and officially certifies the winner of the presidential election.

In modern times, electors simply vote the way the majority of the people voted in the election. In other words, they reflect the popular vote. There were instances in the past when an independent elector voted his or her own way regardless of what the popular vote in his or her state was.

them in his first inaugural speech, "The only thing we have to fear is fear itself."

His actions transformed the role of the national government. Before Roosevelt, most leaders followed the philosophy that people should help themselves when they are down. The government, they said, should not get involved in the personal lives of its citizens. This philosophy changed under Roosevelt. He believed that government should help people in times of crisis. Certainly, the Great Depression was a time of crisis—one of the most severe the nation had ever faced.

While the New Deal policies did help people, they also cost a lot of money and put the government in debt. Government also grew bigger and bigger. It became more involved in the lives of Americans. These negatives have had a profound influence on Americans' attitude toward government spending since the 1980s.

Roosevelt went on to be elected three more times as president, serving from 1933 to 1945. No other president had stayed in office for that long a period, nor will any other president serve as long again. The people kept reelecting FDR because they wanted him to lead them out of the Depression and World War II (1941–1945).

One of Roosevelt's friends and close political advisers was Frances Perkins. (She had known him in New York State and became his secretary of labor.) In her book about Roosevelt, *The Roosevelt I Knew*, Perkins wrote: "He made an indelible impression on his own country and on the world, changing the direction of political thought through knowledge of human needs and suffering and emphasis upon the provision of the good life for the common man. He grew to greatness; . . . he ignored his handicaps, both physical and intellectual, and let nothing hinder him from doing the work he had to do in the world. He was not born great but became great. The words most often on his lips to describe what he regarded as the good democratic society were 'free,' 'fair,' and 'decent.' To his dying day he held the philosophy that, 'If you treat people right they will treat you right—ninety per cent of the time.' "

1. How did the FDR plan to solve the problems of the economic decline the nation suffered through during the 1930s?
2. How did the New Deal change the role of government in the United States?
3. What were the arguments against Roosevelt's program? Explain.
4. Why do you think many people consider Roosevelt to be a great president?

To win the election, a presidential candidate must get 270 out of the total of 538 electoral votes. How is this total arrived at? First, we take the total number of members of the House of Representative, 435. Then, we add to that number the 100 senators. This gives us a total of 535 electoral votes. But where do the extra three votes come from? Because our nation's capital, Washington, D.C., is not part of any state, the people who lived there originally did not vote for president. This flaw in the system was corrected in 1961 when the 23rd Amendment to the Constitution was ratified. It gave the District of Columbia a minimum of three electoral votes. (This is the same number that the state with the smallest population is allowed.) If you divide the total of 538 electoral votes in half and add one more to make it a simple majority, you arrive at 270 as the "magic number" needed to win the presidency.

There have been instances when no one presidential candidate received enough electoral votes to win the presidential race. This may occur when more than two candidates run for office. The Constitution provides for a special procedure in this situation. The House of Representatives elects the president when no one candidate has enough electoral votes. Each state in this case has one vote. Such a situation occurred in the presidential elections of 1800 and 1824.

The Electoral College Affects the Campaign

The Electoral College system of electing a president has a major effect on the way a candidate runs for office. The goal of a presidential candidate is to win the *popular vote* in each state. The popular vote is the total number of votes cast by

Electoral Votes, 2000

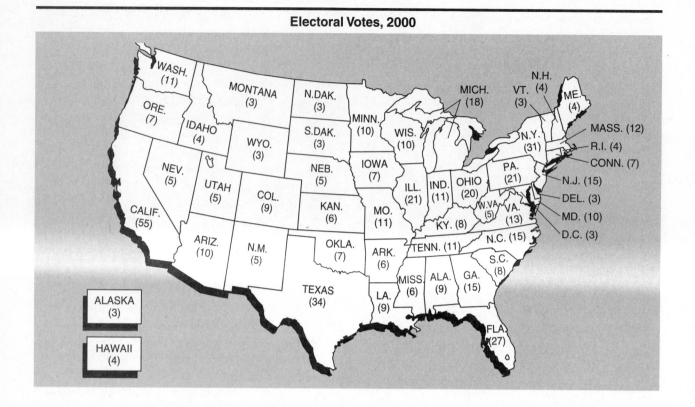

individuals. If a candidate wins the popular vote in a state, he or she will normally win all the electoral votes the state is entitled to. This "winner-take-all system" is used by most states.

Candidates tend to campaign hard and often in the states that have the most electoral votes, such as California, Texas, New York, and Florida. They may ignore or give much less time to states with smaller populations and electoral vote totals, such as Rhode Island, Delaware, and Wyoming. It is possible for a candidate to win the election without receiving the most popular votes. This happened in 2000 when George W. Bush won the presidential election without receiving the majority of the popular vote.

Some people would like to do away with the electoral system and determine the winner with the popular vote only. Others say, if it works, why change it? The debate continues. Americans tend to be slow in making decisions that could bring about major changes in their government.

Let's Think

1. What is the Electoral College?

2. How do we determine how many electoral votes each state has?

3. How many electoral votes does a candidate need to be elected president?

4. What does the Constitution say about elections when no presidential candidate receives the majority of the electoral votes?

5. How does the Electoral College system affect the way candidates conduct their campaigns for the presidency?

Chapter Summary

The job of being president is complex. Although it comes with some privileges and benefits, the office makes many demands on the person who occupies it. The Constitution lists only a few qualifications for president. The person must be at least 35 years of age, a natural-born citizen, and a resident for at least 14 years.

The American voter demands more from the president than the Constitution does. The president must be a good leader and possess qualities that will persuade the nation to follow that leadership. The president must be able to make difficult decisions about both domestic and foreign issues. A very important aspect of the job is the ability to communicate well with the American people.

The president may serve only two four-year terms. This became the law with the passage of the 22nd Amendment.

The vice president serves two main constitutional purposes. The first is to succeed the president if the president dies while in office. The second is to preside over the Senate. In most cases, the nature of the responsibilities given the vice president depends on how much of a role in the government the president wants him or her to assume. A major change in the vice president's responsibility came with the passage of the 25th Amendment. This allows the vice president to assume the role of acting president if the president should become ill or otherwise incapacitated.

The president is the leader of the nation, chief executive, director of foreign policy, commander in chief of the armed forces, ceremonial chief of state, leader of his or her political party, molder of public opinion, and legislative leader. The president also has an influence on the Supreme Court. As chief executive, the president is advised by (among others) the people who serve as the heads of the major departments. These people are included in the president's Cabinet.

Each year, the president is required to give a report to Congress on current conditions in the nation. This has become known as the State of the Union address. In that speech, which is televised, the president reviews the events and accomplishments of the previous year and outlines the legislative agenda for the upcoming year.

Americans do not vote directly for the president. The process we use is known as the Electoral College. When Americans vote for president, they actually vote for electors who, in turn, vote for president. Each state has electoral votes equal in number to its membership in Congress. The number of electoral votes a candidate must capture to win the election is 270. This is one more than half of the total number of electoral votes. Many people have criticized the system as undemocratic because the voters do not select the president directly. Others believe it is a time-honored tradition and should be kept in place.

★ CHAPTER REVIEW ★

A. Matching

Match each term in Column A with its definition in Column B.

Column A

1. chief executive
2. legislative leader
3. treaty
4. State of the Union
5. Cabinet
6. 22nd Amendment
7. War Powers Act
8. ceremonial chief of state
9. 25th Amendment
10. Electoral College

Column B

a. a formal agreement among two or more nations
b. advisers to the president
c. limits the number of terms a president may serve
d. limits the ability of a president to send American troops into combat
e. the role in which the president acts as the symbol of the nation
f. a yearly address given by the president to Congress
g. provides for succession to the presidency
h. the role in which the president proposes laws to Congress
i. the group that officially elects the president
j. the role in which the president directs the daily operation of the government and sees that the laws are carried out

B. Multiple Choice

Select the statement or word that most correctly answers the question or completes the statement.

1. To be president of the United States, a person must be at least this age: **(a)** 25 **(b)** 30 **(c)** 35 **(d)** 50.

2. The amendment that limits the number of terms a president can hold is the **(a)** 23rd **(b)** 22nd **(c)** 21st **(d)** 20th.

3. The vice president is given the constitutional responsibility to act as the **(a)** president of the Senate **(b)** president of the Supreme Court **(c)** chief of state **(d)** chief executive.

4. Who has final responsibility for commanding the armed forces of the United States? **(a)** the president **(b)** the Cabinet **(c)** the vice president **(d)** the speaker of the House.

5. The section of the Constitution that empowers the president to negotiate treaties is **(a)** Article I **(b)** Article II **(c)** Article III **(d)** Article IV.

6. The military conflict that led to the War Powers Act of 1973 was **(a)** the Vietnam War **(b)** the Korean War **(c)** World War II **(d)** World War I.

7. It takes this vote by the Senate to ratify a treaty: **(a)** two-thirds majority **(b)** simple majority **(c)** 75 **(d)** 61.

8. The president will from time to time propose bills to the Congress. In doing so, the president is fulfilling this role: **(a)** director of foreign policy **(b)** chief executive **(c)** legislative leader **(d)** molder of public opinion.

9. The total number of votes in the Electoral College is **(a)** 100 **(b)** 270 **(c)** 435 **(d)** 538.

10. The smallest number of electoral votes any state can have is **(a)** 2 **(b)** 3 **(c)** 4 **(d)** 6.

C. Essay

Write a paragraph about *one* of the following:

1. The job of the president is too much for one person. Discuss why you agree or disagree with this statement.

2. The power of the president can be checked by Congress in several ways.

3. The president of the United States should be a very good communicator.

4. A president must be able to make difficult decisions.

5. The Electoral College tends to favor large states over small states.

D. A Challenge for You

1. The president must play many roles. Select the *two* that you believe are the most important and write an essay explaining why you believe this to be true.

2. Select one role the president plays. Cut out or print out newspaper and magazine articles that show how the president fulfills that role. Place them into a scrapbook. Or you could create a picture essay that shows how the president fills the role. Create a bulletin board display of your articles and pictures.

3. Create a series of campaign slogans that would support a person's candidacy for president in the next election. The slogans could be put on signs or buttons. Or they could be incorporated into a video or PowerPoint presentation.

4. Make a poster summarizing the jobs of the president.

5. Write a letter to a friend describing the qualities that you think a president should have.

Document-Based Question

State the main idea expressed in each document. Then use information in the documents and your own knowledge to write an essay explaining the importance to a candidate for president of being noticed and of projecting a positive personal image.

A Candidate Gets Recognized

The first task facing anyone who wishes to be president is to get "mentioned" as someone who is of "presidential caliber." No one is quite sure why some people are mentioned and others are not. The journalist David Broder has suggested that somewhere there is "The Great Mentioner," who announces from time to time who is of presidential caliber (and only The Great Mentioner knows how big that caliber is).

But if The Great Mentioner turns out to be as unreal as the Easter bunny, you have to figure out for yourself how to get mentioned. One way is to let it be known to reporters ("off the record") that you are thinking about running for president. Another is to travel around the country making speeches

(Ronald Reagan, while working for General Electric, made a dozen or more speeches *a day* to audiences all over the country). Another way is to already have a famous name (John Glenn, the former astronaut, was in the public eye long before he declared for the presidency in 1984). . . .

Once mentioned, it is wise to set aside a lot of time to run, especially if you are only "mentioned" as opposed to being really well known.

From *American Government*, by James Q. Wilson, pages 175–176. Copyright 1989 by D.C. Heath and Company.

The Candidate's Image

The image that candidates project—their personality, appearance, and reputation—certainly affects how people vote. The importance of these qualities explains why modern presidential candidates hire media consultants. The Presidential elections of 1952 and 1956 provide a striking example of "image." Both elections were landslide victories for Republican Dwight D. Eisenhower over Democrat Adlai Stevenson. Eisenhower, a military hero in World War II, had an engaging smile and a "fatherly" image that appealed to many voters. By contrast, the brilliant and scholarly Stevenson projected an image of an intellectual or "egghead." [An intellectual or egghead was thought to be detached or separated from the average citizen.]

The importance of candidate image was also apparent in 1984. From a public relations viewpoint, Democratic challenger Walter Mondale was no match for President Ronald Reagan. Reagan, a former Hollywood actor, was charming and confident in public appearances. Mondale, though a political veteran, had less audience appeal than the incumbent President.

Issues are another factor in voters' decision-making. Voters cast their ballots for candidates whose positions on one or several issues most closely resemble their own. Among the issues that have been crucial in recent elections are inflation, taxes, unemployment, civil rights, social programs, defense spending, and the threat of nuclear war. Candidates may win or lose not only because of their stands on issues but also by the way they present issues and solutions to the voters.

From *Government in America* by Richard J. Hardy. Copyright © 1990 by Houghton Mifflin Company. All rights reserved. Reprinted by permission of McDougal Littell Inc.

CHAPTER 7

The Judiciary

★ CHAPTER FOCUS

1. What powers do the federal courts have?
2. What is the structure of the state and federal court systems?
3. Why is it necessary to have an independent judiciary?
4. What is the importance of the judicial review process?
5. How does a case get to the U.S. Supreme Court?

It is the first Monday in October—the day that the Supreme Court traditionally opens its session. You decide to attend. You enter a large, beautiful courtroom with a high ceiling and carpeted aisles. In front of you is a wide, raised bench with nine high-backed swivel chairs behind it. Suddenly, a voice calls out: "Oyez! Oyez! Oyez! All persons having business before the honorable, the Supreme Court of the United States, are admonished to draw near and give their attention, for the Court is now sitting. God save the United States and this Honorable Court." An air of excitement spreads throughout the room as lawyers, court officers, and spectators stand at their seats. In walk nine men and women wearing long black robes. They take their seats, and the presentations begin.

It is an impressive ceremony to witness, and it occurs in the same way every day the Supreme Court is in session. This distinguished group of individuals is made up of the most powerful judges in the United States. They form the high-est court in the land—the **United States Supreme Court**. It heads the judicial branch as described in the Constitution.

The Constitutional Foundation for the Federal Courts

Article III, Section 1, of the Constitution states: "The judicial power of the United States shall be vested in one Supreme Court, and in such inferior [lower] courts as the Congress may from time to time ordain and establish." These words give life to a very important part of our government. The Framers of the Constitution called for a single high court in the nation. They also saw fit to empower Congress to create lower courts to decide issues of national law.

The Supreme Court Building in Washington, D.C. Over the main entrance to the building are the words "Equal Justice Under Law."

Specific Powers for the Judiciary

The Constitution gives the federal judiciary specific powers. Article III, Section 2, explains them in the following way: "The judicial power shall extend to all cases in law and equity arising under this Constitution, the laws of the United States, and treaties made, or which shall be made, under their authority; to cases affecting ambassadors, other public ministers, and consuls; to all cases of admiralty and maritime jurisdiction; to controversies to which the United States shall be a party; to controversies between two or more States; . . . between citizens of different States, between citizens of the same State claiming lands under grants of different States, . . ."

The federal courts have the power to decide cases after a wrong has been committed. They may also try to keep one party from harming another by issuing an injunction, forbidding an action.

When issues arise involving officials representing foreign governments in the United States, the federal courts have jurisdiction. If a dispute arises between an American citizen and a foreign official, the case will usually be tried in a federal court.

The terms "maritime" and "admiralty" relate to waterways where ships travel and to businesses connected with the shipping industry. One dramatic case was tried in 1842. It involved members of the crew of an American ship, the *William Brown*. While sailing between Liverpool (England) and Philadelphia, the ship struck an iceberg and sank. It had 17 crew members and 65 passengers but only two lifeboats. The larger lifeboat carried many of the passengers and three crewmen, including Alexander William Holmes. Because there was not enough space in the lifeboat and the sea was rough, Holmes and the other seamen threw 16 people overboard in order to save the lives of the others. Only passengers died. All three crew members survived. After they were rescued, Holmes and another crewman, Rhodes, were charged with manslaughter. Rhodes fled, never to be seen again. Holmes was tried in a federal court and convicted of manslaughter. After a recommendation of mercy from the jury, the judge, sentenced Holmes to six months in jail and a $20 fine.

You might not think that states would have disputes with each other. But they do! In the 1990s, New York and New Jersey argued about which state really owns Ellis Island. The island, a former reception center for immigrants, is now a national historic site. It is in New York Harbor close to the New Jersey shoreline. New Jersey argued that the island is in its territorial waters and should be considered part of its state. New York claimed that the island has always been considered part of the state of New York. The

Supreme Court had jurisdiction over the case. In 1998, it awarded 90 percent of the island to New Jersey.

Original and Appellate Jurisdiction

The courts with which we are most familiar are those that hold jury trials. They are lower courts and have what is known as **original jurisdiction** to hear a case. This means that they have the authority to be the first to try the accused or to listen to arguments in a dispute. Let us suppose a store is robbed and someone is arrested. The court responsible for trying the case has original jurisdiction, or primary responsibility, over it. In a case involving ambassadors, a federal court is given the authority to try the case. It has original jurisdiction over this case.

Not all courts have original jurisdiction. Higher courts in both state and federal systems have what is known as **appellate jurisdiction**. (Appellate means relating to or recognizing appeals.) This is the authority of a court to hear and review the cases decided in a lower court. Sometimes, after a jury trial, the parties to the case believe that an error was made during the trial that might have affected the outcome of the case. When this occurs, the case may be appealed to a higher court.

Let us take the example of a criminal trial called *Escobedo* v. *Illinois* (1964). In this murder case, the accused, Danny Escobedo, made statements while being questioned by the police. The statements, which incriminated him, were introduced into evidence at the trial. After his conviction, his attorneys appealed the case to a higher court. They claimed that the trial judge should not have allowed Escobedo's statements into evidence. They said Escobedo had not been given the advice of an attorney when questioned by the police. (Escobedo had asked several times to see his lawyer.) Based on that fact, the higher courts had appellate jurisdiction to listen to the argument and to decide if the evidence had been properly used. The Supreme Court eventually decided that the evidence had not been correctly used. The appeal was not based on the jury's decision.

An appeal cannot generally be made because a lawyer disagrees with the decision of the jury. It can only be made when it is believed that an error was made in the way the trial was conducted or when a misinterpretation of the law formed the basis of the case.

Appellate courts do not hold jury trials. Instead, panels of judges listen to arguments by the lawyers for each case being appealed. Appellate courts do not determine right or wrong or innocence or guilt. They rule on the technical aspects of the law and trial procedure. They decide if an error occurred in the lower court trial. If the judges find that errors were made in the lower court and that these errors affected the outcome of the trial, they may reverse the decision of the lower court. When a decision of a lower court is reversed, the case may be retried in the lower court, this time correcting the errors. If the judges find that no error was made, they are said to uphold, or support, the decision of the lower court.

Let's Think

1. According to the Constitution, what types of cases are tried in federal courts?
2. Explain the meaning of the following terms: appellate jurisdiction, original jurisdiction.
3. Under what circumstances can a case be appealed?

Structure of State and Federal Courts

In the United States, we have two different court systems. There is a state court system and a federal court system. In order to understand this better, examine the diagram on page 111. The structure of the state courts is similar to the structure of the federal system. There are different levels of courts. The lower courts have original jurisdiction, and the higher ones are usually appellate courts. Jury trials are held in the lower courts of both the state and federal systems. They include criminal as well as civil trials.

Civil cases are concerned with disputes be-

Structure of Federal and State Courts

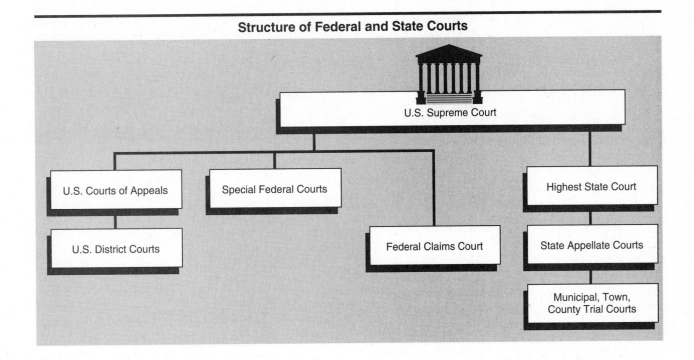

tween two or more parties. The parties can be individuals, states, or major corporations. A civil case might involve a dispute over a contract between two parties. Perhaps you agreed to perform a certain job for a specific price. If the employer does not pay you according to the contract, you can sue. Sometimes a faulty product is sold by a national company. Suing to recover damages is also a civil law issue, called a *product liability case*. The case concerning the ownership of Ellis Island is another example of a civil dispute.

The *criminal cases* that a federal court would try are violations of federal laws. Drug smuggling, kidnapping, murder of a federal official are examples of federal crimes. At the state level, criminal cases involve offenses such as murder, rape, theft, and assault.

Sometimes federal and state courts have overlapping jurisdiction. In those situations, the legal experts work out the jurisdiction in which the case should be tried.

State Courts

State courts are generally organized like the federal court system. Most state court systems are very similar to one another.

The lowest level of courts in the state systems are the municipal courts or town courts. These courts try cases involving small fines and lesser crimes called *misdemeanors*. Some local courts have jurisdiction over juvenile and family cases.

The next court on the ladder of importance is the county court. It is the major trial court in most states. Here more serious crimes, called *felonies*, are tried. Trials in county courts are usually jury trials. This level of courts has original jurisdiction in the state over most matters.

Above the county courts are the state *appeals courts*. They are called intermediate courts because they are the level between the county courts and the highest court in each state. Appeals, or appellate, courts review decisions made by lower courts. Generally, these courts consist of a panel of judges. They will either uphold or reverse decisions of the lower courts.

When we reach the top of the state court ladder, we arrive at the highest court in the state. As in the federal system, many states call this court the Supreme Court. In New York and Maryland, it is called the Court of Appeals. This court performs functions similar to the Supreme Court of the United States but on a state level. Therefore, it interprets matters relating to the state constitution. Decisions in these courts are also made by a panel of judges. The number of judges varies. Once the court makes a decision regarding state constitutional matters, it is final.

Judges in state courts can be either elected or appointed. Some are appointed by the governor with the approval of the state legislature. Very few states allow their governors the sole authority to appoint judges.

Election vs. Appointment of Judges

Which is the better method of selecting judges? Should they be appointed or elected? This question has been debated for a long time. In many states, judges are elected. In the federal system of courts, judges are appointed.

People who support the election of judges believe that running for office keeps judges close to the people. Elections can make judges responsive to the needs of the voters. Others disagree and argue that running for election puts judicial candidates in the position of trying to please the voters. In order to get elected, they might compromise the decisions they make while sitting as a judge.

Voters have a difficult time selecting judges because often little is known about the candidates. A judge may make unpopular decisions and still be a good jurist. Political party endorsements can mean little when several parties endorse the same candidate.

Advocates of appointing judges believe that this system offers the better opportunity to select the best-qualified people. Popularity would not be a consideration, only legal competence. Candidates for judicial positions are usually recommended by respected legal groups or scholars.

Trying to determine which is the better way of selecting a judge is difficult. Since experts disagree on what makes a good judge, it becomes even more difficult to determine which method is more desirable.

Federal Courts

District Level

The lowest court in the federal system is the United States District Court. The district courts are trial courts and have original jurisdiction. There is at least one district court in every state. Some larger states have several districts. The total number of district courts in the 50 states is

89. The District of Columbia has a district court. There are also territorial district courts in Puerto Rico, Guam, the Northern Mariana Islands, and the Virgin Islands. Several judges are assigned to each district court. All federal judges are appointed by the president for life. The appointments must be confirmed by the Senate. Only at the district level in the federal system are jury trials held.

Appeals Courts

The United States Courts of Appeals review cases that come to them from the federal district courts. This court level serves as the intermediate court between the district courts and the Supreme Court.

There are 11 judicial circuits, with one court of appeals in each. In addition, there is a District of Columbia circuit court. The 50 states and the U.S. territories are each assigned to a circuit.

Appeals courts do not conduct jury trials. The cases they hear are those that were originally tried in a lower court. A panel of judges (usually three) listens to the arguments of the attorneys for both sides. Generally, witnesses are not called and evidence is not examined. The judges decide whether to accept the decision of the lower court or say that a new trial should be held.

Most appeals end with the decision of the courts of appeals. But occasionally, the decision is appealed to the highest court in the United States—the Supreme Court.

Special Courts

Several **special courts** have been created to deal with certain types of cases. One such court is the *United States Court of Claims*. Sometimes citizens have a grievance against the U.S. government. It might be that they sold something to a government agency and have not been paid for the goods. In such a case, they have the legal right to file a suit in the Court of Claims.

The *United States Tax Court* has original jurisdiction over cases involving federal taxes. When a citizen disagrees with the Internal Revenue Service about the amount of taxes he or she should pay, the person can appeal the case to this court.

Separate from the federal system is the military court system that tries cases involving people in the armed forces of the United States. Military law is a separate, specialized body of laws. The special federal court dealing with appeals from lower military courts is called the *Court of Military Appeals*.

There are several other special courts. One is the *Territorial courts*, which deal with cases involving United States territories such as the Virgin Islands. The *District of Columbia courts* handle cases arising in the District of Columbia. A District of Columbia Court is required because the district is not part of any state and thus does not have a court system of its own. Veterans of the military services can file grievances against the government relating to veterans benefits with the *Court of Appeals for Veterans Claims*.

Let's Think

1. Make a list of the different types of courts that are found on the state level. What is the function of each?
2. What arguments are made for and against election of judges?
3. Make a list of the different federal courts and outline their functions.

The Makeup of the Supreme Court

At present, there are nine members of the Supreme Court. There are eight associate justices and one chief justice.

The Selection Process

The justices of the Supreme Court are appointed by the president with the advice and consent of the Senate. In deciding who should be nominated, the president turns to his or her top legal advisers for assistance. The Constitution does not list any qualifications for members of the Supreme Court. Most nominees are judges, legal scholars, or lawyers.

Since political thinking and other concerns vary in different parts of the nation, many feel that the makeup of the Court should reflect these differences. They argue that the Court should have members from different geographic locations.

Observers also believe that the ethnic and gender makeup of the Court should reflect the makeup of the nation. In recent years, there has been a conscious effort to include both members of minorities and women as justices.

Usually, the president will interview several people before settling on the final choice. He or she consults with advisers, particularly the attorney general. They help prepare a list of the candidates they think are the best for the job. The attorney general is the logical person to consult because he or she is the person who heads the Justice Department. One organization that may be consulted as the list of potential candidates is put together is the American Bar Association. It is the national association of attorneys. The association rates lawyers and judges and makes recommendations to the attorney general's staff. After the list of the most important candidates is completed, the Federal Bureau of Investigation looks into the background of each potential nominee. The president wants to make sure that nothing in the person's past will disqualify the individual from consideration.

Confirmation

Once the president announces the candidate, it is the job of the Senate to approve the appointment. Hearings are held by the Senate Judiciary Committee. The committee can recommend confirmation or rejection of the candidate. Rejection of a presidential nominee for the Supreme Court does occur. There can be many reasons for the rejection. Sometimes the reasons involve political differences between the Senate and the president or the point of view of the nominee on key or controversial issues.

After the nominee gains the approval of the Judiciary Committee, the whole Senate votes on the choice. If the nominee is rejected, the president must find another candidate.

Members of U.S. Supreme Court in 2009. Front row, from left: Justices Anthony M. Kennedy and John Paul Stevens, Chief Justice John G. Roberts, Justices Antonin Scalia and David H. Souter. Standing, from left: Justices Stephen G. Berger, Clarence Thomas, Ruth Bader Ginsburg, and Samuel Anthony Alito, Jr. Justice Souter has since resigned,

Let's Think

1. Do you think the Constitution should list the qualifications for justices of the federal courts? Why? Why not?
2. What qualifications should a person have to sit on the Supreme Court of the United States?
3. How does the process of selecting justices to serve on the Supreme Court support the idea of checks and balances?

The Need for an Independent Judiciary

Justices are appointed to the Supreme Court for life. You may be thinking, why should they be appointed for life? The judicial branch is called upon to make controversial decisions. These decisions have, at times, angered the members of Congress, the president, and the American people. Granting lifetime appointment assures the members of the Court that they will not be turned out of office if they make unpopular but legally correct decisions. They are also not so easily influenced by the wishes of the executive and legislative branches.

Being independent does not mean that the Supreme Court justices live in a vacuum. They, too, are affected by public opinion, the nature of the times in which they live, and their own personal experiences.

Presidential Control

At times, presidents have made attempts to control the decisions of the Court. Early in 1937, President Franklin Roosevelt became extremely upset with the Supreme Court. It had handed down several decisions that declared some of the president's New Deal laws unconstitutional. Roosevelt called the members of the Court "nine old men" and said that they were undermining his efforts to bring the country out of the Depression.

Roosevelt asked Congress to pass a law giving him the power to increase the number of justices on the Court to as many as 15. He believed that if he could appoint more justices who supported his ideas, he could tip the thinking of the Court in his favor. After a bitter debate, Congress refused to pass the proposed law. The members of Congress did not approve of Roosevelt's efforts to "pack the Court" with people who had the same constitutional philosophy as he did. Had the chief executive been given this authority, the president's influence over another branch of the government might have made him too powerful. Also, the Court's independence might have been severely weakened.

Removal of Judges

You might think that a lifetime appointment for federal judges makes it impossible to remove a judge who is incompetent. This is not true. The Constitution provides for the possibility that a judge might do something that would warrant his or her removal. Any federal judge—from the lowest to the highest court—can be impeached. The procedure for the impeachment of a federal judge is the same as that for other federal officials. The power to impeach gives the executive and legislative branches a check on the power of the judiciary.

Let's Think

1. Why does our government attempt to provide for an independent judiciary?
2. How did President Roosevelt attempt to control the Supreme Court?
3. How can a federal judge be removed from office?

Judicial Review

Most of the cases that come before the Supreme Court involve the question of whether a law conforms to the Constitution. The Supreme Court can declare that a law is in violation of the Constitution. This power to declare laws unconstitutional and therefore void is called **judicial review**.

Judicial review is a check on both the president and Congress. It also serves to check the wrongful acts of state governments. The concept of judicial review is deeply established in the U.S. legal system even though it is not part of the written Constitution. It can be thought of as part of the unwritten constitution that is based on past practice and tradition.

Establishing Judicial Review

One of the most important cases decided by the Supreme Court was *Marbury* v. *Madison* in 1803.

The case involved a government appointment for William Marbury. As John Adams, our second president, was about to leave office, he, at the last moment, appointed William Marbury to the post of a federal justice of the peace. After this "midnight appointment," Thomas Jefferson succeeded Adams as president. James Madison, as Jefferson's secretary of state, was responsible for seeing that Marbury received his appointment. He refused to carry out this duty. Marbury sued in the Supreme Court.

At that time, John Marshall headed the Supreme Court as the chief justice. Under Marshall, the Court ruled that Marbury was entitled to his appointment. It also said that the Supreme Court did not have the power to force Madison to give it to him. In the Judiciary Act of 1789, Congress had given the Supreme Court the authority to handle the problem. But Marshall and the other justices ruled that Congress did not have the authority to grant the Supreme Court powers in addition to those stated in the Constitution.

For the first time, an act of Congress, a section of the Judiciary Act of 1789, was declared unconstitutional. Congress by itself could not amend the Constitution, said the Court. Thus, the case of *Marbury* v. *Madison* established the principle of judicial review.

This decision helped establish the Constitution as the supreme law of the land. As Marshall explained, in a case in which a conflict exists between the Constitution and a law passed by Congress or any other government in the nation, the Constitution must be favored over any law. The Constitution cannot be changed by having Congress pass a law. The only way to change the Constitution is through the amendment process.

Let's Think

1. What is meant by the term "judicial review"?
2. How did the case of *Marbury* v. *Madison* establish judicial review?
3. How does judicial review provide a check by the judiciary on the other two branches of government?

◀REALITY CHECK▶

An Indiana Case Travels to the Supreme Court

A court case may go through several levels of courts before ending up in the Supreme Court of the United States. The process can take several years to complete. For instance, the combined cases of *Crawford* v. *Marion County Election Board* and *Indiana and Indiana Democratic Party* v. *Todd Rokita* had their beginning in 2005. They reached the Supreme Court in 2008.

In 2005, the state of Indiana passed a law requiring voters to show a picture ID at the time of voting. The acceptable forms of identification included a passport, a driver's license, or another government-issued document. If an individual did not have such a document, one would be provided at no charge. However, the person would need a birth certificate to get the ID. In most states, voting procedures require a voter to sign a form that has a sample of his or her signature on it before that individual can cast a ballot. If the signature does not seem to be authentic, the person's identity can be challenged.

The Democratic Party in Indiana believed that the 2005 law, passed by a largely Republican legislature, discriminated against the poor and denied them their right to vote. Generally, this group tends to vote for Democratic Party candidates. The Democratic Party decided to challenge the constitutionality of the law in the Federal District Court for the Southern District of Indiana. The suit was based on the belief that the state law violated the First Amendment and the equal protection clause of the Fourteenth Amendment of the U.S. Constitution. When someone believes that the U.S. Constitution has been violated, that person or group has the right to challenge the action in the federal courts, as in this case.

The suit was based on the following concepts: "(1) the cost of the identification, travel and birth certificate required to obtain identification constitute a poll tax [an illegal tax charged to voters]; (2) the need to go to the county election board to sign an affidavit constitutes an added unnecessary burden; (3) the regulations do not apply to all voters, namely absentee voters, giving rise to disparate [unequal] treatment; and (4) many of the Indiana Bureaus of Motor Vehicles, the only location to obtain valid identification, are difficult to get to, especially in rural counties."

The first step was to file suit in the Federal District Court for the Southern District of Indiana, which has original jurisdiction. The District Court ruled that the **plaintiffs** (those bringing the suit to overturn the law) had not produced enough evidence to demonstrate that people had been hurt by the law. In contrast, the plaintiffs argued, the claim that the state was trying to prevent voter fraud was not valid because voter fraud was not shown to be a common occurrence.

The plaintiffs appealed the District Court's decision to a still higher court, the Circuit Court of Appeals for the Seventh District. The plaintiffs argued that the ruling by the lower court was in error, and that the law did make it more difficult for certain groups of people to vote. The appellate court supported the decision of the lower court, declaring the Indiana voter identification law to be constitutional.

One would think that after two levels of federal courts ruled against them, the plaintiffs would stop their appeals. But they decided to move up to the U.S. Supreme Court. They filed for a *writ of certiorari* (an order by the Supreme Court to have the records of the lower courts sent to it for review). After reading the arguments from both sides of the Indiana case, the justices decided to hear the case. This decision was announced on September 25, 2007. By that time, 20 other states had enacted voter identification laws similar to the one in Indiana. They, too, had an interest in how the Supreme Court would decide.

On January 9, 2008, attorneys for both sides filed into the great chamber of the Supreme Court Building in Washington, D.C., taking their seats at the appropriate tables in front of the bench. All stood as the nine justices entered the room and moved to their seats behind the bench. Both sides presented their arguments and answered questions asked by the justices. Several months later, on April 8, 2008, the Supreme Court announced its 6-3 decision. It ruled that the Indiana law did not violate the Constitution, agreeing with the lower courts' rulings. Thus, the Indiana voter ID law remained in effect.

1. What were the major provisions of the Indiana voter ID law?

2. Why did the Democratic Party decide to challenge the law?
3. Make a chart showing the steps the case went through on its way to the U.S. Supreme Court.
4. Present arguments for and against the amount of time a case normally takes before it can reach the U.S. Supreme Court.

The Journey of a Case to the Supreme Court

Cases originating in the state courts will end at that level unless there are grounds to appeal the decisions to higher courts. After a case has climbed the ladder of appeals through the state system and reached the highest court in the state, the appeals process generally ends there. Each state has a court of last resort. This means that it is the highest court in the state and is the final court of appeal in the state.

In some cases, arguments can be made that the issues being decided are of concern to the nation as a whole. Under these circumstances, the decision in the case may be appealed from the highest court in the state to the United States Supreme Court. In all situations, the court of last resort in the nation is the U.S. Supreme Court.

We cannot expect the Supreme Court to deal with every case that people want it to decide. In large part, the lower courts, the district and circuit courts of appeals, serve as a screening process so that the Supreme Court will have to deal with only a few important cases.

How Do Justices Choose Cases to Hear?

During the course of a year, hundreds of cases are appealed to the Supreme Court. Only a few of them will be heard by the Court. Generally, the justices meet as a group to decide which cases to hear. The justices and their clerks, who are attorneys, read the papers that are filed by those who are appealing cases to the Court. The types of cases submitted cover a wide variety of subjects. They may be criminal or civil cases. The party appealing the case explains to the Court why the case is an issue that should come before the Court.

The justices meet and discuss the cases of greatest interest. If four of the nine justices vote to hear a case, it is placed on the calendar. Generally, the justices choose cases that involve important constitutional issues. Most cases are rejected. If the Court refuses to hear a case, the issue is usually closed. This leaves the decision of the last court in effect.

Deciding a Case

When the day comes for the Supreme Court to hear a case, attorneys for both sides present oral arguments. In their presentations, the attorneys refer to the Constitution, decisions made in other cases, and federal law. The justices sometimes interrupt to ask questions. After they have heard the arguments, the justices meet in closed session to make their decision. They will argue the issue, discuss the legal merits of the case, and come to an agreement. A simple majority vote (five to four) can decide the case.

Decisions are seldom made immediately. The Court takes time to study the issues and write out its decisions. A written document explains the reasoning behind a decision. The document that expresses the ideas of most of the justices is called the **majority decision**. Occasionally, a justice who voted with the majority disagrees with some of the reasoning behind the decision. This justice may issue what is called a **concurring opinion** that gives his or her reasoning. Justices who disagree with the majority often choose to explain, in writing, why they disagree. Their statements are called the **dissenting opinions**. Supreme Court decisions are recorded and studied by attorneys and judges when they are concerned with similar legal issues.

Reversing Decisions

Once the Supreme Court makes a decision, it is normally final. But there are some exceptions. A decision of the Court can be changed in two ways. One is to amend the Constitution. The second is by reversing a decision made in a previous case.

Two cases that demonstrate the latter concept are *Plessy* v. *Ferguson*, decided in 1896, and *Brown* v. *the Board of Education of Topeka, Kansas*, decided in 1954. Both cases centered on the same issue, racial segregation in the United States. From the end of the Civil War in 1865 until the decision of the Supreme Court in the Brown case in 1954, some states passed laws to force blacks and whites to use separate public facilities. As a result, African Americans in these states could only use public bathrooms, water fountains, and other facilities specifically labeled for them.

In the late 19th century, there was a conscious decision to challenge these laws in the courts. Homer Plessy, who was one-eighth African American, boarded a train in Louisiana and sat in a car designated for whites only. He was arrested for violating a Louisiana state law. After he was convicted, he appealed the case through the courts until it eventually arrived at the door of the Supreme Court. The Supreme Court at that time voted seven to one against Plessy. It argued that the law provided for "separate but equal" facilities for blacks and whites. For the next 58 years, the separation of the races in public facilities remained legal.

During the 1950s, African-American students and their families in several states decided to challenge the segregation laws of their states. The states were Virginia, South Carolina, Delaware, and Kansas. Slowly the cases moved up through the various court levels. Eventually, the Supreme Court heard the one known as *Brown* v. *the Board*

of Education of Topeka, Kansas. The decision in the case changed the nation permanently.

The attorneys for the students argued that being forced to attend schools solely on the basis of one's race was a violation of the rights protected by the Constitution in the 14th Amendment. The case for the students was argued by Thurgood Marshall, a prominent African-American attorney who later became the first African-American justice on the Supreme Court. The Court decided by unanimous vote in favor of the students. The opinion said: "We conclude that in the field of public education the doctrine of 'separate but equal' has no place. Separate educational facilities are inherently unequal."

This decision banned any law that required the separation of races in public facilities. In addition, it reversed the decision of the Court in *Plessy* v. *Ferguson*. The Supreme Court under Chief Justice Earl Warren overturned a decision made in a different historical time when the nation thought differently about the nature of social

Thurgood Marshall (center), NAACP special counsel, and his colleagues George E. C. Hayes (left), a Washington attorney, and James Nab, a professor and attorney at Howard University, in front of the Supreme Court Building after winning the decision in the case of *Brown* v. *the Board of Education of Topeka, Kansas*.

justice. The Brown decision corrected a grave mistake that had been made by the nation and an earlier Court.

Let's Think

1. Describe the process the Supreme Court follows in deciding what cases should be heard.
2. What kind of vote is needed to decide a case?
3. What is meant by majority, concurring, and dissenting opinions?
4. Why do you think the written opinions are important?
5. How can a Supreme Court decision be reversed?

The Supreme Court and Controversy

When the Constitution was written, the Framers saw the Supreme Court as the least controversial branch of government. It has not turned out that way. After the Court makes a decision, it has little power to enforce that decision. It is the responsibility of Congress or the president to see that a decision of the Court is carried out. Respect for the Court is strong among the other branches of government and the general public. Even when they disagree with the decisions of the Court, the government and the people usually enforce the decisions. However, the degree of enthusiasm with which the decisions are enforced may vary.

A President Refuses to Enforce a Decision

Occasionally, the Supreme Court has had difficulty getting backing for its decisions. During the early 19th century, the state of Georgia passed a law that forced the Cherokee people off their lands. White settlers wanted the land for farming. The Cherokee sued to keep their land, and the Supreme Court in 1832 ruled in their favor.

The opinion in the case of *Worcester* v. *Georgia* declared that Georgia was wrong to remove the Cherokee from the land they owned. It was an unpopular decision. President Andrew Jackson refused to enforce the decision to make Georgia return the Cherokee's land. The Court had no way to carry out the ruling on its own.

Justices "Make Law"

The Supreme Court has made decisions about a variety of controversial issues, such as abortion, voting rights, segregation, school prayer, and the separation of church and state. A few of these decisions have had a great impact on the lives of many Americans. Some people argue that the Court hands down many decisions that are not supported by the general public. These critics believe that the justices make rulings that, in practice, are treated like laws. It is not the role of the judiciary to make law, they say. Only Congress has that power.

An example of a Court decision that had the impact of a law is the one in the case of *Miranda* v. *Arizona*, decided in 1966. The Supreme Court ruled that people who are arrested must be informed of their rights at the time of arrest. After this ruling, police officers were obligated to read what became known as the "Miranda Rights" to a person who is arrested. These rights inform the accused that he or she can remain silent and have an attorney. If the accused chooses to talk, anything that the person says can be used against him or her in a court of law. This is a clear example of judge-made law, say the critics. Others disagree and say that it is clearly within the power of the Court to make such decisions.

Let's Think

1. Describe the conflict that developed over the case of *Worcester* v. *Georgia*.
2. How does this controversy demonstrate the rivalry between the executive and judicial branches of the federal government?
3. It has been said that the judges make laws. Explain this statement.

POWER *of* ★ ONE

Ruth Bader Ginsburg

If you were to ask successful individuals what the key ingredient in reaching success in life is, many would say that it is the ability to overcome obstacles. If you were to ask Ruth Bader Ginsburg, the second woman to serve on the Supreme Court, this question, she might say the same thing.

Justice Ginsburg was born in Brooklyn, New York, in 1933. On the day before she was to graduate from high school, her mother, who had been seriously ill for some time, died. Ginsburg overcame her sorrow, graduated from high school, and entered Cornell University in Ithaca, New York, in 1950. While there, she met her future husband, also a pre-law student. After attending Cornell, she went to Harvard University Law School, one of nine women in a class of 500. She completed her law studies at Columbia University School of Law because her husband had accepted a job with a law firm in New York City. While in law school, she raised a child and still managed to tie for first place in the graduating class.

In most cases, a law student with such high grades would be actively recruited by major law firms throughout the country. This was not the case with Ginsburg. She felt the sharp arrow of discrimination against her religion (Judaism), sex, and motherhood. She was once quoted as saying: "In the Fifties, the traditional law firms were just beginning to turn around on hiring Jews. . . . But to be a woman, a Jew and a mother to boot—that combination was a bit too much." When asked why she wasn't bitter about the rejections, she replied, "I don't think that being angry or being hostile is very productive."

She served as a clerk to a federal judge. Then she worked on an international law project that focused on Swedish legal procedures and Scandinavian law. Next, she taught law at two universities in the New York City area for 18 years, becoming the first tenured female professor at Columbia. From 1973 to 1976, Ginsburg headed the Women's Rights Project of the American Civil Liberties Union. She won five important decisions before the Supreme Court that protected women's rights. Other cases protected the rights of men, especially husbands of women in the military, who, she argued, deserved the same benefits as wives of men in the military. In 1980, she was appointed as a judge to the U.S. Court of Appeals in the District of Columbia.

Earlier in her career, Ruth Bader Ginsburg thought of herself as a fighter for social justice. She has been very much aware of the problems faced by women who were trying to develop a career. An editorial in a magazine in 1993 said about her: "Commitment to women's rights runs deep in Ginsburg, even into her tenure as a U.S. Court of Appeals judge. In a 1984 speech she advocated universal day care as a step toward gender equality. . . . In a much-publicized lecture [early in 1993] . . . she praised the feminist movement's 'ongoing revitalization in the 1980s and 1990s.' "

In 1993, President Bill Clinton chose her to fill a vacancy on the Supreme Court. The American Bar Association gave her its top rating. The Senate confirmed her by a vote of 96 to 3 to be the second woman to sit as a justice on the U.S. Supreme Court. Ruth Bader Ginsburg, advocate of a better life for women, legal scholar, and now Supreme Court justice, is a shining example of the Power of One.

1. What obstacles did Ginsburg have to overcome to attain success in her chosen career?
2. What qualifications did Ginsburg have that made her an acceptable candidate for the Supreme Court?
3. Why do you think Ginsburg found it necessary to fight for women's rights in this country?

Chapter Summary

The judiciary is one of the three branches of government. The other two are the executive and legislative. The powers of the federal courts are outlined in Article III, Section 2, of the Constitution. The courts have jurisdiction over several types of cases. Among them are issues concerning foreign ambassadors in the United States, disputes between states, disputes between a citizen and a state, and maritime issues.

The courts have two different types of jurisdiction over cases. The first is original jurisdiction. The courts having this responsibility are usually the lower courts. They are the first to try the accused or listen to arguments in a dispute. They hold jury trials.

The second type of jurisdiction that courts have is appellate. Appeals cases are heard by special courts that do not conduct jury trials. Appeals courts hear arguments about cases in which trial procedure may have been violated or a judge may have made an error that affected the outcome of the case.

There are essentially 51 court systems. The first is the federal system, in which the Supreme Court is the highest court. The other 50 are the individual court systems in each of the states. There are also courts in the various U.S. territories.

The lowest level of the state court systems are the municipal or town courts. They try minor cases. On the next level are the county courts. They try most of the more serious civil and criminal cases. The next higher courts, the intermediate courts, are appellate. The highest courts in the state have the last say over state issues. Both the intermediate appellate courts and the highest state courts do not conduct jury trials. Cases taken to them are heard by a panel of judges.

The lowest court level in the federal system is the district court, which conducts jury trials. Each state has at least one. In larger states, there are several districts. The next highest level is the court of appeals. The highest court in the United States is the Supreme Court.

The Supreme Court is made up of nine justices. They are appointed by the president and confirmed by the Senate. All justices serve for life. Lifetime appointments ensure that the justices are not caught up in party politics and are part of an independent judiciary.

Judicial review is a tool used by the Supreme Court to check the authority of the Congress, the president, and the states. It is the power to declare a law or action unconstitutional. The only way that a decision of the Supreme Court can be changed is if the Court itself reverses an earlier decision or an amendment is added to the Constitution.

Cases get to the Supreme Court through the appeals process. These cases may come up through the state courts and through the various levels of the federal courts.

The Supreme Court may decide a case by a simple majority vote. Once a decision is made, the entire nation is expected to abide by it. The president has the responsibility to enforce the ruling.

★ CHAPTER REVIEW ★

A. Matching
Match each term in Column A with its definition in Column B.

Column A
1. Supreme Court
2. judiciary
3. Supreme Court justice
4. jurisdiction
5. original jurisdiction
6. majority opinion
7. *Marbury* v. *Madison*
8. court packing
9. segregation
10. Court of Claims

Column B
a. term referring to courts in general
b. term for the authority to be the first to try the accused or listen to arguments in a dispute
c. the court that hears lawsuits against the government
d. the name for the Supreme Court decision supported by the most justices
e. policy of separating people based on race
f. the highest court in the nation
g. established judicial review
h. member of the highest U.S. court, appointed by the president
i. the authority of a court to hear a case
j. President Franklin D. Roosevelt's attempt to add justices to the Supreme Court

B. Multiple Choice
Select the statement or word that most correctly answers the question or completes the statement.

1. Which statement best describes the role of the Supreme Court in the United States? **(a)** It is the lawmaking body of the government. **(b)** It is the interpreter of the Constitution. **(c)** It is the enforcer of the law. **(d)** It is responsible for changing the Constitution.

2. The section of the Constitution that authorizes the setting up of federal courts is **(a)** Article I **(b)** Article II **(c)** Article III **(d)** Article IV.

3. The federal district courts **(a)** have original jurisdiction when federal criminal laws are broken **(b)** hear only appeals cases **(c)** are the highest courts in the nation **(d)** try cases that involve state law.

4. Appealing a case means **(a)** taking a case to higher court **(b)** making a case interesting for the jury **(c)** accepting the verdict of the jury **(d)** arguing a case before the attorney general of the United States.

5. The Constitution requires this part of the government to give its "advice and consent" to the appointment of a nominee to the Supreme Court: **(a)** House of Representatives **(b)** Senate **(c)** president **(d)** state governors.

6. The power to declare a law unconstitutional is called **(a)** judicial review **(b)** veto **(c)** verdict **(d)** dissenting opinion.

7. Supreme Court justices serve for this period of time: **(a)** four years **(b)** six years **(c)** ten years **(d)** life.

8. The following is the correct order in which a case usually travels through the federal court system on its way to the Supreme Court: **(a)** Federal District Court/Tax Court/Supreme Court **(b)** Federal District Court/United States Court of Appeals/Supreme Court **(c)** State Court/Federal District Court/Court of Claims/Supreme Court **(d)** Federal Tax Court/Court of Veterans' Affairs/United States Circuit Court of Appeals/Supreme Court.

9. The number of justices on the Supreme Court at the present time is **(a)** five **(b)** seven **(c)** nine **(d)** fifteen.

10. When the Supreme Court decides to hear a case, the number of justices voting to hear it must be at least **(a)** four **(b)** five **(c)** six **(d)** nine.

C. Essay
Write a paragraph about *one* of the following:

1. The judicial branch of the government should have greater power to check the legislative and executive branches.

2. The importance of county courts in the life of your community.

3. It is important to have Supreme Court justices appointed for life.

4. The qualifications that you think are necessary for a person to become a justice of the Supreme Court.

D. A Challenge for You

1. Write an editorial giving your opinion about the following topic: "The federal and state court systems should be simplified." You might want to check the Internet for current background information or ideas.

2. Create a scrapbook of newspaper, magazine, and Internet articles that discuss Supreme Court decisions. Summarize them. Explain how the decisions affect our lives. Write an article for the school newspaper about your findings or create a bulletin board display.

3. Prepare *two* speeches for a debate arguing each side of the following topic: "The Constitution should be very specific about the qualifications of Supreme Court justices."

4. Create a cartoon strip that demonstrates the path a case takes to get to the Supreme Court.

5. Select a current member of the Supreme Court and research his or her life. Write a biography of the person that highlights why he or she is qualified to sit on the Supreme Court. Use library resources and the Internet to find current information.

Document-Based Question

State the main idea expressed in each document. Then use information in the documents and your own knowledge to write an essay explaining why judicial review is important in the U.S. system of government.

The Origins of Judicial Review

In the American constitutional system, . . . it is the responsibility of the Supreme Court, though not of the Court alone, to safeguard those values which are essential to the existence of constitutional democracy. . . . This began at least as early as John Marshall's opinion in *Marbury* v. *Madison* in 1803, and has continued to this day.

In this historic opinion Marshall enunciated what came to be described as the doctrine of "judicial review." Only in terms of the application of this doctrine can the American brand of constitutional law be meaningfully defined. As [one professor] . . . puts it:

"As employed in this country, Constitutional Law signifies a body of rules resulting from the interpretation by a high Court of a written constitutional instrument in the course of disposing cases in which the validity, in relation to the . . . [Constitution] . . . of some act of governmental power, state or national, has been challenged. This function . . . involves the power and duty on the part of the Court of pronouncing void any such act which does not square with its own reading of the Constitutional instrument."

. . . On the much debated question whether it was intended by the framers of the Constitution that the Court should Exercise this power, the Constitution itself is silent. Scholars and jurists differ in their interpretation of what the framers intended. It seems to be generally agreed, however, that a number of the most influential members of the Constitutional Convention of 1787 favored such a power and assumed that the Court would exercise it.

From *The Supreme Court and Fundamental Freedoms* by George W. Spicer, pages 2–3. Appleton-Century-Crofts, Inc., copyright 1959.

The Decision in *Marbury* v. *Madison*

. . . a legislative act contrary to the constitution is not law. . . . It is emphatically the province and duty of the judicial department to say what the law is. . . . If two laws conflict with each other, the courts must decide on the operation of each. . . .

So if a law be in opposition to the constitution; if both the law and the constitution apply to a particular case. . . . If, then, the courts are to regard the constitution, and the constitution is superior to any ordinary act of the legislature, the constitution, and not such ordinary act, must govern the case to which they both apply. . . .

The judicial power of the United States is extended to all cases arising under the constitution.

CHAPTER 8

The Living Constitution

★ CHAPTER FOCUS

1. How have the elastic clause and the amending process allowed the Constitution to adapt to changing times?
2. What is the importance of the Bill of Rights?
3. Why is the idea of a living Constitution important to a modern nation?

As the saying goes, change is the one constant in life. What was new and strange one day seems to be a normal part of our lives the next. This is an exaggeration, but think of how the instruments of communication have changed in recent years. To keep up with change, we must be adaptable—willing to adjust our thinking and actions to fit new circumstances. So, too, must government be able to cope with new ideas and new needs.

Fortunately, our basic framework of government—the Constitution—is flexible. The Framers had the foresight to include wording in it that provides for changing circumstances.

The Elastic Clause

One example of the flexible nature of the Constitution can be found in Article I, Section 8. The last clause in the list of powers granted to Congress says that this body has the power "to make all laws which shall be necessary and proper for carrying into execution the foregoing powers,

and all other powers vested by this Constitution in the Government of the United States, or in any department or officer thereof." This clause is called the "necessary and proper" clause or the **elastic clause**. It allows Congress to pass laws it considers necessary to govern the country properly.

An example would be the way the government collects taxes. Constitutionally, Congress has the power to levy taxes. How it collects taxes is spelled out in specific laws. The elastic clause permits Congress to enforce its tax-levying powers and set up the Internal Revenue Service to collect taxes.

The elastic clause does not give Congress unlimited power to pass any laws it wants. What the lawmakers do must fit within the guidelines of the Constitution. The clause, however, does give Congress broad powers.

Strict and Loose Interpretations

At times, controversy has surrounded the elastic clause. It allows Congress to take on what are called **implied powers**. (This refers to powers not specifically named in the Constitution.) Some believe that the clause gives too much power to Congress. This group feels that the words of the Constitution are to be followed exactly, without adding new ideas. If something is not specified in the Constitution, the government should not be allowed to do it. The people who think this way favor a **strict interpretation** of the words of the Constitution.

Others disagree. They believe that the words of the Constitution can and should be stretched to accommodate new situations and new needs. They think of the Constitution as a document that can be interpreted broadly. Their philosophy is termed **loose interpretation**.

Let's Think

1. What is the elastic clause? Explain its importance.
2. Explain the terms "loose interpretation of the Constitution" and "strict interpretation of the Constitution."
3. Why is flexibility in the Constitution considered important by some Americans?

The Amending Process

The Framers of the Constitution realized that the document might need to be changed in the future. Thus, they laid out in Article V the formal process for amending the Constitution. "The Congress, whenever two-thirds of both houses shall deem [think] it necessary, shall propose amendments to this Constitution, or, on the application of the legislatures of two-thirds of the several states, shall call a convention for proposing amendments, which, in either case, shall be valid, to all intents and purposes, as part of this Constitution when ratified by the legislatures of three-fourths of the several states, or by conventions in three-fourths thereof. . . ."

An amendment is an addition to a document that changes some fundamental part of it. Although there have been thousands of proposals for amending the Constitution, it has been changed only 27 times.

Proposing an Amendment

A proposal for an amendment to the Constitution can take two different forms. But only one has been used. Amendments have always been

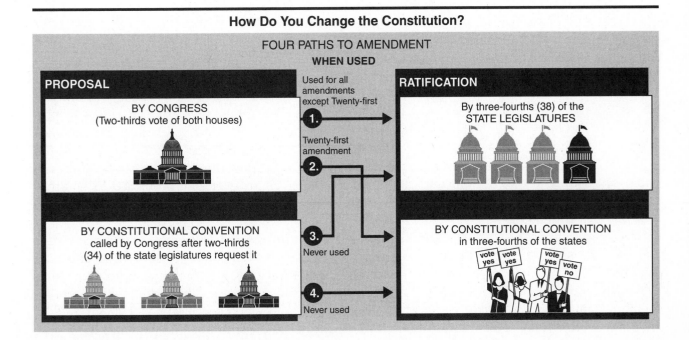

How Do You Change the Constitution?

FOUR PATHS TO AMENDMENT

WHEN USED

PROPOSAL

BY CONGRESS
(Two-thirds vote of both houses)

BY CONSTITUTIONAL CONVENTION
called by Congress after two-thirds
(34) of the state legislatures request it

Used for all amendments except Twenty-first
1.

Twenty-first amendment
2.

3.
Never used

4.
Never used

RATIFICATION

By three-fourths (38) of the
STATE LEGISLATURES

BY CONSTITUTIONAL CONVENTION
in three-fourths of the states
vote yes vote yes vote yes vote no

created and passed by Congress. Both houses must approve a proposed amendment by a two-thirds majority vote.

Another possible way to propose an amendment is to call a national convention. Congress can do this if the legislatures in two-thirds of the states request it. This method has never been used. Since 1789, there have been more than 300 attempts to call a constitutional convention, but none has been successful.

The Ratification Process

The next step a proposed amendment has to go through is approval by the states. This is called the **ratification**, or approval, **process**. Three-fourths of all the state legislatures must vote in favor of an amendment in order for it to become part of the Constitution.

Another way for an amendment to be ratified is to be voted on by state conventions. In this case, special ratification conventions are called in the states to vote on the proposed amendment. Three-fourths of the state conventions must approve the amendment before it can become part of the Constitution. The state convention method was used only once in our history.

The method to be used to ratify a particular amendment is outlined by Congress. Congress can decide to have the ratification process proceed through the state legislatures or through the special state convention method. A time limit for ratification is also established. If three-fourths of the states fail to ratify by the deadline, the amendment is defeated. Including a time limit for ratification makes sense when we consider what happened with the 27th Amendment. It concerns salary increases for members of Congress. First proposed in 1789, it was finally ratified by the 38th state in 1992, more than 200 years later. No time limit had been included in the wording of the amendment.

It may seem that the amendment-ratification process is unnecessarily complex and difficult. That may be so. But it is important to remember that a government represents stability. A government that could change quickly and easily might create a degree of uncertainty among its citizens. A slower process of change allows the people to

reflect on the proposed changes and consider their impact. It may prevent hasty and unwise alterations.

Even with the restraints on the amendment process, the public rethought one amendment that had been popular when it was added to the Constitution. The 18th Amendment banned the manufacture and sale of alcoholic beverages in the United States. It was proposed in 1917 and ratified in 1919. Fourteen years later, the 21st Amendment was passed and ratified within ten months. It repealed, or made void, the 18th Amendment. The ban on alcohol had been difficult to enforce. The public decided that it wanted to be able to buy such beverages.

Let's Think

1. What is an amendment?
2. What are the two ways that amendments to the Constitution may be proposed?
3. What is meant by the term "ratify"?
4. Explain the two methods that can be used to ratify an amendment.

The Bill of Rights

The first ten amendments to the Constitution were added at the same time in 1791. These ten amendments are popularly known as the **Bill of Rights**. At the time the Constitution was ratified, many called for adding a bill of rights to preserve and protect citizens' rights. The amendments did not grant new rights. They limited the power of the government to take away the "inalienable" rights everyone is entitled to. In other words, the Bill of Rights protects the rights we already possess.

Most of the Bill of Rights amendments deal with personal freedoms. Many of them reflect the English Bill of Rights and the writings of John Locke. Originally, the Bill of Rights was intended to apply only to the federal government. In fact, some state constitutions already had their own bills of rights. It was not until the passage of the

14th Amendment in 1868 that the Bill of Rights was uniformly applied to the state governments.

First Amendment

"Congress shall make no law respecting an establishment of religion, or prohibiting the free exercise thereof, or abridging the freedom of speech, or of the press; or the right of the people peaceably to assemble, and to petition the government for a redress of grievances."

This amendment is one of the most important. It prevents the government from limiting rights that are basic to the successful functioning of a democracy.

Freedom of Religion

The First Amendment protects the policy of separation of church and state. The government is not permitted to specify any one religion as the official religion of the country or to use tax revenues to support a religious group. At the time of the American Revolution, most European nations had established national religions. In some, it was Roman Catholicism, and in others, it was a form of Protestantism. People were not permitted to hold government offices if they were not members of the established, or national, religion. Those people who were not members of the established church were discriminated against. Recognizing this injustice, the First Amendment specifically emphasized the idea that the government and all religions should remain apart.

The concept of separation of church and state has been involved with the issue of school prayer. Supreme Court decisions have ruled that it is improper for students to engage in official prayers in public schools. Because public schools are financed with government money, the Court ruled that requiring prayers in public schools would be a violation of the First Amendment. The issue is still being debated.

Residents of the United States are free to worship in whatever way they wish. The only restrictions are that the practices be legal and do not harm anyone.

Freedom of Speech and Press

A pillar of democracy is the right to express even unpopular opinions openly in speaking or writing. This amendment gives everyone the right to criticize government officials and policies without fear of being punished. We cannot, however, deliberately lie or call for actions that would create a "clear and present danger" to public safety.

The Right to Assemble

The right to assemble, to get together to discuss issues, is an important way for people to exchange ideas and learn about one another. If this right were denied, people would not be allowed to attend conventions or public meetings. This right is primarily extended to groups that come together to influence public policy or to demonstrate for or against an issue.

The Right to Petition

This right allows you to write to government officials to criticize their actions or to ask them to do something. Petitions let officials know how individuals, groups, and the public in general feel about the way the government is acting.

An Application of the First Amendment—The Tinker Case (1969)

The Supreme Court handed down its decision in the case of *Tinker* v. *Des Moines (Iowa) Independent School District* in 1969. The case involved a group of students of both junior- and senior-high-school age and their right of free speech.

The case began with an incident in 1965, during the Vietnam War. At this time, the country was bitterly divided over the issue of fighting in the Southeast Asian nation of South Vietnam. American troops had been sent to this nation, and fighting had taken many lives. People in the United States participated in mass demonstrations in cities and on college campuses to protest the war. Those opposed to the demonstrations believed that protesting the war showed a lack of support for the American soldiers who, as good citizens, answered their country's call to fight. It also showed a lack of support for the American government.

Two students, John Tinker, 15, and Christo-

pher Eckhardt, 16, attended high school. Mary Beth Tinker, 13, attended junior high. She was John's sister. The schools were in Des Moines, Iowa. All three teenagers had participated with their parents in protests against the Vietnam War in various locations. The three young people decided that they wanted to voice their objections to the war by wearing black armbands to school. The principals of the Des Moines schools found out about the plan. To stop the protest, they announced a new rule banning the wearing of armbands in schools. If students wore armbands to school, they would be suspended until they promised to return to school without them. John, Mary Beth, and Christopher knew about the regulation and realized what the consequences of their action would be. They wore armbands to school on December 16 and were suspended on December 17. They did not return to school until after New Year's Day.

It should be noted that when the three young people wore the armbands, very few students joined in the activity. There was no disruption of classes.

The Tinkers and Eckhardt, working with their parents, decided to sue the school board. They filed their suit in the U.S. District Court because they believed that the regulation violated the students' First Amendment right to express themselves. Wearing armbands and badges is a form of expression and is considered to be a form of speech.

The district court found in favor of the school authorities. "It upheld the constitutionality of the school authorities' action on the ground that it was reasonable in order to prevent disturbance of school discipline."

Although the Tinkers lost in the district court, they decided to continue the fight. In the Eighth Circuit Court of Appeals, the panel of judges was divided. This had the effect of upholding the decision of the lower court.

The case finally reached the Supreme Court. The central issue focused on the degree of disruption of education in the schools. The Des Moines school officials had anticipated disruption and decided to issue the new regulation to prevent it. As it turned out, the actions of the students in this particular incident did not disrupt the educational process. The justices of the Supreme Court, in a 7–2 majority opinion, argued that the wearing of armbands by the students was symbolic speech, close to what they called "pure speech." As a result, they stated, "First

Mary Beth and John Tinker displaying the armbands they wore in school in 1965 to protest the Vietnam War. The symbol on the band stands for peace.

Amendment rights applied in light of the special characteristics of the school environment are available to teachers and students. It can hardly be argued that either students or teachers shed their constitutional rights to freedom of speech or expression at the schoolhouse gate."

This decision protected the rights of students to express themselves freely in schools. But the right to freedom of expression depended on the atmosphere in the school and the way the students' actions affected normal classroom instruction and other activities in the school building. If the actions of the students had caused a widespread walkout, the students might not have won their case. Students must act as responsible citizens within the school community. When this happens, the law protects their First Amendment right to freedom of expression.

Later, a similar case cited the Tinker case to support a school district's decision to ban buttons that might lead to disruption of a school's educational process. The case of *Guzick* v. *Drebus*, decided in 1970 by a lower federal court, banned buttons and literature of protest in schools. In this situation, there was a history of violent reaction when students wore controversial buttons or armbands to school. The court decided that the First Amendment right to freedom of expression had to be limited. The protests posed a danger to students and created a strong possibility for the disruption of education in the school.

Let's Think

1. Make a list of the freedoms that are protected by the First Amendment. Why is each freedom so important to a democratic society?
2. What were the facts in the Tinker case?
3. What did the Supreme Court mean by the idea that students and teachers do not "shed their constitutional rights . . . at the schoolhouse gate"?
4. Based on the Tinker decision, when might the rights of a student be limited?

The Second and Third Amendments

These two amendments had their roots in the experiences of Americans when they lived under British rule, before their independence. Both related to what might be seen as military matters in areas of self-protection.

The Second Amendment states: "A well-regulated militia being necessary to the security of a free state, the right of the people to keep and bear arms shall not be infringed."

It was designed to protect people from the abuses such as the ones that had been inflicted on the colonies by the British government before the American Revolution. By the mid-1700s, the British government feared colonial unrest. Attempts were made to keep weapons away from the colonists.

The Second Amendment permits states to maintain a *militia* (armed force) made up of ordinary citizens and allows them to own weapons. The regulation of the right to bear arms is not an absolute right for everyone to carry any gun. States and the federal government do have the right to regulate firearms, and have done so. Whether this amendment allows or forbids gun-control laws is widely debated.

In June 2008, the Supreme Court ruled that individuals have the right to own handguns for self-defense (*District of Columbia* v. *Heller*). Many communities around the nation have laws banning individual ownership of guns. Gun proponents are now likely to challenge those laws. The Supreme Court did indicate that gun ownership is not an unlimited right.

The Third Amendment tried to protect Americans from the expense of paying for the military out of their own pockets. It states, "No soldier shall, in time of peace, be *quartered* in any house, without the consent of the owner; nor, in time of war, but in a manner to be prescribed by law."

In 1765 and again in 1774, the British government had passed laws requiring American colonists to house British soldiers at their own expense. Since the soldiers were there to protect the colonists, providing housing was one way the colonists could be made to pay for protection. But colonists resented this action. The resentment was so deep and long-lasting that the people insisted on including an amendment to outlaw such actions in time of peace. Only during wartime could the government require citizens to house soldiers and then only if Congress passed a law to allow it.

Let's Think

1. What abuses by government did the Second and Third amendments attempt to prevent?
2. Why did the Framers of the Constitution decide to add these amendments?
3. Which amendment (the Second or Third) do you think is more important? Write a statement defending your choice.

The Fourth Amendment

Like the First Amendment, the Fourth concerns the rights of the individual. Of particular interest was the *right to privacy*. To protect this right, the Fourth Amendment set up strict guidelines that the government must follow before conducting searches in the houses and private property of individual citizens.

The wording of the amendment is as follows: "The right of the people to be secure in their persons, houses, papers, and effects, against unreasonable searches and seizures, shall not be violated; and no warrants shall issue, but upon probable cause, supported by oath or affirmation, and particularly describing the place to be searched and the persons or things to be seized."

The Fourth Amendment ensures the right to privacy. When law enforcement officials believe there is a need to conduct a search of a home or an automobile, special permission must be given by a judge. After a judge determines that the reasons for a search are appropriate, a **search warrant** is issued. When police officers request a search warrant, they must explain under oath what they are looking for and why they believe a search is needed. The warrant grants police the authority to search a particular place for a specific reason.

An Application of the Fourth Amendment— *Mapp* v. *Ohio* (1961)

The Bill of Rights originally applied only to the federal government. Through time and the addition of the 14th Amendment, the Bill of Rights has been made applicable to state governments as well. One of the legal cases that strengthened this extension was *Mapp* v. *Ohio*, decided by the Supreme Court in 1961.

The facts of the case are as follows. In Cleveland, Ohio, police asked to be admitted to a home to look for a person wanted for illegal gambling. The police had been provided with information that led them to believe that they would also find gambling materials hidden in the house. Dollree Mapp, who lived at the residence, was presented with a piece of paper that was said to be a search warrant. The police grabbed the paper back from her. (The warrant was never produced in court when the case went to trial.) The police then forced their way into her house. After a thorough search, the only things the police found were some obscene books. (Ohio law prohibited the possession of obscene materials.) Mapp was arrested. A trial was held, and Mapp was convicted and sentenced to a prison term. Lawyers for Mapp appealed the conviction and were met with setbacks in the state courts.

Ultimately, the case reached the Supreme Court. In 1961, the Court voted 6–3 in favor of overturning the conviction of Mapp. It ruled that evidence gathered without a proper search warrant was illegal and could not be used against Mapp.

The case was significant because it applied the Fourth Amendment to the states. It also explained that illegal searches and seizures could not be conducted by state officials because they violated the Constitution.

Since this ruling, the Supreme Court has made other decisions that have modified the legacy of the Mapp case to some degree. These decisions permit searches of automobiles and the seizure of material that is in the view of a police officer who does not have a warrant. But the essential idea that a warrant is needed before a search can be conducted is still in force.

Let's Think

1. What are the important elements of the Fourth Amendment?
2. Why do you think people believe the right to privacy is so important in a democratic society?
3. What are the important facts in the Mapp case?
4. Do you think the decision of the Supreme Court was just? Why or why not?

Amendments Five and Six

The next set of amendments address issues centered on the legal process. Each focuses on an issue that deserves close examination.

The Fifth Amendment

"No person shall be held to answer for a capital, or otherwise infamous, crime, unless on a presentment or indictment of a grand jury, except in cases arising in the land or naval forces, or in the militia, when in actual service, in time of war, or public danger; nor shall any person be subject, for the same offense, to be twice put in jeopardy of life or limb; nor shall be compelled, in any criminal case, to be a witness against himself; nor be deprived of life, liberty, or property, without due process of law; nor shall private property be taken for public use, without just compensation."

People accused of crimes are protected by the Constitution. The Fifth Amendment, in particular, prohibits certain abuses that might occur if the government were not given guidelines in this area.

Grand Jury

People charged with having committed a major crime must be brought before a **grand jury**. It is a special jury of citizens who decide if there is enough evidence to hold the accused for trial. If the grand jury decides that the person should be held for trial, it issues a written document containing the charges. This document is called an **indictment**.

In undemocratic societies, people may be arrested without being informed of the charges against them. They may be jailed without going through a trial. The process of grand jury hearings was created to prevent these practices.

Double Jeopardy

A person who is acquitted, found not guilty of a crime, at a trial cannot be tried again for the same crime. To do so would be subjecting the person to **double jeopardy**, which is prohibited by the Fifth Amendment. However, a person might violate both a state and a federal law when committing a crime. If the person is acquitted at the state level, he or she can still be tried at the federal level for the same crime (or vice versa). This would not be a violation of the double jeopardy prohibition.

POWER *of* ★NE

Elizabeth Cady Stanton

Elizabeth Cady Stanton was born on November 12, 1815, in Johnstown, New York. While a young child, she enjoyed visiting her father's law office. There she learned about the problems married women of her time faced regarding property and child custody rights. All her life she refused to accept the idea that women were mentally and legally inferior to men. When she was 11, her father told her that he wished she were a boy. Elizabeth resolved to prove to him that a daughter was as good and as valuable as a son. She tried to do everything boys of her time did—ride horseback, play chess, and study Greek and Latin. She wanted to attend a men's college but was sent instead to Emma Willard's Troy Female Seminary. She graduated in 1832.

Elizabeth Cady developed a deep interest in the antislavery and temperance (antidrinking) movements through her cousin Gerrit Smith. At his home, she saw how slaves who had escaped their masters were hidden for protection and then sent on to freedom in Canada. She attended antislavery meetings and eventually met Henry Brewster Stanton, who made emotional speeches against slavery. Elizabeth and Henry married in 1840. So conscious was she of her status as a 19th-century woman who should have the same rights as men, she refused to allow the word "obey" to be part of the marriage ceremony.

While attending an antislavery conference in England with her husband in 1840, Elizabeth got involved in fighting for women's rights. She protested the ruling that kept women delegates from participating. While in England, she met Lucretia Mott. The two formed a friendship and decided to hold a women's rights convention in the United States.

In 1842, the Stantons settled in Boston, where Henry began a law practice. Elizabeth's interest in the antislavery movement continued. She met such people as Frederick Douglass, the former slave and now active abolitionist. The Stantons moved from Boston to Seneca Falls, New York, in 1847 because of Henry's health.

Protection Against Self-Incrimination

Sometimes a person accused of a crime does not take the stand to testify at his or her own trial. If a person takes the stand, he or she will not only be questioned by his or her own lawyer but will also be questioned by the government's attorney. In answering questions, the person may say something that might incriminate him or her. The Fifth Amendment protects against such situations. The defendant may voluntarily take the stand to testify in his or her own behalf but cannot be forced to do so.

Similarly, police cannot force a person to confess to a crime. In early England and even in some countries today, a person might be tortured into confessing to a misdeed. If a person is in se- rious pain, he or she might say anything to relieve it, even if he or she did not commit the crime. The Fifth Amendment protects us from practices of this sort.

Due Process Under the Law

The "due process" clause is very important because it clearly tells the government how to behave. It states, "No person shall . . . be deprived of life, liberty, or property, without due process of law; . . ." This means that the government cannot take a person's life, freedom, or property without following proper legal proceedings. If someone is arrested, the rules of due process say that the person must be indicted, tried, and if found guilty, sentenced.

During this time, Elizabeth continued to talk about the rights of women. She spoke with legislators and distributed petitions that called for better property rights for women. In 1848, she heard that Lucretia Mott was visiting nearby. At last they were ready to plan a women's rights convention. As part of the agenda for the Seneca Falls Convention, a Declaration of Sentiments was written. It declared that women and men were equal and listed 18 legal limitations placed on women's rights. The well-attended conference began on July 19, 1848. Elizabeth introduced a resolution calling for granting the right to vote to women. Her husband and Mott had tried to stop her. But the resolution was defended by such notables as Frederick Douglass and was passed by the convention. Many, though, ridiculed the idea.

In 1851, Elizabeth began a 50-year friendship with Susan B. Anthony. Together they would make history as they fought to win for women the right to vote.

Stanton wrote newspaper articles and spoke to many reform-minded groups on the need to improve women's rights. She was one of the first women to address the New York State legislature. She fought for more liberal divorce laws for women. During the Civil War, she spoke out against slavery and called for the emancipation of all slaves. After the war, her attention turned again to the rights of women. When the 15th Amendment, granting former male slaves the right to vote, was proposed, Elizabeth fought to include women in it. The effort failed. She made a bid to run for Congress in 1866 but lost by a wide margin. To win support for women's rights, Elizabeth traveled around the country giving lectures. She also wrote articles and books about her causes.

In 1869, Susan B. Anthony and Elizabeth Stanton founded the National Woman Suffrage Association. Elizabeth served as its president for 20 years. In 1878, she persuaded a U.S. senator from California to introduce a federal woman suffrage amendment in Congress. It was brought up in every Congress afterward until it passed in 1919.

Elizabeth Cady Stanton died in 1902. Her "greatest contribution," her supporters said, "was her effort to emancipate women's minds" and free "women from the psychological barriers which hedged them in."

1. In what ways were women treated differently from men in 19th-century America?
2. What did Elizabeth Cady Stanton and Susan B. Anthony fight for?
3. What was the importance of the Seneca Falls Convention?
4. Do you think Stanton would be happy with the rights women have today? Why or why not?

If the government finds it necessary to take your home from you to widen a street, it must follow a special procedure and pay you a fair price for the property. The government's right to take private property for a public purpose is called **eminent domain**.

Think of **due process** as the rules of a game. Due process is the fair rules of procedure that must be followed by the government.

An Application of the Fifth Amendment— *Miranda v. Arizona* (1966)

During the 1960s, a series of Supreme Court decisions involving the rights of the accused were made. One was the Miranda case.

One day in March of 1963, Ernesto Miranda was arrested and accused of kidnapping and forcibly raping an 18-year-old woman near Phoenix, Arizona. The crime had occurred ten days before the arrest. Miranda was taken by the police into a room for questioning. At that time, the police did not inform him of his rights. In addition, the accused did not ask for an attorney. After two hours, Miranda confessed. The statement specifically noted that he had made the confession voluntarily. He was tried, found guilty, and sentenced to 25 to 30 years in prison.

The Miranda conviction was appealed on the grounds that the defendant's constitutional rights had been violated. The appeal reached the Supreme Court. In a 5–4 vote, it struck down Miranda's conviction. The Court found that

"We had to let the animals go. No one informed them of their rights when they were arrested."

although Miranda had not asked for an attorney at the time of his interrogation, the police should have told him that he had a right to have one present. One person facing several police officers in a small interrogation room can be intimidated into saying things he or she would not normally say, said the Court. Miranda might not have confessed if he had been able to speak to an attorney. The Court listed the specific rights that the police must tell suspects about when they are arrested. These rights are: to remain silent, to know that any statements they make could be used against them in court, to have an attorney present during questioning, and to have an attorney provided by the court if they cannot afford one.

Many criticized the Supreme Court's decision. A number of law enforcement officials at the time believed that the Supreme Court was "handcuffing" the police in their ability to solve crimes. Others hailed the case as a decision that would safeguard the rights of the accused.

In recent years, the courts have modified their strict application of Miranda rights in some instances. Incriminating statements have been allowed to be brought up in trials. Statements leading the police to important evidence do incriminate the suspect in spite of any warnings given or not given. Another example of overrid-

ing Miranda rights is when a danger to the public exists. For instance, if a suspect tells the police where a weapon that might endanger the public is hidden, the suspect may be held accountable for the danger. This might be true even if Miranda rights have been given.

The Sixth Amendment

The Sixth Amendment states: "In all criminal prosecutions, the accused shall enjoy the right to a speedy and public trial, by an impartial jury of the State and district wherein the crime shall have been committed, which district shall have been previously ascertained by law; and to be informed of the nature and cause of the accusation; to be confronted with the witnesses against him; to have compulsory process for obtaining witnesses in his favor; and to have the assistance of counsel for his defense."

The Right to a Speedy Trial

A person accused of a crime has the right to be tried within a reasonable amount of time. A person waiting for a criminal trial lives under a cloud even though that person is technically innocent until proved guilty. Sometimes the defendant is held in jail until the trial can begin. Also, witnesses may not be available or may have memory lapses if the wait is too long. Therefore, a speedy trial is in everyone's best interest.

Jury Trial

A second right guaranteed by this amendment is a trial by a "fair-minded" jury. The people called to serve on the jury and the location of the trial must be within the general location of where the crime was committed. As a result, if someone commits a crime in Dallas, Texas, the person would be tried in a Texas state court in the city of Dallas. Sometimes extreme circumstances indicate that a fair trial can be achieved only if the location is changed. Thus, a trial in a state court could be moved from one part of the state to another. This is called a **change of venue**.

Subpoena

Another guaranteed protection is the right to know the specific charges against you. It would be very difficult for the accused and his or her attorney to prepare for the defense at a trial if they did not know why the accused was being tried. It is at the trial that the defendant has the opportunity to face his or her accuser. In criminal cases, the accuser is the "people," the government in the form of the district attorney or, in federal trials, the assistant U.S. attorney. The defendant also has a right to be present when the case against him or her is presented. In addition, the Sixth Amendment grants the defendant the power to summon people to testify on his or her behalf. The summons to testify is called a **subpoena**.

Right to Counsel

It is difficult to decide which of the rights guaranteed by the Sixth Amendment is most important. Certainly, the right to counsel would be high on anyone's list. An attorney helps to protect the rights of the accused at a trial. As a society, we consider the right to an attorney to be important. Even if a defendant cannot afford the fees, an attorney will be appointed to represent the defendant. Organizations such as the Legal Aid Society and the Public Defender's Office specialize in representing those who are poor.

An Application of the Sixth Amendment—
Gideon v. Wainwright (1963)

On June 3, 1961, a man by the name of Clarence Earl Gideon was living in a hotel in Bay Harbor, Florida. He was a drifter and had spent time in prison for a variety of crimes. On that night, a local pool hall was burglarized and $65.00 was taken. An eyewitness told police that he had seen Gideon in the pool hall in the early hours of the morning. The police arrested Gideon, and he was tried two months later in a Florida court.

At the time of the trial, the judge asked Gideon if he was ready for the proceedings. Gideon pleaded not guilty and then indicated that he was not ready for trial because he did not have an attorney to represent him. He asked the judge to appoint one for him. The judge refused on the grounds that Florida law did not allow him to appoint an attorney in this type of case. The judge explained that he was empowered to appoint attorneys only in cases involving capital, or major, offenses.

Gideon acted in his own defense at the trial and was convicted of the offense and sent to prison. While in prison, he researched his rights. He wrote to the Supreme Court, requesting that it hear his appeal. He explained that he had not been given an attorney, which violated his Sixth Amendment rights.

The Supreme Court decided to grant Gideon his appeal. An attorney was appointed to argue Gideon's case before the Court. In a unanimous decision, the Court agreed with Gideon that his Sixth Amendment rights had been violated. The decision stated: "That government hires lawyers to prosecute and defendants who have the money hire lawyers to defend are the strongest indications of the widespread belief that lawyers in criminal courts are necessities, not luxuries." As a result of this decision, states are obligated to provide an attorney for individuals who cannot afford one.

In 1963, another trial was held on the Gideon robbery case. This time, Gideon was represented by a lawyer and was acquitted of the charges.

Let's Think

1. What are the major rights protected by the Fifth and Sixth amendments?
2. Explain why each of these rights is important.
3. *Miranda* v. *Arizona* and *Gideon* v. *Wainwright* were two very important Supreme Court decisions. Explain why each was important.

The Seventh and Eighth Amendments

The Seventh Amendment

This amendment states: " In suits at common law, where the value in controversy shall exceed twenty dollars, the right of trial by jury shall be preserved; and no fact, tried by a jury, shall be otherwise re-examined in any court of the United States than according to the rules of the common law."

The amendment guarantees a jury trial in civil suits in federal courts. Although it makes this guarantee for suits involving at least $20.00, the sum of money in civil suits today is usually much more.

The Eighth Amendment

According to the Eighth Amendment, "Excessive bail shall not be required, nor excessive fines imposed, nor cruel and unusual punishment inflicted."

Bail

When a person is formally charged with committing a crime, a judge sets **bail**. Bail is a sum of money or property of some value that is put on deposit. In exchange for bail, the accused is permitted to remain free while waiting for the trial. Bail serves as a guarantee that a person will appear in court when required. If the accused fails to appear, the bail is forfeited, and a warrant for that person's arrest will be issued. This amendment assures that the bail will not be too high for the type of crime committed.

Cruel and Unusual Punishment

The issue of what constitutes "cruel and unusual punishment" is regularly debated. In earlier times, people lost limbs, were whipped, branded, and in other ways tortured. The "cruel and unusual punishment" clause is there to protect us from such actions by the government. The application of this clause to the death penalty has created much controversy because of some meth-ods that have been used to execute convicted individuals.

Applications of the Eighth Amendment— The *Furman* and *Gregg* Cases

In 1972, the Supreme Court, in a 5–4 decision, voided death penalty laws. This was the *Furman* v. *Georgia* case. According to this decision, the death penalty was being handed out in an unequal way. Judges and juries tended to apply the death penalty mainly to poor or African-American individuals. The decision in the *Furman* case had a major impact on states that had the death penalty at that time. It had the effect of commuting almost 600 death-row sentences throughout the nation. The decision did not ban capital punishment, but it did modify how it could be applied.

In 1976, the Supreme Court turned itself around to some degree in its ruling in the case of *Gregg* v. *Georgia*. In the Gregg case, it upheld a new Georgia law requiring a death penalty for certain crimes. The law gave the jury two tasks. The first task was to decide the innocence or guilt of the defendant. The second task, at a second hearing, was to decide the sentence. The jury would be allowed to consider special circumstances that might keep it from imposing the

Authorities torturing a person on the rack to punish him for a crime or for speaking out against authorities. The Eighth Amendment forbids such "cruel and unusual punishment."

death penalty. The two-stage trial called for by this law was acceptable to the Supreme Court.

The Ninth and Tenth Amendments

The Framers of the Constitution obviously could not anticipate all issues that might arise in the future. So it seemed a good idea to add the Ninth and Tenth amendments, which make general statements about rights and powers held by the national and state governments and the people.

The Ninth Amendment

"The enumeration in the Constitution of certain rights shall not be construed to deny or disparage others retained by the people." This statement is meant to protect all the rights that we have. Even if certain rights are not listed in the Constitution, the people still have them. Two such rights are the right to privacy and the right to travel or live anywhere in the United States.

The Tenth Amendment

The Tenth Amendment is similar in purpose. It states: "The powers not delegated to the United States by the Constitution, nor prohibited by it to the states, are reserved to the states respectively, or to the people." Thus, the rights of the states are protected. Only those powers specifically given to the United States government by the Constitution are the ones the federal government is allowed to exercise. The major source of power in our nation is the states or the people. Therefore, the federal government can have only the powers that the people or the states want to give it. All other powers remain in the hands of the states and the people.

Let's Think

1. What rights are protected by the Seventh and Eighth amendments?
2. What is meant by the expression "cruel and unusual punishment"?
3. How might the issue of the death penalty be affected by the Eighth Amendment?
4. Why are the Ninth and Tenth amendments important?

The Constitution Changes Along With Society

After the Civil War ended in 1865, many issues had to be resolved. How would the victorious Northern (Union) states treat the defeated Confederate states of the South? What was the best way to give the formerly enslaved black people their rights as free citizens? The federal government decided that the best way to handle the new situation was to amend the Constitution. The 13th, 14th, and 15th amendments, passed between 1865 and 1870, have had a far-reaching influence on our country.

The 13th Amendment

"Neither slavery nor involuntary servitude, except as punishment for crime, whereof the party shall have been duly convicted, shall exist within the United States, or any place subject to their jurisdiction."

The 13th Amendment, adopted in 1865, abolished slavery everywhere within the United States and its territories. Involuntary servitude (being forced to work or serve without pay) was also considered illegal. The only time a person may involuntarily lose his or her liberty would be if the person was convicted and punished for committing a crime.

An Application of the 13th Amendment— *Jones v. Mayer* (1968)

Joseph Lee Jones and Barbara Jo Jones were a mixed-race couple. Joseph was an African American, and Barbara was white. They decided that they wanted to buy a house in a development in suburban St. Louis, Missouri. When they spoke to the real estate firm about buying a lot in the development, the firm refused to sell it to them. They could not buy the property because Joseph was black.

The Joneses were determined to fight back. They hired an attorney, who promptly filed a suit against the developer, Alfred H. Mayer Company, and the real estate agent, the Alfred Realty Company. The Joneses argued that the developer and realtor had no right to deny them the purchase on the basis of race. Their attorney cited a section of a civil rights law passed in 1866 by Congress. It stated: "All citizens of the United States shall have the same rights in every State and Territory, as is enjoyed by white citizens thereof to inherit, purchase, lease, sell, hold, and convey real and personal property." In 1965, when the incident occurred, this law was still in effect. The developer and real estate agency claimed that the 1866 law was unconstitutional. Congress, they said, did not have the power to control discrimination practiced by private individuals and companies.

The case was heard first in a federal district court and then in the Court of Appeals. In each instance, the courts ruled against the Joneses. Not giving up, they appealed the case to the Supreme Court. Here, in a 7–2 decision, they were victorious. The Court found that Congress did have the power "under the Thirteenth Amendment . . . to determine what are the badges and the incidents of slavery, and the authority to translate that determination into legislation. Such badges of slavery include restraints on the right to inherit, purchase, lease, sell, . . . property." In other words, the 1866 law applies to private individuals as well as to public authorities.

The 14th Amendment

"All persons born or naturalized in the United States, and subject to the jurisdiction thereof, are citizens of the United States and of the State wherein they reside. No State shall make or enforce any law which shall abridge the privileges or immunities of citizens of the United States; nor shall any State deprive any person of life, liberty, or property, without due process of law, nor deny to any person within its jurisdiction the equal protection of the laws. . . ."

The 14th Amendment, which was passed in 1868, has become very important in the areas of civil rights, states' rights, and the application of the Constitution and the Bill of Rights to state governments. It is important to note, though, that Native Americans were not given citizenship by this amendment.

Citizenship and Due Process

The opening words of this amendment define citizenship. The purpose was to make clear the legal status of the freed slaves. It also recognized that naturalized citizens have the same rights as those who are citizens by birth.

The first section of this amendment also relates to issues involving states. In the past, states argued that portions of the Bill of Rights did not apply to them. These portions applied only to the federal government. In examining the first section of the 14th Amendment, we see a direct attempt to resolve this issue. It specifically says that the states cannot limit citizens' rights without "due process" and that states must apply the "equal protection of the laws" to everyone.

The due process clause in the 14th Amendment is similar to the due process clause in the Fifth Amendment. Many believed that the due process clause in the Fifth Amendment applied only to the Congress and the federal government. The wording of the 14th Amendment makes it clear that the states cannot violate the Constitution when making judgments about the individual rights of their citizens.

Equal Protection of the Laws

The concept of "equal protection of the laws" is a necessary ingredient for a successful democratic society. All people must be treated equally in the eyes of the law. Governments cannot set up special categories of people and treat them in an unreasonable manner. The fight to make sure that people are treated equally is a constant battle. In the past, there was more open discrimination against women in the job market. Often women were hired for jobs that men also held, but the women received a lower wage than the men. Equal pay for equal work is an important right protected by the 14th Amendment.

Let's Think

1. What did the 13th Amendment accomplish?
2. How did the Jones case relate to the 13th Amendment?

3. Describe the major provisions of the 14th Amendment.

Voting Rights and the Constitution

The question of who has a right to vote is addressed in several amendments. Until 1870, only white males over 21 years of age could vote. Then the privilege was extended to African-American males over 21.

It took until 1920 for women to be given this basic right. Why it was denied to them for so long is difficult to understand now. Two additional amendments have further extended voting rights.

The 15th Amendment

"The right of citizens of the United States to vote shall not be denied or abridged by the United States or by any State on account of race, color, or previous condition of servitude."

The 15th Amendment, adopted in 1870, was added to the Constitution to make sure that male freed slaves would be able to exercise their right to vote. The amendment made it illegal to deny the right to vote to any male based on race.

Even though the wording did not specifically exclude women, few at the time would have assumed that the amendment applied to females. Women were not thought to be capable of exercising the right to vote in a rational way.

It took more than the amendment to protect the voting rights of African-American males. In the late 1800s, a number of states passed voting regulation laws that included what are called **grandfather clauses**. Their purpose was to deny African Americans the right to vote. Such laws stated that if a person's grandfather had voted in previous elections, the person could vote in current elections without having to pass a new test to show that he was qualified to vote. Obviously, if you had been a slave, you would be denied the right to vote because it is most likely that your grandfather had also been a slave and had been prevented from voting.

Such laws are no longer legal in the United States. Through a series of federal laws and Supreme Court decisions, discriminatory laws like these have been abolished.

The 19th Amendment

"The right of citizens of the United States to vote shall not be denied or abridged by the United States or by any State on account of sex."

One large group of U.S. citizens continued to be left out of the voting process. Voting rights applied only to males over the age of 21. Women could not legally vote in national and most state elections.

The struggle for women's **suffrage**, the right to vote, was a long, hard-fought battle. No argument women made convinced male legislators to allow them to vote in elections at any level until the late 1800s. Wyoming Territory passed a law in 1869 that gave all women the right to vote in territorial elections. In 1890, when Wyoming became a state, the law remained in effect. As the 19th century came to a close, several other states granted women the right to vote in state elections. But Congress failed to act.

One significant event that aided the cause of women was the involvement of the United States in World War I (1917–1918). During this time, many men were by law required to join the military. Who would replace them in jobs in offices, factories, and government agencies? Many of these jobs were filled by women. If they could fill jobs traditionally held by men, women argued, they could also vote in a responsible way. Public demonstrations put pressure on Congress. Finally, in early 1919, the 19th Amendment was passed by Congress. By the following year, the required number of states had ratified it, and it became part of the Constitution. The changing role of women in the United States was recognized in a formal way.

As the 20th century continued, the need to protect and expand the right to vote became evident. The 24th Amendment (1964) eliminated **poll taxes** and **literacy tests** for citizens. (In some

◀REALITY CHECK▶

Amending the Constitution—A Slow Process

In recent years, the government has had to deal with issues that would have boggled the minds of the Framers. In the mid-20th century, we sent men to the moon, and now we are building a new space station. The government has wrestled with the morality of funding stem-cell research. It has tried to enact laws so the country could become more energy independent. None of these issues were mentioned in the Constitution. What has given our government the ability to respond to modern issues is the built-in flexibility of the Constitution. One provision that allows the document to change is the amending process.

Over the years, there have been many attempts to amend the Constitution. It is a deliberately slow process. The Framers did not want to encourage hasty changes. History has shown that only long-term issues of great importance to the nation are added to the Constitution in the form of amendments. Two examples are the expansion of voting rights to most adult citizens and the orderly succession of power in case of a tragedy occurring to the sitting president. In more than 220 years, our Constitution has been amended only 27 times. This is a tribute to the Framers, who created a farsighted document that was meant to last. With advances in science and changes in society yet to come, we cannot begin to know what the future holds and what amendments may be needed to meet new challenges.

In each session of Congress, new amendments are proposed because someone is not satisfied with the current document and believes that the elastic clause cannot provide a solution. In recent years, none has been ratified. In the 108th Congress (2003–2005), there was a proposal to lower the minimum age for a member of Congress from 30 in the Senate and 25 in the House of Representatives to age 21 for both houses. Another idea involved the territories and commonwealths of the United States. It would have allowed citizens living in those locations to vote for president. At the present time, they do not have this right even though the people who live in these areas are U.S. citizens.

In the 109th Congress (2005–2007), one proposed amendment called for the government to balance the budget every year, with provisions to change that rule by a three-fourths vote in each house of Congress. Some believe that the government should not overspend and borrow money to pay its debts. This amendment would have forced the government to spend only an amount equal to the money it receives each year. Except for special circumstances, the government could not go into debt or borrow money. Another proposed amendment would grant a naturalized citizen who has lived in the United States for 20 years the right to run for president.

Some proposed amendments are introduced multiple times. In the various sessions of Congress in the 1990s, the number of proposed amendments ranged from a low of 60 to a high of 214.

1. Why do you think some of the proposed amendments never went through the ratification process?
2. Why do you think there have been only 27 amendments added to the original Constitution?
3. Give arguments for and against simplifying the ratification process so that amendments can be added to the Constitution more easily and quickly.
4. If you were to propose an amendment to the Constitution, what would it be and why would you want it as an amendment?

Freedmen lining up to vote in New Orleans, Louisiana, in 1867.

states, voters had to pay a fee, a poll tax, to vote.) These practices had been put in place to limit the voting rights of African-American citizens. A few years later, the 26th Amendment (1971) extended the right to vote to 18-year-old citizens.

Let's Think

1. What are the major provisions of each of the following amendments: 15th, 19th, 24th, and 26th?
2. How did each expand the idea of democracy?
3. How does each amendment demonstrate the flexibility of the Constitution to change with the times?

Chapter Summary

The Constitution is a flexible document that can change as American society changes. This is one reason why it has been able to survive for more than 200 years and still serve us today.

The elastic clause gives Congress the authority to pass laws it considers necessary to govern the country properly. The laws have to fit into the guidelines of the Constitution. But the clause does make it possible to meet changing circumstances.

People's views of how government should work determine what the wording of the Constitution means. Some people believe that the Constitution should be carried out exactly as written. These people believe in strict interpretation. Others believe that the Constitution should be stretched and interpreted broadly. This is known as loose interpretation.

Another way the Constitution has been changed to fit the times is through the amendment process. An amendment is an addition to the original Constitution. The Constitution has been amended 27 times. Generally, the amendment process is slow. Amendments can be proposed by Congress or by a constitutional convention. No such convention has been held since 1787. Congress must approve an amendment by a two-thirds vote. Then the proposal is submitted to the states. Three-fourths of the state legislatures must vote for the amendment before it can be added to the Constitution. The process by which amendments are approved is called the ratification process.

The first ten amendments added to the Constitution are known as the Bill of Rights. These amendments are designed to protect individual rights such as freedom of speech, religion, and press, and the right to a fair and speedy trial and due process. A number of Supreme Court decisions have reinforced these rights: *Tinker* v. *Des Moines*, *Mapp* v. *Ohio*, *Miranda* v. *Arizona*, *Gideon* v. *Wainwright*.

After the Civil War, several amendments that dealt with the rights of former African-American slaves were enacted. They ended slavery (the 13th), gave African-American males the right to vote (the 15th), and applied the Constitution and the Bill of Rights to the states (the 14th).

Gradually, the right to vote was expanded. This was accomplished through the 19th, 24th, and 26th amendments.

★ CHAPTER REVIEW ★

A. Matching
Match each term in Column A with its definition in Column B.

Column A
1. elastic clause
2. 13th Amendment
3. due process
4. suffrage
5. Bill of Rights
6. grandfather clauses
7. *Miranda* v. *Arizona*
8. freedom of speech
9. Fourth Amendment
10. 19th Amendment

Column B
a. this amendment extended the right to vote to women
b. right found in the Fifth and 14th amendments
c. the name given to the first ten amendments to the Constitution
d. this amendment protects the right to privacy
e. a decision that requires police to tell suspects of their rights at the time of arrest
f. allows Congress to pass laws necessary to govern the country properly
g. this amendment abolished slavery
h. a right protected by the First Amendment
i. policies used after the Civil War to deny former slaves the right to vote
j. the right to vote

B. Multiple Choice
Select the statement or word that most correctly answers the question or completes the statement.

1. Congress has the power to levy taxes. The part of the Constitution that allows Congress to pass laws that establish the procedure for collecting taxes is **(a)** the elastic clause **(b)** Article II **(c)** the First Amendment **(d)** the Eighth Amendment.
2. This amendment protects against excessive bail: **(a)** First **(b)** Second **(c)** Eighth **(d)** Tenth.
3. Due process **(a)** allows the government to take action to ensure the safety of the nation **(b)** limits the actions that government can take when depriving a person of life, liberty, or property **(c)** limits the ability of the government to declare war **(d)** provides for shelter for all people.
4. Powers that are not listed in the Constitution are given to the **(a)** Congress **(b)** president **(c)** Supreme Court **(d)** states or the people.
5. The case of *Mapp* v. *Ohio* centered on the following issue: **(a)** cruel and unusual punishment **(b)** illegal searches and seizures **(c)** the right to counsel **(d)** excessive bail.
6. In the case of *Gideon* v. *Wainwright*, the Supreme Court ruled that **(a)** those who cannot afford an attorney must have one appointed to defend them **(b)** in most cases an attorney is not needed during the trial **(c)** an attorney is guaranteed by the Tenth Amendment **(d)** a jury is not necessary in a trial.
7. The case of *Jones* v. *Mayer* stated that this amendment should be applied to this case: **(a)** Sixth **(b)** Ninth **(c)** 13th **(d)** 19th.
8. The Sixth Amendment protects each of these rights *except* **(a)** speedy trial **(b)** trial by jury **(c)** right to counsel **(d)** grand jury.
9. This amendment has been used to apply the Bill of Rights to the state governments: **(a)** 15th **(b)** 14th **(c)** Seventh **(d)** Fifth.
10. The vote of the states that is necessary to ratify an amendment is **(a)** majority **(b)** three-fourths **(c)** three-fifths **(d)** one-fourth.

C. Essay

Write a paragraph about *one* of the following:

1. The elastic clause makes the Constitution flexible.
2. The Bill of Rights protects individual freedoms.
3. Amendments help the government change with the times.
4. The first ten amendments are the most important.
5. The amending process is too complicated.

D. A Challenge for You

1. Write an editorial on the following topic: We need a new Constitution for the 21st century.

2. For a two-to-four-week period, watch newspapers and magazines for articles about issues related to the Bill of Rights. Cut the articles out or photocopy them. Create a graph to show the frequency and amount of coverage each issue is given. Also indicate whether the rights are related to local, state, or national events.

3. Prepare *two* speeches, one for each side, in a debate on the following topic: The elastic clause gives the government too much power.

4. Create a cartoon strip that outlines the steps in the process of proposing and ratifying an amendment.

5. Create an amendment that you believe should be added to the Constitution. Put the proposal in the form of a petition. Gather signatures in support of the amendment. If your idea appeals to a fair number of people, you might send it to your representative in Congress.

Document-Based Question

State the main idea expressed in each document. Then use information in the documents and your own knowledge to write an essay explaining the arguments for and against calling a national constitutional convention to propose an amendment.

"James Madison Wouldn't Approve" by Melvin Laird*

The only precedent we have for a constitutional convention took place in Philadelphia in 1787. That convention, . . . violated specific instructions from Congress to confine itself to amending the Articles of Confederation and instead discarded the Articles and wrote our present Constitution. Moreover, that convention acted in violation of the existing Articles of Confederation by devising a new method for ratifying the proposed Constitution, specifically prohibited by the Articles of Confederation.

Reputable scholars have recently grappled with these complexities, but the realistic fact remains that 200 years later there is no certainty that our nation would survive a modern-day convention with its basic structures intact and its citizens' traditional rights retained. The convening of a federal constitutional convention would be an act of the greatest magnitude for our nation. I believe it would be an act fraught with danger and recklessness.

*[Laird was a congressman from Wisconsin and later served (1969–1973) as secretary of defense under President Richard Nixon.]

"Constitutional Convention: Oh, Stop the Hand-Wringing" by Griffin Bell*

Also, we are bombarded with ominous stories about a "runaway" constitutional convention that, presumably would repeal the Bill of Rights, dismantle the Constitution and install some sort of totalitarian regime. Well, while we have not had a federal convention since 1787, there have been over 200 conventions held in various states, many of whose constitutions provide for periodic conventions to propose amendments. Such gatherings have brought out the best, not the worst, in people's government.

. . . Thomas Jefferson, . . . assumed that we would have a new convention about every 20 years. . . .

Those who wring their hands over the prospects of a convention run the risk of exposing their elitism, implying that the average citizen cannot be trusted. . . .

*[Bell served (1977–1979) as attorney general under President Jimmy Carter.]

Both from "Do Ordain and Establish This Constitution for the United States of America," *A Bicentennial Chronicle*, Fall 1984, No. 4, pages 18, 32. Published by the American Historical Association and the American Political Science Association.

CHAPTER 9

State and Local Government

1. How do the national and state governments share power under federalism?
2. How does the state government affect our lives?
3. What are the differences among state, county, and city governments?
4. What is the importance of the initiative, recall, and referendum?

State governments existed long before the Constitutional Convention met in 1787. At that time, the states reluctantly decided to share power with the national government. Then, as well as now, the people wanted to keep public policy decisions closer to home. The federal system that the Constitution set up divides power between the national government and the state and local governments. This sharing of power is called federalism.

The Constitution *delegates*, or gives, certain powers to the national government alone. (Some, for example, are coining money, regulating interstate commerce, and declaring war.) The Tenth Amendment declares that the states have reserved powers. These are powers that have not been denied to the states nor given to Congress. (Some, for example, are establishing educational systems and regulating marriage and divorce.) A third category of powers is called concurrent, or shared. This means that both the national and state governments can exercise these powers. (For example, both can levy and collect taxes.)

Federalism: A Constant Tug of War

As the cartoon on page 145 shows, balancing power in our nation is a constant struggle. The states complain that the federal government imposes too many rules and regulations. The federal government, on the other hand, claims that the states too often try to ignore or find a way around federal directives.

144

Tug of War

"BUT THE 10TH AMENDMENT GIVES US THE POWER!"

Line of Power

Federal Government

State Governments

A Test of Federalism

Normally, the states and the federal government just argue about rights and power. But in the 1830s, the country nearly went to war over the right of a state to nullify a federal law, to declare that it had no legal standing. A compromise law finally resolved the issue. The federal government did not have to use force to get the state to obey the spirit of the legislation.

Nearly 30 years later, in 1861, the country did go to war. Southern states decided to secede from, or leave, the federal Union over disputes about states' rights, slavery, and economic issues. President Abraham Lincoln believed that the Union must be preserved, and he sent federal troops to fight against the South. The Civil War ended in 1865 with a Northern victory over the Southern Confederacy. In 1870, the last of the Southern states were readmitted to the Union. No state since has seriously threatened to secede. The Civil War resolved the issue of the supremacy of the federal Constitution.

Shifting Power

From 1865 until the early 1900s, the federal government imposed few rules on the states. State laws affected the people and businesses within its borders. Residents looked to their state capital rather than to Washington, D.C., for guidance.

The Progressive Movement of reform-minded leaders gained political influence after 1904. They called for national laws to protect people from the damaging practices of major national industries. Such industries included drug companies, food-processing plants, and the railroads. Congress passed a number of laws that continue to this day to make our lives safer.

Not until the Great Depression of the 1930s, though, did the national government take on the powers that we are familiar with today. Extraordinary times called for extraordinary measures to deal with the economic crisis. Programs were created in Washington and regulated by national agencies. Funds came from federal taxes. Federal laws required states to take certain actions and follow specific guidelines.

While this policy worked fairly well for many years, states began to rebel. They felt that Washington did not always know what was best for each of the 50 separate states. State government, state leaders said, was closer to the people and could spend tax money more wisely than the federal government.

In the mid-1990s, the effort to shrink the national government gained strength. This movement wanted to put more decision-making power in the hands of the states. Federal funds would be most acceptable to the states in the form of grants of lump sums of money. These grants might be for specific purposes, such as health care for the elderly. But the state would determine how to spend the money within the state. No longer would Washington control all of the details.

Let's Think

1. What is federalism?
2. How did the states in the early 19th century attempt to weaken the power of the federal government?
3. How did the Great Depression lead to a change in the relationship between the state and federal governments?
4. Why was there an effort to shrink the national government in recent decades?

State Government

Each of the 50 states has its own government. All state governments have three branches. As you would expect, these branches are the executive, legislative, and judicial. State governments fashion themselves along the lines of the national government.

The state constitutions follow an organization similar to that of the U.S. Constitution. They contain an introduction called a preamble, which states the purpose of the document. Other common features of state constitutions include a bill of rights and an outline of the various powers of the three branches of the state government.

State constitutions tend to be much more detailed than the federal Constitution. Thus, they are much longer. The U.S. Constitution contains about 7,000 words. One of the longest state constitutions, that of Alabama, contains 357,157 words. Most contain 15,000 to 30,000 words.

State governments, like the federal government, have found it necessary to change their constitutions. State constitutions, though, have been amended many more times than the national Constitution. Throughout its history, Alabama has adopted 798 amendments, South Carolina, 463, and Indiana, only 8. Many states have totally revised their constitutions more than once. For instance, Alabama has rewritten its constitution 6 times, Georgia, 10 times, and Louisiana, 11. State constitutions may be amended so often because it is easy to do so. In some states, it takes only a simple majority of the voting public for an amendment to be added to the state constitution.

The Executive

The **governor**, as the chief executive, is charged with the responsibility of carrying out state laws. You can think of the governor as the "president" of the state. The governor's role on the state level is similar to the role of the president on the national level. The governor is elected by the people who are residents of the state and are eligible to vote in the state. Almost all governors are elected to four-year terms. In some states, the governor is limited to serving two terms in office.

Governors are responsible for formulating policies. They work closely with the legislatures to enact laws that bring the policies to life. Laws are proposed to the state legislatures in the same way that the president proposes laws to Congress. Like the president, governors have the power to veto laws passed by the legislature. Most governors also have the *line-item veto* power. This enables them to strike out the portion of a spending bill they do not like without having to veto the entire bill.

State Government

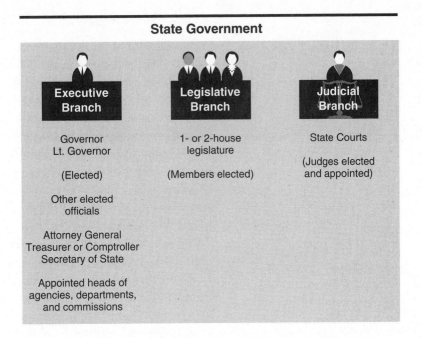

Executive Branch	Legislative Branch	Judicial Branch
Governor Lt. Governor	1- or 2-house legislature	State Courts
(Elected)	(Members elected)	(Judges elected and appointed)
Other elected officials		
Attorney General Treasurer or Comptroller Secretary of State		
Appointed heads of agencies, departments, and commissions		

Governors have broad appointment authority. They decide who should head various government agencies. For instance, a governor might appoint the commissioner of motor vehicles, the head of the state department of education, and the head of the state department of transportation. In most cases, the state legislature has the power to approve the appointments.

Other appointments that generally do not require legislative approval are the governor's executive staff. These individuals assist the governor in carrying out his or her responsibilities. Therefore, the governor's appointments secretary, chief of staff, and press secretary, for example, are appointed by the governor and are directly responsible to him or her.

Qualifications for Governors

What kind of person is likely to be a governor? As of 2009, 43 of the 50 governors were men. Almost all were white and middle-aged. To run for governor, a person must satisfy a residency requirement. This requirement varies from only one year in the state of Minnesota to ten years in Missouri. The minimum age requirement varies as well. The range starts at 18 for Washington and California to 31 for Oklahoma. The majority of the states set the age at 30.

Most governors are little known outside of their states. Occasionally, one will stand out be-cause of personality or successful state policies. These individuals may be pushed for a high national office. Bill Clinton, governor of Arkansas, was elected president in 1992 and 1996. George W. Bush was elected president in 2000 and 2004 after serving as governor of Texas.

Assisting the governor is the **lieutenant governor.** Like the vice president, the lieutenant governor is responsible for helping the chief executive carry out policy. If the governor is unable to perform his or her duties or is unable to complete the term of office, the lieutenant governor takes over the responsibilities. In some states, the lieutenant governor acts as governor when the governor is out of the state. Usually, the lieutenant governor has the duty of presiding over the state Senate.

Other Elected Officials

The number of elected officials who hold state-wide office varies from state to state. Almost every state has an elected official called the *attorney general*. This person handles legal matters within the state. The attorney general determines law enforcement policy and monitors matters involving violations of statewide business practices. If a citizen is unhappy about how a company handled a problem or feels that a company has engaged in unscrupulous practices, the citizen can contact the attorney general to help resolve the problem. The people who hold this office have large staffs of lawyers who specialize in different areas. Some try cases. Others work with law enforcement officials such as state police to conduct investigations into alleged criminal activity or government corruption.

Another elected state official is the *treasurer*, or *comptroller*. This person is concerned with the financial affairs of the state. The office monitors state spending and businesses that hold state contracts. The treasurer makes sure that the companies doing business with the state meet their financial obligations. In addition, the treasurer monitors tax revenues and determines that state funds are spent in the way laws require them to be spent. For instance, if a tax is earmarked to be spent for education, the treasurer monitors these funds to be certain that they are spent on educational matters.

The *secretary of state* is the official in charge of keeping state records. If a business wants to structure itself as a corporation, its officers will apply to the secretary of state for the proper state documents to achieve that goal. In addition, the person who occupies this office is responsible for seeing that the election laws are properly administered. They certify ballots and petitions. States that do not have such elected officials are Alaska, Hawaii, and Utah. In Pennsylvania and Virginia, the office is called the secretary of the commonwealth.

Civil Service Workers

Many people who work for the state are not elected. They are employed in departments such as state law enforcement, finance and taxation, and the motor vehicle bureau, among others. These civil servants make up a major portion of state workers and are responsible for the day-to-day operation of government.

In order to be considered for public-service jobs (the civil service), individuals take competitive examinations. They are then hired on the basis of their test scores. Part of the reason for requiring tests for such jobs is to remove them from political influence.

The Legislature

The legislative branch of a state, like the Congress of the United States, is responsible for making laws. The difference is that the laws apply only to one state. The legislative branches of the states have different names. Many are called the General Assembly. Others are simply named the Legislature. The State of Massachusetts officially calls its lawmaking body the General Court.

Forty-nine of the 50 states created bicameral (two-house) legislatures. Only one, the state of Nebraska, has a unicameral (one-house) legislature. Most of the legislative houses have the same names. One is the Senate. Generally, it is considered to be the "upper" house, the one with more prestige. This is because there are fewer senators in the Senate than there are representatives in the other, or "lower," house. Senators represent a larger population base and tend to have longer terms of office than members of the lower house.

The other house is given different names, depending on the state. One name is the House of Representatives. Another is the Assembly. The table on page 149 lists several states, the names of the houses of their legislatures, and the size of each of the houses.

Qualifications for State Legislators

Like other elected officials, state legislators must meet certain qualifications for office. Most state constitutions have residency and citizenship requirements. Usually, a candidate must live in the district he or she may represent as well as in the state. The length of residency varies from six months to two years.

Age requirements for officeholders also vary from state to state. Some state constitutions require only that the individual be eligible to vote. In this case, the person who wanted to run for office would have to be a resident and at least 18 years old. The requirements for each house of the legislature may be different. Terms of office tend to be two or four years.

Each state legislator represents the people of a particular district in a state. Senatorial districts contain more people than house districts. The boundaries of the districts may be reshaped after each census.

STATE	POPULATION*	NAME OF LEGISLATURE	MEMBERS IN EACH HOUSE
Alabama	4,627,851	Legislature	Senate, 35; House,** 105
California	36,553,216	Legislature	Senate, 40; House, 80
Colorado	4,861,515	General Assembly	Senate, 35; House, 65
Florida	18,251,243	Legislature	Senate, 40; House, 120
Iowa	2,988,046	General Assembly	Senate, 50; House, 100
Maine	1,317,207	Legislature	Senate, 35; House, 151
Massachusetts	6,449,755	General Court	Senate, 40; House, 160
Michigan	10,071,822	Legislature	Senate, 38; House, 110
Texas	23,904,380	Legislature	Senate, 31; House, 150
Wisconsin	5,601,640	Legislature	Senate, 33; Assembly, 99

*Estimated, 2007

**Full name for House label: House of Representatives

Enacting Laws

As it is for Congress, the primary responsibility of a state legislature is to pass laws. The laws a state legislature passes must comply with the provisions in the state's constitution. They cannot violate the federal Constitution either. As you remember, the federal Constitution is the supreme law of the land. For example, suppose a state legislature passes a law declaring a certain religion to be the official religion of the state. This law cannot be enforced because it violates the First Amendment of the federal Constitution.

The process by which most states enact laws is similar to the lawmaking process in Congress. Bills, or proposed laws, have to be introduced into one house of the legislature for consideration. State legislatures also use committees to handle the work more efficiently. In general, a bill introduced in a state legislature goes through the following steps on its way to becoming a law. The bill is assigned to a committee, which holds hearings. The committee then decides the fate of the bill. It can kill it, pigeonhole it, or recommend it to the entire house of the legislature for a vote. If the bill is passed, it is sent on to the other house where it will be assigned to a committee there. (Sometimes both houses will consider the same bill at the same time.) If this committee recommends passage of the bill, it is then voted on by the second house. As in the national government, bills often come out of each house in a different form. When this happens, a conference committee consisting of members of both houses will decide the final form of the bill. Both houses must pass the same version of the law. Once voting has been completed, the final bill is sent on to the governor, who will either sign or veto it.

Checks and Balances, State Style

Checks and balances are just as important at the state level as they are at the federal level. Many of the checks are similar. Governors have the power to veto bills. Legislatures can override the veto. They can also institute and carry out impeachment proceedings against state officials. In most states, the legislature must approve appointments of certain government officials. State courts may declare state laws unconstitutional.

State Finances

All governments need money to operate. On the state level, revenue comes from several sources: 53 percent from taxes of various sorts, 22 percent from federal government funds, and 23 percent from insurance trust revenue. Insurance trust funds are earmarked for the pensions of state workers, such as state police and teachers.

Three types of taxes provide the largest portion of state revenue. They are: income (levied on private individuals and businesses), sales, and excise. Other revenue comes from license fees, tolls, and lotteries.

How does a state spend this money? One area that states spend a great deal of money on is education: 21.4 percent on elementary and secondary education and 10.4 percent on postsecondary education. Another large expense is for public assistance and Medicaid (23.3 percent). States spend about 8.1 percent on highways and various forms of public transportation. The amount of money spent on corrections, including running the state prison system, is 3.4 percent. The remaining 33.4 percent of the budget covers items such as running the government, taking care of parks and forests, providing recreation, and repaying state debt.

In most states, the people urge the government to keep expenses down. Few see a way to increase revenue to meet new needs.

The Judicial Branch

A person commits a crime that violates a state law. Perhaps it is a robbery or passing a bad check. When arrested, that person will be tried in a state court. In general, as discussed in Chapter 7, state courts are organized in a way similar to the federal system.

Judges for the various courts are elected in some places. In others, they are appointed by state officials with the advice of state bar associations (groups of lawyers). Most state courts are faced with more cases than they can handle in a timely fashion. There is little effort to expand the number of courts or judges because of the expense involved.

The State Affects Our Lives

Motor Vehicles

One way the state affects your life is by regulating the licensing of drivers. It decides the age that you must reach before you can drive. That is why a friend of yours in another state may drive at the age of 15, but you have to wait until you are 17. The state also prepares the test that you must pass before you get your driver's license.

All motor vehicles must be registered by the state government. This means that the owner of each vehicle is identified and issued license plates for the vehicle. States also mandate that car owners carry insurance for their cars. This protects both owners and passengers in case of accidents.

States regulate the inspection of motor vehicles. These inspections are designed to keep the family car safe to drive. Many states regulate the amount of pollutants allowed into the atmos-

phere by automobiles. These regulations are in addition to federal laws.

Education

It is commonly believed that public schools are financed primarily by funds from the local community. This is only partly true. Public schools receive a large portion of their income from state funds. A state has a great deal of authority over the education of young people. It establishes the age at which young people must start school and the age they must reach before they may leave school. The state determines the curriculum that will be studied and the requirements for graduation. State rules establish the standards that teachers must meet to be licensed or certified to stand in front of you in your classroom. In addition, states may have something to say about the size and shape of school districts.

Marriage and Divorce

Some of you may have a close family member who is about to be married. Did you know that it is the state government that sets the minimum age for marriage? This age standard varies from state to state. Teenagers may marry in some states without the consent of parents, while in other states, they must have the consent of parents. State governments may even require that the bride and groom have physical examinations or blood tests. If certain diseases are present, the couple may be denied a license.

Just as states establish marriage laws, they also set divorce laws. The states empower the courts to decide divorce cases, child custody rules, and property settlements.

Voting

Another area that the state has control over is voting. Although the voting age is now established by the federal Constitution, the states determine voting registration requirements, where people can vote, and the method of voting. State governments decide when elections for state officials will be held.

Prisons

States are also responsible for maintaining a prison system. People who commit minor offenses might be kept for short periods of time in a municipal jail. But those who must serve more than one year in jail for committing a felony are sent to a state prison. State prisons require a large workforce to maintain them, from prison guards to educators to experts in criminal behavior. Many prisons are overcrowded. Some states are looking for alternative ways of dealing with their criminal populations.

Let's Think

1. What is the purpose of each branch of state government: legislative, executive, and judicial?
2. Describe the main job of each of the following state officials: governor, lieutenant governor, secretary of state, attorney general.
3. What types of checks and balances are built into state constitutions?
4. What are the major sources of revenue in states?
5. Describe a typical state's expenditures.

Counties and the States

The states are divided into parts called **counties**. Alaska calls these divisions "boroughs," and Louisiana calls them "parishes." The population of counties can vary widely. The range can be as great as 10 million–plus people in Los Angeles County in California to as low as 67 people in Loving County in Texas. The square mileage of counties is equally varied. The county with the largest area outside of Alaska is San Bernardino County, California, with an area of 20,053 square miles. The smallest county in area is Kalawao County, Hawaii, which has just 13 square miles. Each state decides the size of its counties. Some large cities, such as New York, contain several counties within their boundaries. If you are looking for a pattern to the size of counties, you will not find one. For example, Delaware has the fewest counties (3); Texas has the most (254). There are 3,401 counties in the 50 states and 30 city-

county governments. Cities such as Denver, New York, and San Francisco have combined government functions with the counties in which they are located.

Function of Counties

Counties provide the main structure of government for rural areas within a state. County officials are responsible for furnishing state services to county residents. This could mean law enforcement, a court system, social services, education, road building and maintenance, and park systems. In addition, the county is empowered to "assess" property value. It sets a value on property, which is then used as a basis for taxing the

Illinois Counties

POWER *of* ★NE

Maynard Jackson

Have you ever wondered what it would be like to be the first one to do something? The first one to accomplish something that no other person has ever done? It takes a person with courage, determination, and a vision of what he or she wants to accomplish in life to be the first. Such a person was Maynard Holbrook Jackson, Jr. In 1974, he became the first African-American mayor of the city of Atlanta in Georgia.

Maynard Jackson was born on May 23, 1938, in Dallas, Texas. When Jackson was seven, his family moved to Atlanta, where his father became pastor of a Baptist church. Seven years later, Jackson was admitted to Morehouse College on a special early admissions scholarship. After he graduated in 1956, Jackson began selling encyclopedias. He worked his way up from salesperson to assistant district sales manager within a short time. In 1961, he decided to try a new career and entered law school. While a law student, Jackson earned the designation by the New York Bar Association as one of the outstanding debaters in the United States.

In 1968, Maynard Jackson decided to enter the political arena. At this time, few African Americans had been elected to public office in any state. He unsuccessfully tried to be nominated to run for the U.S. Senate from Georgia. Although he lost the primary election, Jackson gained a great deal of respect as a political candidate for the way he ran his campaign and for the number of votes he received. His efforts enhanced his reputation and increased his recognition among voters. Jackson saw this as a victory for himself and other African Americans. It would, he believed, encourage others to get involved in the political system. Jackson declared that a "historical victory has been achieved. . . . Georgia has told the world that any American—black or white, rich or poor, liberal or conservative—can run for public office in this state."

Jackson then decided to enter the race for vice mayor of Atlanta. The person occupying this office was second in command to the mayor. He was elected Atlanta's first African-

---

property. Counties also maintain voting records for those living within their jurisdiction.

County responsibilities vary considerably from state to state. In Maryland, for instance, counties oversee financing of schools, sewers, and parks. But in Illinois, separate government authorities, called districts, manage schools, parks, sewers, and other services. Counties have no involvement with them.

Today, counties are moving into new areas. Some are working on programs involving child welfare, consumer protection, economic development, and employment and training.

County governments are the "children of state governments" as are most other forms of local government within the state. This means that they are created and regulated by the states. Policies and programs administered by the county are often mandated by the state government. In some cases, counties and other local governments must ask permission of the state government to carry out a policy. Many states have decided to give more power to local governments through **home rule**. Home rule gives local governments the authority to enact and carry out programs on their own, without direct guidance by the state. If, for instance, a local government wanted to raise the sales tax in its jurisdiction, it would be able to do so on its own if it had home rule.

American vice mayor with the support of many white voters as well as African-American voters.

At the same time, Jackson held several other positions, including president of the city's board of aldermen. He also helped to found Georgia's first and largest African-American law firm.

Jackson made plans to run for mayor. In 1973, he was elected Atlanta's first African-American mayor. When he assumed the office, the position of mayor had been strengthened through a new city charter that had recently been ratified. The composition of the new city council, which replaced the board of aldermen, was evenly divided between whites and African Americans. This election demonstrated that candidates could be elected regardless of racial or ethnic background.

With the new city charter in operation, Jackson set about reshaping Atlanta's government. One of his major concerns was to lower the crime rate in the city. He waged an unsuccessful attempt to remove the city's police chief. Appointed by the previous mayor, the chief had been blamed for not reducing the crime rate. Furthermore, the black community believed that he had unfairly demoted several black officers. Eventually, the police chief bowed to pressure and stepped down. Jackson then appointed his own choice to the position.

Within a short time, new law-enforcement policies brought about a sharp drop in the city's crime rate.

In 1982, after two terms as mayor, Jackson had to leave office. (Atlanta has a legal limit on the number of successive terms a mayor can serve.) Seven years later, the voters of Atlanta returned him to the office of mayor. During what would become his third and final term of office, Jackson worked hard to aid African-American businesses in the city.

One of the most publicized achievements of the Jackson administration was persuading the International Olympic Committee to hold the 1996 Summer Olympic Games in Atlanta. Many saw this as a great accomplishment that brought much publicity to Atlanta and improved the economy of the city.

Maynard Holbrook Jackson, Jr., died in 2003. He was another fine example of the Power of One. He made a difference in the lives of the people of his city and state.

1. What were the "firsts" that Maynard Jackson accomplished?
2. What programs did he work on that made a difference in the lives of the people of Atlanta?
3. Why was his leadership significant?

The Form of County Governments

Counties are generally governed by an elected **board** or **commission**. These boards usually have five to seven members. The officials may be called commissioner, supervisor, or freeholder. The board passes laws and monitors the people who carry out the responsibilities of the county.

Counties have a number of other elected officials. The most common ones are the sheriff, district attorney, treasurer, and clerk. The *sheriff* supervises the county police force. The *district attorney* protects the interests of the state in civil lawsuits as well as criminal prosecutions. The *treasurer* collects the taxes for the county, keeps the tax records, and pays the bills. The *county clerk*

maintains records of births, deaths, marriages, and *deeds* (documents that establish ownership of property). The diagram on page 154 shows how a typical county government is structured. Details may vary from county to county.

Let's Think

1. What is a county?
3. What are its functions?
2. Define home rule.
4. Describe the main duties of the following county officials: district attorney, treasurer, clerk.

A Typical County Government

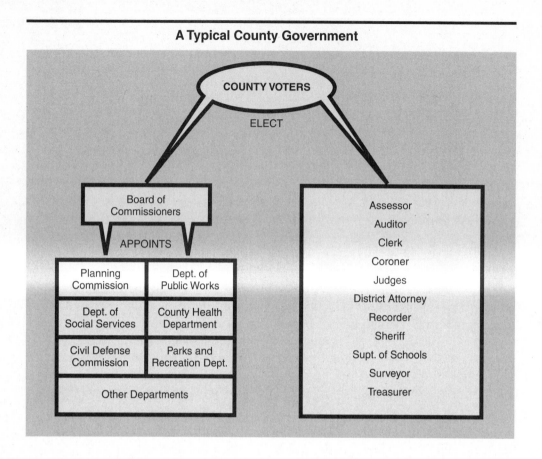

Cities—Centers of Population

A city is an urban center—a **municipality**. Cities vary in size. They range in population from thousands to millions. Each has its own government and provides many services. These services include public schools, law enforcement, sanitation, hospitals, recreation facilities, and a water system.

Cities exist because they are granted **charters** by the state government. This is an authorization or a license to operate as a city. Once a city has this authorization it is said to be **incorporated**. Most cities create a constitution, usually called a *city charter*. Like other constitutions, the city charter outlines the responsibilities and limits of the city government. The charter includes the duties of the branches of government and specifies which officials will be elected and the length of their terms of office.

Major cities around the nation such as Boston, Chicago, San Francisco, and Nashville are examples of incorporated communities. When a community is not incorporated, it is governed by the county. People living in unincorporated communities are, of course, obligated to follow state laws and county regulations.

Types of City Governments

The government of a city has a structure similar to those of the county, state, and federal systems. There is a legislature, often called a **city council**, a chief executive—the **mayor**, and **courts**. (See the diagrams on page 155 for examples of typical city government structures.)

The most popular city government structure is the **mayor–council**. The mayor is elected in a citywide vote. Council members are usually elected from districts within the city. Smaller cities may elect council members through citywide ballots.

In some cases, the system is called a "strong-mayor–council plan" because the mayor appoints the heads of the administrative departments of the city government. These include sanitation, police, fire, consumer affairs, and housing, among others. A "strong" mayor

Two Forms of City Government

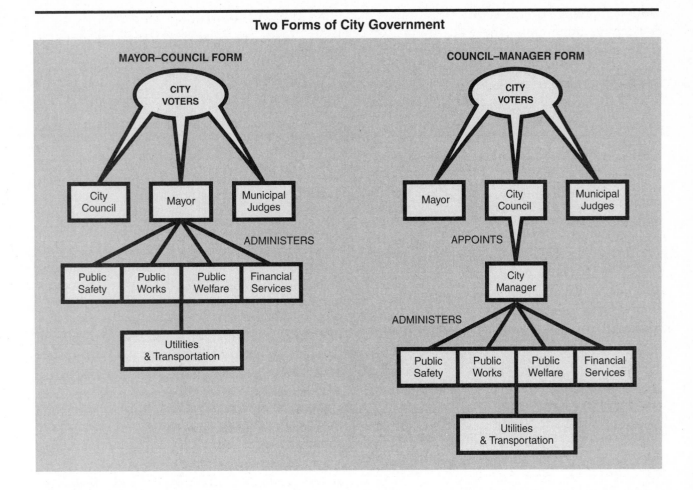

prepares the city budget and has a central role in making policy.

Another form is the "weak-mayor–council plan." Under this arrangement, the mayor has more limited power than under the strong-mayor–council system. The council is the dominant force. It chooses department heads and may even appoint the mayor.

A second city government structure is the **council–manager** type. In this case, the city council hires a city manager who is responsible for operating the government on a day-to-day basis. Given authority by the council, the city manager is actually the chief executive and supervises the various city agencies. The concentration of power is in the hands of the city council. A mayor may be elected to handle ceremonial duties.

Cities Provide Many Services

A primary function of a city is to provide for the needs of the people who live and work within its

boundaries. Local roads and traffic laws are needed to help people move efficiently and safely from place to place. A school system is necessary to educate young people. A health-care system helps maintain the well-being of residents.

Safety in the city is the responsibility of the police. The city government also administers local jails that hold those people accused of crimes and awaiting trial and convicted criminals who receive short sentences.

Waste management is another service provided by the municipal government. It finances and operates a sanitation department and a sewage-treatment system. Issues relating to recycling are also handled by the municipal government.

Like all other governments within the state, the city government is responsible for carrying out the policies and laws established by the state. It also tries to exercise some independence in meeting its own needs and deciding its own future. Planning for low-cost housing and the development of an industrial park are the types of decisions that a city government must make to maintain the social and economic health of the community.

Zoning

Community planning is an issue that affects all members of a community. People do not like to travel far to reach a shopping center. Yet they do not necessarily want one near their homes because it might attract too much traffic. How does a community decide where various businesses, factories, and residences should be located? To accommodate the desires and needs of communities, local governments have set up planning committees or boards. They have devised rules, **zoning**, that determine what should be built where. Zones are areas designated for specific land use. For instance, an area zoned for residential purposes can have only homes in it. Some zones permit only private one- and two-family homes. Other zones are designated for multiple-dwelling buildings, such as apartment houses. In commercial zones, businesses are permitted to build facilities for offices and stores. A mall may be built in such a zone. Industrial zones are also set up. They are designated for manufacturing facilities.

Where to place the different zones is an issue of concern to all citizens. Zones shape the character of a neighborhood. (Think what a community would look like if private homes and manufacturing plants were mixed together.) How do communities decide what to locate where? Planning boards hold hearings. Residents can voice their opinions at the hearings. They can also influence the city council, which usually has the final vote on zoning changes.

Municipal Courts

Most cities set up municipal courts to handle specific types of cases. Housing courts hear tenant–landlord disputes about rent, repairs, or services. Family relations courts specialize in domestic problems, such as child abuse. Juvenile courts take care of cases involving young people below an age set by the state. As the name implies, traffic courts handle violations of traffic laws. These courts do not use juries. A judge hears the case and makes a decision.

Suburbs

Close to larger cities are communities called **suburbs**. They are often small cities themselves. Many of the people who live in them work in the larger central city. They commute to their jobs, sometimes by private automobile but often by bus or train.

Suburbs tend to be made up of private homes and apartments, shopping areas, school systems, and some office buildings and industrial areas. Most do not have downtown areas. These cities provide the same services to their residents as any other city. Their governments are based on the patterns established in other cities.

Commuters use services in the place where they live and the city where they work. Many pay taxes in both places. But most pay taxes only where they live. This situation deprives the central city of needed funds.

It has been suggested that suburbs and central cities should cooperate more to cope with regional problems. Rather than having each city pass regulations to lessen pollution, for instance, a metropolitan area authority might regulate the problem. Similar area-wide authorities could coordinate fire departments and services for water, sewage, and garbage disposal.

Let's Think

1. What is a municipality?
2. What is the meaning of each of the following terms: city charter, incorporated community?
3. Describe the two most common forms of city government.
4. Why is zoning in a community an important issue?

Towns and Villages

Many people in the United States do not live in cities. They live in rural areas or smaller commu-

How a Small Midwestern City Spends Tax Dollars

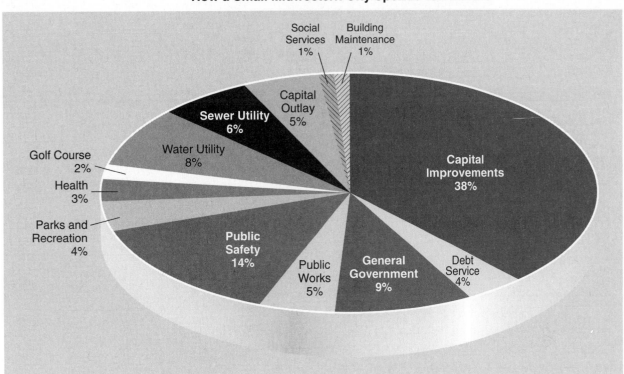

nities called **towns** or **villages**. Most towns have their own government and carry out responsibilities similar to those of cities. Other towns look to the county for services.

One expert describes the powers of towns in this way: "About 16,690 towns and townships exist in 20 states in the Midwestern and Eastern United States. Some have powers that don't go far beyond distributing aid from the federal government, while others are so strong that they virtually render county government useless. Even more so than counties, towns and townships are considered to be the government 'closest to the people.'"

In the Northeast, the town is the main form of noncity government. It carries "out the duties of a county or school district for a region of villages and unincorporated land. In Connecticut, for instance, towns and cities are the premier [main] forms of government, and counties have depreciated to merely running local court systems. Residents in many towns still can attend town meetings and vote directly on local issues simply by raising their hands."

Just as other local governments do, towns

have their own elected and unelected officials. These officials may include a board of selectmen, usually made up of three to five members. In addition, there are normally a treasurer, a town clerk, and an assessor.

In New England, the Middle Atlantic states, and the Middle West, another local government exists. It is called a **township**. Townships are divisions of counties. Each has an elected governing body, usually called a board of trustees. There may also be other elected officials. Townships take care of roads, some property records, and some law enforcement. They may administer the public school system in the area.

Town Meetings

Historically, the town has been recognized for its role in furthering the cause of democracy in the United States. New England towns gave birth to a form of direct democracy known as the **town meeting**. All voting age residents gather at the annual town meeting to decide local issues and elect local officials.

An agenda is set and the citizens participate in debating and voting on the issues taken up at the meeting. These decisions may concern major issues such as when to rebuild a bridge or the amount by which taxes should be raised as well as relatively minor issues.

Some large towns may have too many eligible voters to bring them all together in one location to make decisions. In these places, the townspeople elect representatives to attend the town meetings and make decisions for the community.

Financing Local Government

When we look at all the services that local governments provide, it is clear that they need a great deal of money to function. Taxes are an important source of revenue for all governments. Local governments depend for the most part on property taxes for income. Such taxes account for more than $390 billion in local revenue nationally, according to the U.S. Census Bureau. Property tax bills are usually based on the value of a piece of property or a building. Other sources of revenue for local government may include license fees for certain businesses and services and sales taxes.

Let's Think

1. What is a township?
2. What functions do town governments perform?
3. Who are some of the officials in a town government? What are their duties?
4. How are most local governments financed?

Special Districts

There is yet another division within a state. It is known as a **special district**. Special districts are formed to carry out special tasks. They may be within one county or community or overlap several.

An example of a special district is a school district. Sometimes it is inconvenient or too costly for one town or village to maintain a school system by itself. In these cases, several communities will be allowed to band together to form a special school district. Such districts spread the tax burden of operating a school system over a larger number of people.

Other special districts might provide fire protection for an area or monitor environmental health or develop a system to bring clean drinking water to an area. Regardless of the purposes of special districts, they are usually administered by an elected governing board.

Let's Think

1. What are special districts?
2. What functions do they serve?
3. Why are they important?

Bringing Democracy Close to Home

Participating in the democratic experience is an activity Americans hold close to their hearts. There are several ways in which state and local governments have attempted to bring democracy closer to the people. These processes are the initiative, referendum, and recall.

The Initiative

An **initiative** is a proposal by a group of citizens for a law, constitutional amendment, or regulation at the state or local level. The process begins by creating wording to go on a petition. This petition must be signed by an appropriate number of voters, as established by law. After the proper number of signatures is obtained, the proposal will be placed on the ballot at the next election. The number of signatures for a petition for an initiative varies according to the state or the locality. For instance, in California a statute (law) initiative needs signatures from 5 percent of the number of citizens who voted in the previous

States That Allow Ballot Initiatives

Allow Ballot Initiatives

Do Not Allow Ballot Initiatives

state election. An amendment to the state constitution must get signatures from 8 percent of that number. In Arizona, the signature requirement is 10 percent for any legislative measure and 15 percent for a constitutional amendment.

A wide variety of subjects have been proposed as initiatives. They range from a law requiring a state to balance its budget to one limiting services to illegal aliens. In 1996, voters in Maine managed to pass a campaign finance reform initiative that the state legislature had rejected year after year.

Once the appropriate number of signatures has been gathered in support of an initiative, the petition is given to the legislature for consideration. If the legislature approves the proposal, it becomes law. If the legislature does not pass the proposal, it is placed on the ballot for the citizens of the affected area—state, town, or city—to vote on. A majority vote is all it needs to be passed.

A current complaint is that out-of-state organizations are proposing initiatives that may not be beneficial to the citizens of the state. These groups often use paid signature collectors instead of volunteers. This may make it easier to collect the required number of valid signatures by the legal deadline to put the initiative on the ballot.

Generally, people campaign for the passage of an initiative just as they campaign for a candidate for political office. You can think of the in-

itiative as an election of a particular issue instead of a candidate. If the proper number of votes is obtained, the proposal becomes law or the suggested amendment is added to the constitution.

The Referendum

Another way that voters get involved with approving or rejecting laws is through the **referendum**. Under this process, certain laws or actions approved by a state legislature must be submitted to the voters before becoming legally effective.

An example of a referendum that is common in many states is the submission of an amendment to the state constitution to the voters. In these states, an amendment approved by the state legislature must be put on the ballot in the very next election. If the legally required number of voters give their approval, the amendment takes effect and becomes part of the state constitution. In most states that provide for a referendum, the requirement for passage is that the majority of the voters approve it.

Another common referendum concerns bond issues. (See page 190 for a fuller discussion of bonds.) Voters must approve these proposals to raise money for projects such as building schools or prisons.

◄REALITY CHECK►

Local Government at Work in Plymouth, Massachusetts

Lights! Camera! Action! These words associated with the film industry in California may be coming east to the historic town of Plymouth, Massachusetts. Some members of the community are trying to bring a movie studio to the community. Most of the townspeople are excited about the prospect of seeing movie stars walking down their streets, shopping in their stores, and eating in their restaurants. Others are reluctant to allow the studio to move into the area. They fear it might change the character of their hometown by increasing the pace of life and raising prices. These are some of the issues that have to be resolved by the town government.

Plymouth was founded in 1620 when the Pilgrims first landed in Massachusetts. Its population now is about 58,000. It is governed by a council–manager system. The manager is hired by the council, an elected body called the Board of Selectmen. The board makes the decisions for the town. In considering whether to attempt to persuade a business to move to the town, the board must consider the costs and the benefits of

doing so. They hope the benefits will outweigh the costs.

State lawmakers have offered tax benefits to attract the movie industry to Massachusetts. This effort has met with some success as film companies have been set up in other areas of the state. The effort to persuade Plymouth Rock Studios to move to Plymouth is an example of this initiative.

In July 2008, Plymouth Rock Studios announced that it had purchased the 240-acre Waverly Oaks Golf Club, located in Plymouth. The development the studio wants to build on this site would include sound stages, a hotel, back lots, and office buildings. Town officials announced that the area had to go through a rezoning process. This area had been designated for one type of use: a golf course. It would now have to be redesignated for use as a movie studio.

If the zoning issue is resolved, Plymouth Rock Studios would have to submit its building plans to the town officials for approval before construction could begin. In addition, new roads would have to be built and utilities such as electric power and sewers would

The Recall

Sometimes the citizens in a community are unhappy with a government official's work. They do not want to wait until the next election to remove that person from office. Many state and local governments provide for a system known as **recall**. It is a citizen-initiated movement to remove a public official from office.

People create a petition that states the reasons why they believe the person should be removed. As with an initiative, a required number of people must sign the petition. If the proper number of signatures is collected, the recall proposal is placed on the ballot for people to vote their approval or disapproval of the recall. A vote for the recall removes the officeholder from office. In

2003, Governor Gray Davis of California was removed from office as a result of a recall initiative placed on the ballot. As a result of the election that was held simultaneously, Arnold Schwarzenegger was elected governor.

Let's Think

1. Explain the initiative and referendum.
2. What procedures must be followed to get an initiative and a referendum on the ballot?
3. What is the recall? How is the recall a check on elected officials?

have to be provided. In combination, these items are known as **infrastructure**.

The company wants to begin construction as soon as possible so that the studio can open for business in two years. Unresolved issues regarding the granting of permits may require town meetings at which members of the public can voice their opinions. Earlier, the town held a vote to approve the studio's plan, but that vote concerned a parcel of land that is no longer under consideration. The golf course represents a new parcel of land. Some argued that the town should have to vote on this new site because it is different from the original.

The studio had hoped to speed up the process and not have to go through a permitting process. But because the site is on a former golf course, some members of the town government believe that it would be unfair to allow the company to begin the project without letting those who live near the site to express their opinions.

There are many reported benefits to the project. It is believed that the new studio would become a large source of revenue, bringing in millions of dollars each year. In testimony before the board, one official estimated that the project would create 3,000 jobs and $147 million in wages. Nearly $4 million in property taxes might be generated annually, plus revenue from hotel room taxes and permit fees. In contrast, the cost to the town is estimated at about $786,000 in services, mostly police and fire, each year. The project would also bring in some $30 million to $50 million in state funding for road, water, and sewer improvements, which the town will need even if the studio project is not built.

The board did approve a proposal for tax breaks for the company over a 20-year period. Numerous other commercial projects in Plymouth have received similar tax breaks. Some question whether the tax break would cost the town too much in lost revenue in the long run.

This account illustrates the types of decisions local governments have to make. They hope they will make wise ones that benefit their communities.

1. What issues must be considered before the town approves a major project or development?
2. What benefits might the movie studio project bring to the town?
3. Why might people oppose the project?
4. Why are the operations and decisions of the local government so important to the lives of the people in the community?

Recent Trends in Local Government

Since the 1980s, there have been periodic efforts to **downsize** government (reduce the number of its responsibilities and employees). Supporters of this view believe that government on all levels has become too big and too involved in people's lives.

When federal spending is cut across the board, there is a reduction in the amount of money going to the states. If the states receive fewer funds, they have less to spend on a variety of programs. They have to cut back on their services. This challenge became even more serious during the economic downturn that began in 2008.

Privatization

To find more money and to make tax dollars go further, state and local governments are taking steps to become more efficient. The major concern is to give services to the people in the most cost-effective way possible. To accomplish this goal, governments are experimenting with different ideas. One of these ideas is called **privatization**.

Privatization means replacing government agencies with private companies. These companies contract with the government to provide a service normally carried out by a government agency. When services are provided by a government agency, the people who do the work are employees of the government. Their wages, health insurance, pensions, and other benefits are paid for by the government. Under the system of privatization, a privately owned company takes over the function of the government agency, and the government workers are replaced by private employees.

It is widely believed that private companies can deliver many services more efficiently and at a lower cost than government can. Many government workers and their unions have objected to the idea for fear of losing their jobs.

New Trends

In the mid-1990s, the city of Indianapolis created a system that is somewhat different from, yet similar to, privatization. The mayor claimed that the new system reduced the number of city workers on the government payroll by as much as 25 percent. This was accomplished not through firing employees. Instead, city agencies just did not hire new people to replace those who retired.

The mayor also went to the government agencies and asked workers to find ways to reduce the cost of operating their agencies. If a government agency could "underbid" a private company in delivering a service, the agency would continue to do the job. If the private company underbid the agency, the company would get the contract.

Competition will benefit everyone, officials believe, by providing better services at reduced costs. Government will thus be smaller, more efficient, and less expensive. If this can be accomplished, taxes might be reduced.

Some states have privatized the management of some of their prisons. According to recent statistics, 7 percent of the nation's prison population is housed in privately operated prisons. In Colorado, one in every four prisoners is in a private facility.

The state of Indiana recently held an auction and received a large payment from a private company in exchange for a lease that allows the company to collect tolls and maintain the toll roads. The company was given a long list of "dos and don'ts" to make sure that its operation of the roads would be efficient. The money from the auction helped finance other state government operations.

The city of Chicago auctioned off the Skyway Bridge, a 7.8-mile toll road. The city received about twice as much as the original estimate. The company that won the 99-year lease is responsible for operating and maintenance costs. It keeps the tolls. Chicago also hopes to privatize Midway Airport. If the plan can be carried out, Midway would become the first major U.S. airport to be privatized under a 1996 program developed by the federal government. Other municipalities are looking to privatize either the airports or the management of the airports in their areas.

Another service that has been privatized is waste (garbage) management. Local governments have contracted with private companies to haul and process waste. Several state-owned power plants have been turned over to private companies as well.

Opposing Views

The opponents of privatization believe that it does not result in the most efficient or safe system. "Some areas of government responsibility don't lend themselves to privatization, regardless of competition or how well the companies' operations are monitored by public officials. Switching to private from public operators at airport control towers, for instance, could undermine the confidence of the flying public and severely disrupt service. In addition, politicians often shun privatization because they fear losing control over any activity for which they have been responsible," said the national director of public sector services at a national accounting firm.

Another argument made against privatization is that it only works when there is competition to provide a particular service. For instance, if several companies compete for the government contract, then the cost might be lower. When there are limited choices, the cost will usually rise.

Cost-cutting ideas are part of what became a popular political slogan of the 1990s, "reinventing government." It gained renewed support in the economic downturn of 2008–2009. The idea has come to mean that people would like to alter the role of the government by limiting its size and the extent to which it is involved in the lives of the citizens. Increasing efficiency and eliminating waste are major aims of this policy. Officials also hoped to weed out programs that had outlived their usefulness or only served special interests.

Let's Think

1. What is meant by privatizing government services?
2. What are some of the reasons why people have supported the idea of privatization?
3. How does the idea of privatization reflect the concept of "reinventing government"?

Chapter Summary

A delicate balance of responsibility and power exists between the state and federal governments. The system is called federalism. The Civil War was a major challenge to federalism. During the Progressive Era and the Great Depression, federal authority expanded.

State constitutions outline the structure of the state governments. They also have a section similar to the Bill of Rights that protects civil liberties. Most state constitutions have been revised and amended many more times than the federal Constitution.

The organization of state governments mirrors the structure of the federal government. They both have executive, legislative, and judicial branches. The governor is the chief executive of the state. Each state establishes its own qualifications for governors and legislators. In most cases, these qualifications include age and residency requirements.

The executive branch includes other elected officials besides the governor. Some are the lieutenant governor, secretary of state, attorney general, and treasurer.

State legislatures are responsible for passing laws for the states. The process of lawmaking at this level is almost the same as the process in the U.S. Congress.

State constitutions have built-in checks and balances. These include the governor's veto power, the legislature's right to impeach officials and approve executive appointments, and judicial review of state laws.

As is true for the federal government, a state government must have sources of revenue in order to operate and provide services. Most state revenues come from income taxes on individuals and corporations and sales taxes. Most collect fees for various licenses. Some receive money from lotteries. Expenditures for public education, welfare, highway building and maintenance, and law enforcement take up the largest chunks of state revenues.

States have established systems of courts that have jurisdiction over state laws. The local courts in towns and cities are often called municipal courts. The lowest state court is usually the trial court. At the next level is an intermediate appellate court. A supreme court is the highest court in a state. The names of the courts vary from state to state. Generally, the structure of the state court systems resembles the federal court structure. Judges at the various levels may be elected or appointed.

The state affects our lives directly through the funding of many services. The state is responsible for education, the licensing of many professionals, including teachers, and rules about driving, marriage, and voting. States have a major responsibility for maintaining an effective prison system.

States are divided into counties. They are responsible for providing services to county residents—welfare, education, law enforcement, parks. Counties are generally governed by an elected board or commission consisting of five to seven members. Other elected officials include the sheriff, district attorney, treasurer, and clerk. Many counties and cities have been given home rule authority by the states.

Cities exist because they have been granted charters by the state government to incorporate as a city. Constitutions, also called charters, set up the form of government for cities. The most popular form of city government is the mayor–council system. In some places, there is a strong-mayor–council system and in others, a weak-mayor–council plan. Some cities are governed by the council–manager form. Municipalities also have court systems that have jurisdiction over relatively minor matters. City governments are responsible for providing such services as the maintenance of local roads, garbage removal, a school system, and a health-care system. Zoning laws in cities regulate how land is used.

Towns and villages are smaller communities and divisions in the states. Citizens in these jurisdictions may vote directly on the laws they want and the way tax money is to be spent in the area. Cities, towns, and villages finance their operations mainly through property and sales taxes.

Special districts have been created to carry out specific purposes. In rural areas, special districts could be school districts that encompass several towns and villages. Other types of special districts provide for law enforcement, fire protection, and water systems.

In some states, citizens can directly affect policy making through the initiative, referendum, and recall. Initiatives allow citizens to suggest their own laws or amendments to the state constitution. The referendum allows citizens to vote on issues proposed by the legislature. For instance, if the legislature proposes a constitutional amendment or a bond issue, citizens have a right to vote for or against it. Recall makes it possible for citizens to remove a public official from office before the person's term is up.

Recent trends in local government promote cost cutting and efficiency through privatization of some services.

★ CHAPTER REVIEW ★

A. Matching
Match each term in Column A with its definition in Column B.

Column A
1. initiative
2. governor
3. Assembly
4. attorney general
5. selectman
6. city manager
7. mayor
8. recall
9. town meeting
10. city charter

Column B
a. name for one house of many state legislatures
b. elected chief executive of a city or village
c. process used to remove an elected official from office
d. a form of direct democracy
e. a way for citizens to propose a law
f. the constitution of a city
g. an official selected by a city council
h. chief executive of a state
i. elected government official in a town or township
j. official who handles a state's legal matters

B. Multiple Choice
Select the statement or word that most correctly answers the question or completes the statement.

1. The division of powers between the states and the federal government is called (a) federalism (b) checks and balances (c) concurrent (d) initiative.
2. This amendment leaves all powers not given to the federal government to the states: (a) Fourth (b) Fifth (c) Tenth (d) 14th.
3. The only unicameral state legislature is that of (a) Indiana (b) Colorado (c) Nebraska (d) Florida.
4. Many states elect a chief financial officer who is often called a (an) (a) governor (b) lt. governor (c) comptroller (d) attorney general.
5. This state subdivision helps deliver state services to residents of the subdivision: (a) township (b) county (c) special district (d) city.
6. Large urban centers are known as (a) counties (b) municipalities (c) townships (d) villages.

7. City courts are called (a) municipal courts (b) supreme courts (c) appellate courts (d) district courts.

8. In a strong-mayor–council government, the heads of city agencies are appointed by the (a) city council (b) Assembly (c) mayor (d) comptroller.

9. This type of district is often thought of as a special district: (a) municipal district (b) school district (c) county (d) city.

10. A voter-created movement to propose a law is called a (an) (a) recall (b) referendum (c) initiative (d) vote.

C. Essay
Write a paragraph about *one* of the following:

1. Privatization is the answer to government budget problems.
2. Voters should pay more attention to state and local issues than to national issues.
3. The relationship between the state and federal governments.
4. The town meeting is an effective way of governing a community.
5. The initiative and referendum are important tools that the average citizen can use to get involved in government decision making.

D. A Challenge for You
1. Write an editorial for a newspaper about the following topic: Counties and cities should be able to make policy decisions independently of the state.
2. Collect articles from newspapers, the Internet, and magazines that describe new trends in city government (for example, privatization). Summarize the articles. Explain how these trends might affect your community.
3. Attend a meeting of your city council or local governing body. Keep notes on the proceedings and report about your experience to the rest of the class.
4. Create a cartoon strip that explains how the town meeting works to further democracy.
5. Prepare a petition recommending a new law that you think should be passed. Explain how you would use the initiative process to get it on the ballot in your state.

Document-Based Question
State the main idea expressed in each document. Then use information in the documents and your own knowledge to write an essay on whether privatization makes sense.

The Drive Toward Privatization

Hundreds of municipalities have sold their garbage trucks and squeezed out public employees in favor of hiring companies to pick up, and dispose of, household trash. Small villages have turned to private contractors for fire protection and ambulance service. Large cities, including Atlanta and Los Angeles, have contemplated permitting the private sector to run, or even own, their sprawling international airports. The California state government has hired developers to build and operate toll roads. Private interests have studied construction of a magnetic-levitation train to flash back and forth from Orlando's airport [Florida] to the city's tourist center. In all cases, officials contemplate the possibility that outsiders can perform public services at less cost and with more efficiency than government.

Today's drive toward privatization is a reversal of earlier trends. A seemingly endless flow of federal and state funds to municipalities, beginning with Democratic President Franklin D. Roosevelt's Depression strategy in the 1930s and continuing through Democratic President Jimmy Carter's administration in the late 1970s, encouraged government expansion into nearly all areas of service delivery. The so-called new federalism of President Ronald Reagan's Republican administration in the 1980s brought that trend to an abrupt end, and federal funds to state and local governments dried up.

A survey of 1,100 counties and cities by . . . [a major] international management consulting firm, showed that virtually every government had privatized at least one service by the end of 1987. Privatization became exceptionally popular in the economic recession of the early 1990s, when cash-strapped governments embraced virtually any idea that could save them money.

Not a New Idea

The concept of privatization is not a new one. It has been tested and tinkered with since before the federal government contracted for pony express riders to deliver the mail. But many governments seemed to have forgotten this proven tool during the 1980s as they scrambled for solutions to their primary dilemma: meeting citizen demands for more services at a time when revenue sources were drying up.

While many governments not long ago began to tap privatization, private sector groups felt their potential to help governments was not being realized. In 1985, a group of individuals working in the fields of law, insurance, investment banking and consulting decided to play matchmaker and show both the public and private sectors why they were right for one another. They formed the Privatization Council as a forum for discussion between public and private administrators.

"Our philosophy holds that there are many problems that could be better resolved through public-private partnerships than through purely private or purely public efforts," explained Roger Feldman, Privatization Council vice chairman. "We believe that when private capital is involved in part of the solution of problems, there will be a high likelihood that efficiency of the process will be improved and benefits realized by the public will be improved." The council seeks to promote that message through research, education and debate, added . . . a council board member.

Both from *Issues Confronting City & State Governments* by Andy Oakley, pages 39–40, 43–44. Copyright 1994 by P.O. Publishing Co., Skokie, Ill.

UNIT 3

The Government and the Economy

How the Economic System Works

★ CHAPTER FOCUS

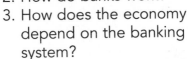

★ 1. How are the market, command, and mixed economic systems different from one another?

2. How do banks work?

3. How does the economy depend on the banking system?

4. What role does the Federal Reserve System play in the U.S. economy?

Just like the people in the cartoon on page 170, you and almost everyone else you know make decisions about money every day. You decide what to buy. You choose which bills to pay and when to pay them. You determine how much money to put into savings. Why do we have to make these decisions? It is because money, our income, is limited. Most people don't have enough to cover every want, and many cannot even meet their needs. So, everyone has to make choices about how to use his or her income. These choices affect each person's well-being—and the well-being of the whole economy.

The people in every nation produce and sell goods. Some of the goods may be manufactured in factories. Some may be grown in fields. People also provide and use services—from mowing lawns to setting broken legs. Producing and selling goods and services form the basis of the economy of a nation.

Every nation has to answer for itself the following questions: What goods and services should be produced? What quantity of each is needed? What methods should be used to produce the needed goods and service? How should the goods and services be distributed to the population? Who should receive the profits?

Over the centuries, these questions have been answered in a variety of ways. Some economic systems have proved to be more successful than others. The three most common systems that exist today are market, command, and mixed.

A Market Economy—Capitalism

Under a **market economy** system, the private citizen is given the most freedom to make decisions about how goods and services are produced. Other names for a market economy are **capitalism** and **free enterprise**. In a free enterprise system,

Budgeting and buying wisely helps keep us out of debt and prepared for the future.

people may choose the occupations they want to work in. They can own property and can dispose of it as they wish. They have the opportunity to study and work toward their own economic goals. Maybe you dream of opening your own business one day. It might be a travel agency, a diner, or a sheep farm. Under a capitalist system, private citizens can own and operate their own businesses. They have the opportunity to make and keep a profit from the business they run.

Production: What and How Much?

An important issue in an economic system is what to produce and how much to produce. When Nick and Suzette started Fast Trak Sneakers, they decided that their product would be fashionable and comfortable. They found a terrific location for the factory. The building is near major highways, so it is relatively easy to ship goods to customers and receive materials needed to make the sneakers.

Once they were ready to begin production, they had to establish the selling price of each style of sneaker. Under the free enterprise system, the amount they will manufacture and the selling price are really determined by the popularity of their sneakers. Nick and Suzette have the freedom to decide how much to charge. But they will base the prices on what buyers are willing to pay for the product. If consumers do

not like the sneakers, they will not buy them. If the sneakers do not sell, the company will not survive because it will not be able to meet expenses. Prices also reflect the cost of production, the profit they want to make on each pair, and what the competition is selling similar items for.

In a market economy system, the consumer is the ruler. This means that the consumer determines what products will be produced. If consumers like a product and believe that the price is reasonable, the product will sell. On the other hand, if consumers believe that the price is too high, the product will not sell even if they like the product. If the product does not sell, the manufacturer will not make a profit. The manufacturer may have to lower prices or create another product that will appeal to consumers. If none of these tactics works, the company may have to go out of business.

Profits

When people work for others, they earn wages in exchange for their labor. This is how people support themselves. People who own their own businesses need to earn a living, too. But how do business owners support themselves? They hope that their business will be successful and will make a profit. Profit is the money left over after a business pays for the cost of manufacturing a product or producing a service. The size of the

P O W E R *of* ★NE

Bill Gates

A free enterprise system allows the individual to take the initiative in business and to market the goods he or she thinks will appeal to consumers. The reward is profit. A person who has taken full advantage of the  free enterprise system—a capitalist—is William Henry Gates, III. He is a co-founder and chairman of the board of Microsoft, arguably the most successful computer software company in the nation, and possibly the world. Gates and Microsoft are revolutionizing how we communicate, how we do business, how we learn, and even how we socialize. How did he do it?

Born in Seattle, Washington, in 1955, Gates showed an interest in computers and in business at an early age. He and some friends (one was Paul Allen, a cofounder of Microsoft) started the Lakeside Programming Group. They went to their high school's computer center as much as they could. The group developed a computer program for their school's class schedules.

"Gates and his friends became so enamored of computers that they began rummaging through the trash bins at the nearby [computer company], hunting for scraps of paper left by programmers. 'Paul would hoist me on the garbage cans,' Gates recalled . . ., 'and I'd get the notes out with the coffee grounds on them and study the operating system.'" Gates and his friends found errors in the company's programs. After Gates wrote a 300-page manual outlining these errors, the company hired the boys. Gates and his friends later developed payroll systems and systems to measure the volume of vehicular traffic. Their efforts to sell traffic counting systems to cities met with some success at first. But when potential customers found out that the group was still in high school, they were reluctant to do business with the teenagers.

Gates took time off from high school to join a software company. (Software is a program that tells the computer how to perform a task the user wants it to do.) Within a year, he decided to finish high school and go on to Harvard University to study pre-law. But the attraction of computers proved to be too strong. Gates left Harvard and joined Paul Allen in another business venture.

They decided to adapt the computer language BASIC to a microcomputer that needed software. The business took off, and the name Microsoft was born. Other large companies asked Microsoft to develop software for them. Then came the huge boost that would eventually put the name Microsoft on the lips of almost every American. IBM (International Business Machines) asked Microsoft to develop a software system for its new line of microcomputers. After buying the rights to an existing program, Gates improved it and renamed it Microsoft Disk Operating System, or MS-DOS. Soon, other companies began to develop software that would be compatible with the MS-DOS system. Every time a company needed MS-DOS to develop software, it had to pay Microsoft for the rights. This made Microsoft very profitable.

By the time Bill Gates turned 31, he had become the youngest billionaire in the nation's history. His story is a classic account of how the free enterprise system allows an individual with good ideas to build a successful business. Gates's unique talents revolutionized the computer industry.

1. Why did Bill Gates decide to go into the software business?
2. How does a capitalist system allow a man like Gates to succeed?
3. Would he have been as successful under a command system such as communism? Why or why not?

profit depends on the health of the business and the overall economy. Under a free enterprise system, individuals who own businesses are free to make as large a profit as they can. If enough people are willing to pay for the item or service, the business will make money.

What is done with the profit depends on the owner. Some of the money goes to the owner for personal needs. A portion may be used to buy a new machine, hire a new employee, or increase the advertising budget. In a capitalist system, the individual is free to make these decisions. The government does not dictate what is to be done.

Competition

In a free enterprise system, anyone can set up another sneaker business to compete against Fast Trak. No one person or group controls the production of a particular good or service. The competitor's footwear may sell for less than Fast Trak's products. To keep their customers, Nick and Suzette must make sneakers that are better or cheaper than anyone else's. To do this, their manufacturing process may have to become more efficient to keep costs down. Thus, competition helps provide consumers with more choices at lower prices.

Let's Think

1. Define the following terms: economic system, market economy, free enterprise, capitalism.
2. Three elements of a market system are production, profit, and competition. Explain how each affects the way this system operates.
3. Competition is a major factor in determining the selling price of an item. Is this statement true? Why or why not?

The U.S. Government and the Market Economy

The Constitution gives Congress the power to regulate interstate commerce (trade between the states). In the 1800s, the government stood back and watched businesses grow larger and more powerful. Little was done to curb this power or to make sure that products were safe. Nor were the rights of workers protected. This "hands-off," or laissez-faire, attitude started to change in the early 1900s. Congress passed anti–big business and consumer protection laws. Government regulation gained strength in the 1930s through New Deal measures passed to combat the Great Depression. This trend lasted until the 1970s. Then a movement to cut back on the number of rules in order to increase competition and reduce the cost of doing business began to gain strength.

Deregulation

Starting in the 1970s, a number of industries that had been closely regulated by the federal government were **deregulated**. (This means that the government eliminated or reduced the number of rules that told businesses how they should or should not conduct their affairs.) These industries include communications, airlines, trucking, and utilities. At one time, AT&T provided both local and long-distance telephone service in almost all parts of the nation. In most areas, it was the only provider. A lawsuit allowed new companies to compete with AT&T to give people a wider choice of service with lower rates. Today, many cable television companies have gone into the telephone service business. In turn, phone companies such as Verizon have gone into the cable television business.

In the late 1970s, the regulations that limited airlines to certain routes and similar fare schedules were dropped. This deregulation of the airline industry allowed new airlines to be formed to compete with the older, larger airlines.

State government regulations on providers of electricity and natural gas have been lifted in many states. Competition in those industries has increased.

By giving consumers choices, competition allows them to seek out better service at lower prices. In order to compete successfully, companies will find less expensive ways of operating their businesses. Lower costs can also translate into increased profits.

AGENCY	FUNCTION
Food and Drug Administration (FDA) (Part of the Dept. of Health and Human Services)	Regulates the food and drug industries; establishes standards for the sale of healthy food and medical products
Federal Aviation Administration (FAA) (Part of the Dept. of Transportation)	Regulates the safety standards of the airline industry; operates air traffic control system
Federal Trade Commission (FTC) (Independent agency)	Promotes competition in interstate commerce; protects consumers; provides economic reports
Federal Communications Commission (FCC) (Independent agency)	Grants licenses to those who own and operate radio and television stations; supervises cable television, cellular phone services, satellite transmission facilities; regulates local telephone services

Continuing Regulation

Through a number of government agencies, the federal government continues to involve itself in the regulation of business. State and local governments have also passed laws that affect business operations. In many cases, the government has assumed a protective role—to prevent dangerous or unhealthful products being sold. The table above lists several major government agencies and their functions that affect businesses.

Another way the federal government involves itself in businesses is through the programs that provide pensions and medical care to people. Individual workers contribute part of their wages to Social Security and Medicare funds. Their employers must also put money into these funds on behalf of workers.

All levels of government affect businesses through their tax policies. High taxes cut into profits. Lower tax rates may make it possible for a marginally profitable operation to exist.

Regulation of business is a controversial issue. Some believe that regulations are unnecessary government interference that increases costs. Others disagree, saying that regulations are necessary to protect workers and the public in general from dishonest and unsafe practices.

Let's Think

1. What is meant by deregulation?
2. Why has deregulation caused much debate in the United States?

Command and Mixed Economies

A **command economy** is one in which the government makes almost all of the essential decisions about economic policies. This means that many of the major industries in a country are owned and operated by the government. Under such a system, decisions about how much and what to produce are made by the government. This was the type of system that existed in the Soviet Union before it broke up in 1990. The People's Republic of China also imposed a command system on its people until the mid-1990s. Cuba operates under this type of system, as does North Korea. The name for the command system in these countries is *communism*. A Communist country is normally headed by a dictator. The people cannot own property privately, and profits, in theory, cannot be made by individuals.

Socialism is another type of command system,

How Do Economic Systems Differ?

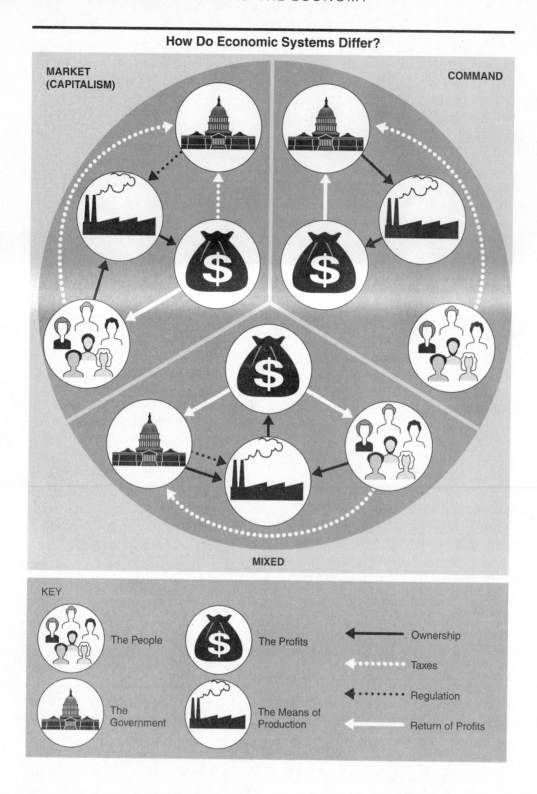

but it is less extreme than communism. Many governments, such as Sweden, that have this type of economic structure are democratic. Under socialism, major industries are owned and operated by the government. But many smaller businesses are in the hands of private individu-als. These businesses react to market conditions and consumer demand. Individuals can own property and make profits.

Today, most nations throughout the world have **mixed economies**. Under a mixed economy, government makes some economic decisions while the market system makes most others. The government may subsidize some industries, regulate business practices to protect the environment, and provide a wide variety of social welfare services. But economic power is mainly in the hands of private business owners. Some mixed-economy countries may be more command or socialist while others may be more market driven.

Let's Think

1. What is a command economy?
2. What is a mixed economy?
3. In which economy does the consumer have more power? Explain.

Money and Banks

People everywhere expect something of value in return for the products or services they create. Usually, the "something" is money. In the United States, money takes the form of bills and coins, both manufactured by the federal government. Money is a medium of exchange. This means that people are willing to accept coins or bills in exchange for products (goods) and services.

A person earns money through labor or receives it as a gift. The money is used to pay for necessities—food, clothing, and shelter—and other items that an individual needs or wants. A portion of earnings may be set aside as savings for future needs and wants.

Banks and the Economy

Have you ever thought about what happens to money after you purchase something for yourself? Money is used over and over again. The dollars you spend at the local record store for the latest CD will travel far. Some of the money may be set aside to pay a worker's salary, purchase more merchandise for the store, or settle the rent bill. The worker may take the money and use part of it to buy lunch. The cashier at the restaurant may give some of it in change to someone

else, who may use it to buy another product, and so on. Before a dollar bill is retired and replaced, it may have been in the hands of thousands of people and have traveled from one end of the country to another. (Of course, most people now use checks, credit cards, or debit cards rather than cash to pay for goods and services.) The flow of money from one person to another helps fuel the economic system. You can think of it as the gasoline that makes the engine that we call the economy run.

How does the money get from place to place? It is usually moved along by banks through our checking and credit card accounts.

How the System Works

Banks in our country operate under two different systems. All banks are given the right to operate by permission of either the federal or state governments. The right to operate is called a charter. Banks with a federal charter are members of the Federal Reserve System, which will be examined shortly. Banks granted state charters conduct business under state law within one state.

To see how the banking system works, let's assume that you want to buy a car that costs about $12,000. How do you pay for it? You could pack a suitcase with $12,000 in large bills and deliver it to the car dealer in person. Of course, you might be looking over your shoulder all the way to the dealership to check for potential robbers. Once the automobile dealership gets the case of money, it will have to find a safe place to put the cash in.

Paying for the car is made easier by banks. Instead of taking that suitcase full of money to the automobile dealer to purchase the car, all you have to do is take your checkbook and write a *check*. A check can be thought of as another form of currency.

To be able to use checks, you have to open a checking account in a bank. Here is how it works. You place, say, $15,000 into your checking account. Then, after negotiating the purchase of the automobile, you write a check for $12,000 and give it to the dealer. You shake hands, and the keys to the car are given to you. This is not the

Parts of a Check

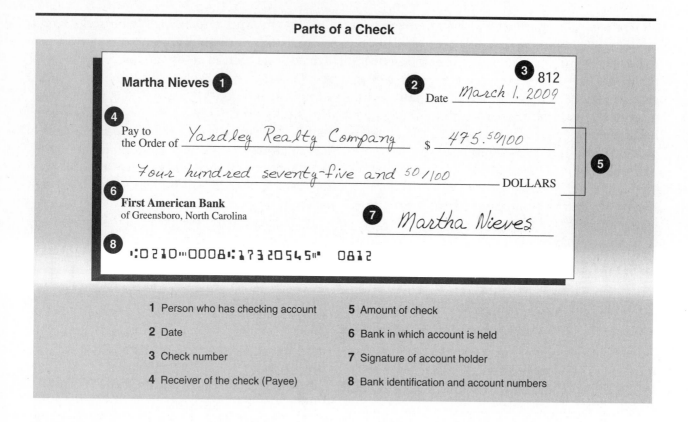

1 Person who has checking account	**5** Amount of check
2 Date	**6** Bank in which account is held
3 Check number	**7** Signature of account holder
4 Receiver of the check (Payee)	**8** Bank identification and account numbers

end of the story. The automobile dealer deposits the check in the checking account of the business. This means that it goes to the dealer's bank.

The check serves as a safe way to transfer money. When you write a check, you designate who will receive the funds. So, with proper identification, the person or business can cash the check or deposit it in a checking or savings account in a bank. Let us say that the dealer deposits the check in the Security Bank. The check was drawn on your bank, the More Money Bank. A check says that you have a certain amount of money on deposit in your checking account. Once the Security Bank gets the check, it has the money transferred to the dealer's account from your account in the More Money Bank. The $12,000 is now deducted from your account. The balance remaining is $3,000.

Checks provide a convenient method of moving money from one place to another in a safe and efficient way. They are used by individuals as well as by businesses. It is important to remember that if a person writes a check to pay a bill, he or she must have that amount of money deposited at the bank. Writing checks when you know that you do not have funds in the account is illegal.

How Banks Make Money

At this point, you may be wondering how a bank makes money. After all, banks are in business just like the factory in town or the movie theater or the local restaurant. They need money to pay their expenses. To get this money, banks make loans to people and businesses. In order to understand how lending money makes money, let us return to the Fast Trak Sneakers factory. Sales are up, and Suzette and Nick want to expand the business. They need money for the expansion. How will they get it? They go to their bank and ask for a loan. Because they have a good credit history and the business is sound, their application for the loan is approved.

When bankers examine a borrower's credit history, they are looking into the borrower's past ability to pay back loans. They ask such questions as did the borrower make payments to the lender on time? Did the borrower pay back the loan completely? Records are kept of this information, so a lender will check the record before granting a request for a loan. After all, if a borrower owes too much money, he or she might not be able to pay back a new loan. Suzette and Nick get the loan and go ahead with their expansion plans.

In exchange for the loan, Fast Trak has to pay back the amount of the loan plus an amount of money over and above the original loan. The original amount borrowed is called the *principal*. The extra amount above the principal is called **interest**. Fast Trak borrows $10,000 and agrees to pay the loan back in one year. For the use of the money, the bank adds on interest equal to 7 percent of the $10,000. By the end of the year, Fast Trak must pay to the bank a total of $10,700. The $700 is the profit the bank makes on this loan.

The money to make loans comes from savings accounts, extra funds in checking accounts, and bank earnings. In return for your permission to allow the bank to lend out your money, the bank promises to pay you a fee. This fee is also called interest. Therefore, by putting money into a savings account, you can earn money on your savings. The bank lends this money to others and charges them interest on their loans.

Let's Think

1. What kinds of services does a bank provide?
2. Why do banks charge interest on the loans they make?

3. Why would a lender check a person's credit history?

The Federal Reserve System

In the early 1900s, the nation recognized a need for a uniform national banking system. To meet this need, Congress passed the Federal Reserve Act in 1913. It set up the Federal Reserve System. The purpose was to create a solid currency and give people confidence in the banking system.

The Federal Reserve System (Fed) can be thought of as a bank for bankers. It lends money to member banks. Through its loans and the interest it charges on the loans, the Fed has the power to influence banks throughout the United States and the economy in general. The Fed requires banks to follow certain procedures when they make loans and conduct their business. The requirements apply mainly to federally chartered banks and those state chartered banks that have chosen to be part of the system.

The Structure of the Fed

The Federal Reserve System is organized into 12 District Reserve Banks. As you can see from the map below, the banks are located in several

Districts of the Federal Reserve System

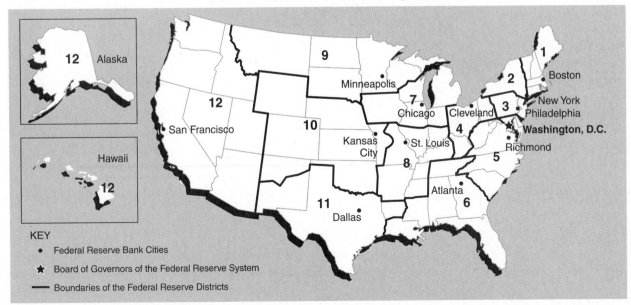

KEY
● Federal Reserve Bank Cities
★ Board of Governors of the Federal Reserve System
— Boundaries of the Federal Reserve Districts

◄REALITY CHECK►

The Credit Crisis of 2008–2009

Imagine what life might be like if you or your parents could not borrow money. How could you buy a home or car or finance a college education? How might a business owner run a business or expand it if she or he could not obtain loans? Individuals would not be able to make major purchases. Businesses would not be able to operate. The economy might come to a standstill. This is what came dangerously close to happening in the United States and countries throughout the world in 2008–2009.

Many say this economic crisis had its roots in the housing market. During the 1990s and the first half of the 2000s, the prices of homes rose to new heights. More and more people were eager to buy homes before they were outpriced. Some of those people did not have enough income to be able to obtain a conventional **mortgage** from a bank or another lending institution. (Such a mortgage is a loan agreement that calls for the buyer to make a cash down payment of a certain amount, often 10 or 20 percent, and then the bank lends the balance of the purchase price to the buyer at a fixed interest rate. The loan must be repaid within a certain number of years, usually 20 or 30.)

Many home buyers did not have the best *credit rating*. This is a measure of one's ability to repay loans. Some people had debts that were too high for their income. Others might have defaulted on a debt in the past. Because a mortgage is a loan that is guaranteed by the home that is purchased, banks that grant a mortgage in effect become partners with the purchaser of the home.

Unfortunately, many people took out mortgages under conditions that were less than ideal. Banks and mortgage companies, seeing that the value of homes had skyrocketed, believed they could make profitable loans to people who could not really afford the terms of the loan. Many of these mortgages are called *subprime loans*. This means that the borrower had less than the financial resources required for a conventional mortgage. Some mortgages were the type that kept monthly payments low for only a few years, and then borrowers had to make much higher payments. People took out such mortgages in the belief that their income would increase and that they could afford the higher payments in the future. They also felt that if this did not happen, they could sell the home at a profit and still pay back the bank.

The "gambles" by both lenders and borrowers backfired. Many homeowners soon found that they could not pay their mortgages, and banks began foreclosure proceedings against those properties. Many people's homes were foreclosed on.

The defaults on the loans proved to be a problem for the banks. They were not getting their money back. If banks do not receive ongoing payments, they cannot make loans to others. Banks do not want to be owners of homes because their business is to lend money. There-

---

major cities throughout the United States. Each of the banks is supervised by its own board of directors.

A seven-member governing body directs the activities of the Fed. It is known as the Board of Governors. Each member is appointed by the president with the approval of the Senate for a 14-year term. One of the members is named chair for a period of four years. The term can be renewed.

The Functions of the Fed

The Fed monitors banks by making rules about the reserve amount of money each must keep on hand. It sets interest rates through the amount it charges banks for loans.

Reserve Ratio

All banks that are members of the Federal Reserve System are required to follow specific

fore, they needed to sell foreclosed properties as soon as they could. Foreclosed houses were priced lower than comparable homes that were for sale in a neighborhood. This had the effect of lowering the value of *all* houses on the real estate market. Soon, there was a glut of houses for sale and few buyers.

Many banks found themselves without the ability to lend money. This situation can cause banks to go out of business. The whole economy faced the danger of a major slowdown because businesses and individuals could not borrow money. Some major financial institutions began to falter. Many other companies foundered. One of the largest insurance companies in the United States nearly imploded. Some banks failed. Others were bought by banks that were in better financial shape.

The money problems soon produced a lack of confidence in the banking and financial system. The entire economy went into crisis mode. Stock prices plummeted. The situation became so serious that many feared a depression similar to the Great Depression of the 1930s.

In the fall of 2008, the Federal Reserve Bank took action to reduce the pressures on the economy. It lowered the interest rate at which banks borrow money from the Fed. But this did not calm the crisis. Congress was forced to step in. It passed a $700 billion "bailout" bill, which was signed by President George W. Bush. Among other things, this Emergency Economic Stabilization Act of 2008 authorized the secretary of the treasury to purchase the bad debts of banks so banks would have cash to conduct their business. The hope was that if the government stepped in and helped banks and other financial institutions, money would become available to circulate throughout the economy.

Another provision provided help to many people in danger of losing their homes. A relatively small number of home owners were permitted to renegotiate their mortgages if they faced foreclosure. In order to restore confidence in the banking system, the government (through the Federal Deposit Insurance Corporation—FDIC) temporarily increased the protection for individual savings accounts from $100,000 to $250,000.

Critics of the government's efforts said that it was doing too little, too late. They said that there should have been more government regulations to prevent the financial system from collapsing as it did. Critics also did not think so much money should be spent to bail out banks. "Bail out Main Street, not Wall Street!" and "Protect the average citizen, not big business!" were common slogans in late 2008.

By the time Barack Obama became president in January 2009, only half of the $700 billion from the bailout act had been spent. Obama got Congress to pass the $789 billion Economic Stimulus Bill. He and many others felt that the government was not doing enough to stimulate the economy. What was needed, they claimed, was massive spending. The Economic Stimulus Bill was soon passed.

1. What problems occurred when banks could not lend money to people and businesses?
2. How did the lending practices of banks lead to the banking crisis?
3. What steps did the Emergency Economic Stabilization Act of 2008 call for to help restore confidence in the banking system?
4. Why were there differences of opinion about the steps taken by the federal government in 2008 and 2009?

---

rules established by the Fed. As you know, banks handle large amounts of money every day. To make sure banks stay healthy, the Fed does not allow a member bank to lend out all of its money. A bank is required to deposit a certain amount with its regional Federal Reserve Bank. This is called the *reserve ratio*. Having a reserve ratio makes sure that money is available for the needs of a bank's customers. Through the reserve ratio, the Fed can monitor the amount of money in circulation. If the reserve ratio is raised, the Fed banks have less money to use to make loans. This action has the effect of removing money from circulation.

Discount Rate

At times, banks themselves need loans. They get the money from the Fed. The amount of interest banks pay to the Fed for the loans is called the *discount rate*. When the Board of Governors determines that there are indications of inflation, it raises the discount rate. This takes money out of circulation and stabilizes prices.

Inflation is seen as an undesirable condition that makes it more costly to do business and that creates higher costs for consumers. Generally, inflation means that prices are rising. When this happens, the value of money declines. How does the Fed determine if the rate of inflation is too high? It looks at several economic indicators. A few are how much manufacturers are selling their goods to retailers for, the unemployment rate, and how much debt consumers are accumulating (through credit card purchases, for example). By conducting such studies on a regular basis, the Fed can determine the direction interest rates should take to keep the economy healthy.

If the cost of loans to banks increases, banks may borrow less money. Or, if they do go ahead with the loans, they pass along the increased costs of their loans to the consumer. They increase the interest rates on loans they give out. The higher costs most likely cause consumers to slow their borrowing rate. This also takes money out of the economy.

Once the economy slows down, there may be a need to increase the amount of money in circulation. This can be accomplished by lowering the discount rate and allowing member banks to borrow more money and charge lower interest rates to customers.

Lower prices tend to help the economy. When the economy is slow, the Fed reduces the discount rate. This leads to more loans because member banks have more money to give out to customers.

Let's Think

1. What is the Federal Reserve System?
2. What is the length of the term for members of the Federal Reserve Board and the Chairman of the Board?
3. Identify the following terms: reserve ratio, discount rate.
4. What role does the Federal Reserve System play in maintaining a healthy economy in the United States?

Chapter Summary

Producing and selling goods and services form the basis of the economy of a nation. The type and quantity of goods produced and how they are distributed are determined by the economic system of the nation. The three most common types of economic systems today are the market, command, and mixed systems.

The system that provides for the greatest freedom of individual decision making is the market system, or capitalism. In it the means of production and distribution are privately owned. The owners can keep the profits they make. The consumer determines what is manufactured and what is sold. If the consumer does not buy an item, the manufacturer will not produce it. The United States, to a large degree, functions under a market system. It is also called the free enterprise system. Competition keeps prices down and quality up.

In the United States, the government regulates certain types of businesses and business practices. It protects workers' rights and collects taxes from businesses.

Another economic system is the command system. In it the decisions about what to produce are made by the government. Communism is an extreme form of command system. Under communism, the government owns all the major industries and determines what will be produced. A Communist country is usually a dictatorship. The former Soviet Union operated under this system. Today, the nations of Cuba and North Korea have Communist economies.

Socialism is a milder form of command system. In socialist countries, the major industries are owned and operated by the government while private ownership of smaller businesses is permitted. Some European nations operate under such a system.

A mixed economy operates under the principle that some government decision making is needed and should be blended with the private enterprise system. In a mixed economy, government-sponsored social welfare programs are created. Most industrialized nations today follow a mixed system.

Banks are an essential element of the economic system of the United States. They provide a safe place to keep money, and they give out loans to businesses and private individuals. The borrower pays a fee called interest on a loan. Checks are an efficient and convenient means of moving money from place to place.

The Federal Reserve System is called a bankers' bank. It is the national banking system of the United States. The Fed is divided into 12 districts and is headed by a Board of Governors and a chair. It helps regulate the flow of money in the United States. Most banks are required to follow the regulations set by the Federal Reserve System. When banks need money, they can borrow from the Fed. Banks that borrow money from a Federal Reserve bank pay an interest rate called the discount rate. Banks are also required to maintain a certain amount of money in their accounts. This is known as the reserve ratio.

The Federal Reserve Board meets periodically to examine the health of the national economy. Sometimes it finds that it must make adjustments in interest rates or loans to prevent inflation. Sometimes the economy is sluggish, and the Fed may decide to give it a boost. How does the Fed do this? It raises or lowers the interest rates. This increases or limits the amount of money in circulation and tends to raise or lower prices.

★ CHAPTER REVIEW ★

A. Matching
Match each term in Column A with its definition in Column B.

Column A
1. market economy
2. command system
3. bank
4. communism
5. mixed economy
6. deregulation
7. socialism
8. reserve ratio
9. interest
10. check

Column B
a. system in which the government controls the means of production and makes almost all economic decisions
b. free enterprise system is another name for this type of economy
c. an extreme form of command economy
d. business that provides loans and checking and savings accounts for customers
e. system in which both the government and markets make economic decisions
f. fee paid for a loan
g. the amount of money a bank must keep at a regional Federal Reserve Bank
h. the process of reducing or eliminating laws that affect business practices
i. a convenient and efficient means of transferring money
j. economic system in which only the major industries are controlled by the government

B. Multiple Choice
Select the statement or word that most correctly answers the question or completes the statement.

1. The way a nation makes decisions about producing and distributing goods and services is called a (an) **(a)** economic system **(b)** deregulation system **(c)** banking system **(d)** Federal Reserve System.

2. The money the owner of a company has left after paying expenses is called **(a)** interest **(b)** reserve ratio **(c)** profit **(d)** discount rate.

3. The U.S. government affects the economy most directly through **(a)** inflation **(b)** the Federal Reserve System **(c)** government ownership of industries **(d)** the Agriculture Department.

4. The economic system that promotes the idea that the government should not regulate the economy is **(a)** socialism **(b)** communism **(c)** mixed economy **(d)** laissez-faire capitalism.

5. Private ownership of property is generally not permitted in this economic system: **(a)** capital-

ism **(b)** communism **(c)** monarchy **(d)** dictatorship.

6. One of the few nations that still operate under a Communist system is **(a)** Thailand **(b)** Canada **(c)** Cuba **(d)** France.

7. Communism is an example of this economic system: **(a)** capitalism **(b)** command economy **(c)** federal reserve **(d)** laissez-faire capitalism.

8. Banks affect the economy in the following way. They **(a)** tell factories what to produce **(b)** help circulate money **(c)** provide for the general welfare of all people **(d)** create the federal budget.

9. The number of regional banks in the Federal Reserve System is **(a)** 5 **(b)** 10 **(c)** 12 **(d)** 15.

10. Inflation brings about **(a)** decreasing prices **(b)** increasing prices **(c)** balanced budgets **(d)** early repayment of loans.

C. Essay

Write a paragraph about *one* of the following:

1. In a market economy, the consumer is "king."

2. Capitalism provides more freedom for the individual than communism.

3. Socialism is a blend of economic systems.

4. The Federal Reserve System helps control the amount of money in circulation.

D. A Challenge for You

1. Write an editorial for a newspaper on the following topic: "Deregulation of the American economy is an important economic issue."

2. Create a scrapbook of articles about the policies established by the Federal Reserve System for a period of a few months. Summarize the articles. How will these policies affect you and your community?

3. Create a pictorial display for the bulletin board to show what happens to a paper bill or a check after either is used to purchase a product or service.

4. Get a loan application from a bank. Describe the type of information that the bank asks for. Why do you think the bank wants all of this information? Should banks be allowed to ask for this type of information? Why or why not?

Document-Based Question

State the main idea expressed in each document. Then use information in the documents and your own knowledge to write an essay explaining why the Federal Reserve System was created.

The Need for a Central Banking System

Banking in the America of 1863 was far from easy or dependable. The First Bank (1791–1811) and the Second Bank (1816–1836) of the United States were the only official representatives of the U.S. Treasury—the only sources that issued and backed official U.S. money. All other banks were operated under state charter, or by private parties. Each bank issued its own individual "banknotes." All of the state and private banks competed with each other and the two U.S. Banks to make sure that their notes were redeemable for full face value. As you traveled around the country, you never knew exactly what kind of money you would get from the local banks. With America's population growing in size, mobility, and economic activity, this multiplicity of banks and kinds of money soon grew chaotic.

In 1863, Congress passed the first National Bank Act providing for a supervised system of "National Banks." The act set up [operating] standards for the banks, established minimum amounts of capital to be held by the banks, and defined how the banks were to make and administer loans. In addition, the Act imposed a 10 percent tax on state banknotes, thus effectively eliminating non-federal currency from circulation.

From *The Federal Reserve System, History, Function & Organization*. Copyright 1999 by About.com, Inc.

The Fed Is Created

Put most simply, the Federal Reserve System is the central bank of the United States. Congress created the Federal Reserve through a law passed in 1913, charging it with **a responsibility to foster a sound banking system and healthy economy**. . . . To accomplish its mission, the Fed serves as a banker's bank and as the government's bank, as a regulator of financial institutions and as the nation's money manager, performing a vast array of functions that affect the economy, the financial system, and ultimately, each of us. . . .

With this complicated system of checks and balances, the Federal Reserve is the unmistakable offspring of the American political process. Congress created the System in 1913 in an effort to respond to the needs of a growing U.S. economy, and to avoid cyclical patterns of booms and busts that had characterized much of the 1800s. By the early 1900s there was general consensus that the country needed a central bank, but little agreement on how to structure it. As a result, the creation of the Federal Reserve turned into a legislative tug-of-war marked by frequent disagreement, occasional suspicion, but in the end, compromise. Eventually, the Fed—basically a creature borne of compromise—emerged with a structure designed to reconcile the needs, fears, and prejudices of many different interests.

From *The Fed: Our Central Bank*, Federal Reserve Bank of Chicago, April 1994.

CHAPTER 11

How Government Is Financed

1. Why do governments need money?
2. How do governments raise revenue?
3. What are the different types of taxes?
4. How do governments borrow money?

Your community needs to repave a busy street and build a new elementary school. State officials are talking about repairing the bridge on the turnpike outside of town and developing a new state park nearby. The federal government wants to give a raise to National Park Service employees who work in the parks. It also wants to buy new equipment for the scientists at the Disease Control Centers who are working on a cure for AIDS. Where does the money come from to pay for these and other government expenses?

The Government Needs Money to Function

Just as your family needs money to pay for food and housing, governments also require money. They must pay their operating expenses and provide services we need and want. Where do the

funds come from? Governments can't just print money whenever they need it. To do so would make money worthless and cause chaos in the economy. To get funds to operate, all levels of government impose taxes on individuals and businesses.

Article I, Section 8, of the U.S. Constitution gives Congress the "power to lay and collect taxes, duties, imposts and excises to pay the debts and provide for the common defense and general welfare of the United States. . . ." It also gives Congress the power "to borrow money on the credit of the United States." Thus, the Constitution provides for a centralized method of raising and borrowing money when needed.

State and local governments share the power to tax. The Tenth Amendment gives them this concurrent power. If states were not permitted this function, they would be completely dependent on the federal government for funds. The Framers of the Constitution and the state leaders did not believe that this would be a desirable situation.

Citizenship and Taxes

Everyone hates to pay taxes. Then why do we pay them? First of all, it is against the law not to. Also, we know that governments provide services that we want. It takes money to supply the services. So, if people refuse to pay taxes or if the government did not have the power to levy taxes, it could not function. Paying taxes, then, is an obligation that goes along with being a good citizen.

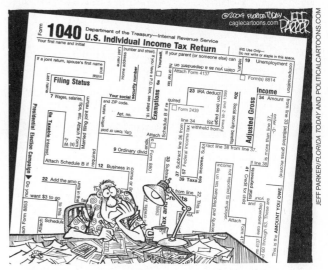

The IRS may not be liked by every taxpayer, but it is considered to be one of the most efficient tax collection agencies in the world.

Let's Think

1. Which section of the Constitution allows Congress to collect taxes?
2. Which amendment to the Constitution permits the state governments to collect taxes?
3. Why do both the state and federal governments need the power to levy taxes?

Types of Taxes

All levels of government use a variety of types of taxes to raise revenue. The two types of taxes that bring in the most money are the income tax and the sales tax.

Income Taxes

A major source of revenue for the national and state governments is the personal **income tax**. This is a tax placed on the money we earn. For most people, it is collected during the course of the year by our employers. They withhold money from our paychecks and send it on to the various levels of government. The federal agency that collects and monitors income taxes is the *Internal Revenue Service (IRS)*. Federal tax rates are set by Congress.

Most states also collect income taxes. As of 2009, only Alaska, Florida, Nevada, South Dakota, Texas, Washington, and Wyoming had not levied such a tax. (New Hampshire and Tennessee only tax income from interest and dividends.) Each state determines its own tax rates and method of collection.

Corporations also pay taxes on income. Such taxes are imposed on the profits the corporation makes from selling products or services. Both the federal and state governments tax corporations. Tax rates vary.

The income tax is a **progressive tax**. A progressive tax is one that increases in percentage as one's income goes up. Those who earn more money each year will, in theory, pay more taxes because their tax rate is higher. Those who earn less money annually will pay a smaller amount of taxes because their tax rate is lower.

Criticism of Income Taxes

In recent years, the federal income tax has come under criticism. Many say that the tax laws are very complicated and the forms a taxpayer must fill out are hard to understand.

Part of the problem is related to the system of

TYPES OF REVENUE TAXES

TYPE OF TAX	STATE	FEDERAL
Income	Yes	Yes
Excise	Yes	Yes
Sales	Yes	No
Inheritance	Yes (some states)	Yes
Estate	Yes (some states)	Yes
Gift	Yes (some states)	Yes

deductions taxpayers are allowed to take to lower their tax rate. Certain expenses, such as charitable contributions and interest on home mortgages, can be subtracted (or deducted) from your income before taxes are paid to the government. This has the effect of lowering the income that would be taxed. The lower the income, the lower the tax that will be paid. Some argue that the current system of deductions is unfair. This is because those with higher incomes have the ability to take more deductions than those with more modest incomes.

Others argue that the federal income tax rate in general is too high and should be lowered. The government, they say, does not need to spend so much money. It should cut expenses so that it can lower taxes.

Flat Tax

To counteract the criticism aimed at the current income tax system, some have proposed a **flat tax**. This means that all incomes, high or low, would be taxed at the same rate. Therefore, if you earned $10,000 and the rate was 8 percent, you would pay $800. If you earned $100,000, you would also pay 8 percent, or $8,000.

Those who support the flat tax argue that it would simplify the system. It would eliminate or greatly reduce the number of loopholes and deductions that exist in the current income tax system. Others claim that a flat tax would lower the taxes paid by the wealthy and increase the burden on the less well-to-do.

Excise Taxes

Excise taxes are taxes placed on the manufacture or sale of certain goods and services. Among the most common types of items subject to excise taxes are tobacco, alcohol, gasoline, and airline tickets. The tax has the effect of increasing the sales price of these goods. This type of tax does not make allowances for the level of income of those who use the products that are taxed. Rich or poor, you pay the same tax when you buy a gallon of gasoline. Obviously, a person earning $50,000 a year would find it less of a burden to pay a 50-cent-a-gallon tax than a person earning

$15,000 a year would. Thus, an excise tax is termed a **regressive tax**. Because an excise tax is part of the selling price, people do not always notice that they are paying it. Such a tax that seems to be hidden is said to be an **indirect tax**.

Customs Duties

The federal government also collects revenue on goods brought in from other countries. These **custom duties**, also known as **tariffs**, are paid on goods manufactured outside of the United States. For example, imported clothing, television sets, and automobiles all have a tariff placed on them.

Sales Taxes

The **sales tax** is a tax on goods and services. This tax is set at a fixed percentage of the selling price. The U.S. government currently does not levy a sales tax on goods and services. However, state and local governments use the sales tax to raise revenue for their expenses. Five states have no general sales tax.

The items that are taxed vary from state to state. Food items and prescription and nonprescription drugs are not usually taxed. The sales tax is another example of a tax that applies equally to all people regardless of their income level. In other words, it is a regressive tax.

Estate and Gift Taxes

Most people try to save part of their income for future use. They plan for retirement, to buy a home, or to have funds on hand in case of an emergency. Sometimes people accumulate more money than they spend during their lifetime. When they die, the money is passed along to their loved ones and to charities. This is an example of one economic right that all Americans enjoy. It is the right to "transfer and dispose of their property as they see fit." The people who receive such gifts have to pay a federal **inheritance tax** if the value of the gifts or inheritance is more than $3.5 million. Property that might be taxed includes real estate, cash, jewelry, and other personal possessions. Both federal and state govern-

P O W E R *of* ★ NE

Christina Romer

Imagine that you are distinguished professor of economics at a major university. One day you get a call offering you a job in the administration of the newly elected president of the United States. It would be your responsibility as head of a team of experts to come up with policies to prevent an economic collapse. Such an offer came to Professor Christina Romer of the University of California at Berkeley shortly after Barack Obama was elected president in 2008. Romer had actively supported Obama during the election campaign. Obama respected Romer and her ideas.

The actual position she was asked to assume was chair of the Council of Economic Advisers. The Council is composed of three people the president deems qualified to give advice and ideas about economic matters. It is the Council's responsibility to study the state of the nation's economy and prepare a report for the president. The Council also gives the president and the budget director ideas about what to include in the annual national budget. The Council's members hope their ideas will keep the economic life of the nation on a healthy course.

Born Christina Duckworth on December 25, 1958, in Alton, Illinois, Romer went on to attend the College of William and Mary in Virginia. There she earned a bachelor's degree in economics in 1981. Four years later, she earned a Ph.D. in economics from the Massachusetts Institute of Technology (MIT). Then Romer obtained a position as Associate Professor of Economics at Princeton University in New Jersey. In 1988, she moved west to teach at the University of California at Berkeley, eventually becoming a full professor.

Romer is a *macroeconomist*. This means that she views economic issues from a wide perspective, often trying to analyze how certain factors affect the entire nation, not just one area. She has written many scholarly articles on monetary policy and economic ups and downs in the 20th century. A recent book of hers is about the impact of the New Deal on the United States. The New Deal was the economic plan created by President Franklin D. Roosevelt in the 1930s to help the nation climb out of the Great Depression. Many scholars have praised her work. At a time in U.S. history when the nation was faced with serious economic problems, it seemed appropriate to President Obama to bring into the government an economist who had studied the Great Depression. Although the circumstances were different, the problems were similar. As a major player on the president's economic team, Romer has much to say about the government's economic policies.

Newspaper columnists and political observers praised the selection of Romer to be part of the new administration. She has broad appeal among both Democrats and Republicans.

1. What is the Council of Economic Advisers?
2. What qualifications did Christina Romer have to become chair of the Council?
3. What are Romer's responsibilities as chair?

ments collect inheritance taxes. They are also called **estate taxes**.

Large monetary gifts are also taxed. As you might guess, such levies are called **gift taxes**. Any gift over $12,000 is taxed by the federal government. Some states also collect a gift tax. The purpose of the tax is to prevent people from trying to avoid the estate tax by distributing large portions of property before they die. By doing this, the value of the estate would be decreased, and the taxes due on it would be less.

Social Security and Medicare

We have learned that a certain amount of money is withheld from our paychecks for federal and state income taxes. Other deductions are made for Social Security and Medicare insurance. Social Security is the program that provides retired workers and their spouses with a pension. In addition to the pension, it provides for survivor's benefits, payments for workers who are disabled, and benefits for the spouses and children of workers. As of 2009, Social Security taxes were levied on all income up to $106,800. Employers match the contributions made by workers.

Medicare is a federal medical insurance program for citizens 65 and over. It was created to ensure that people would have medical and hospital care in their later years. For Medicare, all earned income is taxed.

Property Taxes

An important source of revenue for state and local governments is the **property tax**. This tax is levied on the value of real estate (property). The types of property taxed include homes, office buildings, farms, malls, and factories. Officials called assessors determine what the value of a piece of property is. The tax rate is decided by the local legislature.

Other Sources of Revenues

States collect tolls on roadways and bridges. These funds are often used to help maintain the transportation system of the state.

Another way states raise money is through li-

cense fees. They include driver's licenses and professional licenses. Professional licenses are needed to practice dentistry, medicine, and pharmacy. One also needs a license to sell real estate or be a hairdresser. These license fees not only raise revenue, they also help maintain standards within a profession or occupation. Generally, one must pass a state-sponsored examination to obtain a professional license.

In recent years, states have resorted to nontraditional methods of raising revenue. Many states have instituted lotteries. An increasing number of states also allow casino gambling in a limited number of locations.

To participate in a lottery, people buy tickets. They hope that the numbers they select will be chosen in the daily or weekly drawings and that they will win large sums of money. The money the states receive from the sale of the lottery tickets is greater than the amount of prize money they give out. The states keep the difference. This money is used to pay for various government expenses or special programs. Many states use the funds to help finance education.

Lottery programs have their critics. People argue that those who can least afford to spend income on lottery tickets are the ones who buy them. Some people are addicted to gambling. State-sanctioned lotteries make it easy for individuals with this problem to spend too much on a bad habit.

States that permit casino gambling carefully regulate this industry. The taxes collected from casino operations are another source of revenue for states.

Let's Think

1. What is an income tax?
2. Why is the income tax said to be a progressive tax?
3. Explain each of the following taxes: excise, sales, inheritance.
4. Why are excise and sales taxes considered to be regressive taxes?

Taxes Serve Several Functions

Governments use the tax system to do more than raise revenues. Tax policies can promote or restrict certain personal and social behaviors. They can also affect the health of the economy.

Taxes and Behavior

Taxes may be used to influence the way people behave. High taxes on certain products may keep people from buying these items or, at least, from purchasing them in large quantities. Governments may want to discourage the use of cigarettes and alcoholic beverages, so they put high taxes on these products.

Traditionally, the government has promoted the building of private homes. It also wants to encourage people to buy homes. In order to buy a home, most people take out a bank loan called a mortgage. They pay interest on the loan. The government allows a home owner to deduct the amount paid in mortgage interest from his or her income. Thus, the income subject to tax is reduced as is the amount of tax that must be paid. By allowing the mortgage interest deduction, the government gives people an incentive to buy their dream houses. Home owners are thought to be stable citizens who will take an interest in keeping their communities in good shape.

By following certain guidelines and formulas, a taxpayer can deduct from taxable income the amount contributed to legitimate charitable organizations. Such a policy on the part of the government encourages gifts to charities, educational institutions, and other nonprofit groups.

Taxes and the Economy

It is usually in the government's and the nation's interest to encourage businesses to expand their production or develop new products. When businesses are successful, they employ more people and help keep the economy healthy. Corporate tax laws may allow deductions for money used to develop new products, buy more modern machinery, or build new factories.

Tax policies may help dreams come true.

Let us return to the Fast Trak Sneakers company for a moment. Nick and Suzette, the principal owners of Fast Trak, recently applied for a loan to expand the business. Corporate tax laws allow business owners to deduct the interest on business loans from their income when determining how much they owe the government in taxes. If Nick and Suzette could not have deducted the interest, they might not have taken out the loan or expanded the business. In a sense, you might say, the tax system encouraged them to expand.

The federal government can influence the amount of money in circulation through the tax system. Assume there is inflation. If the income tax rate goes up, people will have less money to spend. If there is less money in circulation, prices tend to stay the same or decrease. Sometimes, the economy needs to be stimulated and consumer spending encouraged. When this is the case, the government may decide to lower taxes. If taxes go down, people have more money to spend or save.

Let's Think

1. Name three functions of a tax policy.
2. How does tax policy influence the way people behave?
3. How can tax policy help or hurt a business?

The Government Borrows Money

United States Savings Bonds are issued in various amounts.

Your family wants to buy a new automobile or a new house. How do they get the money? Most of us need to borrow the funds from a bank or another lending service. Even when we go to buy clothes or new CDs, we borrow the money to make our purchase if we use a credit card. People borrow money all the time to pay for things they need and want. It is hoped that they make wise buying decisions and are able to pay the loan off in the proper amount of time.

Just as people take out loans to pay for purchases, the government finds it necessary to borrow money to pay its expenses. Although the government collects taxes of all kinds to pay for its operations, it does not always collect enough. To bridge the gap between the revenue that the government receives and what is actually needed to make ends meet, the federal government takes out loans. It is authorized to do this under Article I, Section 8, of the Constitution. This gives Congress the power "to borrow money on the credit of the United States." State and local governments also borrow money to meet expenses.

Securities

The government borrows money by issuing paper notes for sale to individuals, corporations, and banks. These promises to pay are called *securities*. Federal government securities include savings bonds and treasury bills, notes, and bonds. Savings bonds can be bought in small or large amounts. This encourages people at many different levels of income to invest in them.

The interest paid by the government is not usually as great as that paid by private companies. Investors are willing to make a little less

money on their investment in exchange for safety. After all, the government is less likely to go out of business than a private company is, and it has its taxing power to use to pay back the loan.

States Borrow Money

State governments also find it necessary to borrow money. One method of borrowing is to issue **bonds**, a type of security. Bonds are usually earmarked for special purposes. A few examples are environmental cleanup, new college dormitories, new school buildings, bridges, and highways. The legislature may pass a law authorizing the sale of bonds, or the public may vote on whether or not to borrow the money. (This vote is called a referendum. See page 159.) If approved, the bonds will be put up for sale. The interest on the bonds is guaranteed to the lender over a specified number of years. At the end of this time, the holder of the bond can turn it in and receive the original investment plus the interest.

Let's Think

1. Why do governments find it necessary to borrow money?
2. How does the federal government borrow through savings bonds and treasury securities?
3. What kinds of instruments do states use to borrow money?
4. Why do individuals find government securities attractive investments?

The Federal Government Prepares a Budget

Your family earns a certain amount of money each week or month or year. This money is spent to pay the mortgage or rent, buy food, and purchase clothing. Other expenses include paying the gas and electric companies, meeting loan payments for a new car, and saving for a vacation and college.

Budgeting

We need to make choices when we spend money. There is usually not enough money for all the things that we want or need. Then we have to decide what is necessary and what we can get along without. Families often create a plan to help them spend their money wisely. This plan is called a **budget**. In creating a budget, people decide the length of time it will last, how much money is available, and the amount of the bills that must be paid. A budget helps us approach spending in an organized way.

In much the same way that individuals create budgets, the national government develops a spending plan. It takes months to put together. The federal budget projects the amount of money that will be collected from taxes. Then it shows the amount of money the government expects to spend. The federal budget is for one year, which begins on October 1 and ends on the following September 30. This is called the **fiscal year**. We can think of it as the economic year instead of the calendar year, which begins on January 1 and ends on December 31.

The President Prepares the Budget

Preparation of the budget for any fiscal year begins with the executive branch of the government. The president, as head of the executive branch, needs money to carry out the responsibilities of the government. Congress must approve any spending plans.

The major responsibility for creating the budget proposal is in the hands of the *Office of Management and Budget (OMB)*. Input comes from the president's Council of Economic Advisers. The OMB also gathers the budget projections of all the administrative agencies of the executive branch. The Cabinet departments and agencies tell the OMB how much money they believe they will need for their operations during the fiscal year. The Office of Management and Budget spends countless hours reviewing these requests. Then it prepares a proposal that reflects the president's ideas about how the money should be spent.

After the president reacts to the proposal, the OMB holds more meetings to analyze the proposal and shape it to conform to the president's policies. The OMB then returns the modified budget to the various departments and agencies. They study the changes and make proposals for additional modifications. When the final draft of the budget meets with the executive branch's approval, it is submitted to Congress. Even though the fiscal year does not begin until October 1, the budget by law must be submitted to Congress 15 days after Congress begins its session in January of each year.

Congress Considers the Budget

The Constitution makes it clear that Congress has the power to raise revenue and pass laws involving how it is spent. This means that Congress has the authority to pass on the budget because it involves spending money and raising revenue. All bills relating to the raising of revenue must begin their journey through Congress in the House of Representatives.

Just as the president has the help of the Office of Management and Budget, Congress has the help of an agency called the *Congressional Budget Office (CBO)*. Although it is an independent arm of the government, its primary purpose is to provide Congress with information relating to the spending plans in the budget. This information is used to check the information that the OMB gives to the president. The CBO develops its own set of projections of how much money the government can expect to receive in the coming fiscal year. It also projects how much money each new program will cost.

Congressional committees review the budget and hold hearings. Modifications are likely to be made in how the revenue is apportioned among the programs and departments. After the budget bill is passed by both the House and the Senate, it goes to the president to be signed.

It is extremely unlikely that the budget proposed by the president will be passed without being changed by Congress. The political and economic thinking of the members of Congress may be similar to the ideas of the president or may be very different. Thus, passing a budget can be a difficult, complicated, and sometimes bitter process.

A Budget Crisis

In the fall of 1995, a crisis developed over the fiscal 1996 budget. President Bill Clinton (a Democrat) and Congress (controlled by Republicans) could not agree on the budget. Congress wanted to make deep cuts in federal spending, and President Clinton, although agreeing to cuts, wanted to protect programs such as Medicare. Congress wanted to lower taxes, but the president thought that the proposed tax rates would not bring in enough revenue to meet expenses.

Another controversial issue was how to balance the budget. Increasingly, Americans have become concerned about government spending and the growing national debt. Over the years, the government has spent more than it takes in and has had to borrow money to make ends meet.

As a result, the United States government has accumulated a very large debt. Interest payments on the loans take up a large percentage of the budget. Everyone agrees that something must be done. They just cannot agree on what to do.

A major focus of the budget negotiations in 1995 and 1996 was on how to balance the budget. Balancing the budget means that the amount of money the government plans to spend must be no more than the amount of money it expects to receive. Part of the discussion centered on how long it would take to balance the budget. Congress wanted to balance the budget within seven years—by the year 2002. President Clinton believed that it should take more than seven years to balance the budget.

By September 30, 1995, the end of the fiscal year, no budget agreement had been reached. This meant that the government was not authorized to spend money much beyond that date. In effect, the government would have to shut down because it did not have permission to spend money. As the days passed, no agreement was reached, and the government actually did shut down. Those people who worked in what were considered to be nonessential jobs were told to stay home. National parks closed, as did most government offices that served the public. Cabinet members warned that if the crisis was not resolved soon, the government might not be able to pay its debts. The stock and bond markets

Visitors to a museum in Washington, D.C., in November 1995 are disappointed to find it closed. The budget disagreement between Congress and the president shut down government-financed operations throughout the country for a number of days.

National Debt Since 1930

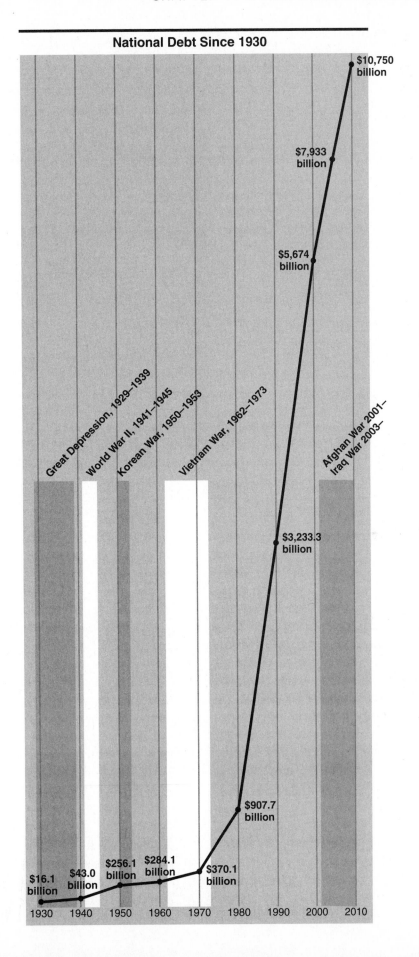

$10,750 billion

$7,933 billion

$5,674 billion

$3,233.3 billion

$907.7 billion

$370.1 billion

$284.1 billion

$256.1 billion

$43.0 billion

$16.1 billion

Great Depression, 1929–1939

World War II, 1941–1945

Korean War, 1950–1953

Vietnam War, 1962–1973

Afghan War 2001–
Iraq War 2003–

1930 1940 1950 1960 1970 1980 1990 2000 2010

◀REALITY CHECK▶
States Try to Make Ends Meet

Each year, every state government prepares a budget (plan for income and spending) for the coming year. The plan estimates the amount of money the state will spend to maintain the proper operation of the government and to provide services to the people of the state. The budget will include estimates of what will be spent on salaries for state workers, health care for the poor, and grades K–12 and higher education. It also shows the amounts to be spent on road and bridge maintenance, pensions for those who have retired from state employment, prisons, and law enforcement. Because states often borrow money for expenses, budgets must also provide for the payment of older debts. These are only the major expenditures that a state budget may include.

The process by which a state budget is approved is unique to each state, but it generally follows the process the federal government goes through. The governor, like the president, prepares a budget and submits it to the state legislature. The legislature usually rewrites the budget. Often there are spirited debates about how to spend money. Usually, many compromises have to be made before the budget can be passed. Once everyone

agrees on the budget, it goes into effect for what is called the fiscal year.

If the economy is good, all should go well. Revenue comes into the treasury of the state as the various taxes are collected. They include income taxes, sales taxes, fees, and other sources such as tolls on roads and bridges. The federal government also contributes funds to each state.

There are times, however, when the best of plans don't work. What happens when the economy takes an unexpected slide downward? How does that affect the budget and the state's ability to pay for all the goods and services that the state planned for? A downturn in consumer sales would lower the expected revenues from sales taxes. What would happen if there was a slump in the housing market and fewer new homes were built, as happened in 2007–2009? This could lead to a lowering of expected income from real estate taxes. Economic downturns cause businesses to lay off workers. In 2009, the national unemployment rate rose to 9.5 percent. According to the Bureau of Labor Statistics, this meant that the number of people out of work was about 15 million. Unemployed people usually do not have much

became nervous. The public could not understand why Congress and the president could not reach a compromise.

Temporary agreements finally let all employees go back to work. But no permanent solution was worked out by the time the 1997 budget had to be submitted. The fact that 1996 was a presidential election year made the disputes even more intense. Agreement between the White House and Congress on the budget was finally announced in April 1996. This was the budget that should have been in place for the fiscal year beginning October 1, 1995.

The public let Congress and the president know that they were annoyed about the 1996 budget crisis. The executive and legislative leaders got the message and reached an agreement on the 1997 budget in a timely fashion.

A shutdown of the government has not occurred since the mid-1990s. In 2009, though, an economic recession caused states and cities to cut government services severely and lay off employees. Some states were so short of funds that they asked the federal government for assistance.

Let's Think

1. What is a budget?
2. Why do governments need budgets?
3. Make a list of the steps the federal govern-

income and thus do not buy many things nor pay as much in taxes. Thus, revenues to the state decline. When this happens, a state faces a difficult decision. It has to revise its budget to cut back spending or, at the very least, get money from other sources to pay the bills. It might also consider raising taxes.

To reduce spending, a governor may ask government departments to prepare plans to save money. In effect, the departments are asked to operate more efficiently. Perhaps it means they will do with fewer supplies or cut back on services. Sometimes, as employees retire, their positions may not be filled. Sometimes the number of employees is cut back, so people lose their jobs. Needed repairs to roadways and bridges might have to be postponed.

Sometimes a cut is made to all departments equally. This means that if there is an "across-the-board-cut" of, for example, 3 percent, all departments must reduce their operating expenses by that percentage. Difficult decisions must be made.

How do you cut a budget? If the spending part of a budget is cut, what impact will the cuts have on people? Lawmakers want to protect the interests of their constituents. They may disagree with the plans a governor makes. Unions representing public employees may pressure the government to keep cuts to a minimum so that their members will not lose their jobs. Law enforcement officials become concerned that they might receive less money from the state. Public safety might be affected. Public colleges and universities realize that if their funding is cut, they might have to raise tuition. This would put a burden on their students. Public hospitals also fear that funding cuts would make it difficult to serve patients properly.

During the recession of 2007–2009, many states lost revenues and could not meet their expenses. They faced the problem of making drastic cuts in the services they provide. Some feared a shutdown of the government. California, for example, found that it had a budget gap of $22.2 billion. It had no way to get more revenues, so the governor said he might ask the federal government for more help.

The hard part for governors and legislators is to make the budget cuts seem necessary and fair. The citizens of a state need to feel that the cuts are applied in an evenhanded way.

1. What decisions must state governments make when creating a budget?
2. What types of spending cuts do states consider when they find they cannot balance a budget?
3. What problems develop when public employees are laid off from their jobs?
4. If you were the governor of a state with economic problems, how would you go about cutting spending or raising revenues to make sure the state is able to pay its bills?

ment takes to pass a budget and write a brief description of each step.
4. What are the roles of the Office of Management and Budget and the Congressional Budget Office?
5. What is meant by the term "fiscal year"?

The National Debt

Over the years, the United States has accumulated a large debt. In most years, it has spent more than it received in revenues. In 2009, the national debt amounted to some $11.3 trillion. If the total debt were divided by the population, every person in the United States would owe some $37,000. Calls for cutting spending and reducing the debt have grown louder and louder.

Roots of the Debt

Many believed that the national debt has its roots in the New Deal. President Roosevelt in the 1930s put forth government programs to pull the nation out of the Great Depression. Then came World War II, the Korean War, the cold war, and the war in Vietnam—all of which made huge defense outlays necessary between 1942 and 1990. In addition, social welfare programs cost more as the population increased. In the early 2000s, the country became involved in wars in Afghanistan and Iraq.

Spending on those wars added to the debt. During the recession of 2008–2009, federal funds were used to stabilize weak financial institutions, also adding to the debt. The public has not supported raising taxes to fund the programs fully. It became easier for Congress to borrow money to meet spending needs than to cut popular programs.

Solving the Problem

Various attempts have been made to force the government by law to balance the budget. Many of these laws were declared unconstitutional. Efforts to pass a constitutional amendment to require a balanced budget have so far failed in Congress. But the idea has many supporters.

Critics of the amendment believe that it would force the government to make choices unacceptable to citizens even if they believed in the need to cut spending. Economists think that a balanced-budget amendment should include a provision for flexibility. What would happen, they ask, if there are emergencies and the government needs funds for unexpected situations?

Reducing the federal debt and balancing the budget require us to make many difficult decisions. Part of the problem is that the government must spend less money. If it spends less money, it must decide what to cut. A delicate balance must be developed between the need and the desire the American people have for services and their willingness to pay the bill for the services.

Let's Think

1. Define national debt and budget deficit.
2. Why are citizens and government officials concerned about both?
3. What can be done to reduce spending and still take care of our defense and human welfare needs?

Chapter Summary

Governments, like individuals, need money if they are to survive. They too must pay for goods and services.

Taxes are a major source of revenue for all governments. For the federal and most state governments, the income tax on earnings provides the greatest amount of money. Income tax rates rise with the level of taxable income. Because people with larger incomes pay a higher rate than those with smaller incomes, the income tax is called a progressive tax. Some local governments also levy income taxes.

A different method of taxing income is through the flat tax. Under this system, all people would pay the same proportion or percentage of their income. Flat tax supporters believe that it would simplify the tax system.

The federal government uses several other types of taxes to raise revenue. They include excise taxes, customs and duties, estate and gift taxes. Excise taxes are placed on goods such as alcohol and tobacco. Customs and duties are paid by individuals or businesses that import goods into the country. Estate and gift taxes are levied on the transfer of property from one person to another, usually a family member.

Federal taxes to pay for Social Security and Medicare benefits are deducted from workers' paychecks. Social Security is a pension program that almost all working citizens are eligible for upon retirement. Medicare is a medical and hospital insurance program for the elderly.

Local governments rely heavily on property taxes. This is a tax based on the value of real estate of all kinds.

Sales taxes provide large amounts of revenue for state and local governments. In areas that impose a sales tax, most items except food and drugs are taxed. The sales tax is considered to be a regressive tax. This means that it is more burdensome to lower-income people than to higher-income people.

To raise even more money, especially for education, many states have turned to lotteries. Casino gambling is also allowed in some areas and provides revenue mainly to the state and local levels of government.

Tax policies can influence behavior patterns. The federal government has established income tax deductions that favor home ownership and charitable contributions.

Tax policies also influence the economy. When taxes are low, people have more money to invest, spend, or save. This influences the amount of money in circulation and has some impact on the health of the overall economy.

Like many of us, governments find it necessary to borrow money. The federal government borrows by issuing various securities such as U.S. Savings Bonds and treasury notes and bills that individuals may purchase. After the securities mature, interest is paid on the investment.

State governments borrow money by issuing bonds. These bonds have a specific life and pay interest when they mature. They are usually designated for specific purposes such as education, building new roads, college dormitories, or cleaning up the environment.

All governments plan how to spend their money. The process of planning is called budget making. The budget-making process of the federal government requires the teamwork of the president and Congress. Usually the president proposes the budget, which does not go into effect until it is agreed to by both the president and Congress. The Office of Management and Budget (OMB) helps the president prepare the national budget. The Congressional Budget Office (CBO) aids Congress in analyzing the president's proposals. The budget-making process involves proposals, hearings, debates, and compromise. States follow a similar process. Governors usually propose budgets, and legislatures approve them.

Because governments often spend more than they have, they tend to owe money. The total accumulation of debt that the federal government owes is called the national debt. A substantial percentage of each year's budget goes for paying interest on that debt. When the yearly budget plans call for spending more money than the government receives, there is a deficit. The budget deficit adds to the national debt. Money must be borrowed to make up the difference between expenses and revenues. One proposal to do away with the deficit by forcing the government to balance the budget is to add an amendment to the Constitution. So far this proposal has not met with success.

★ CHAPTER REVIEW ★

A. Matching
Match each term in Column A with its definition in Column B.

Column A	Column B
1. flat tax	a. a major source of state and local revenues
2. income tax	
3. excise tax	b. period covering a 12-month budget
4. sales tax	
5. Social Security	c. a tax policy that requires everyone to pay the same fraction of their income
6. bond	
7. budget	d. the federal pension system
8. fiscal year	e. a tax on money people earn
9. Office of Management and Budget	f. a federal tax on particular goods
10. national debt	g. plan for income and expenditures

h. financial paper sold by governments to raise money

i. advises the executive branch in the budget-making process

j. total amount of money the federal government owes lenders

B. Multiple Choice
Select the statement or word that most correctly answers the question or completes the statement.

1. Taxes serve the following function: They **(a)** pay for the cost of running the government **(b)** increase the deficit **(c)** make people wealthy **(d)** promote good relations with foreign countries.

2. This is a tax on many types of goods sold in stores: **(a)** excise **(b)** income **(c)** progressive **(d)** sales.

3. A federal gasoline tax is an example of a (an) **(a)** excise tax **(b)** income tax **(c)** proportional tax **(d)** tariff.

4. The federal agency that collects income taxes is the **(a)** Congressional Budget Office **(b)** Office of Management and Budget **(c)** Internal Revenue Service **(d)** Customs Office.

5. An income tax on businesses is called a **(a)** sales tax **(b)** corporate income tax **(c)** personal income tax **(d)** tariff.

6. One effect of income taxes is to **(a)** increase the deficit **(b)** influence people's behavior **(c)** make the president rich **(d)** decrease the amount of government revenue.

7. This part of the federal government must approve the president's budget: **(a)** the Supreme Court **(b)** the Cabinet **(c)** Congress **(d)** the Internal Revenue Service.

8. The organization that helps Congress analyze the budget is the **(a)** Congressional Budget Office **(b)** Office of Management and Budget **(c)** Attorney General's Office **(d)** Secretary of the Treasury.

9. The fiscal year for the federal government is the same as the **(a)** calendar year **(b)** president's term of office **(c)** budget year **(d)** session of Congress.

10. A way many states raise money without levying taxes is by **(a)** running a lottery **(b)** encouraging tourism **(c)** coining money **(d)** charging for advertising.

C. Essay

Write a paragraph about *one* of the following:

1. Taxes serve many functions.
2. Governments find it necessary to borrow money to pay expenses.
3. Many Americans favor a balanced federal budget.
4. The budget-making process is complicated.

D. A Challenge for You

1. Write an editorial for a newspaper that explains why you are for or against the idea of a flat tax.

2. Research the types of taxes levied in five or six states and the current rate of the taxes. Create a table or graph to show how the tax levels in these states compare with the levels in your state. Check the Internet for up-to-date information.

3. Research the proposals for a balanced-budget amendment. Prepare two speeches, one for each side of the issue.

4. Create a cartoon strip that demonstrates your understanding of the budget process.

5. Interview members of your community's legislature to find out what the budget-making process is like in your community. Report on your interview to the class. Suggest how local residents can influence the process.

Document-Based Question

State the main idea expressed in each document. Then use information in the documents and your own knowledge to write an essay explaining how the flat tax system would both solve and create problems for American taxpayers.

Flat Tax Fever

Although it was [once] a largely unknown academic concept. . . , the flat tax today is one of the most talked about policy reforms in Washington. . . . It now looks increasingly possible that the current income tax system will be junked in favor of this simple, fair, pro-growth plan. The present system suffers from three major problems, each of which would be solved by the flat tax:

Problem #1: High tax rates that discourage work, savings, and investments. Flat Tax Solution: The . . . flat tax replaces the current discriminatory system of tax rates with a simple, low rate that treats all taxpayers equally.

Problem #2: Needless complexity that imposes $200 billion of compliance costs [expenses of keeping records and filling out forms]. Flat Tax Solution: The . . . flat tax allows all taxpayers to fill out their taxes on a postcard-sized form.

Problem #3: Multiple taxation of capital income that penalizes economic growth. Flat Tax Solution: Not only are all individuals treated equally, so is all income. No longer would some income escape taxation while other types of income are subject to as many as four levels of taxation.

The flat tax solves all these problems by creating a tax system that treats all citizens equally, rewards productive behavior, and gets the government out of the business of using tax law to micromanage the economy.

From *Flat Tax Fever* by Dan Mitchell, McKenna Senior Fellow in Political Economy at the Heritage Foundation, in June/July *Insider*, 1996. By permission of the Heritage Foundation.

The Failing of the Flat Tax

Our current tax code, while far from perfect, does a reasonably good job of ensuring that people with similar total incomes pay similar amounts in taxes . . . , and that people with higher incomes pay more in taxes. . . . Eliminating any taxation of capital income [return from investments] at the individual level, as would the flat tax, will make the tax code far less equitable. Families with the same total income will bear vastly different individual tax burdens, depending on how they earn that income. The family that earns a larger share of its income from labor will pay a higher personal tax than the family that collects more of its income from interest, dividends, and capital gains [increase in value of investments]—even though it is no better off. Similarly, two families with vastly different total incomes may pay the same individual tax if both families have the same amount of labor income. The flat tax, in short, produces a bias against labor, in much the same way that the current tax code produces a bias against saving. . . .

Flat tax proponents argue that by eliminating the individual tax on capital source income, we will stimulate future savings and investment. But the proposal would exempt from tax not only income from future savings and investment, but also income from *existing* saving and investment. This would represent a huge tax windfall to current investors, most of whom are in the top 5 percent of the income distribution. . . .

The flat tax would simplify the system, but not because it ends progressive rates, but because it ends deductions, credits, depreciation allowances, and so on. *This simplification is equally consistent with a single rate or progressive tax rates.* Remember, the complicated part of figuring one's taxes is calculating taxable income; once you've done that, calculating the taxes owed is easy, whether there is one marginal tax rate or several. . . .

From *The Failing of the Flat Tax* by Jeff Hammond, PPI Economic Policy Analyst. The Democratic Leadership Council (DLC) and The Progressive Policy Institute (PPI), 1996.

CHAPTER 12

Business and Labor— The Foundation of the U.S. Economy

★ CHAPTER FOCUS

1. What are the main types of business organizing structures?
2. What is the relationship between business and government?
3. How do labor unions function?
4. What is the relationship between government and organized labor?

Have you ever dreamed of opening your own business? You like the idea of being your own boss. You may hope to make a lot of money. Possibly, you may expect to become famous. Owning your own business offers you many opportunities and allows you to be the "master of your own fate."

A variety of decisions have to be made before a person is ready to open the door to a new business. When Nick and Suzette decided to begin Fast Trak Sneakers, they, too, had many things to consider. They needed to determine how much start-up money they required, where they would locate the plant, and where they would get people to work in the business. They also had to decide what sort of business organizing structure to operate under.

Types of Business Organizing Structures

Starting a business is complicated. Suzette and Nick couldn't just open a store, rent an office, or buy a factory building and hang out a sign. They had to find out what local and state, even national, regulations they must follow. Some types of businesses require special licenses or permits. If you were to open a restaurant, you would need approval from the local board of health. You probably would need a sales tax certificate in order to collect the required taxes that get passed along to local and state governments. The business might have to be located in a certain part of a community because of zoning laws.

200

Business Organizing Structures

Sole Proprietorship

"Mine, all mine!"
(including profits and debts)

Partnership

"Ours, all ours!"
(including profits and debts)

Corporation
Stockholders
"Ours! We share in profits and debts."

How do you find out what to do? You can start with the local Chamber of Commerce. It is an organization of businesses whose purpose is to help businesspeople and the community. Consulting an attorney who specializes in helping businesspeople operate their establishments would also be a good idea.

After Nick and Suzette made the decision to open Fast Trak, they investigated the types of business organization they could operate under. They had several choices. Not all were practical for Suzette and Nick, but they decided to investigate them all. They examined the benefits and liabilities of the business structures called sole proprietorship, partnership, and corporation.

Sole Proprietorship

Some individuals want to own a business all by themselves. When one person owns and operates a business all alone, the business is called a **sole proprietorship**. The advantage of this form of business structure is that one person has complete decision-making power over the company. He or she decides what to produce and how to produce it, or if it is a store, what to sell and how it will be sold. The sole proprietor bears the responsibility for the success or failure of the business and can do what he or she wants with the profits. Most businesses in the United States are sole proprietorships.

There are, however, several disadvantages to a sole proprietorship. The first is that the owner of the company is held personally responsible for all debts the business may accumulate. Sometimes all does not go well for a business. It can have a problem paying its bills.

What happens when the business does not have the resources to pay its bills? Creditors, the individuals and businesses who are waiting for payment, have the right to claim the *assets* (cash and property) of the business. They also have a right to go after the personal property of the owner. Personal property includes the owner's house, savings, and other possessions. A sole proprietorship makes the owner of the company personally liable for all debts and any lawsuits that might be brought against the business.

Another disadvantage is that a sole proprietorship has a limited life. When the owner of the business retires or dies, the business usually goes out of existence.

Partnership

Suzette and Nick could not use a sole proprietorship for Fast Trak because they are two people. The type of business structure they seriously considered was a **partnership**. A partnership is a business owned by two or more people. Partners may have more funds available to invest in the business than a sole proprietor. Each person can contribute money to develop the enterprise.

Another advantage to a partnership is the sharing of ideas. The partners can share philosophies about how to make the business a success and "bounce" ideas off each other. Sometimes one partner has talent in one area and another has talent and training in another area. This allows the partners to specialize in different aspects of the business. For instance, Nick is a good salesperson, so he manages the sales force and the marketing of the sneakers. Because Suzette has had training as an accountant, she is focusing her attention on the technical and financial side of the business.

Partnerships also have several disadvantages. A partnership has a limited life. When a partner dies, the partnership must be reorganized or go out of existence. The share of the business owned by the deceased partner can be transferred to heirs, but the process is complicated.

Another disadvantage of a partnership is that it, too, has unlimited liability. Partners are held personally accountable for the debts created by the business. If Fast Trak were to amass large debts and could not pay them off, Suzette and Nick would be obligated to pay the debts themselves. This means that any savings or property they have could be claimed by creditors.

Corporation

After learning about the risks of a partnership, Suzette and Nick wanted to look into another type of business structure, a **corporation**. A corporation is a business that is given life when it is granted a charter, a statement of incorporation, by the state in which the corporation operates. The charter, or license to operate, allows the business to issue shares. A person can become an owner by purchasing a share of stock in the company. People who own shares are called **stockholders**. There can be many owners of a corporation or just a few.

A corporation has several advantages over the other forms of businesses. One of the biggest advantages is that it offers limited liability to the stockholders, or owners. If a corporation goes bankrupt and owes money, the stockholders could lose the investment they made when they bought the stock. However, they will only be held liable for debts up to the value of their stocks and no more. The personal property of each stockholder is protected. State laws recognize that only the corporation as an organization is responsible for its debts, not the individual owners.

Another advantage to the corporation structure is that it has an unlimited life. If one or more stockholders die, the business does not cease to exist. The stocks can be sold to others or inherited by survivors.

When a corporation needs to raise money for expansion or other business purposes, it can issue more shares of stock. It does not have to rely on loans from banks.

A corporation has some drawbacks. It can be complicated to set up and operate. In order to follow various regulations and tax requirements, a corporation needs the services of lawyers and accountants. This increases the cost of doing business. Also, a corporation pays taxes on its profits before dividends are distributed. Stockholders, who may be the ones running the corporation, also pay taxes on the dividends. Stockholders of large corporations have little control over those who manage the business. Suzette and Nick decided that a corporation best suited their situation. Their business name became Fast Trak Sneakers, Inc. (Inc. is short for incorporated.)

Multinational Corporations

A phenomenon of the late 20th century was the development of the *multinational corporation*. Such companies have spread their operations (whether it be service or manufacturing based) across national boundaries. Although they may have their headquarters in one country, subsidiary companies exist in various parts of the world. The development of such companies has led to the globalization of the economies of the nations of the world. Multinational corporations are having a growing influence on the economies of the nations in which they do business.

Let's Think

1. What types of decisions does a person have to make before he or she starts a business?

2. Describe the advantages and disadvantages of each of the following types of business organizations: sole proprietorship, partnership, corporation.

Production of Goods

The mouse on your computer is broken. Almost automatically you or a member of your family pays a visit to a computer store to purchase a new one. You bring it home and attach it—it fits and works. Each mouse for your type of computer fits because each one made by the manufacturer is exactly alike. This is accomplished by a process called **mass production**.

Through mass production, large numbers of goods are made quickly by machines. Each item that is produced is identical to the one made before and the one made after. The parts used to make the mouse are *interchangeable*. Each screw, for example, or each wire is interchangeable with another screw or wire. An individual worker is responsible for a specific task in assembling the mouse. One worker connects the internal wires. Another attaches the external wires and plug to the mouse. A third secures the housing to the mouse and completes the task. This is called *division of labor*. Each worker has a particular task to do. He or she does only the one job all day rather than perform all the steps in creating the product. Division of labor and interchangeable parts make it possible to create more products in a shorter time. Now machines handle the manufacturing steps for most products. Individual workers monitor the machines and the quality of the products.

Most products are complicated combinations of parts and material that must be put together. The mass production process makes use of the assembly line to put products together—assemble them. For example, an automobile starts out at the beginning of the assembly line as a frame. As the frame moves down a long line of workers and machines, parts are attached to it. The motor is put into place, wheels, doors, fenders, bumpers, etc., are put on. By the time the car reaches the end of the line, it is fully assembled. When the

A robotized automobile assembly line. Humans monitor the work of the robots.

process was first used, human workers stood at various points on the line to put all the parts on. Now robots perform many tasks with humans monitoring the work of the machines. Now, too, the assembly line has been modified to allow teams of workers to put together a whole car.

Getting the Product to Market

Producing goods is important, but if you don't have a practical way of getting the goods to market—to the buyers—you would be in trouble. The United States has a well-developed transportation system that enables people and goods to move easily throughout the country. Getting goods to stores where consumers may buy them is called *distribution*. As we drive on the highways of our nation, we see large trucks rolling along full of products that we use. They may be carrying refrigerators, stereo equipment, or food products. Railroads actually carry a higher percentage of the freight traffic than trucks. Airlines move very little freight.

Selling Goods

The process of selling goods to the public is called *marketing*. Most often a buyer purchases a product in a store. Large-scale selling through department stores, superstores, and catalogs is called mass marketing. Products are also offered for sale through electronic catalogs on the Internet, home shopping networks on television, and ads on television. The buyer uses the telephone to order the item and pay for it with a credit card.

Advertising acquaints us with products and brand names. It whets our appetites for a wide variety of goods and services. Mass marketing helps to make mass production profitable.

Let's Think

1. Explain the meaning of the following terms: mass production, interchangeable, distribution, marketing, division of labor.
2. Explain the importance of interchangeable parts to mass production.

Government Regulation of Business

During the 19th century and part of the early 20th century, the federal and state governments allowed businesses to grow without much interference. Most people believed that this was the correct course of action. But some thought that the growing businesses needed to be carefully watched.

Problems With Railroads

Farm production increased rapidly after the end of the Civil War in 1865. More and more people moved to the central area of the United States to open land to cultivation. Aiding the settlement was the expanding national network of railroads. The crowning achievement of the railroad builders was the completion in 1869 of the transcontinental railroad. It linked the eastern part of the United States with the West Coast. Farmers found the railroad to be a fast and efficient way of shipping goods to markets. They quickly became dependent on the railroad line nearest to them.

Railroads were giant companies that usually had no real competition. There was no other way to transport goods quickly long distances over land. If a farmer lived near a river or canal, goods could be transported by water. Not many had

that choice. Small farmers began complaining about the high rates the railroads charged. This increased the farmers' costs and decreased their profits. Another complaint was that those who owned large farms received better shipping rates because they shipped more. A two-tiered system of pricing developed.

Interstate Commerce Act

After much pressure from the farmers and their supporters, the federal government responded to the complaints about the railroads by passing the *Interstate Commerce Act* of 1887. Article I, Section 8, of the Constitution gives Congress the power to regulate commerce "with foreign nations, and among the several states." Interstate commerce refers to goods that are sold in more than one state and to businesses that operate in more than one state. The regulation of business within a particular state is generally left to the state.

The passage of the Interstate Commerce Act was pushed forward by a decision of the Supreme Court. The case was known as the *Wabash, St. Louis and Pacific Railway Company* v. *Illinois*. Protesting farmers prodded several states to pass laws to regulate the railroads. But a state could control only what a railroad did within the state. In the Wabash case, the Supreme Court ruled that the states could not regulate a business that was involved in activities across state lines. Only the federal government could regulate interstate commerce. The decision left the nation without any laws to curb the railroad industry. Congress reacted to the Wabash case by passing the Interstate Commerce Act in 1887, just one year after the Wabash decision.

The new law regulated the pricing practices of the railroads throughout the nation. It stated that the railroads could not charge one price to one customer and a different price to another customer. The act mandated equal rates for all customers.

In addition, it created the Interstate Commerce Commission. The ICC had the responsibility of supervising interstate commerce and enforcing regulations on railroads and shipping and, later, trucking within the United States. In a move to cut back on expenses and get the government out of the regulation business, Congress abolished the ICC in 1995.

Business Grows in America

Toward the end of the 19th century, powerful individuals came to control companies in several different industries. John D. Rockefeller headed the oil business. His company, Standard Oil, soon controlled most of the oil production within the United States. Andrew Carnegie created a power base in the steel industry. His company, Carnegie Steel, developed new and improved methods of producing steel that other firms could not duplicate.

Remember that a cornerstone of the American economic system is free enterprise. The philosophical basis of capitalism is competition. Competition results in fairer prices to the consumer and a wider choice of products.

As the owners of the large businesses grew in power, they became richer and richer and their companies became more profitable. They implemented practices that limited competition. One method was the **merger**. A merger is the combination of one or more companies into a single company. In the last half of the 19th century, railroad companies grew through mergers. Small railroads were bought and combined. Soon large companies controlled the industry, setting prices that farmers found expensive.

Today, if mergers are not seen as limiting competition, the government allows them to take place. Late in 1996, the Boeing Corporation, this country's largest manufacturer of commercial aircraft, announced a merger with McDonnell Douglas Corporation, a major producer of military aircraft. Because there is foreign competition, the merger was seen as a positive move for the American aircraft industry.

Another method aimed to control an entire industry. This attempt to be the only company to produce and market a product or service is called a **monopoly**. Monopolies are now illegal. Any attempt to limit competition has come to be called a monopolistic practice.

Some monopolies, though, are legal. The government permits utilities (suppliers of electricity or natural gas) to be the only supplier in a partic-

Electricity utility workers repairing a downed line after an ice storm. Deregulation laws are taking away the monopoly status of utilities in many states.

ular area. Such a practice seemed to be in the best interests of the consumer. In recent years, there has been a move toward relaxing the laws that permit such monopolies. Utilities have begun the process of deregulation and are competing with other companies that supply electricity and gas. This deregulation met some obstacles, most notably the allegation of fraud in the Enron energy company case that hit the headlines at the end of 2001. As a result of the Enron scandal, Congress passed the Sarbanes-Oxley Act in 2002. It provides for severe penalties for acts of fraud by public corporations. Deregulation of utilities has taken different forms in the states. Not all states have adopted a program of deregulation of the energy industry.

A third method of combining businesses is by creating a **holding company**. A holding company buys shares of stock in a number of companies. It acquires money by selling its own stock. Then it uses the money to purchase controlling interests in other companies. A controlling interest is ownership of 51 percent of the total number of shares issued by a company. Each share of stock represents one vote at a stockholders' meeting.

Holding companies do not manufacture anything. Their purpose is to accumulate stock and gain control of a majority of the stock in a number of different companies. Then they can direct the policies of these companies. A holding company might have power over several companies that are in competition with one another, or it might purchase controlling interests in several

POWER *of* ★ ONE

Cesar Chavez

Called "one of the heroic figures of our time," Cesar Chavez dedicated his life to the improvement of the lives of others. He was born in 1927 and died in 1993. During his early childhood, he lived on a farm near Yuma, Arizona. When lack of rain and low crop prices caused the Chavez farm to fail, the family became migrant farmworkers. Migrant workers move from one large farm to another to harvest crops. The Chavez family traveled mainly between Arizona and California, harvesting various crops at different times of the year. The family lived in a series of labor camps in poorly built houses. Chavez attended more than 30 elementary schools. When he dropped out of school in the seventh grade, he could barely read and write. The family members worked hard from dawn until dusk for very little money. Sometimes employers did not pay them. Often they were discriminated against because of their Hispanic background.

While a young man, Chavez watched his father join union movement after union movement in an attempt to better his life, but without success. Chavez stated many times that his father's perseverance made a lasting impression on him and shaped his later life.

During World War II, Chavez served in the Navy. After he returned home, he again became a migrant worker in California and Arizona.

In the early 1950s, Chavez developed an interest in organizations that helped underprivileged people. He aided people in Mexican-American communities to register to vote, deal with immigration problems, and work with welfare boards. "At first, because he was then frail and boyish looking and lacking in confidence, people tended to dismiss him as a 'kid,' but he soon learned techniques for recruiting members and developing leaders," said one biographer.

By 1958, Chavez had become director of the Community Service Organization (CSO). Increasingly, he gained the support of groups of middle-class people who were interested in improving the plight of the poor. He urged the CSO to think about organizing migrant farmworkers. In 1962, the CSO voted down a proposal to do so. In protest, Chavez resigned as director.

He then decided to form the National Farm Workers Association. Chavez traveled through the agricultural areas in California to speak to migrant farmworkers. He wanted to get a sense of their feelings about their working conditions. Chavez worked on weekends as a ditchdigger, and his wife, Helen, worked in the fields. Even then, he could not always make enough money

unrelated companies. When holding companies dominate several companies within the same industry, the effect is to limit competition.

Trusts, in some ways, were similar to holding companies. Both involved the transfer and ownership of stock by one company in another. Stockholders agree to turn the stock they own in a certain company over to the trust. The trust, in turn, gives them certificates that represent ownership in the trust company. A trust is then able to

control many different companies. If you owned trust certificates, you owned a part of the trust that in turn controlled many other companies.

In some cases, the business combinations increased the efficiency of businesses. But primarily, the combinations had the effect of limiting competition and making it possible for the new, larger companies to increase their profits. If mergers were successful, they might control the major share of the market and therefore dictate prices.

to support his family. At times, he had to beg for food from the very workers he was trying to help.

Gradually, more and more workers came to him to handle problems they had with employers. Chavez talked to local community leaders, such as priests and ministers, to bring pressure on employers to correct problems. Although the National Farm Workers Association was growing in size and influence, Chavez did not believe it was ready for large-scale action.

In September 1965, a group of 800 Filipino grape pickers went on strike in California. They belonged to the Agricultural Workers Organizing Committee (AWOC), which was part of the AFL-CIO. Chavez's organization decided that it had to support this strike. He raised funds from various civil rights organizations to help the strikers. Within a short time, other unions in industries not related to agriculture were making contributions to sustain the AWOC. By July 1966, Chavez's National Farm Workers voted to merge with AWOC.

Cesar Chavez used nonviolent tactics to win concessions from employers. They included many of the peaceful protest techniques devised by Mohandas Gandhi of India and Martin Luther King, Jr. Chavez also dramatized his cause with such events as church meetings, sing-ins, bilingual theatrical performances, a 300-mile march from Delano to Sacramento in California, and fasting. (*Fasting* means to go without food.) To gain sympathy and support for the union demands, Chavez fasted on a number of occasions, once for 25 days.

A series of labor contracts were successfully negotiated. The contracts increased the wages of the workers and allowed them to have a union hiring hall for placing workers in jobs. But not all farmworkers benefited. The table grape growers refused to negotiate. (Table grapes are the ones people buy to eat as opposed to the grapes that are used to make wine.) Chavez urged a nationwide boycott of table grapes grown in California. The national boycott was effective. People across the country refused to buy grapes and participated in rallies to protest the actions of the growers. Almost 20 percent of the grape market was taken away by the boycott.

The dream of Chavez to create a truly national organization to represent all migrant farmworkers was never achieved. However, those he was able to help are now living better as a result of his efforts. Migrant workers became eligible for medical insurance, employer-paid pensions, unemployment insurance, and other benefits. Unionization gave them a formal way to challenge employer abuses. Chavez was also successful in persuading the California state legislature to pass an important collective bargaining law for farmworkers in 1975. Chavez's actions touched the lives of individuals throughout the nation. He was an inspirational leader who achieved important goals.

1. How did Chavez's early life influence his desire to organize migrant farmworkers?
2. How successful was Chavez in reaching his goals?
3. In what ways does Chavez's life demonstrate that one person can make a difference in the lives of people?

Competition and You

How does a lack of competition affect you, the consumer? Let us look at this example. When you shop for a sweatshirt, you can choose from many different brands, which vary in quality and price. You may shop at two or three sporting goods stores or casual wear stores that carry similar items. You will probably try to buy the best quality garment for the cheapest price. But what happens if there is only one store selling sweat-shirts or one company that manufactures them? You have fewer choices. You have to take what is available at whatever price is asked. Competition provides us with choices.

Legal Curbs on Monopolies

The Interstate Commerce Act regulated transportation and freight rates, but it had little impact on monopolistic business organizations. To curb the power of big business, Congress passed the *Sherman Antitrust Act* in 1890. It outlawed monopolistic practices.

Almost 25 years later, the *Clayton Antitrust Act* of 1914 attempted to close some loopholes in the Sherman Act. The Clayton Act made it easier to identify illegal monopolistic practices. It forbade the limitation of competition, held the individual directors of corporations criminally responsible for their companies' wrongdoings, and took a first step to protect labor unions.

Congress also passed the *Federal Trade Commission Act* in 1914. This law created the Federal Trade Commission (FTC), an independent agency of the federal government. It is responsible for making sure that businesses engage in fair practices. The commission also enforces the Clayton Act and other federal trade laws. If the FTC detects violations, it investigates and, if necessary, refers the offending companies to the Justice Department for prosecution.

Through these laws and others, the federal government tries to promote fair business practices. It does not allow businesses to act in any way they choose. Consumers want to feel that their interests are being protected and that they have somewhere to turn to if they have a problem.

Let's Think

1. Explain why the Interstate Commerce Commission was needed. What effect did it have?
2. What methods did 19th-century corporations use to limit competition?
3. How did the federal government attempt to curb monopolistic practices?

Government Deregulation of Business

During the last 20 years of the 20th century, government regulatory policies came under attack. Sectors of the business community believed that government regulations limited the ability of businesses to conduct their affairs as they saw fit. Some believed that less government regulation would increase competition, which would benefit consumers and aid the growth of business. With more competition, prices might be lower and service might improve.

Deregulation is the idea that there should be fewer rules created by government regarding the conduct of business. Many argued that the economy was overregulated and that businesses were finding it increasingly difficult and expensive to compete with other companies, especially companies in other countries. According to one report in the mid-1990s, government regulations cost the U.S. economy $1 trillion a year.

One of the first industries to be deregulated was the airlines. At one time, the airlines were regulated so extensively that they could not change airfares or schedules without the approval of the now defunct Civil Aeronautics Board (CAB). As a result of deregulation, several older airlines went out of existence because they could not compete. Low-price airlines sprang up, and several have continued to be successful. The government still maintains oversight of the industry through the Federal Aviation Administration (FAA).

In the late 1990s, Congress deregulated the banking industry, allowing it to expand into financial services. This meant that banks could not only be a repository for savings but could also sell mutual funds, 401(k) plans, and insurance. Deregulation resulted in many mergers between banks and financial services companies. Banks that were originally regional expanded nationwide and grew larger.

Part of the deregulation process provided for the expansion of mortgage lending into areas that had not had access before. As a result, mortgages were approved for people who had less than ideal credit ratings. Many say that this "subprime" mortgage lending helped bring about the financial meltdown of 2008–2009.

During the presidential race of 2008, the candidates debated about how they would solve the financial crisis that came to a head that year. Each said he wanted to preserve the concept of the free enterprise system to allow businesses to flourish. Most experts agreed on the need to investigate the practices of banking and financial services organizations in order to prevent similar financial crises in the future. The trend is to increase what is called transparency. *Transparency* is opening up the books of financial institutions to allow the government and investors to see better how the financial institutions are conducting business. Some say that transparency would reduce the possibility that these institutions might make questionable investments or engage in risky business transactions.

Let's Think

1. What are the arguments for and against government deregulation?
2. What happened when the airline industry was deregulated?
3. How did deregulation of the banking industry create problems for the U.S. economy in 2008–2009?

Labor Unions and Their Importance

During the last half of the 19th century, the number of people employed in factories increased. More and more people flocked to the cities to fill the many jobs that had become available in manufacturing centers. New machinery and new methods of production appeared on the scene.

As eager as people may have been to seek new opportunities, they found their working conditions to be less than ideal. People worked long hours for low wages, often in dirty and poorly ventilated and lighted buildings. The machinery they used caused many injuries.

Such conditions, coupled with the abusive treatment they received from many employers, caused workers to seek changes in their working environment. They also demanded higher wages. To achieve these goals, workers banded together in organizations called **labor unions**.

Purpose of Unions

Unions operate under the assumption that there is power in numbers. Think about what might happen if you go in alone to ask an unpleasant boss for a raise. You may be a good worker, but there are many others who could do your job. Even if the boss decides to hear your request, it is likely that it will be turned down. What is your alternative? Either you go back to work or threaten to quit. Either way you would not achieve your goal.

On the other hand, if you joined with other workers and spoke as one, your voice would be louder. Now the boss would have to deal with perhaps 50 people instead of just one. The boss might hesitate to fire everyone or risk having everyone quit at the same time. He or she might decide to give everyone a raise or correct an unsafe condition.

Unions try to achieve their demands through negotiations with the owners of individual businesses. The negotiation process is called **collective bargaining**. Representatives from the union and the workers sit down with management and try to reach an agreement through discussion. If both sides agree on the issues, they formalize the terms in a **contract**, a legal document.

A contract is in force for a specified period of time (usually two or three years). During that time period, the two sides agree to abide by the terms of the contract. The agreement spells out what raises the union members are to get, the

An AFL-CIO march to help janitors organize a union and recruit Hispanic members. Unions use a variety of tactics to publicize their benefits and attract new members.

number of sick, holiday, and vacation days they are entitled to, and various other conditions of work. Normally, union members cannot be fired except for unruly or illegal behavior. The contract also sets forth procedures for handling disputes between management and labor.

Union Weapons

What happens if negotiations stall and neither the union nor management will budge on its demands? Then the union takes steps to increase pressure on management to get it to agree to union demands or, at the very least, make some compromises.

Boycott

One way to create such pressure is to implement a **boycott**. This action asks consumers to stop buying goods from a particular company. Union members might distribute flyers explaining the reason for the boycott. Unions may also place advertisements in newspapers, in magazines, and on television to publicize their cause.

Mediation

Through **mediation**, the disputing sides call in a mutually acceptable third party to help them come to an agreement. The mediator listens to both sides, engages in fact finding, and proposes possible solutions. Mediation is voluntary, and the proposals put forth can be accepted or rejected by either side.

Arbitration

In **arbitration**, the two sides also call in a third party they both respect. They agree beforehand to accept the arbitrator's settlement. The arbitrator listens to arguments from both sides, tries to find out the facts in the case, and comes up with a fair proposal. Agreeing to go to arbitration doesn't happen often. Neither side wants to lose control of its future by placing the settlement in the hands of a third person.

Strike

The most dramatic weapon a union can use is the **strike**. Strikes are work stoppages. Workers refuse to perform their jobs. The strike is usually the weapon of last resort. Why? When workers are on strike, they are not paid. When workers strike, businesses cannot operate. Both sides suffer economically. Sometimes a union provides money to its members to help them pay bills during a strike. Usually this payment is much lower than a worker's regular wage. When a union resorts to a strike, it is hoped that management will understand the depth of their feelings and finally sit down at the bargaining table to reach an agreement.

In September 2008, the Boeing Company, the world's second largest manufacturer of commercial jetliners, faced a strike by its machinists. The strike lasted 52 days. As a result, the company could not operate at full capacity and the strikers could not earn their wages. A major issue, according to the machinists' union, was *job security*. The union wanted assurances from management that the machinists who currently worked for the company would not lose their jobs as a result of Boeing's seeking outside companies to do some of the work for them. Other issues were wage increases, health-care costs, and pensions. The company demanded increased productivity. This would require a change in the way the machinists did their work. It was estimated that the strike cost Boeing $100 million per day. The machinists also suffered financially. The strike shut down production on more than 1,000 jetliners.

The strike spread over three states and involved about 27,000 workers. Ultimately, a federal mediator assisted both sides in reaching an agreement on a four-year contract. The dispute illustrates how both union and management can be hurt by such a job action.

During a strike, workers picket their place of business. Lines of workers march near the entrances and hold signs that explain to the public the reasons for the strike and their demands. Picketers attempt to prevent nonstriking workers from entering the place of business and carrying on the work of the business. The pickets also discourage suppliers and customers from doing business with the firm.

Logic tells us that the only way any dispute can be resolved is to bring the two sides together so that they can discuss their differences and reach an agreement. Negotiations generally require compromise on both sides. Most labor-management disputes are settled before either side finds it necessary to use the weapons described here.

Management Weapons

Management also has a battery of weapons it can use to pressure labor unions to reach an agreement. One threat a business owner can make is to move to another location. The new spot would likely be in an area that has few unions. Wage rates are generally lower in such areas. The owner might also talk about having work done in another country by low-wage workers.

Sometimes employers will lock out their workers. A **lockout** occurs when the owners close the doors of the business to prevent workers from coming to work. During a lockout, union members do not get paid.

When a union goes on strike, it sometimes takes greater risks than a loss of pay. Some business owners hire **strikebreakers**. They are nonunion workers who are willing to perform the jobs of the union workers who are on strike. If the business is successful in hiring enough replacement workers to keep the business open during a strike, it puts the union at a great disadvantage. After all, when a business is open, management is in a position to hold out for a long time. If strikebreakers perform satisfactorily, management may decide not to call the strikers back to work at all.

Strikes and the Public

Workers and their employers are not the only people affected by labor disputes that result in strikes. Consumers are also affected. When a manufacturer is closed down, the product it makes is in short supply. Retailers that sell the item are also hurt. If a service industry is struck, people are inconvenienced. If a strike against one airline company occurs, bookings for the remaining companies are tough to get. People may not be able to go where they want to when they want to.

Whether the public will look favorably on a strike depends on the issues. Job security or health insurance might be the kinds of issues that

the average person could identify with. A push for higher wages by well-paid workers or for special privileges might not arouse much sympathy. Whether public opinion supports a strike or not does not lessen the inconvenience caused by the job action.

Let's Think

1. What is a labor union?
2. Why do workers find it desirable to join unions?
3. Define the following terms: collective bargaining, contract, boycott, mediation, arbitration, strike, lockout, strikebreaker.
4. How is the public affected by labor disputes?

Labor Union History

Workers' associations or labor unions have existed for a very long time. But not until the Industrial Revolution brought about the factory system did unions grow into powerful forces. In the United States, the influence of workers' organizations became stronger in the latter half of the 19th century.

Knights of Labor

One of the earliest national labor organizations was the Knights of Labor, formed in 1869. It was open to people who had different types of job skills—specialists and unskilled workers. There was no discrimination by sex, race, or national origin. After 1879, its membership vastly increased under the leadership of Terence Powderly. Throughout the 1880s, the Knights fought for fewer working hours per day (eight instead of ten or more), better working conditions, and higher wages for its members. After winning several labor disputes, it reached its peak of 700,000 members in 1886.

The Knights of Labor declined after the Haymarket Riot in Chicago in 1886. Unionists and their supporters held a rally in Haymarket Square to protest police actions that had occurred the night before. A fight had broken out between striking workers at an industrial plant and strike-breakers. While stopping the fight, the police had killed and injured a number of the strikers. When the police appeared at the Haymarket rally to break it up, a bomb exploded. Seven policemen were killed, and many in the crowd suffered injuries. Mass arrests of unionists and outside activists took place. Eight nonunion men were tried and convicted for the bombing even though the evidence against them was weak. Four were executed, and the others were given long prison terms.

Although the people convicted were not members of the Knights of Labor, the public associated the Haymarket Riot with that organization. It soon lost support and faded into oblivion.

Covered with coal dust, John L. Lewis, president (1920–1960) of the United Mine Workers Union, answered reporters' questions after spending eight hours underground investigating an accident that killed 119 coal miners in Illinois in 1951.

American Federation of Labor

Another union organization, the American Federation of Labor (AFL), was formed in 1886. One of its most prominent leaders was Samuel Gompers. Unlike the Knights of Labor, the AFL admitted mainly skilled workers. In a strike situation, skilled workers are more difficult to replace than unskilled workers. The AFL fought for the eight-hour workday, better working conditions, and fringe benefits such as sick leave and vacation pay. Under Gompers, it gained 2.5 million members by 1917.

Like the unions that came before, the AFL faced opposition. This opposition forced the organization to take steps that led to several strikes. The actions turned violent and brought negative publicity to the union. However, it outlasted the setbacks and remains as one of the major labor organizations today.

Congress of Industrial Organizations

By the 1930s, a large number of workers around the United States still did not have union representation. Unskilled workers, in particular, had no champion to fight for them. Labor unions also did not encourage women and minorities to join.

In 1935, John L. Lewis, the head of the United Mine Workers Union, led a movement to separate from the AFL. Joining the mine workers were other unions and union leaders. Lewis believed that the time had come to change the face of organized labor in the United States. He wanted to organize unions as industrial groups that would include both skilled and unskilled workers within a particular industry (for example, mines, automobile, steel, clothing). His group formed a separate organization called the Committee of Industrial Organization. Later it changed its name to the Congress of Industrial Organizations (CIO).

The two major union organizations (AFL and CIO) co-existed independently of each other until the 1950s. In 1955, the two groups merged to form one major association of labor unions. It is now known as the American Federation of Labor–Congress of Industrial Organizations, or the AFL-CIO.

In 2008, unions represented 16.1 million workers, some 12 percent of the labor force in the United States. Unions lost strength as the factory system, traditionally the backbone of the labor movement, underwent major changes. People who work in the professions, offices, and service industries are not widely represented by unions.

In order to be more competitive, businesses have seen the necessity of giving good wages and a solid benefit package to workers. (A benefit package usually includes such items as pay for vacation time and sick days, health insurance, and life insurance.) Such an attitude helps to keep talented employees and give them a reason to be more productive. If they are well treated, workers are less inclined to turn to unions to represent them.

Let's Think

1. What were the aims of the Knights of Labor?
2. What was the American Federation of Labor?
3. What was the Congress of Industrial Organizations?

Government's Relationship With Labor Unions

Early labor unions did not enjoy government support. The government, along with the general public, thought that unions disrupted the normal order of things. Big business had great influence over politicians. Businesses, of course, resented unions. They did not want employees telling them how to run their affairs. Business owners also wanted to keep expenses down. Union demands, they thought, would cut into profits.

Early attempts at organizing were met with court decisions that outlawed most union activity. The government and the courts also used the Sherman Antitrust Act against unions. The act supported the claim that strikes limited the ability of a business to conduct its activities in the way it thought best.

When labor unions went on strike in the early 1900s, management quickly applied to the courts for help. Courts granted **injunctions**, rulings that ordered the strikers back to work.

The Clayton Act of 1914 protected labor unions by recognizing that they had a right to exist. It stated that unions could not be stopped from striking by the claim that the work stoppage restrained, or limited, trade. Most laws aimed at businesses tried to encourage competition. Anti-labor government officials tried to use these laws to restrict labor practices, particularly strikes. Strikes, they said, prevented businesses from conducting business. Therefore, strikes were considered to be in restraint of trade. Although many union leaders hailed the Clayton Act as a step forward in protecting labor rights, more help was needed. The courts tended to interpret the law in favor of the business owners.

The table on page 214 lists the significant laws that have affected government-labor relations in the United States since the 1930s.

Other Government-Labor Relationships

An important gain for American workers that originated during the Great Depression is unemployment insurance. The program was created to help people who have been laid off or fired from a job to find a new job. While they are looking, they receive payment from the state for a period of time. These payments end after a certain amount of time or when the person finds a job.

Unemployment compensation programs are administered by the states with federal assistance. They are financed by employer contributions. In Alaska, Pennsylvania, and New Jersey, employees also contribute. Benefits are distributed through state offices. During 2008, more than $30.5 billion was paid to 9.8 million people. They received an average weekly benefit of $287.73. Under normal circumstances, an unemployed person gets 26 weeks of unemployment benefits. Because of the poor economy in 2008 and 2009, the federal government extended benefits to cover more weeks.

Disability insurance is part of the Social Security package. When a worker is disabled temporarily or permanently, he or she may be entitled to certain benefits. The children under 18 of a disabled worker are also entitled to benefits.

Public Employees and Unions

Millions of people in the nation work for all levels of government. Public sector employees—government workers—include police officers, firefighters, teachers, sanitation workers, air traffic controllers, paramedics, file clerks, and policy

NAME OF LAW	MAJOR PROVISIONS	IMPACT
Norris-LaGuardia Act, 1932	1. Restricted the use of the injunction against labor unions. 2. Outlawed *yellow dog contracts*. (See 2 at right.)	1. Strikes were legalized. 2. Employers could not force workers to promise not to join a union.
National Labor Relations Act (Wagner Act), 1935	1. Management must allow workers to join a union. 2. Management required to negotiate with the designated union. 3. Created the National Labor Relations Board (NLRB).	1. The Wagner Act was one of the most important pro-labor laws ever passed. 2. Blacklists outlawed—they branded some workers as undesirables, thus keeping these workers from being employed. 3. The NLRB hears charges made by labor unions regarding unfair practices by employers.
Taft-Hartley Act, 1947	1. Banned *closed shops*, which required a worker to be a member of the union before he or she could be hired 2. Supported the legality of the *union shop*. 3. Unions can be held responsible for damage caused during a strike. 4. Unions have to file financial records, the background of union officials, and other information with the government. 5. Unions have to announce the possibility of a strike 60 days in advance. 6. The president can call for an 80-day *cooling-off period* if a strike might be harmful to national health or security. 7. Unions are prohibited from making financial contributions to political campaigns. 8. The law created the Federal Mediation and Conciliation Service.	1. The law underscored the importance of labor-management collective bargaining. 2. In union shops, workers who are not members of a union can be hired, but the person has to join the union within a short time after being hired. 3. Pro-union forces believed that the law took away the gains made by labor over the years. 4. Pro-business groups hailed the restrictions.
Landrum-Griffin Act, 1959	1. Unions required to file financial reports with the government. 2. A bill of rights was created to protect union members from leaders who might engage in illegal activities.	1. During the early 1950s, labor unions were being infiltrated by gangsters. Landrum-Griffin aimed to remedy the problem. 2. The purpose was to curb corrupt practices in unions.

makers. They too join unions to improve wages and working conditions.

Many public sector employees provide services that are considered essential to the health and welfare of society. We could not get along very easily without firefighters, police officers, and sanitation workers. Governments at all levels have attempted to regulate public-employee unions in order to remove the right to strike as a weapon. Many states have laws that outlaw strikes by workers in the public sector. They impose severe penalties if a public-employee union goes out on strike.

Many public employees are protected by civil service laws. These laws provide a system of promotion through job performance as well as examinations. Civil service workers are also protected by an elaborate procedure that must be followed if a worker is to be fired.

Let's Think

1. Describe the major provisions of each of the following laws: Clayton Act, Wagner Act, Norris-LaGuardia Act, Taft-Hartley Act, Landrum-Griffin Act.
3. How are the rights of public service employees protected?

Chapter Summary

Businesses can be organized in different ways: sole proprietorship, partnership, and corporation. Sole proprietorship gives the owner complete control over his or her business. The owner is responsible for any debts that the business cannot pay. The partnership is similar to the sole proprietorship in that the partners are personally responsible for the debts. When a partner retires or dies, the partnership ends. When a sole proprietor retires or dies, the business also ends.

The corporation provides greater financial safety for the owners of the business. This is because people own shares, or stock, in a corporation. The responsibility for debt if the business goes bankrupt is limited to the value of the stock a person owns. Personal property and savings are safe. A corporation can last indefinitely.

Goods are produced in great quantities through the mass production process. Most are produced on assembly lines. This is an efficient way of putting the parts of a product together as it moves along an automated track.

As important as it is to produce goods, it is just as important to get the goods to the places where they will be sold. A good transportation system is essential to moving goods to market. Trucks and railroads carry the greatest amount of freight.

Marketing goods is an essential aspect of operating a business. Good marketing practices will result in good sales. Today, many companies rely on mass-marketing outlets to sell their goods.

In 1887, the government passed the Interstate Commerce Act, which regulated the pricing practices of railroads. The Interstate Commerce Commission was created to regulate the transportation industry.

As large businesses developed, they engaged in practices that limited competition. These practices included mergers, holding companies, and trusts. To curb these monopolistic practices, the federal government passed the Sherman Antitrust Act of 1890 and the Clayton Antitrust Act of 1914. Also in 1914, the Federal Trade Commission Act was passed to ensure that businesses engage in fair trading practices.

After decades of promoting regulations for businesses, the government has begun to eliminate many rules affecting business practices. Deregulation has its supporters and critics.

In the early stages of industrialization, conditions in the factories were poor and wages low. Soon workers banded together to form organizations called unions. The major function of a union is to secure better working conditions, higher wages, and job security for its members. Having one organization to speak for all the workers in a company increases the power of the workers.

In order to secure agreements between labor and management, unions use several approaches. The most important is negotiation. Both sides to a labor dispute sit down together, discuss the issues, and try to reach an agreement, or contract. When they are unsuccessful in reaching an agreement, unions might engage in a

◀ REALITY CHECK ▶

Google, a Business Success Story

Perhaps you have a term paper to write. Your teacher wants you to use documents, statistics, and even graphs. Or perhaps you want to get the best possible price on the latest electronic game you want your parents to buy for your birthday. For these and other tasks, all you have to do is sit down at the computer to find the information you need. You just "google" the right words, and a list of references appears in front of you. We take search engines such as Google for granted now. But not long ago, search engines did not exist. Your parents and grandparents might have had to hike over to the library and spend hours searching through printed reference materials to find the right information for the term paper. They might have had to visit several stores before finding the best price for the electronic game. Now, life has been made much easier through the computer and the use of search engines.

One of the most interesting success stories of innovation in business is the formation of Google. In a few years, it became a leader in Internet browsing. The company began after two close friends, Larry Page and Sergey Brin, met while attending graduate school at Stanford University, in California. There they set out to create a search engine for information that was already on the Internet. Their search engine proved to be better than the ones already in existence. It is now used worldwide, and the search clues have been translated into more than 100 languages.

In order to move their idea forward as a business, Page and Brin needed capital. They managed to raise money from several professors at Stanford and from others willing to invest in the hope of making a profit. With those funds in hand, they began the development of this now corporate giant.

One question remained: How does a company that provides a vehicle for searching the Internet make money? The answer was to solicit advertisements. Google sold ads to companies that could be associated with the information people might be searching for. As an example, one might be searching for information about a favorite sports team. On the page with the search results, there would appear ads for companies associated with sports. The ads might be from a sneaker company, a golf club manufacturer, or a company that makes baseball gloves. The placement of an ad link or the size of an ad did not determine how much the advertiser would have to pay to Google. The fee was based on how many times consumers clicked on the ad to link to the advertiser's page. In this way, Google took into consideration customer interest in the product or service.

As the company grew, Brin and Page built a huge business campus in Mountain View, California, in Silicon Valley. Known as the Googleplex, it is a unique place in which to work. The company does not impose a dress code on employees. There are several restaurants where the employees can eat gourmet food for lunch and dinner, sometimes at no cost. Google provides scooters for employees to get around the campus. The complex also includes workout rooms, washers and dryers, a massage room, assorted games, a wave pool, and volleyball courts. Twice a week, roller hockey is played in the parking lot. It is Brin's and Page's belief that an informal atmosphere, recreational facilities, and good salaries help foster creativity. The company prides itself on "out-of-the-box" thinking and being on the "cutting edge" of innovation.

1. How did Page and Brin begin their business?
2. Why might people think that working at Google is a unique experience?
3. Give arguments for and against the idea that the work atmosphere at Google fosters creativity.

boycott or agree to bring in a mediator or arbitrator to help both sides come together. Both sides agree to accept the proposed solution before the arbitration begins. The most drastic tactic used by a union is the strike, a work stoppage. This is considered to be a last-resort maneuver.

Management also has several ways of bringing pressure on a union. They include negotiation, the use of strikebreakers, and lockouts.

The Knights of Labor was an important labor union in the late 1800s. After it was falsely accused of setting off a bomb at a labor rally in Chicago in 1886, its support faded away. The next important union was the American Federation of Labor, formed mainly of skilled laborers. During the 1930s, a union of unskilled workers was founded—the Congress of Industrial Organizations. In 1955, the AFL and the CIO merged to become the AFL-CIO.

The Clayton Act of 1914 recognized the right of unions to exist. Other laws that protected unions were the Norris-LaGuardia Act of 1932 and the Wagner Act of 1935. The Taft-Hartley Act of 1947 and the Landrum-Griffin Act of 1959 regulated unions more closely in a less favorable way.

Public employees have formed unions. But many government workers, such as police officers, firefighters, and teachers, are considered to perform essential services. They cannot legally go out on strike.

★ CHAPTER REVIEW ★

A. Matching
Match each term in Column A with its definition in Column B.

i. the combination of two or more businesses into one
j. organization of workers

Column A
1. sole proprietorship
2. corporation
3. mass production
4. Interstate Commerce Act
5. merger
6. union
7. negotiation
8. arbitration
9. Wagner Act
10. lockout

Column B
a. the process of manufacturing large amounts of goods
b. use of third party to impose a solution to a dispute
c. the closing of a business by management to prevent workers from working
d. law that established the National Labor Relations Board
e. type of business organization that limits liability in case of bankruptcy
f. the process of bargaining between labor and management.
g. law first passed to regulate railroads
h. a one-person business

B. Multiple Choice
Select the statement or word that most correctly answers the question or completes the statement.

1. The type of business in which people can buy shares of stock is called a **(a)** corporation **(b)** partnership **(c)** sole proprietorship **(d)** principal ownership.

2. Individuals and businesses that are owed money are called **(a)** proprietors **(b)** creditors **(c)** debtors **(d)** charters.

3. Getting goods to market is called **(a)** separation **(b)** stocking **(c)** distribution **(d)** monopolizing.

4. This law was enacted in 1887 to regulate railroads: **(a)** Taft-Hartley Act **(b)** Clayton Act **(c)** Landrum-Griffin Act **(d)** Interstate Commerce Act.

5. A company that buys shares of stock in other companies to gain control of these companies is a **(a)** holding company **(b)** sole proprietorship **(c)** partnership **(d)** superstore.

6. The process of negotiation by a union for a contract with management is called **(a)** collective bargaining **(b)** striking **(c)** boycotting **(d)** picketing.

7. An action taken by a union as a last resort to pressure management in a labor dispute is the **(a)** boycott **(b)** merger **(c)** strike **(d)** lockout.

8. This union organized mainly unskilled workers: **(a)** AFL **(b)** Knights of Labor **(c)** NLRB **(d)** CIO.

9. This law provides for a "cooling-off period" if a strike is seen as hurting the national health or security: **(a)** Landrum-Griffin Act **(b)** Taft-Hartley Act **(c)** Wagner Act **(d)** Clayton Act.

10. The ability of this group of union workers to strike is limited or banned by law: **(a)** unskilled workers **(b)** private employees **(c)** public employees **(d)** television reporters.

C. Essay

Write a paragraph about *one* of the following:

1. It takes much planning to start a business.

2. As businesses grew in the United States, the government found it necessary to pass laws to regulate certain business practices.

3. Competition is important to American businesses and consumers.

4. Deregulation of industry has sparked debate in the United States.

5. Unions are important for workers.

D. A Challenge for You

1. Create a scrapbook or a bulletin board display of articles about important issues facing American businesses today. Summarize the articles. Discuss why these issues are important to the public.

2. Choose the most important law regulating business, in your opinion, and write a three-minute speech explaining the reasons for your choice.

3. Create a cartoon strip that depicts the history of labor unions in the United States.

4. Interview several leaders or members of unions to find out how each union helps its members. Discuss what actually happens during the negotiation process. Report your findings to the class.

5. Interview several owners of businesses. Prepare questions in advance to help you find out what type of business structure each chose and why. Report your findings to the class.

Document-Based Question

State the main idea expressed in each document. Then use information in the documents and your own knowledge to write an essay explaining how companies try to compete today.

Local Company Tries to Compete Nationally

Have you ever had Blue Bell ice cream? It depends almost entirely on where you live.

In Texas and a number of nearby states, chances are you've had a scoop. In some markets, more than half the ice cream sold is Blue Bell. Its regional might is so great that even though it is not available in most the of the country, it is the nation's No. 3 ice cream.

What is the secret to Blue Bell's sweet success? To Howard W. Kruse, chief executive of Blue Bell Creameries Inc., it is simple. "We make the best ice cream in the country," he said. "The milk we use is so fresh, it was grass yesterday."

But part of the formula is surely Blue Bell's homespun appeal, with constant reminders of its folkloric "little creamery in Brenham." . . .

The question now is whether this almost cultish mystique can survive as Blue Bell strives to become a true national brand, gradually stretching its radius as it enters one new market after another.

A local favorite can easily make it big in the wider world, . . . or it can face a rougher journey.

For one thing, cutting corners on quality can backfire. Harder to control, though, is that regional tastes vary. New Yorkers may not crave the same ice cream Texans do. And some products just can't make it if they lose their down-home image.

Blue Bell hopes it can cope with all this, partly by maintaining strict oversight on production, and still grow outside its regional base. . . .

With $3.3 billion in sales, the market for store-bought ice cream is filled with plenty of contenders defending their turf. . . .

Its greatest difficulty in pursuing a wider market has been distribution. Like so many other small food and beverage companies, Blue Bell has had difficulty gaining shelf space.

From "Maintaining Local Flavor" by Kate Murphy. Copyright © February 7, 1998, by the New York Times Co. Reprinted by permission.

Boeing Prepares for the Future

The Boeing Company announced yesterday that it planned to acquire the McDonnell Douglas Corporation in a $13.3 billion deal, the 10th largest merger in American history and the largest ever in the aerospace industry.

The acquisition would make Boeing the only manufacturer of commercial jets in the United States while catapulting it ahead of Lockheed Martin Corporation as the world's largest aerospace company and . . . [strengthening] its status as the nation's leading exporter. . . .

Yesterday's announcement signals that aircraft manufacturing will increasingly be a competition among nations. Airbus Industrie, the European Consortium [association of companies] that sold its first jet in 1974, has grown to be a formidable [impressive] competitor behind Boeing.

So far this year, by some measures, Boeing has won roughly 60 percent of new commercial orders and Airbus has won 35 percent, leaving McDonnell Douglas with about 5 percent of the new orders.

Executives in Boeing and McDonnell Douglas, as well as industry experts, said the deal made sense. Boeing is predominantly a commercial aircraft builder that hopes to continue expanding its presence in military contracting while the bulk of McDonnell Douglas's business is already in the military field. With a rich history in commercial aircraft and substantial manufacturing capacity, McDonnell Douglas also can help Boeing meet increased worldwide demand for new planes. . . .

From "Boeing Offering $13 Billion to Buy McDonnell Douglas, Last U.S. Commercial Rival" by Adam Bryant. Copyright © December 16, 1996, by the New York Times Co. Reprinted by permission.

CHAPTER 13

Wise Participation in the Nation's Economy

★ **CHAPTER FOCUS**

★ 1. How do you participate in the nation's economy?
2. What does it mean to be a wise consumer?
3. How can you plan for a secure financial future?

★

Do you know how you influence the economy? You can start to find out by taking the following quiz. Check "yes" or "no" for each action to indicate whether you think it does or does not influence the economy.

ACTION	YES	NO
Opening a savings account in a bank		
Purchasing and downloading the latest music by your favorite artist		
Buying a loaf of bread		
Taking out a loan		
Buying something with a credit card		
Investing in stocks, bonds, or mutual funds		

If your answer in each case was "yes," you are correct in thinking that the action influences the economy. You and everyone you know are all consumers. As consumers, you are the driving force in the nation's economy. Even if you save or invest instead of buying, you are a participant.

As a participant, you help to determine the present and future course of the nation's economic health. You have a great deal of power.

Making Wise Economic Decisions

Good citizenship includes being a responsible participant in the economy. As a good "economic citizen," you should spend wisely, avoid getting too deeply in debt, and plan for your future. Sharing information is another aspect of being a good "economic citizen."

Affecting the Market

Your purchase of goods makes you a driving force in the nation's economy. Your decisions about whether to buy or not to buy an item affect the seller (retailer) and the manufacturer. This is true whether you are making a large purchase for an automobile or a small purchase for a compact disc (CD).

To illustrate how your actions may affect the market, let us assume that you are going off to college and want the most up-to-date cell phone. When the X-phone first came out, it was in great demand. The original X-phone sold for more than $200. Other cell phones were less expensive, but the X-phone was innovative and fashionable. Many people paid the asking price. Within a year, though, a new, less expensive model was developed.

What would happen if you and your friends and others around the country decided not to purchase the new phone because of the high cost? Probably nothing, you think. Others will likely buy it no matter what the price is. This is a common thought. But many people will react as you did and will refuse to buy the phone when it first comes out. As smart shoppers, you and others might decide to wait for the phone to go on sale or look for a less expensive cell phone with similar features.

If more and more people hold off on buying the X-phone, its sales will likely fall. Retailers may drop the price in order to make the item more attractive to buyers. If the reduced price is more acceptable to the buying public, sales may increase because the product is still in demand. Your action, combined with similar actions by thousands of others, might affect the income of the retailer. (Of course, putting off buying the item may not always result in lowering the price.)

A real example of how demand affects prices occurred in the early 1980s. A major toy manufacturer created the Cabbage Patch Dolls. They were cute and pudgy and were each given a name and a "birth certificate." These dolls became so popular that people paid almost $100 for one that normally sold for about $40. Why? Children begged for the dolls, and parents and grandparents wanted to make the children happy. In time, as with many other crazes, the demand died down and prices dropped. Why? Individual shoppers refused to pay the higher price for the doll, leading to fewer sales. Store owners want merchandise to move out of the store, not stay on the shelves. By buying or not buying, we affect the profitability of a business. We are "players in the economy."

A sign in a New Jersey store in November 1983 announces that it has no more Cabbage Patch dolls. The dolls were an extremely popular gift item for the holidays that year.

Managing Your Money

You get an allowance. Perhaps it is $20 a week. There are many things you want to do with this money. Perhaps you plan to go to the movies at the end of the week and go out with your friends for a hamburger. Then you want to buy your mom or dad a birthday gift at the end of the month, and you need to save some money for that purpose. Making sure that you will have money for all this requires budgeting. Creating a plan to guide you in how to spend your allowance is wise decision making.

In a similar way, adults plan how they will spend their money. They determine how much income they have and what bills they must pay in a certain period of time (a week or month). Before they spend, they decide what to buy, how much to spend, and when to spend.

Smart Shopping

Learning how to shop wisely makes you a responsible consumer. It also helps you to get the most for the money you spend. The following are suggestions that will help you become a more knowledgeable consumer.

Study Advertisements

Advertisements are messages and campaigns created by businesses to persuade consumers to use a particular product or service. They are designed to attract you, the consumer, to a product"—to make you think you need it. Ads promote everything from breakfast cereal to political candidates and charities.

Are ads truthful? Will you get what they promise? The only way to tell is for you to do your homework as an intelligent consumer. Sometimes it means reading books and articles in magazines and newspapers about products and companies. Becoming an intelligent consumer may require you to make telephone calls to appropriate public or private agencies to get information. (Much information may be available on the Internet.) What it all comes down to is that you must actively seek out information and question the claims of advertising promotions.

Advertisements can be very attractive. After all, they are designed to capture our interest and appeal to our imagination. They promise romance, adventure, pleasure—all the good things in life. A wise consumer will look behind the color and fun and determine what the product can actually do. The following checklist will help you analyze the accuracy of advertisements.

Advertising Checklist

1. What does the advertisement claim the product will do?

2. Is the information accurate?

3. Does the advertisement imply that the product will do more than it is supposed to?

4. Does the wording of the advertisement really give you the information you need to make a wise decision?

5. Is there a message in the advertisement that appeals more to your emotions than to your practical need for the product?

Read the Fine Print

Be sure to look at all parts of an ad. Print ads often use large-size type to attract your attention. Sometimes, though, the most important information is in the tiny type at the bottom. It lets you know the limitations of the offer.

Get Advice

An informal method of discovering who advertises reliably is to speak to friends and relatives. You may discover that they have had experience doing business with a company. Recommendations by someone you respect may go a long way toward helping you make wise buying decisions.

Compare Offers

It is also important to research the price and quality of an item. You can do that by going to different stores to look at different brands. Ask questions of salespeople, and above all, don't be afraid to take notes so that you can compare one brand with another. Comparison shopping helps you get the most for your money.

A good source of information about products is *Consumer Reports* magazine. It is published monthly by the Consumers Union (CU), a national nonprofit organization. The Consumers Union tests products and reports its findings in the magazine. *Consumer Reports* does not accept advertising. The tests determine the durability of a product, how well it functions, and if it does what it promises to do. The articles also tell what prices are charged for a product in a variety of stores. Several brands are compared. If you are making an important purchase, you can bet that somewhere along the way, the Consumers Union has tested it. Your local library should have back issues of the magazine. The magazine also has a Web site, which gives some free information (www.consumerreports.org).

Another organization to contact is the Consumer Federation of America (CFA). Located in Washington, D.C., it produces many consumer-oriented publications. Visit the Web site at www.consumerfed.org.

More and more Americans are shopping on the Internet. Many of the same good practices that apply to shopping in stores also apply to purchasing items on the Internet. It is important to know the reliability of an Internet seller. Make sure the company is reputable. Check the site and read the "All About Us" link that appears on most sites. Compare the prices and companies that advertise on the Internet.

Stopping Crime

A serious problem that shoppers and store owners face is shoplifting—stealing items from a store. Shoplifting costs stores millions of dollars a year. It also hurts consumers. When this crime causes businesspeople to lose money, they are forced to install security measures to curb the practice. The cost of these measures along with the cost of the stolen goods is passed on to the consumer in the form of higher prices.

Laws Protect the Consumer

Claims in advertising are regulated by state and local laws. In some cases, Federal Trade Commission rules affect advertising practices. In order not to be taken advantage of by merchants, one should be aware of laws concerning improper selling practices.

What Is a Sale?

Laws define what is meant by a "sale." We see signs in windows of stores claiming "Sale! Prices slashed 40%!" Most communities have laws requiring that the reduction in price must be taken from the regular price of an item. One practice a store owner is not allowed to do is raise listed prices just before a sale is about to begin. It is illegal to raise prices and then lower them to the original prices and call the change a sale. For example: A shirt usually sells for $35.00. The owner of the store raises the price to $43.50 just a week before the sale. The following week, the sale starts, and the store owner puts the shirt on sale at $35.00. This is considered to be a deceptive sales practice and is illegal. Records must show that an item was marked at a certain price for a specified period of time before it can be called the regular price. Sometimes, stores claim that the price was "reduced" to $35.00 when it was never any higher!

It is difficult to prove that these practices are occurring. One way to be sure is to watch the pricing of something you need and determine the price before it goes on sale. If you suspect that the sale is deceptive or untrue, you can make a complaint to your local department of consumer affairs.

Bait and Switch

Another illegal and deceptive sales practice is called **bait and switch**. This occurs when you are lured into a store by an advertisement that offers an item at a great price (the "bait"). When you

An announcement of a sale in a store. The sign tells customers how much the markdowns are and how long the sale will last. Note the terms "ticketed price" and "orig. (original) price." They help customers judge how much they may be saving.

ask about the item, the salesperson says that the advertised item isn't available or is inferior to others. The salesperson may then quickly steer you to another, usually higher-priced item (the "switch"). The use of this practice is almost universally outlawed.

Know Product Warranties

A wise consumer should know about product **warranties**. A warranty is an assurance by a manufacturer that a product will perform as expected for a specified amount of time. Some products have 90-day warranties. Others may have ones that last a year or longer. Many automobile manufacturers warrant their cars for three years or 36,000 miles, whichever occurs first, while a few actually offer 10-year or 100,000-mile warranties, whichever comes first. One must carefully read the car warranties to see what coverage is offered. Many warranties do not provide complete or so-called "bumper to bumper" protection.

It is important to read the terms of a warranty. Each product carries a different set of rules. If a product breaks or fails to perform as expected within the warranty period, you will need to contact the manufacturer to ask for satisfaction. The store where you purchased the item is not usually responsible for the warranty.

Before You Complain

Sometimes people create their own problems because they don't use a product in the way it was intended to be used. Certainly you would not purchase a CD and use it as a Frisbee! If it became scratched and consequently did not play well, you couldn't really complain to the record store that you had been sold faulty goods. Even though this example is exaggerated, it demonstrates a point. Read labels and be sure you understand what a product can and cannot do before you purchase it. Labels also often tell us how to care for a product. It is our responsibility as wise consumers to study labels.

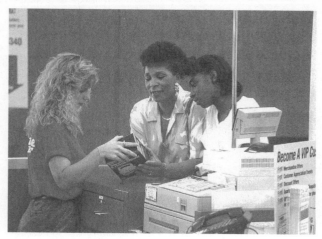

Customers getting help with a problem from a clerk in an office supply store.

Where to Go for Help

Consumers have several places to complain to when they believe they have fallen victim to deceptive or illegal business practices. Most of these avenues can be found locally in your community. If not, there are state offices you can turn to. Both private and government organizations exist to help. When you have a complaint, there are several steps you should take before initiating formal legal action.

Step One—Contact the Store

First, you should speak with store personnel—the sales clerk, the manager, even the president or owner, if necessary. Be polite but firm. State clearly the problem and how you want it remedied.

Most stores want to maintain goodwill with their customers and will usually try to resolve any problems quickly. Most reputable stores will give a refund for defective merchandise or replace it if you follow the terms of their refund policy. You should find out what the refund policy of the store is before you make a purchase. If it is not stated on signs near the cash register, be sure to ask.

Sometimes clerks or managers will not give you satisfaction. If this happens, you should try to speak to the store owner. If it is a large chain store, you may need to contact the customer relations head or the president of the chain. If you still are not able to get satisfaction, go to Step Two.

Step Two—Public and Private Help

Most local governments have a department of consumer affairs that monitors businesses to make sure that they are not engaging in deceptive practices. In addition, many state attorneys general are responsible for protecting consumers from deceptive advertising and other illegal business practices. Both of these arms of the government have the power to impose fines on businesses or bring legal action against them. You can contact these officials if you have a problem with a business. Their phone numbers can be found in the telephone directory.

Another organization that can be helpful to consumers is the local *Better Business Bureau (BBB)*. Better Business Bureaus are associations supported by most reputable businesses. They maintain records of complaints against commercial establishments. You can contact the BBB by phone or online to check the reputation of a business you want to deal with. It will tell you how many complaints about a business have been registered with it.

Calling in the Media

Many local television stations have a consumer reporter who investigates consumer problems of general interest. An account of how the problem was solved may be featured on a newscast. Such reporters may also handle stories about false advertising and other questionable or illegal business practices. To avoid negative publicity, businesses are generally willing to resolve a

◀REALITY CHECK▶

Dealing With Consumer Fraud/Identity Theft

You get your monthly credit card statement and see that it includes purchases for hundreds of dollars of goods and services you did not make. Later, you get statements from credit card accounts that you did not open. You get calls from companies saying that you owe money for items you bought, but you have never been to those stores. These examples demonstrate what happens if you are a victim of **consumer fraud**.

In 2007, the Federal Trade Commission (FTC) published a report on the types of consumer fraud that come to its attention. According to the report, 813,899 complaints were filed in 2007. People who were victims of **identity theft** made the largest number of complaints. They accounted for 32 percent of all complaints, numbering 258,427. The report stated that credit card fraud was the most common form of reported identity theft (23 percent), followed by utilities fraud (18 percent), employment fraud (14 percent), and bank fraud (13 percent). According to the report, fraud losses amounted to $1.2 billion.

The FTC encourages consumers to file a complaint with the agency if there has been evidence of wrongdoing. The agency gathers information in an effort to develop patterns of fraud. Eventually, the information could lead to criminal prosecution.

The FTC Web site contains a great deal of information that helps educate consumers and assist them in making wise decisions. People are victims of many types of crimes. Some, such as consumer fraud, can be very damaging to one's credit rating.

If people gain access to your Social Security number, they can wreak havoc on your credit rating. They can take out loans by using the stolen identity. They can clean out bank accounts. With the information stolen from you, thieves can open new accounts at different addresses. These thieves use the accounts without your knowledge. These criminals have no intention of paying the bills they run up. Suddenly, you might be contacted by a collection agency asking for money owed

on purchases you did not make. Once the thefts are discovered, the victims have to spend a lot of time and money trying to prove that they were not the ones who borrowed the money in the first place. It can take months and sometimes years to straighten out the problem.

It is extremely important that you always keep your credit and debit cards secure. You should also keep your personal information private. There are times when you may have to provide your Social Security number—on a credit application or another form, for example. Just be sure the number will be kept secure. Never give out your Social Security number in an e-mail or a telephone call. Never provide personal information to people or organizations you do not know. Call the institution that claims to need the information and verify that it is actually requesting the information. These steps will help keep your credit records in order and protect you from many hours of resolving problems related to debts piled up by people who have stolen your identity.

Another action to take is to check your credit reports periodically. These reports are free. Doing this will ensure that the information in a report is accurate. If you see discrepancies, you should contact the credit agencies, submit written explanations, and put fraud alerts on the accounts. You can also discover which accounts listed on your credit report are not yours. Then you can have them closed as fraudulent.

The electronic age has made life easier for us in many ways. But the use of electronic devices can also complicate our lives. As a wise consumer, you must be very careful to protect sensitive information.

1. Define consumer fraud.
2. What is the most common consumer fraud crime reported to the FTC?
3. How does identity theft hurt you?
4. What steps can you take to prevent identity theft?

dispute once they understand the nature of the problem.

When you have a problem, don't think you can immediately contact your local station for help. The consumer reporter will expect you to have taken steps to resolve your problem before you come to him or her. You will be expected to have:

1. copies of contracts and sales receipts

2. a record of all telephone calls and the names of people you spoke to

3. copies of all letters you wrote and received

4. records of governmental or private organizations you contacted, such as the BBB, your community's department of consumer affairs, or the Federal Trade Commission.

Small Claims Court

Many communities have what is known as a **small claims court**. This court allows people to institute a lawsuit that concerns only a small amount of money without involving a lawyer. Many small claims courts set a ceiling on the amount a person may sue for. (Check your local laws before bringing a lawsuit to small claims court.) Cases concerning amounts above that ceiling would have to be filed in a higher civil court.

A small claims court, for the most part, is a low-cost, "do-it-yourself" court. Anyone may go to the local court office and complete papers that will be delivered to the person being sued. The papers require the parties to be in court on a certain day to answer the charges. You do not have to bring a lawyer with you. The case is usually heard by a judge or a hearing officer who is empowered to decide who is right and who is wrong.

Let's Think

1. How does creating a budget help a person spend wisely?
2. What should a wise consumer look for in an advertisement?
3. What is comparison shopping?
4. Identify the following terms: sale, bait and switch.

5. Describe the steps one should take to settle a dispute over a sales transaction.

Buying on Credit

So you want to buy a new stereo system for your room or a new bicycle equipped with all the latest features. You do not have the money on hand to buy these items with cash. But the sales are so good that you would save a lot of money by making the purchase now. Your solution is to buy on credit. Making a purchase on credit is like taking out a loan. Whether you get the loan from a bank or charge it on a credit card, the idea is the same. You are using someone else's money to make the purchase.

Applying for a Credit Card

People often get mail that says they have been preapproved for a credit card or that urges them to apply for a low-interest credit card. Ask your parents to show you some of the mail they get from credit card companies. Such mail includes applications and information about the amount of interest charged and the annual fee for the right to use the card. The application asks for certain information about you to help the credit card company decide whether it should take a chance on you. (See page 227.) Here is some of the information that you will be asked to provide:

Name and address

Social Security number

How long you have lived at your present address

Whether you own or rent your home

Your monthly rent or home mortgage payment

Where you work

How long you have worked there

What your monthly income is

What credit cards you currently have

After you submit your application, the credit card company will investigate your background

Invitation   **Popular** BANK CARD

NAME AND ADDRESS
NOTE: Your name and address will appear on your account as shown below. Please make corrections below, if necessary.

PLEASE TELL US ABOUT YOURSELF

007834322

JANE DOE
8860 MAIN STREET
FLUSHING, NC 21374

Years at Current Address	Own Home		Condo/Co-op
	Rent	Parents	Other

Social Security Number

Date of Birth (Mo./Day/Yr.)

Mother's Maiden Name

Home Phone No. with Area Code

Gold Invitation: **#89355141**	Credit Line: **up to $10,000**

Name on Phone Bill

Previous Home Address	Street		Years There
	City	State	Zip

PLEASE TELL US ABOUT YOUR WORK

Employer/ Business Name	Years at Job	Check Here if Applicable:	Retired	Self-Employed
Position		Business Phone No. with Area Code		

ABOUT YOUR INCOME

You do not have to include alimony, child support, spouse's yearly income, separate maintenance or other income unless you want us to consider it in connection with this application. Your total **yearly** income from all sources must be at least **$25,000** to be considered for Gold cardmembership, and at least $8,000 to be considered for silver cardmembership.

Your Total Personal **Yearly** Income	Other **Yearly** Household Income
$, .00	$, .00

Source(s) of Other **Yearly** Household Income

ABOUT YOUR EXISTING ACCOUNTS

Please check those that apply. Be sure to specify Bank/Institution Name.

Money Market/Investments	Yes	No
Checking Acct.	Yes	No
Savings Acct./CD/Treasuries	Yes	No
Stocks/Bonds	Yes	No

Visa®/MasterCard®	Diners Club	American Express Card
Department Store/Sears	Gasoline	Other

Please Fill In Your Total Monthly Loan Payment, Including All Applicable Auto, Personal And Home Improvement Loans. $, .00

WOULD YOU LIKE AN ADDITIONAL CARD AT NO CHARGE?

If yes, please print the full name of the family or household member.

PLEASE SIGN HERE
By signing below, I certify that I have read the Disclosures, agree to and meet all the Terms and Conditions of Offer stated on the reverse side of this Invitation.

Applicant's Signature	Date
X	

AP-GN7R7-04

A sample credit-card application form.

and determine if you are a good credit risk. If they allow you to borrow their money, can they be reasonably sure that you will repay the loan? People can have trouble getting credit if they have never borrowed before. One reason is that the creditor, the company making the loan, doesn't know whether you can be counted on to pay back the loan. If you have never borrowed money, you don't have a credit history, or a track record of meeting repayment obligations.

Once approved, you will be sent a credit card for your use. Using a credit card carries a lot of responsibility. It is important for you to know the terms of the agreement you have entered into.

POWER *of* ★ ONE

Ralph Nader

Today you decide to take a ride with your parents to the local mall. You get into the car, and your parents buckle their seat belts and start the car. Mom turns to you in the back and tells you not to forget to fasten your seat belt. Without giving it another thought, you buckle up. Most cars today also have air bags to protect passengers. These safety features and others are in automobiles because one man waged a campaign that woke the nation up to vehicle safety problems. His name is Ralph Nader.

Ralph Nader was born in Connecticut in 1934. His parents had come to the United States from Lebanon. They were involved in local politics and believed that it was the responsibility of all citizens to work for justice in a democratic society.

Nader graduated from Princeton University in 1955. While there, he showed that he was not afraid to "paddle upstream against the current." He stood up for causes he believed were right no matter who opposed him. One of the causes was to stop the spraying of campus trees with DDT. DDT is an insecticide that was eventually banned for use in the United States because of its harmful effects on humans and animals.

In 1958, Nader earned his law degree from Harvard Law School. He then established a private law practice in Hartford, Connecticut, and set up an informal legal aid program. This is a program that provides free or low-cost legal services to the poor.

During his time at Harvard, Nader became interested in automobile safety after studying automobile injury cases. He found that the law usually blamed drivers for accidents, never assuming that the automobiles might have been unsafe. Nader began to write magazine articles calling for improved safety standards in automobiles. He also made speeches and testified at hearings held by the state legislatures of Connecticut and Massachusetts.

To make a greater impact in the area of auto safety, Nader decided to take his fight to the nation's capital. He became a consultant at the Department of Labor. Nader bombarded U.S. senators with information about the need for greater automobile safety. After a while, he devoted all of his time to writing a book about auto safety in the United States. In 1965, *Unsafe at Any Speed: The Designed-In Dangers of the American Automobile* was published. It attacked the American automobile industry in general but focused in on one particular automobile, the

---

The back of the application contains a list of rules and terms that you are agreeing to abide by when using the card. It lists the interest rate and explains how the interest will be computed. The maximum amount you can charge is also listed, as are the fees for late payments.

Using Credit Cards

Normally, you get a credit card bill once a month. It lists your purchases, where they were bought, the amounts charged to the card during the previous month, when the payment is due, and what the minimum payment is. The minimum is the least amount of money you can send to the company without being penalized. The minimum is usually a small percentage of what you owe.

Many cards will not charge interest if the entire balance is paid by the date the payment is due. Sometimes people decide to stretch the repayment of a credit card balance over a period of time. It is then that owning a credit card becomes expensive. If you pay only a portion of the balance,

Corvair, produced by the Chevrolet division of General Motors. It was, he wrote, "one of the nastiest-handling cars ever built." The Corvair was unstable and prone to spinning out of control. The book quickly became a best seller.

Government officials and private citizens became concerned about the safety of the automobiles they drove. Shortly after the book's publication, Congress held hearings about automobile safety. President Lyndon B. Johnson called for a highway safety act.

Nader accused General Motors of investigating and harassing him. He continued to criticize Ford and General Motors for equipping their cars with unreliable seat belts and other companies for faulty designs. Automobile manufacturers, he said, should reveal all defects discovered in their models.

The National Traffic and Motor Vehicle Safety Act became law in 1966. The *Washington Post* editorialized, "Most of the credit for making possible this important legislation belongs to one man—Ralph Nader. . . . Through his book, *Unsafe at Any Speed*, his determination, and his seemingly limitless energy, he won; a one-man lobby for the public prevailed over the Nation's most powerful industry." Today, there are laws that require automobile manufacturers to recall automobiles when safety flaws are discovered and repair the machines at no cost to the owner. This is an outgrowth of Nader's crusade for auto safety.

Nader, supported by researchers called "Nader's Raiders," later turned his attention to other areas of concern: safety in mining, safety of natural gas pipelines, reducing the amount of X-rays we receive at the dentist's office, improving the quality of life for Native Americans. He also pushed for a law to improve federal inspection standards in slaughterhouses and meat-processing plants. Nader obtained a long-buried Department of Agriculture study of horrible conditions in these facilities and passed it along to the press. To keep the pressure on Congress, Nader organized a letter-writing campaign, gave speeches across the country, and wrote critical magazine articles. The Wholesome Meat Act passed in 1967.

In 1971, Nader founded Public Citizen, a consumer's watchdog organization. It has concerned itself with fighting for such things as safe medicine (drugs), safer medical devices, and cleaner and safer energy.

In 1996, 2000, 2004 and 2008, Nader campaigned to be elected president of the United States. On his Web site, he listed the following as some of his accomplishments. "Founder of 28 non-profit citizen advocacy groups; including Center for Study of Responsive Law, Public Interest Research Group, Center for Auto Safety, and Clean Water Action Project." Nader's aim is to make people aware of problems, to get businesses and the government to act responsibly, and to improve life for all.

1. What did Nader do to make the automobile industry change?
2. What can other citizens do to bring about changes in society?
3. In your opinion, why was Nader so successful?

---

the company begins to charge you interest on the unpaid balance. This is good for the credit card company and bad for the consumer. The credit card company makes a profit from the interest it charges you on the loan. Interest rates charged by credit card companies are generally higher than the rates charged by banks for consumer loans.

Some credit card companies charge an annual fee. The fee can range from $35 to $50 or more. Many companies do not charge an annual fee. You must do your homework and shop around for the terms that are best for you.

Pros and Cons of Credit Cards

A credit card can be a good source of instant buying power. It provides us with funds when we need to make an unplanned, but necessary, or bargain-rate purchase. A credit card can help us handle emergencies. Perhaps the family car broke down while you were on a trip. The unexpected expense to repair it might have drained the family of the cash you needed to continue on the trip. Using a credit card to pay for the repair may have saved the trip. A credit card can also offer you protection. If something goes wrong with the purchase or the repair, and the merchant won't correct the problem, you can inform the credit card company and explain the nature of the dispute. It will investigate and hold up payment to the merchant until the dispute is settled.

There is also a downside to using a credit card. You may go on a buying spree. Without thinking of how you will pay for the purchases, you just hand over your credit card and charge the items. When the bill comes in, you may be shocked by how much you charged. You realize that you won't be able to pay the bill in full this month. You could, of course, just write a check for the minimum payment. The balance is then carried over to succeeding months. Depending on how much you owe, this could go on for some time. All the while, the credit card company collects interest on the outstanding balance. So, paying just the minimum can make your purchases very costly by the time they are finally paid for. It's easy to fall into the trap of spending more than you should when you use a credit card. The important question to ask is: "If I charge this, will I be able to pay it off quickly?"

Many young people get their first credit card when they go off to college. For some, this easy access to credit gets them into trouble. They charge everything—books, pizzas, "in" clothing, vacations. At first, they keep up by making only the minimum payment each month. As time goes on, though, the debt gets larger and larger—sometimes reaching into thousands of dollars. Even making the minimum payment gets to be a burden. If they stop paying, they end up with a bad credit rating. This may prevent them from getting a loan in the future when they really need it for a car or a house.

Many people prefer to use a *debit card* instead of a traditional credit card. A debit card is linked to your bank account. With a debit card, the amount of a purchase is deducted right away from your bank account, most often the checking account. A debit card can be thought of as an electronic check. When the transaction is complete, the money is transferred to the merchant's bank account and deducted from your checking account. The advantage is that you, in effect, are paying in cash. You do not accumulate debt that must be paid at the end of the month because you

are immediately spending the funds that are on deposit in your account.

Taking Out a Loan

Sometimes using a credit card will not suit your purpose. Credit cards set a limit on the total amount of money you are able to borrow. If a person wants to purchase a house or an automobile, he or she will need many thousands of dollars. To get the money for large purchases, many people go to a lending institution such as a bank to take out a loan.

When a person applies for a home mortgage or car loan, the person will complete a credit application similar to the credit card application. The major difference is that the bank loan is usually for a specific amount of money to be paid back over a set period of time in exact payments. The life of a home mortgage loan may be from 15 to 30 years. The life of a car loan usually averages about five years.

The federal government and most states have passed **truth-in-lending laws**. They explain your rights when you take out a loan. Such laws require lending companies to make clear what the actual cost of the loan will be (the amount of the loan plus the interest), the annual percentage rate, and the charges for handling the loan.

Responsibilities of Taking Out Loans

Taking out a loan is a big responsibility. You are legally bound to repay the principal and interest according to the terms of the contract. If you fail to repay a loan, you are said to *default*. When this happens, the lending institution may take a portion of your paycheck. If you agreed in advance to use the item you bought as security, the lending company may take the item from you. For instance, if you fail to repay your home mortgage, the mortgage holder has the right to repossess the house.

The consequences of not repaying a loan follow you for a long time. When you do not pay a debt, the failure is noted on your credit record. If you attempt to take out another loan or apply for a credit card in the future, the default will appear on your background check. This will make it much more difficult for you to obtain loans or credit cards.

Sometimes when you are in default, the lending institution will ask a collection agency to attempt to recover the debt from you. It is important to know that even under these conditions, you have certain rights. Collection agencies do not have the right to make pestering or threatening phone calls. Usually, you can work out a payment program that you can handle and that will satisfy the lending institution.

Remember, it is better to make the payments on schedule. If there are special circumstances such as illness or sudden loss of a job, lending institutions will usually work with you to set up a different payment schedule. The important thing to remember is to inform people of your situation.

Let's Think

1. What happens when a person buys on credit?
2. What kind of information does a creditor want to know before you are granted credit?
3. What are the advantages and disadvantages of purchasing items with a credit card?
4. How do truth-in-lending laws protect the consumer?

Making Wise Decisions for the Future

Matt and Lisa were married a year ago. They are happily living in their two-bedroom apartment in a nice part of town. Both are established in their chosen professions. They feel they need to set up a savings and investment program to help them meet future needs. They want to buy a house before starting a family. Once they have children, they will need to set aside money for the children's education. Another goal is to save so that they will be financially secure when they retire from their careers. In the meantime, they want to have some money to spend on special vacations. One day, Matt and Lisa began to discuss how they will achieve these goals.

Setting Priorities

Of course, Matt and Lisa cannot achieve all of their goals quickly. Some are long term and may have to be adjusted as circumstances change. They decided to make a list of all the goals they have set for themselves in the order in which they hope to achieve them.

Put money away for emergencies

Buy a house

Furnish the house

Plan for a family (children)

Save for the children's college education

Save money for their retirement

Buy a retirement home in a part of the country that has a warm climate

They realize that they will have to work out a good savings plan that they can realistically stick to. To do this, they must decide how much they can afford to save. Then they must research various ways of investing their money so that it will grow safely.

In addition, both Matt and Lisa need to check what types of retirement savings plans are offered through their places of employment. Many employers have pension plans that are financed by the employer through insurance companies. In some cases, employees can also contribute money to the plans.

A 401(k) plan is a different type of retirement savings program. It is set up by an employer for its employees. The employees contribute money from their paychecks before taxes are deducted. Some employers contribute to the employee accounts. Funds are usually invested in stock, bond, or money market plans. Earnings from the investments are not taxed until they are withdrawn. Even small contributions can grow substantially over time.

Making Investments

Soon after their discussion, Matt brought home a book about a variety of options that they can consider for saving and investing money. The following is a list of the methods described in the book:

Savings accounts at a bank

Investing in stocks

Investing in U.S. Savings Bonds

Investing in mutual funds

Investing in insurance

Investing in IRAs

Each method required both Lisa and Matt to do some homework. It is important to know the benefits and dangers of each. During the next few weeks, they borrowed books from the library and spoke to friends and financial experts to determine what the best investment program for them should be. The more they read and investigated, the more they realized how complex the issues are. They examined the pros and cons of each option very carefully.

Bank Savings Accounts

One way to save money is to put it into a savings account in a bank. A savings account pays you interest on the money that is on deposit in the account. The method of computing the interest may vary, depending on the type of account you hold. The interest rate is usually low. It is important to get information from several banks to see how much interest each offers on savings accounts. You can take money out of or deposit money into a savings account at any time without being penalized.

Sometimes you can earn more interest by depositing your money in a **certificate of deposit (CD)**. These accounts guarantee you a certain interest rate for a particular period of time. Certificates of deposit can have a life of three months to five years. You agree to leave the money on deposit for the length of time specified by the certificate. You cannot add to the initial deposit nor can you withdraw money before the due date without paying a penalty. To find out what interest rates various banks are offering, watch for ads in your local newspapers or collect literature from banks.

Savings accounts and certificates of deposit are insured. This makes the investment relatively safe. If the bank fails, the money you have on deposit is insured up to $250,000 per account by the Federal Deposit Insurance Corporation (FDIC).

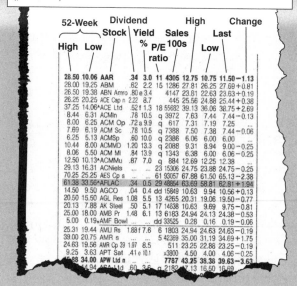

Stock exchange listing:

(AFLAC insurance highlighted): Reading from left to right, the listing presents the following information:

52-week high and low prices ($61.38 and $33.56).

Company name.

Dividend: Dollar amount of company's per-share earnings paid to stockholders ($.34).

Yield: Per-share dividend divided by per-share stock price, expressed as a percentage (0.5).

Price-Earnings ratio: Compares the stock's current market price to the company's earnings per share of stock (29).

Sales volume: Number of shares bought and sold on the previous day, in hundreds (add two 0's: 4,885,400 shares).

Prices paid for stock during the previous day: highest, lowest, and closing ($63.69, $58.81, $62.81).

Net change: Difference between the past two days' closing prices (plus $1.94).

Investing in Stocks

Savings accounts are conservative investments that grow slowly. Lisa and Matt would like to see some of their money grow faster. They see investing in stocks as a possible option. Stocks, you remember, are shares of ownership in a corporation. The companies that offer stock for sale are listed on stock exchanges. The two largest, the New York Stock Exchange and NASDAQ (National Association of Security Dealers Automated Quotations), are located in New York City.

Understanding the benefits and risks of stock investments is very important. People can make a great deal of money by investing in stocks. They can also lose a great deal of money. The individual investor must make many decisions before deciding what stocks to purchase. You need to decide how much to invest and whether you want to invest for the long term or the short term. Long term means buying stocks and holding them for months or years. Short term means buying stocks for a low price and selling them as soon as the price increases. In this way, you turn a profit quickly. It is important to remember that profits on stock sales are subject to taxes.

Because prices rise and fall, you should try to buy or sell at the right time. Your aim is to buy when the stock is at a low price and sell when it increases in price. If you need cash when the stock is lower in price than when you bought it, you will lose money. If you sell your stock when the price is higher than when you bought it, you will make a profit. The price of stock in certain businesses such as telephone companies and utilities is generally steady. The stock of companies that make trendy products may rise or fall in price very rapidly.

At the end of the year, many companies declare stock *dividends*. They are cash payments that are made when the company is profitable. The dividend is declared for each share. The more shares you have, the greater the dividend you will receive. This is one way of earning money while owning a stock. Some people prefer to buy stocks that produce income through dividends.

Buying Stocks

Most people purchase stocks through stockbrokers. They are licensed individuals who work for companies that buy and sell stocks for their clients. When a person decides to purchase stocks, he or she opens an account with a stockbrokerage house. Brokers charge a fee for their service called a *commission*. The amount of the commission depends on the value of either the purchase or the sale of the stock. The more a person purchases or sells, the higher the commission.

Individuals can buy and sell stocks via the Internet without using a broker. The fees for online trading are generally lower than brokers' fees.

Lisa picked out several stocks she thought would be good buys and followed their price ups and downs for a couple of weeks. Each day the local newspapers list the prices of stock shares.

This information can also be picked up from the Internet and some television channels.

Stock prices change almost daily and reflect supply and demand. If people want more stock than the amount available, the price of the stock will increase. If a stock becomes unpopular, the share price is likely to decrease. The idea is to buy stock when the price is low and sell when it is high. This aim is difficult to achieve, so most people try to invest a particular amount of money in stock on a regular basis so that the price averages out. You only make or lose money on stock when you sell it.

When choosing a stock, it is important to learn about the company. Federal law requires all companies that issue stock for sale to be registered with a "watchdog" agency of the federal government. This agency is the *Securities and Exchange Commission (SEC)*. The SEC was created during the Great Depression of the 1930s to regulate the trading of stocks. As an enforcement agency, it punishes those who violate the rules of stock trading.

Each company that offers stock for sale issues a summary of its activities for review by the public. This summary should be read so you can determine if the business of the company is the right one for you to invest in. The report includes the assets of the corporation, any debts it has, and any other liabilities it may possess. You should be able to make some judgment about the health of the company from the summary. If you are going to invest in the stock of a business, you want to make sure that business will be around for a while and will make a profit.

Investing in stocks carries greater risk than putting money into a savings account. There is no guarantee that the money you invest in stocks will grow. If a company loses money or fails, the investor runs the risk of losing his or her investment. Stock accounts are not insured. You are less likely to lose your money in a savings account. On the other hand, stocks may increase in value more rapidly than money does in a savings account. For the past 50 to 60 years, investments in the stock market have outperformed other types of investments. The return has been greater than the return on safer types of investments.

Investing in Bonds

Another way to invest money is to purchase bonds. *Bonds* are "loans" to corporations or governments. Many people like to invest in government bonds because they are seen as relatively safe investments. Examples of government bonds are United States Savings Bonds and state and municipal bonds. Government bonds carry an extra advantage because the interest income on them is not usually taxed.

Bonds exist for a fixed life and have a fixed rate of return (interest). This makes bonds attractive to many people. When individuals purchase bonds, they know in advance how much they will get when the bonds mature. If a company remains healthy, it will pay back the bondholders when the life of the bond ends (matures). Government bonds are backed by the taxing power of the government that issues them.

One advantage of a corporate bond over a stock is that if a company fails, a bondholder is paid before a stockholder. A bond is considered a debt, and a company is legally obligated to pay any and all debts before it divides any remaining assets among its owners, the stockholders. Both corporate and government bonds can be purchased through brokers who deal in these securities. United States Savings Bonds can be purchased through most banks or on the Internet at www.treasurydirect.com.

Investing in Mutual Funds

Many people find investing in individual stocks and bonds too complicated. They may not have the time to research each company and do not know what types to purchase for their needs. Also, they may not have a great deal of money to invest at any one time. This was Matt and Lisa's situation. So they decided to look into the possibility of investing in a **mutual fund**. Mutual funds are investing companies that own stocks and bonds of corporations that engage in many different fields of business.

People buy shares of stock in mutual funds. The value of the shares reflects the demand for the shares and how well each fund performs its investing function. There are hundreds of mutual funds to choose from. Each puts out a *prospectus* that tells the potential investor about the fund. The prospectus outlines the way the mutual fund invests money, the types of investments it makes, and the performance of the fund over the last several years.

Some mutual funds specialize only in stocks, others in bonds, and still others in both. The prices of the shares of mutual funds are published daily in many newspapers throughout the country. The information is also available online.

Mutual funds allow individual investors to set up a purchasing program. Usually funds require an initial investment of a few hundred dollars or more. Then, an investor may elect to purchase shares on a monthly schedule directly from the fund. This type of investment program helps people with limited means to enter the stock and bond market. There is, however, no guarantee that investments will increase in value. Mutual fund companies can fail. As with stocks and bonds, mutual fund shares can be sold at any time.

Buying Insurance

Purchasing insurance is another way to save for future needs. **Insurance** policies pay out money on the death of the insured, for disability, or for retirement. The money is paid to a designated person, the **beneficiary**. Many types of policies pay dividends to the policyholder over the life of the policy. Dividends increase the value of the policy.

Straight life insurance pays out money on the death of the holder. It also accumulates a cash value as the policy matures. To be covered by this type of insurance, the holder pays an annual premium from the time the policy is purchased until the holder dies. If a person decides not to continue paying for the policy, it can be cashed in. This cash value is normally much less than the face amount that would be paid on the death of the holder. This is the cheapest type of insurance and can be purchased in amounts ranging from a few thousand dollars to hundreds of thousands of dollars. It is considered the cheapest because the premium will not increase as you grow older. If you take out a straight life policy when you are in your 20s, you will pay lower premiums than you would if you purchased it at age 45.

Term insurance is different. It is in force for a specified period of time. At the end of that period, it expires unless it is renewed. When it is renewed, the premium increases as the age of the insured increases. The policy does not have a cash value. Term insurance is good for a person with a young family and a modest income. When the children are young, money is needed to provide for their financial security until they reach adulthood. Therefore, a parent may purchase term insurance to cover the first 16 to 18 years of the children's life. When the children are grown, the family may no longer need that much insurance and may choose not to renew it.

An *annuity* is often taken out by people to save for their retirement or for another future goal. In this case, a person pays premiums for a fixed number of years and then receives an income at regular intervals after reaching a certain age. There are a variety of annuities and payment plans.

Insurance companies are licensed by the individual states to sell policies within that state. You can purchase policies from insurance company salespeople or from companies directly. Sometimes, insurance companies run into financial problems and go out of business. If this happens, the policy you purchased may have a limited value or no value.

Investing in IRAs

Traditional *Individual Retirement Accounts (IRAs)* are tax-deferred savings accounts that can be set up by individuals and couples who earn a salary. They allow people to build up income for retirement. Taxes do not have to be paid on the earnings until the money is withdrawn. The maximum per year that can currently be put into an IRA changes periodically. The savings can be invested in a variety of types of accounts, such as stocks and bonds.

A second type of IRA is the *Roth IRA*. It is like a traditional IRA except that you buy it with money that has already been taxed. When you are retired and withdraw income from a Roth IRA account, you normally do not have to pay taxes on the withdrawals.

Financial Planners

Making intelligent financial plans and decisions for oneself is difficult and time-consuming. Finding objective and reliable information can be challenging. As a result, many people seek help from professionals known as *financial planners*. These people study the economy and background information on investment plans. They use this information to help others manage their finances.

A financial planner will have a conference with you, determine how much money you have to invest or should invest, and help you make plans to reach your financial goals. Financial planners do charge fees or receive commissions on what you buy and sell. It is important to know the background of a financial planner, his or her reputation, and the person's track record in giving useful advice.

As you can see, the choices open to Matt and Lisa are many. Knowing how to spend, when to spend, how much to save, and what to invest in takes discipline and planning. It is now up to Matt and Lisa to use the information available to them and make a savings and spending plan they can live with.

Let's Think

1. What are the advantages and disadvantages of each of the following types of investments: bank savings accounts, stocks, bonds, and mutual funds?
2. How does life insurance protect a person's family?
3. What is the role of a financial planner?

Chapter Summary

As a consumer, each individual is an important contributor to the economic well-being of the nation. Being a good citizen also means being a wise and responsible spender and saver.

Spending wisely means smart shopping. As an intelligent shopper, a person will study advertisements, carefully analyze them, and comparison shop. Getting advice from friends and relatives about what and where to buy can be helpful.

Laws protect the consumer from deceptive sales practices, such as bait and switch and fake sales.

It is important to understand the warranty provided for a product. Knowing warranty limits will assist in solving problems that may arise if the product does not perform satisfactorily.

Consumers have rights. Organizations exist to help resolve problems with merchants. To settle a disagreement, you should follow a sequence of steps. You should keep all receipts and know the refund and replacement policies of the stores where you purchase items. Speak firmly and politely to the salesperson at the store where you purchased the problem item. If necessary, talk to the manager and then to higher-level executives. You may need to write to the head of the company about your complaint. Suggest how you would like the problem remedied.

Several government and private organizations can be contacted when the consumer still does not get satisfaction. They include the local department of consumer affairs, a state attorney general's office, the Federal Trade Commission, the Better Business Bureau, and television and radio stations. When all else fails, consumers do have the right to sue in small claims courts.

Buying on credit through using credit cards is one way to make purchases. It is important to know the terms of the credit agreement. Making only the minimum payment on a credit card bill can be costly over time. The interest rates charged on installment purchases are generally quite high. Many credit card companies charge an annual fee. If you have a problem with an item purchased with a credit card, some companies will withhold payment to the merchant or help you resolve the dispute. It is easy to overspend when using a credit card. Debit cards can also be used to purchase items. They are like electronic checks.

If you want to buy something that costs many thousands of dollars, you usually go to a bank to take out a loan. The interest rate is less than that charged by credit card companies.

Truth-in-lending laws require lenders to explain your rights when you take out a loan. Lending companies must tell you the terms and actual cost of the loan. You have a legal obligation to pay back a loan. Otherwise, you will be in default and have a poor credit history.

Planning for the future when a person is young provides economic security. Budgeting and saving on a regular basis help you meet your life and financial goals. You have many investment choices: savings accounts, stocks, mutual funds, bonds, and IRAs. Life insurance is used to protect one's family income or provide for retirement income.

Stocks, bonds, and mutual funds can be purchased through stockbrokers or Internet sites. The federal Securities and Exchange Commission regulates the trading of stocks. Federal, state, and local governments issue bonds backed by the taxing power of the various governments.

In order to get help with making investment decisions, you can consult professionals who are experts in planning investments. They are called financial planners.

★ CHAPTER REVIEW ★

A. Matching
Match each term in Column A with its definition in Column B.

Column A
1. budget
2. sale
3. warranty
4. Better Business Bureau
5. credit
6. creditor
7. default
8. SEC
9. mutual fund
10. prospectus

Column B
a. marketing goods at a reduced price
b. description of a mutual fund
c. an investing company that purchases shares in many different companies
d. an assurance that a product will perform as expected
e. failure to pay a debt
f. federal stock market watchdog agency
g. a person or company that lends money
h. organization of businesses
i. funds that can be borrowed
j. an income and spending plan

B. Multiple Choice
Select the statement or word that most correctly answers the question or completes the statement.

1. The major purpose of advertisements is to **(a)** provide pretty pictures **(b)** persuade people to buy a product **(c)** criticize the competition **(d)** provide false information.

2. Checking the price of a product in different stores is called **(a)** buying on credit **(b)** credit shopping **(c)** comparison shopping **(d)** bait and switch.

3. An advertisement offers an inferior product at a special price. When customers come to the store to purchase the sale item, the salesperson steers them to a more expensive product. This deceptive practice is called **(a)** default **(b)** bait and switch **(c)** sales **(d)** warranty.

4. The product you just bought breaks within a week. The first thing you should do is **(a)** call the local television station **(b)** complain to the Better Business Bureau **(c)** take it back to the store **(d)** file a complaint with the Federal Trade Commission.

5. A court that is often used to resolve consumer problems when the value of the item is relatively small is the **(a)** supreme court **(b)** appellate court **(c)** small claims court **(d)** federal court.

6. The amounts of money a person owes to lenders and the pattern of repayment are set out in the person's **(a)** credit record **(b)** truth-in-lending statement **(c)** investment record **(d)** prospectus.

7. A major reason why young parents make investments that will be paid out in the future is to **(a)** save for their children's elementary education **(b)** make purchases of luxury items **(c)** save for their children's college education **(d)** purchase stocks.

8. A bank account that guarantees a certain rate of interest on your money for a specific amount of time is called a **(a)** mutual fund **(b)** prospectus **(c)** certificate of deposit **(d)** bond account.

9. When purchasing stocks, people usually seek the assistance of a (an) **(a)** insurance broker **(b)** stockbroker **(c)** banker **(d)** Securities and Exchange commissioner.

10. A person who helps people plan their economic future is called a **(a)** federal trade commissioner **(b)** bank teller **(c)** financial planner **(d)** referee.

C. Essay
Write a paragraph about *one* of the following:

1. The average citizen influences the American economy in many ways.
2. To be a wise consumer, an individual should be aware of good and bad business practices.
3. Both public and private consumer organizations exist to help the buying public.
4. Credit cards are useful but dangerous tools.
5. Planning for a sound economic future takes time and discipline.

D. A Challenge for You

1. Select several different types of advertisements. Use the checklist on page 222 to ana-

lyze the message in each ad. Decide if you would purchase the products or services advertised. Create a booklet that others can use to evaluate ads.

2. Select five stocks and check the financial pages in the newspaper or on the Internet to follow their progress. Record their daily high and low prices over a period of time, such as a couple of weeks or a month. How have they risen or declined in price? When would have been the best time to have bought or sold the stocks?

3. Create a series of questions to ask a stockbroker about how the stock market works and about how he or she buys and sells stocks for clients. Interview the person, write down the answers, and report your findings to the class.

4. Search newspapers and magazines or the Internet for information about the best ways to save for college. Summarize the information. Then create a list of the most frequently named suggestions or the ones you think are most practical and post it on the bulletin board. You could also turn your findings into an article for the school newspaper.

5. In a personal journal, keep track of what you spend your allowance and earned money on—everything from a candy bar to new sneakers. Do you think you are a wise spender and saver? Do you make and keep a budget? How influenced are you by ads in the media? Do you always shop around for the best price on costly items?

Document-Based Question

State the main idea expressed in each document. Then use information in the documents and your own knowledge to write an essay about the advantages and problems of investing in mutual funds.

The Ease of Investing in Mutual Funds

Mutual funds are good investments for a number of reasons. For starters, they allow beginners to place their money in the same expert hands as the big guys. Corporate pension dollars aren't given any better treatment in a mutual fund than the scraped-together savings of a high school student.

It's convenient to invest in a fund too. With postage-paid envelopes, a busy woman can write a check to the fund of her choice and have it on its way before she begins the day's errands. Or she can use a toll-free phone number to call the fund and have money transferred directly from her bank account. There's no waiting in lines to invest in a mutual fund.

Mutual funds are an easy way for small-timers to diversify their investments. It wouldn't be wise to risk all of your money on a single stock, hoping that it pays off. Without mutual funds, people with little money to invest would have few choices because they couldn't afford to own a bunch of different investments. . . . In a fund, however, every dollar sent in is spread across many different investments, sometimes even international ones. That way if a single investment does poorly, the rest can keep the losses to a minimum. Mutual funds can earn more money than bank accounts but are safer than owning individual stocks.

From *Neatest Little Guide to Mutual Fund Investing* by Jason Kelly, page 4. Copyright 1996 by PLUME, Penguin USA.

Being a Wise Mutual Fund Investor

Deciding when to get out of a mutual fund may be the most difficult task of investing in mutual funds. Once your money is committed, emotions often come into play, tempting you to either hold on to winning funds long after they have peaked or to bail out of losers just before they bounce back.

To recognize the right time to sell or switch to another fund, continually compare the funds you own with others. And don't forget your personal financial goals. As long as your fund is meeting your objectives, hold on to it. But don't hesitate to move your money if another fund promises to do the job better.

From *Mutual Funds—Winning Strategies for the 90's* by the editors of *Money Magazine*, page 55. Copyright 1994 by Money Personal Finance Library, Money Magazine.

UNIT 4

Making a Difference

CHAPTER 14

Responsibilities of a Citizen

★ CHAPTER FOCUS

1. What does it mean to be a citizen of the United States?
2. What are the major steps in the voting process?
3. What are the responsibilities of a good citizen?
4. How do you become an informed citizen?
5. How do you become a naturalized citizen?

hat does being a citizen of the United States mean? Test yourself. Decide if each of the following statements is true or false.

1. You can be a citizen of a community and, at the same time, a citizen of a state and a nation.

2. All citizens have the same rights.

3. Laws apply to all citizens equally.

4. Citizenship does not make distinctions regarding gender, age, race, religion, or cultural background.

If you answered true for each statement, you are already on the way to understanding what being a citizen of the United States means. Citizenship in the United States places all people on an equal level. No one citizen has more legal privileges than any other.

The Meaning of Being a Citizen

Being a citizen means that a person can participate fully in the political process of the government. Two vital aspects of participation are voting and holding public office. Not every citizen has the opportunity to hold public office, but every citizen can vote. It is much easier to go to your local voting place and vote than it is to run for public office. Voting is one of our most important rights and responsibilities.

Democracy, as you know, is rule by the people. This means that the power of the government lies with its **citizens**. But holding the power is only part of the story. We must exercise that power. One of the easiest and most important ways to wield power over government officials and policies is to vote. If the right to vote was not so potentially powerful, why has it been withheld from large groups of citizens in this country and elsewhere over the years?

Expanding Voting Rights

Although the United States after the American Revolution was seen as a great experiment in democracy, democratic rights were not extended to all people. Only adult, white males who owned property worth a certain amount could vote and hold office. The Constitution did not grant suffrage, the right to vote, to everyone. Those who were left out—primarily women, African Americans, and Native Americans—had to fight for the right to vote over a long period of time.

We saw in Chapter 8 how the 15th, 19th, and 26th amendments to the Constitution expanded voting rights. But they did not stop the states from continuing to put obstacles in the way of voters. The Constitution allows states to regulate elections—determine when and how elections should take place within their jurisdiction.

Throughout the 20th century, federal laws were passed to enforce the rights given in the amendments. In 1924, the Snyder Indian Citizenship Act was passed. By gaining citizenship, all Native Americans could participate in the political process and exercise their right to vote.

When the government passed the Civil Rights Act of 1964, it took a big step toward eliminating discriminatory practices in many areas, including the voting booth. It banned the unequal application of literacy tests. (To register to vote a person had to prove that he or she could read and understand passages from the state or federal constitutions. In some states, African Americans were given more difficult passages than whites to read.)

The 1964 act did not end all restrictions. African Americans in many southern states continued to be discouraged from registering and voting. In the summer of 1964, three civil rights workers who were registering African-American voters in Mississippi were murdered. It became apparent that stronger protective measures were needed. Thus, Congress passed the Voting Rights Act of 1965. It focused on correcting discriminatory practices specifically related to voting. The law forbids the use of any type of poll tax (payment to vote) in state and local elections. It provided for federal inspectors to help register voters and for stiff criminal penalties for those

The passage of the Voting Rights Act of 1965 encouraged prospective voters to register. Long lines of African Americans wait to fill out voter registration forms in Alabama in 1966.

who attempted to restrict a person's right to vote. The government could send federal officials to states to oversee elections and make sure that all sections of the law were followed.

The Voting Rights Act of 1970 banned the use of any literacy test as a requirement for voting in any election. Five years later, Congress passed another voting rights act. It provided for ballots to be printed in languages other than English, depending on the requirements of the community.

Let's Think

1. Describe what it means to be a citizen.
2. Why is exercising the right to vote important?
3. What is the importance of the Civil Rights Act of 1964 and the Voting Rights Act of 1965?

Becoming a Registered Voter

Before a person can vote in an election, he or she must get on the voting lists. In order to do that, the person must register to vote. When registering to vote, you provide the board of elections in your state with information that helps identify you. Qualifications, generally, are that you must be 18 years old, a citizen of the United States, and a resident of the state and local area in which you are registering. Each state has its own length of residency requirements. Proof of identity must be provided. One type of proof is your driver's license. Other official government documents may also be used. To register, you can go to the local board of elections office or the local motor vehicle bureau. Many organizations, such as the League of Women Voters, carry out voter registration drives on a regular basis.

The board of elections checks the information provided on the registration form. After the information is verified, a voter registration card is sent to you. This card is shown to poll workers at the polling place to prove that you are a registered voter.

Technology has made it easier than ever to register to vote. Web sites such as Vote411.org provide detailed instructions about how to regis-

ter to vote. These sites even provide you with an online form that can be sent to your state. The state will then send you an application that you can complete and send back. In some cases, states allow you to register to vote online. Washington and Arizona were the first states to permit online registration.

Let's Think

1. Why is it necessary to register to vote?
2. Describe the process of registering to vote.

The Details of Voting

Federal and state elections are held on the first Tuesday after the first Monday of November. Primary elections, school board elections, and other special-purpose votes may be held at other times of the year. On election day, people who are on the voting lists go to their local **polling places** to cast their ballots. Polling places are generally open for a long period of time on election day. The hours vary by state, but they are generally from early morning until evening. Some states, such as New York, allow voters more than 12 hours to get to the polls.

Voting in Secret

You may be wondering why you go into a private place to cast your vote. In this country, we believe that a person's vote should be private. There is no need for others to know how you vote. Since the late 1800s, the **secret ballot** has been used. It is also known as the **Australian ballot** because the idea of the secret ballot originated in Australia. Before ballots were secret, a voter could be pressured into casting a vote for a particular candidate or issue even if the voter did not want to make that choice. Anyone could tell how anyone else voted because the ballots for each party's candidates would be printed on a different color paper. Once the ballot became secret, voters could make their decisions without fear of retaliation.

◄REALITY CHECK►
Getting Out the Vote

One of the great mysteries of a participatory democracy is why more voters don't turn out to vote in elections at all levels of government. Presidential elections normally bring out the most voters. Yet many who are eligible to vote do not do so in any election—local, state, or national. Not all who are eligible to vote even register. Registering to vote is the first step in the voting process.

In 1993, the federal government attempted to make it easier to register by passing the National Voter Registration Act (NVRA). This law required government offices, such as motor vehicle bureaus and welfare agencies, to offer voter registration forms and help in filling out the forms. But very often, it is the individual, working with others on what we call a "grassroots level," who makes a difference.

The presidential election of 2008 generated a lot of passion and caused those concerned about the outcome to make every effort to register eligible voters and get them to the polls on election day. The following are a few examples of what ordinary citizens did to involve potential voters.

In September 2008, students at the University of Memphis in Tennessee were excited about voting for president. Several school organizations got together to provide students and faculty (and other employees of the university) the opportunity to register to vote in the November election. They ran an all-day voter registration drive at the campus's Panhellenic Ballroom. The student organizations managed to get funds to provide refreshments and music in order to create a "happening." The event's ultimate purpose, claimed the organizers, was to get everyone to vote, no matter what political party a voter supported.

Who would think that it would be possible to register to vote at a local beauty parlor? Workers in a hair salon in Bakersfield, California, turned it into a voter registration site. They wanted to make it easy for eligible voters in the nearby African-American community to register. In 2004, voter turnout in Kern County, where Bakersfield is located, was very low. The salon workers hoped to increase the percentage in 2008. They managed to register more than 200 new voters.

In Blackman High School in Murfreesboro, Tennessee, three students volunteered to run the voter registration drive. The student body president, one of the organizers, said that the purpose of the drive was to inform kids and get them active in government and politics. The students hoped to register many of the 120 who they knew were eligible. At the end of the drive, they had signed up 200.

Nationwide voter turnout in the presidential election of 2008 increased approximately 1.6 percent over the turnout in 2004. Many people who believed that the 2008 turnout would show a greater increase were disappointed. According to Curtis Gans, an authority on election turnout and the director of the Committee for the Study of the American Electorate, more people were registered to vote in 2008 than in 2004. As a result, the percentage of voter turnout did not show a dramatic increase over the previous election. Even so, 6.5 million more people were registered to vote in 2008 than in 2004. Furthermore, the total number of ballots cast in 2008 was the highest ever. Thus, the hard work of registering new voters by the high school and college students, the beauty salon workers, and countless others did pay off.

Very often, it is the little things we do that make us good citizens. The individuals described in these accounts remind us how simple, responsible actions can support democracy and make our society better.

1. Why is it important for people to register to vote?
2. How did each example of a voter registration drive demonstrate how people can carry out their civic responsibilities?
3. What was different about voter turnout in 2008 compared with that in 2004?

Casting an Absentee Ballot

People sometimes have to be away from home on election day. Some people may be temporarily living out of their home state but are still legal residents of the home state. They may not be able to return to vote. Fortunately, there is a way to vote even if you are out of town on election day or if you are ill or otherwise unable to get to the polls. You can contact the local Board of Elections and ask to be sent an **absentee ballot**. (See page 247.) When the ballot arrives, you complete it and mail it back by the deadline, which is before election day. The ballot remains sealed until election day and is then counted and added to the votes cast in the voting booths. You must make your own arrangements to get an absentee ballot.

Early Voting

A more recent development in elections is the concept of early voting. This means casting your ballot at a polling place days or weeks before the actual election day. Traditionally, people voted at polling places during designated hours on election day. Often they had to wait on long lines,

and some were discouraged from voting by the long wait. More and more states decided to make it possible for people to cast ballots before the official election day, particularly in presidential elections.

Early voting should not be confused with absentee ballot voting, which has been in place for a long time. Absentee ballot voting is done entirely by mail. Under the early voting procedure, people go early to designated polling places to cast their ballots. This can be done several weeks before the actual election is held.

Currently, 32 states allow no-excuse early voting. Fourteen other states allow early voting with an excuse as to why it is necessary to vote early. (A typical excuse is having to be out of town.) One state, Oregon, has mail-in voting only; it does not have polling places. Four states do not allow any in-person early voting.

Voting in Local Elections

Voters' enthusiasm for elections tends to peak every four years during the presidential race. National elections attract more attention than local

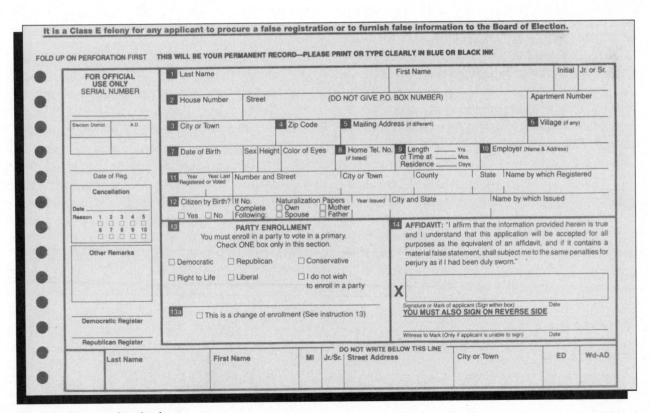

One type of voter registration form.

contests. Yet some of the most important issues in your daily life are decided by state and local officials. Where to locate the new garbage dump, how to finance a new school, what to do about traffic tie-ups on Main Street are all issues decided by local officials. These problems may not be the focus of lead stories on the evening news, but they are of more immediate interest to you than, say, the budget for the State Department. Thus, it is important that we pay attention to local and state election races. We need to choose the best-qualified individuals for public office at this level, too.

Let's Think

1. What are polling places?
2. What must you do before you can cast a ballot?
3. What is an Australian ballot; an absentee ballot?
4. Why is it important to vote in all elections?

The Importance of Carrying Out Responsibilities

Voting in elections, whether they are national, state, or local, is essential to maintaining the democratic process. To this end, many organizations, such as labor unions, citizens' groups, the League of Women Voters, and the Urban League, promote and carry out voter registration drives. The theory is that if one is registered, one is more likely to vote.

Congress recognized this theory in 1993 when it passed the National Voter Registration Act (NVRA), commonly called the Motor Voter Law. It requires government offices, such as motor vehicle bureaus, to make voter registration forms available to people who use the services of the offices. Help must be given to those who request aid in filling out the forms. The law also allows potential voters to register by mail. The NVRA has encouraged millions to become eligible to vote. In 2007, the Federal Election Commission reported to Congress the results of the National

Voter Registration Act for the 2004–2006 elections. It stated that motor vehicle bureau voter registration accounted for 45.7 percent of the total of voter registration applications received by boards of elections nationwide.

Actual Voter Turnout

Does registration always translate into votes? Not in recent elections. Take a look at the table on page 248. It shows the percentage of the voting age population who cast ballots in presidential elections from 1932 to 2008. From 1932 to 1968, a person had to be 21 or older to be able to vote, so the voting age population included everyone who was 21 years of age and older. In 1971, the 26th Amendment lowered the voting age to 18. Thus, the voting-age population increased.

In 2004, about 60.7 percent of the voting-age population voted in the presidential election. In 2008, the number voting rose to 61.6 percent. The increase from 2004 to 2008 can be attributed, in part, to dissatisfaction with the performance of the Bush administration and concern about poor economic conditions.

Why Not Vote?

People do not vote for a variety of reasons. Sometimes they do not have an interest in government or the issues. They may not like or trust government. Others do not like any of the candidates on the ballot. Or they may feel that they do not know enough about the candidates to make an intelligent decision. Some believe that their vote will not make a difference, so why bother. This apathy, or lack of interest, tends to be translated into neglecting a fundamental right and a basic responsibility.

Those who do vote have a very different outlook. They consider it to be their civic duty. Voters believe, that by casting their ballots, they can influence both the present and the future of the nation. Voting selects candidates for office. The process also decides issues.

Your vote is so important that at election time candidates become very visible. They seem to be everywhere seeking support from potential voters. Candidates want your vote. They need it in

ABSENTEE BALLOT APPLICATION

Sec. 8-400-Rev. 07/92

County _____ Town or City _____, Ward/A.D. or Leg. Dist. _____, Election District _____

Registration Serial Number _____   Party Enrollment _____
(To be Filled by Board)

Primary ☐   General ☐

☐ Due to Duties, Occupation, Business, Studies or Vacation (Sec. 8-400)
☐ Due to Illness or Physical Disability (Sec. 8-400)
☐ Due to Permanent Illness or Permanent Disability (Sec. 8-400)

_____, an applicant for an Absentee Primary/General Ballot, States as follows:
(Print or type name)

I reside at _____, and I am a REGISTERED (and ENROLLED) voter of the
(Street, number, name of post office and zip code)

Town or City of _____, County of _____
I KNOW OF NO REASON WHY I AM NO LONGER QUALIFIED TO VOTE.

DUTIES, OCCUPATION, BUSINESS, STUDIES or VACATION

I expect in good faith to be absent from the County of _____, State of New York, on Primary/General Day,
_____, 19____,
_____, 19____ because my duties, occupation, business, studies or vacation require me to be elsewhere as follows:

1. Explain briefly your position and nature of duties, occupation, studies or business requiring such absence and give dates when you expect to begin and end your absence.
_____

2. Place or places where you expect to be on business, studies or on vacation. _____

3. Name and address of employer, if any. _____
(If self employed or unemployed, so state-If student, give name of school)

4. If this application is based by reason of accompanying your spouse, child or parent: would such spouse, child or parent, if a qualified voter, be entitled to apply for the right to vote by absentee ballot? _____,
(Yes or No)
_____ _____
(Name of such spouse, child or parent) (Relationship to you)

5. If this application is based by reason of being or expecting to be an inmate or patient of a veteran's administration hospital, give name and address of hospital.

6. If application is based on confinement pending trial in a criminal proceeding or for conviction of a crime or offense other than a felony, give particulars:

✱ ☐ I will be absent continuously between the dates of the primary election and general election and request that, based on the information provided above, an absentee ballot for the general election also be sent to me.

DUE TO ILLNESS OR PHYSICAL DISABILITY

I certify that I have been advised by my medical practitioner or Christian Science practitioner:
_____
(Name and address of medical practitioner or Christian Science practitioner)
that I will be unable to appear personally at the polling place of the election district in which I am a **REGISTERED AND ENROLLED** voter on the day of the next Primary Election because of my ☐ illness ☐ Physical Disability and will be confined ☐ at Home, in a ☐ Hospital. If hospital confinement is expected, state name and address of Hospital. (check appropriate boxes)
_____ _____
(Name of Hospital) (Address of Hospital)

DUE TO PERMANENT ILLNESS OR PERMANENT DISABILITY

☐ I hereby certify that such illness or disability is permanent and request that Absentee Ballots be mailed to me for future elections without my making further application. The nature of my permanent illness or disability is _____

Check if applicable (See instruction No. 2)
☐ I hereby certify that my illness or disability began not more than nine days before the election for which I am requesting this ballot.

ALL APPLICANTS *MUST* FILL OUT FOLLOWING

Delivery of primary election ballot (check one)
☐ Deliver to me in person at board of elections.
✱ ☐ Deliver to _____ whom I hereby authorize to receive my ballot.
(Name)
☐ Mail ballot to me at _____
(Address)

Delivery of general election ballot—if applicable (check one)
☐ Deliver to me in person at board of elections.
✱ ☐ Deliver to _____ whom I hereby authorize to receive my ballot.
(Name)
☐ Mail ballot to me at _____
(Address)

APPLICANT MUST SIGN BELOW
I CERTIFY THAT THE INFORMATION IN THIS APPLICATION IS TRUE AND CORRECT AND UNDERSTAND THAT THIS APPLICATION WILL BE ACCEPTED FOR ALL PURPOSES AS THE EQUIVALENT OF AN AFFIDAVIT AND, IF IT CONTAINS A MATERIAL FALSE STATEMENT, SHALL SUBJECT ME TO THE SAME PENALTIES AS IF I HAD BEEN DULY SWORN.

Date _____   Signature of Voter _____

(If applicant is unable to sign application because of illness or physical disability, the following statement must be executed): By my mark, duly witnessed hereunder, I hereby state that I am unable to sign my application for an absentee ballot without assistance because I am unable to write by reason of my illness or physical disability or because I am unable to read. I have made, or have received assistance, in making my mark in lieu of my signature.

Date _____   _____ Mark
(Name of Voter)

I, the undersigned, hereby certify that the above named voter affixed his mark to this application in my presence and I know him to be the person who affixed his mark to said application and understand that this statement will be accepted for all purposes as the equivalent of an affidavit and if it contains a material false statement, shall subject me to the same penalties as if I had been duly sworn.

_____ _____
(Address of witness to mark) (Signature of witness to mark)

VOTER TURNOUT IN PRESIDENTIAL ELECTIONS SINCE 1932

YEAR	CANDIDATES	VOTER PARTICIPATION % OF VOTING AGE POPULATION
1932	Roosevelt (Dem.)* — Hoover (Rep.)	52.4
1936	Roosevelt (Dem.)*— Landon (Rep.)	56
1940	Roosevelt (Dem)*— Willkie (Rep.)	58.8
1944	Roosevelt (Dem.)*— Dewey (Rep.)	56
1948	Truman (Dem.)*— Dewey (Rep.)	51.1
1952	Stevenson (Dem.) — Eisenhower (Rep.)*	61.6
1956	Stevenson (Dem.) — Eisenhower (Rep.)*	59.3
1960	Kennedy (Dem.)* — Nixon (Rep.)	62.8
1964	Johnson (Dem.)* — Goldwater (Rep.)	61.9
1968	Humphrey (Dem.) — Nixon (Rep.)*	60.9
1972	McGovern (Dem.) — Nixon (Rep.)*	52.2
1976	Carter (Dem.)* — Ford (Rep.)	53.5
1980	Carter (Dem.) — Reagan (Rep.)*	54
1984	Mondale (Dem.) — Reagan (Rep.)*	53.1
1988	Dukakis (Dem.) — Bush (Rep.)*	50.2
1992	Clinton (Dem.)* — Bush (Rep.) — Perot (Ind.)	55.9
1996	Clinton (Dem.)* — Dole (Rep.) — Perot (Ind.)	49
2000	Gore (Dem.) — Bush (Rep.)* — Nader (Green)	51.3
2004	Kerry (Dem.) — Bush (Rep.)* — Nader (Ind.)	60.7
2008	Obama (Dem.)* — McCain (Rep.)	61.6

*The winner of the election.

Dem. = Democrat; Rep. = Republican; Ind. = Independent

order to be elected. Even after they are in office, they think about your voting support when they make policy.

At election time, voters are often called upon to decide a variety of issues. Such issues may concern borrowing by government agencies, land use, immigration, and civil rights. Do we want to have only a small percentage of the population deciding such important questions? All potential voters need to make their voices heard in the voting booth. The close presidential election in 2000 demonstrated the importance of every vote.

Responsibilities Beyond Voting

Being a good citizen goes beyond just voting. While this right and obligation is one of the most important, other actions also show what kind of citizen you are. Do you go to school every day, turn in your homework on time, show an interest in class, attend student government meetings? How you handle responsibilities such as these indicate how good a "school citizen" you are.

When you ride your bike, do you wear the required safety gear and follow traffic rules? Obeying the laws of your community and state shows that you know how a good citizen should behave.

Serving on public committees and supporting groups that promote good government are other ways to show that you are a good citizen. Being called for jury service is a visible civic obligation. People are needed to make decisions in criminal and civil cases. Showing up when called for jury service may help make the justice system work better.

Another aspect of being a good citizen is to keep a watchful eye on those we elect. A good citizen tries to keep track of how legislators voted. He or she also tries to let legislators know what he or she thinks about issues through letters, phone calls, and e-mail messages.

Respect for others is a key element of good citizenship. We can honor other people's rights and differences. Just because someone has different ideas about an issue, it doesn't mean that the per-

NON-VOTERS OF THE PAST

VICTIMS OF RACISM

VICTIMS OF SEXISM

NON-VOTERS OF THE PRESENT

IT DOESN'T MATTER WHO WINS... IT'S JUST ONE VOTE...

VICTIMS OF CYNICISM

The cartoonist seems to be saying that nonvoters of today do not have a good excuse for not voting and that every vote is important in an election.

son is wrong or ignorant. Life experiences give us different perspectives on events and ideas. Skin color, ethnic background, or religious beliefs should not be reasons to discriminate against anyone. Each person is unique and should be valued for that uniqueness and what we can learn from it.

How far does respect extend? Should we respect lawbreakers or those who harm others through their speech or actions? We can respect their basic rights. But we should not stand idly by and let many be hurt by the actions or ideas of the extreme few. We can speak out and let law enforcement officials or others in authority know about potentially dangerous situations.

Let's Think

1. What is the importance of the Motor Voter Law?
2. Why do a variety of organizations work to increase voter registration?
3. In addition to voting, how else can a person show that he or she is a good citizen?

Becoming Informed

How do we know which person to vote for? How do we know whether to vote yes or no on an initiative or a proposition? Where can we find reliable information on issues?

Voting makes you an active participant in the political process. To be a wise voter means that you should learn as much as you can about the candidates and the issues. The more you know, the more likely you are to vote. There are many sources of information that you can turn to for facts and opinions: newspapers, magazines, television, radio, and the Internet.

Print Media

Newspaper reporters write articles about candidates who are running for office. Usually, the accounts are about people seeking major offices, such as senator, mayor, or president. Some newspapers print selections from candidates' speeches. Editorials may be written about issues and the candidates' stands on issues.

National news and commentary magazines also carry information about election campaigns. Magazines usually come out weekly or monthly. Therefore, they try to find information that will provide more background or analytical information than most newspapers can on a daily basis.

Sound and Visual Sources

Television and radio are also sources of information about candidates and their positions. Reports may be carried on local and national news programs, depending on the nature of the election. Or there may be background programs on candidates and issues. Radio and television also carry advertisements for political candidates. These ads are designed to persuade us that one candidate deserves our vote more than another does. It must be remembered that these short "sound bites" and generalizations provide little "hard" information.

Candidates are often criticized for not giving the voters enough information in answers to questions posed by television reporters. But the candidates complain that the televised reports don't allow them enough time to give a good answer. Extended news programs provide more information. Many show in-depth interviews with candidates or debates among the rivals for a public office.

POWER *of* ★ ONE

Walter E. Fauntroy

Walter E. Fauntroy believes that citizens must participate in civic life. As a civic leader in Washington, D.C., he has worked on several fronts to give meaning to the idea of good citizenship.

Fauntroy was born in 1933 in Washington, D.C., one of seven children. Growing up in a poor section of the city, Fauntroy proved to be a tough-minded young man who earned the respect of those around him by participating in athletic activities. "I was always smaller," he said, "and I guess that helps to make you try harder."

At an early age, he became involved in the New Bethel Baptist Church near his home. He worked for the church, helped it raise money, and decided that he would like to become a minister. As a "thank you" for all his efforts, the church gave him enough money to pay for his first year's expenses at college. After graduating from Virginia Union University in Richmond in 1955, he attended the Yale University Divinity School. While at Yale, he proved to be a standout as a student. He was noticed by the president of Yale and offered the deanship of the Divinity School when he completed his degree. Instead of accepting the deanship, Fauntroy chose to be the pastor of the New Bethel Baptist Church.

As a follower of the Reverend Dr. Martin Luther King, Jr., Fauntroy became an activist in the civil rights movement of the 1960s. He became the director of the Washington, D.C., bureau of the Southern Christian Leadership Conference, the most influential civil rights group of the time. Founded by Dr. King and others, it advocated a nonviolent approach to further civil rights for minorities.

Fauntroy lobbied for the passage of two laws that expanded voting rights for African Americans: the Civil Rights Act of 1964 and the Voting Rights Act of 1965. He helped to

---

Talk shows on television and radio may invite candidates for less formal interviews than those on news programs. Through these programs, the public may learn more about the personal side of the candidate than the policy side.

In recent years, radio talk shows have become very popular. Some talk show hosts have gained a wide following and exert great influence on the opinions of their listeners. Many cover the major issues of the day. Sometimes they stress one point of view over another. The listener must carefully weigh the information he or she gets. Most of these shows allow listeners to call in and speak on the air to the host or guests. The voter can learn much about the opinions of others from listening to these programs.

The Internet

Information about candidates is easily available on the Internet. Political parties, candidates, and many public-interest groups maintain Web sites that provide a great deal of information about issues and candidates' backgrounds and views. It is important to analyze who is sponsoring a Web site to determine its accuracy. For instance, if you are reading information on a political blog, you should research the sponsors of the

arrange freedom rides in 1961. (On freedom rides, African Americans volunteered to board interstate buses to sit in whites-only sections to protest segregation laws.) In addition, Fauntroy organized protest marches on Albany, Georgia, in 1962; on Birmingham, Alabama, in 1963; and on Selma, Alabama, in 1965. He was a key person in organizing the massive March on Washington in August 1963 in which 200,000 people peacefully demanded jobs and freedom. It was before this group that Dr. King gave his stirring "I Have a Dream" speech. In recognition of Fauntroy's efforts, President Lyndon B. Johnson called on him for advice on how to make the new civil rights legislation work.

Even after Dr. King's assassination in 1968, Fauntroy continued his efforts to expand voting rights and protect the civil rights of African Americans throughout the nation. In addition, he worked locally in Washington, D.C., to make life better for African Americans. He and others put together the Model Inner City Community Organization in 1966. It promoted urban renewal programs that considered the needs and desires of African Americans and the use of African-American professionals and workers in creating projects.

In 1970, President Richard Nixon signed a bill that gave the District of Columbia a nonvoting delegate in the House of Representatives. Although the odds were against him, Fauntroy ran for that seat and won the election. A major theme of his campaign platform was full home rule for the capital.

Fauntroy fought hard to get Congress to pass a bill that would give the District of Columbia the right to establish its own city government. In 1973, Congress passed a limited home rule law for Washington, D.C. Those who lived in the city could now vote for local officials, such as the mayor. Fauntroy retired from Congress in 1990.

Walter Edward Fauntroy has worked tirelessly all his life to involve African Americans in the life of the nation. He values the importance of the right to vote and impresses on people the need to take an active role in making society better. No one else will do it for them, he says.

1. How did the New Bethel Baptist Church influence Fauntroy's life?
2. What was his role in the civil rights movement?
3. What was Fauntroy's goal for Washington, D.C.?
4. What does Fauntroy urge all people to do? Why?

---

blog and who is writing the content. You need to ask yourself if you can trust the information and opinions being provided by the individuals posting on the blog.

Campaign Literature

One can also get information from the campaign headquarters of candidates. If you can, it is a good idea to visit the offices located in your community. There you can pick up brochures that outline the candidates' positions on many issues. You may meet volunteer campaigners at busy places in your community—a mall, a bus stop, a factory. They will be handing out campaign literature designed to help you get to know the candidate better. Remember, the information in this literature is one-sided. It portrays the candidate in the most favorable light possible, and it might even "stretch" the truth.

Analyzing the Media

Just as it is important to be an informed and intelligent shopper and analyze advertisements (see Chapter 13), it is vital to be an intelligent and informed voting citizen. When we read articles, listen to radio, and watch television, we learn about candidates and issues. But how do we know if the information is accurate and objective? Below is a guide to help you decide the fairness and accuracy of the information.

Evaluating Media Coverage of Politics

1. Watch for exaggerations in claims.

2. Separate fact from opinion. Make a list of the major facts and points of view.

3. Compare the listed facts with other facts you have learned about the same issue or candidate.

4. Determine whether the information is one-sided. Does it favor or cover one candidate more than another? (Note: sometimes an article is about one side of an issue. In that case, learn what you can and watch for information about the other side of the issue or the other candidate.)

5. Test the information by comparing it with information from other sources.

Let's Think

1. Where can voters get information to help them make intelligent decisions about voting?
2. How should you analyze information obtained from the media?

Becoming a Citizen

The United States is a nation of immigrants. From the early days of the colonial period until today, people from all over the world have come to this country in search of a dream. Some came in search of freedom, others in search of wealth. Those who loved adventure came in search of the new and unknown. Immigrants have helped to create a unique society in this country. But not all who come to live here permanently decide to become citizens.

Starting the Process

For people to truly participate in the democratic process, they must be able to vote. To vote, they must be citizens. The United States has set up a system that allows immigrants to become citizens. This process is called **naturalization**. Becoming a citizen requires a person to go through certain steps and complete forms from the *U.S. Citizenship and Immigration Services*, a division of the Department of Homeland Security.

An individual requesting an application for citizenship is required to be at least 18 years of age and to have lived in the United States continuously for five years (three years if married to a citizen). Many first file a *declaration of intention* to become a citizen. When the petition for naturalization is completed, it is filed with a federal district court.

The applicant must be a person of "good moral character" and must believe in the principles of the U.S. Constitution. The person must also demonstrate an ability to read and write simple English and a knowledge of U.S. history and government. The English requirement is set aside for a person who is over 55 years of age and who has lived in the United States for 15 or more years.

Taking the Oath

The application for citizenship is closely looked over by the Citizenship and Immigration Services. Once the information is proved to be correct, the applicant is well on the way to becoming a U.S. citizen. The final step is to swear or affirm an oath of allegiance to the United States. The federal judge who conducts the swearing-in ceremony also gives each new citizen a certificate of citizenship.

The oath of allegiance (see page 253) carries with it several important obligations. It requires loyalty to the United States government. It also requires the new citizen to give up any legal allegiance he or she may have had to the former home country. Another obligation is to defend the nation when it is necessary.

Even after naturalized citizens have received a certificate of citizenship, they may not vote in elections until they have registered to vote. After registering, all follow the same voting proce-

Immigrants in New York City studying for a civics exam. To become a citizen, immigrants need to show that they have a basic knowledge of how the U.S. government works.

dures as any other citizen would. In the eyes of the law and according to the 14th Amendment, a naturalized citizen is the same as a native-born citizen. The only thing that a naturalized citizen cannot do is serve as president or vice president of the United States.

The Oath of Allegiance Taken by Newly Naturalized Citizens

I hereby declare, on oath, that I absolutely and entirely renounce and abjure all allegiance and fidelity to any foreign prince, potentate, state or sovereignty, to whom or which I have heretofore been a subject or citizen; that I will support and defend the Constitution and laws of the United States of America against all enemies, foreign and domestic; that I will bear true faith and allegiance to the same; that I will bear arms on behalf of the United States when required by the law; that I will perform noncombatant service in the armed forces of the United States when required by the law; that I will perform work of national importance under civilian direction when required by the law; and that I take this obligation freely without any mental reservation or purpose of evasion; so help me God.

Let's Think

1. What is meant by the term "naturalization"?

2. Make a list of the steps a person must take to become a citizen of the United States. Describe the importance of each step.
3. What are the most important ideas contained in the oath of citizenship? Explain why you think they are important.

Chapter Summary

All citizens have the same rights. Under American democracy, no one group has more privileges under the law than any other. Over the years, there has been a gradual expansion of voting rights. When the Constitution was first written, several groups in American society were denied the right to vote, in particular, women, African Americans, and Native Americans.

Through the 19th and 20th centuries, several constitutional amendments were ratified that gave former male slaves, women, and 18-year-olds suffrage—the right to vote. Federal laws had to be passed to ensure that states did not continue to deny people the rights protected by these amendments. These laws included the Snyder Indian Citizenship Act, the Civil Rights Act of 1964, and the Voting Rights acts of 1965 and 1970.

Exercising the right to vote is essential in a democracy. In order to be listed on the voting rolls so that one can vote, a person must go through a process called registration. Once a citizen reaches the voting age of 18, he or she may obtain a voter registration form to complete. The 1993 Motor Voter Law allows people to register at state motor vehicle offices and other government agencies.

All voters are assigned a polling place where they cast their ballots. The act of voting is secret. This is to ensure that voters are not unduly influenced by others. The Australian ballot is another name for the secret ballot. If a voter is away from home at election time, he or she may vote by absentee ballot.

While exercising the right to vote is the mark of a good citizen, one may also show good citizenship in other ways. You can take school seriously, obey public laws, treat others with respect, speak out when wrongdoing occurs, and be willing to become involved in community activities.

Being an informed voter is a major responsibility of all citizens. Several sources of information shape our opinions about issues and candidates. They include the print media, television, radio, and campaign literature. We can also obtain much information from the Internet. It is important to clarify our understanding of issues and candidates by analyzing the accuracy and objectivity of media coverage.

People who were not born in this country but now live here have the opportunity to become citizens of the United States. The process of becoming a citizen is called naturalization. Potential citizens must satisfy a residency requirement and be of good moral character. Naturalized citizens have the same rights as native-born citizens.

★ CHAPTER REVIEW ★

A. Matching
Match each term in Column A with its definition in Column B.

Column A	Column B
1. suffrage	a. information put out by a candidate's supporters
2. registering	
3. polling place	b. federal agency that supervises immigration policies
4. Australian ballot	
5. naturalization	c. legislation that outlawed literacy test requirements for voters
6. National Voter Registration Act	
	d. process of placing one's name on the voting lists
7. U.S. Citizenship and Immigration Services	e. the right to vote
	f. the process through which an immigrant becomes an American citizen
8. campaign literature	
9. absentee ballot	g. law allowing people to register at motor vehicle bureaus and other government offices
10. Voting Rights Act of 1970	
	h. a location where people vote
	i. secret ballot
	j. allows people to vote even when they are away from home on election day

B. Multiple Choice
Select the statement or word that most correctly answers the question or completes the statement.

1. A citizen is defined as a person who (a) just arrived in a country (b) can participate fully in the political process of government (c) is a member of the Internet (d) leaves his or her country.

2. In order to keep citizens from being denied certain rights, Congress took this action: (a) repealed an amendment (b) passed voter protection laws (c) changed election day (d) overrode the president's veto.

3. This law gave Native Americans the right to vote: (a) Voting Rights Law of 1965 (b) Civil Rights Act of 1964 (c) Australian Ballot Law (d) Snyder Act of 1924.

4. This practice was used to deny African Americans the right to vote: (a) requiring literacy tests (b) filing absentee ballots (c) applying the 15th Amendment (d) increasing voter registration.

5. Evaluating the accuracy of information about issues requires that you (a) pay close attention to rumors (b) read only literature from lobbyists (c) accept the views of your favorite talk show host (d) separate fact from opinion.

6. One objective way to evaluate a public official's performance in office is to look at (a) campaign literature (b) the person's voting record (c) responses on interview programs (d) attendance at fund-raising events.

7. When a person registers to vote, he or she has the option to (a) declare a party affiliation (b) vote for a Supreme Court justice (c) serve on a jury (d) run for public office.

8. This amendment lowered the voting age to 18: (a) 15th (b) 19th (c) 22nd (d) 26th.

9. A single person applying for citizenship in the United States must have lived in the country continuously for (a) 90 days (b) two years (c) five years (d) ten years.

10. People under the age of 55 who apply for citizenship must (a) show a knowledge of English and United States history and government (b) serve in the United States military before becoming a citizen (c) marry an American citizen (d) campaign for public office.

C. Essay

Write a paragraph about *one* of the following:

1. The most important obligation of a good citizen.
2. The best ways to stay informed about issues and candidates for public office.
3. Naturalized citizens should be allowed to run for president of the United States.
4. Ways to persuade people to vote.

D. A Challenge for You

1. Create a cartoon strip that shows potential voters how to register and what happens at the polling place.
2. With your friends, prepare a plan for becoming a more active good citizen. Put the plan in writing. Keep a log of how you carried out your plan and how people reacted to your efforts.
3. For a week or two keep track of the coverage on the radio, television news, and the Internet, and in newspapers and magazines, of a public issue that concerns you. Clip or download the articles and jot down the main points in the radio and TV programs. Then analyze the information, using the steps given on pages 252. Which source of information seems to be the most accurate, factual, and objective? Did any one report affect your opinion more than others? Why? Write a report about your findings.
4. Contact your local League of Women Voters or another organization that promotes good government practices. Conduct an interview with one of its officials. The interview should focus on the way the organization works, what it sees as its main purpose, and how it carries out its mission. Report to the class on what you learned or write an article for the school newspaper.

Document-Based Question

State the main idea expressed in each document. Then use information in the documents and your own knowledge to write an essay about how the Motor Voter Law affected voter registration and turnout.

Five Million Added to the Rolls

In what political experts say is the greatest expansion of voter rolls in the nation's history, more than five million Americans have registered to vote in the eight months since the National Voter Registration Act was enacted.

Several states report that the Act—popularly known as the "Motor Voter law" because it permits people to register while obtaining a driving permit"—has generated three-fold increases, and greater, in the pace of registration compared with earlier years. . . .

Estimates are that [early in the 21st century], if the surge generated by the new law continues, at least four of every five adult Americans will be registered to vote, compared with about three of every five [in the mid-1990s]. . . . .

Whether the voting act has encouraged fraud, what is certain is that the expanded rolls include duplications. Some new voters are actually re-registrations by people who have moved from one address to another and have failed to send back word of their switch to registrars in their old neighborhoods. . . .

"I'm impressed by the registration surge thus far, but I'm not ready to predict there will be a significant increase in the percent of people actually voting," said Curtis B. Gans, the director of the Committee for the Study of the American Electorate, a Washington-based organization.

"Certainly the Act can't hurt," he said. "It surely reaches out to young people, and it surely opens up opportunity to register in some states where opportunity has been lacking somewhat, as in parts of the South. But that's no guarantee that people will actually vote in greater numbers."

Motor Voter or Motivated Voter?

Motor Voter represents the most recent attempt to make voting easier by removing restrictions imposed in the early years of [the 20th] century. Its promise is that it specifically targets those groups now least likely to be registered voters—the mobile, the young, the poor, and citizens of color—by linking registration to particular agencies with whom these groups deal. For example, although 89 percent of 25- to 29-year-olds have driver's licenses, only 65 percent claim to be registered and 54 percent to be voters, according to a Department of Transportation study. In the course of a five-year driver's license cycle, most citizens will have an opportunity to get on the voting rolls. By extending mail-in registration to the 33 states where mail-in procedures did not exist before, Motor Voter facilitates opportunities for outreach by activist public officials such as the secretaries of state of Connecticut, Florida, Ohio, and New Mexico, plus advocacy groups such as First Vote, which coordinates voter registration of high school senior classes in some 3,000 schools. . . .

For sure, Motor Voter will yield increases in turnout in states such as Florida where "in person" registration requirements were a significant deterrent to voting. Yet while a broader and more representative slice of the electorate will surely get on the voter rolls, particularly to the extent registration in public assistance offices is effective, a significant national impact will depend on the extent to which political strategists take advantage of the new opportunities Motor Voter affords to motivate registrants by mobilizing them to turn out to vote. . . .

By making registration easier, Motor Voter creates voter rolls that are more inclusive of everyone—lower-income citizens and citizens of color as well as young people and movers. Because of new updating and reporting requirements these lists will be more accurate and more likely to be computerized. They are also more likely to be available well before the election, something that is not the case with election day registration. This means parties, campaigns, and interest groups can more easily contact a broader and more inclusive slice of the electorate. . . .

People are most motivated to act when contacted by people whom they know rather than by pieces of direct mail, telemarketers, and television commercials. . . .

In other words, what is required is to contact these citizens and persuade them that turning out to vote could make a big difference to them. . . . Motor Voter helps because in most states newly registered voters will at least receive mailings from the state: a voter card, sample ballot, and an election pamphlet. This provides them with basic information and lets them know that their participation [voting] matters enough to merit a piece of mail from the state.

CHAPTER 15

The Active Citizen and Public Policy

★ CHAPTER FOCUS

1. How do important issues come to our attention?
2. What steps can we take to become an active citizen?
3. What are the different ways people can get involved in civic life?

Why do you think the people in the cartoon on page 258 are so frustrated? What sorts of issues is the average person likely to face every day? There are personal issues concerning individual and family matters. There are public issues. They concern our schools, neighborhoods, communities, states, nation, and the world. Personal issues tend to be handled privately—by the individuals involved. Public issues affect a broader range of people and are likely to be resolved by national organizations or the government.

Views on how issues should be handled form the basis of public policy. Shaping and reshaping public policy is a major task for government at all levels. In a democratic society, the shaping is also a major task for its citizens.

Public policies attempt to create courses of action that will solve problems and serve people. By their nature, policies come about as the result of compromise. Through compromise, policy makers attempt to benefit or satisfy the greatest number of people. The process implies "rule by majority" and aims to win over the support of the largest number of people.

The system of democratic government that we support emphasizes the importance of "rule by the people." One aspect of "ruling" is citizen participation. Participation allows us to influence government officials on public policy issues. Our Constitution provides the mechanism for participation. It is built into the Bill of Rights, particularly the First Amendment. This amendment protects freedoms such as those of speech and the press and the rights of petition and assembly. Signing a petition demanding a new traffic light at an intersection, debating important questions at a town meeting, voting at election time, and volunteering in community activities are all examples of participation.

The danger to the democratic process develops when individuals fail to take notice of issues and do not express their reasoned opinions. If we refuse to participate, we are not meeting our civic responsibility. To get involved, we need to understand how issues become important.

How Do Issues Come to Our Attention?

We read about issues such as those depicted in the cartoon at right in newspapers and magazines. We see reports about the issues on television and the Internet. Issues arouse emotions and ignite debate. Soon the public calls for a public policy to be formulated.

How Issues Develop

An issue may be created by a single action, a series of actions, or a gradual development that gains significance over time. As people become aware of an issue, they show various degrees of concern about it. Certainly, when our daily lives are affected, an issue becomes more immediate, and we show more interest in it. For instance, there may have been several bad accidents at an intersection near your school. People may have been severely injured. Soon community residents demand a traffic light on that corner or a more visible police presence to cut down on speeding. Or there may be a call for the building of a sewage treatment plant to prevent dumping of untreated sewage into the local waterways. Such issues may move people to sign petitions to get government officials to take action.

Other issues come to the surface slowly and push into our consciousness over a period of time. As our nation became more dependent on motor vehicles, the number of vehicles on the roads increased. Scientists began to warn us that exhaust fumes from cars and trucks were becoming a major source of pollutants in the atmosphere. During the 1960s, laws were passed to regulate the amount of polluting exhaust new vehicles could produce. Later the lead content of gasoline was regulated. When the automobile was invented, no one thought about the consequences of exhaust emissions. As pollution became more of a problem over the years, public officials decided to act.

Sometimes health questions spark public concern about an issue. For instance, when the general public first heard about AIDS (Acquired Immuno-Deficiency Syndrome), people panicked. They feared what would happen if they

"Issues, Issues, Issues—Will they never end?!"

were exposed to the virus that causes AIDS, and they feared that the virus could be anywhere. The public wanted information and called on the government to do something.

The federal government responded by setting up research and education programs. The Centers for Disease Control and Prevention (CDC) in Atlanta coordinated the ongoing research. It also provides information about prevention and treatment of AIDS. Local and state governments set up treatment centers and education programs.

Court decisions often have long-term consequences. One that stirred up a great debate was a decision by the Supreme Court in 1973. The Court's ruling in the case of *Roe* v. *Wade* permitted abortions in the first six months of pregnancy. Abortion is an emotional issue that people have strong feelings about. Two different camps have developed. One, known as the "Right-to-Life" group, opposes abortions. Supporters of this point of view think abortion is morally wrong and a form of murder. The people on the other side of the issue believe in "Pro-Choice." This group thinks that a woman should have the right to privacy and be able to make the decision to have an abortion herself without outside interference. A major area of controversy centers on whether government funds for medical insurance, such as Medicaid, should be used to finance abortions. People on both sides of the issue lobby Congress constantly to achieve their goals.

When events threaten the lifestyle of Americans or shatter the order of things, new issues come to the surface. The bombing of the federal building in Oklahoma City in 1995 made people realize that terrorist acts could occur anywhere and affect any citizen. The bombing led to a call for a federal law to deal harshly with terrorists who commit such crimes in the United States. Congress passed the Comprehensive Terrorism Prevention Act in 1996. The terrorist attack that destroyed the World Trade Center on September 11, 2001, triggered government actions. Airport security was increased. More stringent screening of passengers and baggage was set in motion. The federal government took over the supervision of airport security personnel, and airplane security was improved. In addition, the U.S.A. Patriot Act was enacted in 2001. It is designed to provide the government with broader powers to deal with terrorism. Stricter airport security measures were put into place. These measures slowed check-in procedures. But the public accepted them to get a greater feeling of safety.

The NRA is a powerful lobby force at all levels of government. Its loyal members are active voters. This billboard near Houston, Texas, shows that the organization uses a variety of ways to promote its message.

Lobby Groups Publicize Issues

Lobbies and other pressure groups work to keep issues in the public eye. In order to influence Congress, state legislatures, and town and city councils, they publicize their causes in the media and through direct mailings to the general population. Such campaigns are designed to marshal people to take action—demand laws—to right wrongs.

Many of the people profiled in the "Power of One" features in this book used lobbying techniques to bring the issues they promoted to the attention of the public and legislators. For instance, Ralph Nader wrote a book about defects in automobiles. It gained support for his campaign to increase safety standards in the manufacturing of automobiles. The public outcry pushed Congress into passing a motor vehicle safety law in 1966.

After a young man tried to kill President Ronald Reagan in 1981, calls for restrictions on access to handguns grew louder. Also injured in the shooting was James Brady, Reagan's press secretary. Brady and his wife, Sarah, set up an organization to promote gun control. The opposite point of view was vigorously put forth by the National Rifle Association. The NRA spent a great deal of money to lobby legislatures and for campaign contributions to defeat candidates who supported gun control. Both sides have sent out countless mailings to solicit money and win public support. The debate goes on, but Congress did pass a gun control law in 1993. President Clinton signed the Brady law in 1994. It put restrictions on the purchase of handguns. A 1994 Crime Control law contained curbs on the sale of various types of guns to certain groups of people and banned the sale of assault weapons.

For years, cigarette manufacturers used lobbyists and campaign contributions to prevent antismoking legislation from being passed. Antismoking forces gained strength after scientists found more and more compelling evidence to link smoking with the development of various cancers and heart and lung diseases. In the 1990s, the antismoking lobby finally persuaded local and state legislatures across the country to ban smoking in many public places.

The antismoking forces continued to gain strength. In the late 1990s, the tobacco industry faced a number of lawsuits about the harmful effects of tobacco, smoking, and secondhand smoke. Juries often decided against the tobacco companies and awarded millions of dollars to states and individuals. The money was used by the states to repay health care costs.

Current issues kept in the spotlight by various lobbies are health care reform, Medicare and Social Security reform, and campaign finance reform. Public debate will presumably lead to solutions to the problems. Or the public will tire of the arguments and the issue will fade away or be ignored until something happens to stir up emotions again.

Public Opinion Polls

Through polls, political and business leaders can find out what the general public thinks about a particular issue or candidate. Polls might help bring issues to the attention of leaders. For example, a candidate for public office finds out that the voters are more concerned about building new schools than about a new park. The candidate most likely will come up with a proposal about new schools. If the candidate is elected, the proposal will probably become part of a legislative package.

Polls also allow people to see how others feel about issues. Knowing the opinions of others may cause you to alter your point of view. Or the knowledge may help you better understand a differing view. For instance, if you are among the 59 percent who think that the public transportation system in your community is good, you might wonder why 41 percent think it is poor. Once you learn more about others' experiences, you realize that your area of the community is better served than most areas. Perhaps you will consider asking your city council representative to do something to make the service more equal. Who knows, you might even join a group that promotes better transportation service.

Poll results may help us understand, to some extent, why our decision makers support certain policies over others. Why should a government official go out on a limb to demand television coverage of court trials when the majority of his or her constituents oppose the idea? We can also learn that some issues have greater significance in one area of the country than in another.

Participation and Acceptance

Participation by the public in the formulation of public policy is essential to make democracy work. Without individual input into the major issues of the day, democracy would be limited. If only a few make decisions for all, we could not call our system a government by the people.

Public policy is a blend of ideas. Usually, it represents a compromise among the views of many groups. No public policy will satisfy all of the people. Most are designed to satisfy the largest number of people or to meet the greatest need. Even if we disagree with a policy, we, as good citizens, bow to the wishes of the majority. But we retain the freedom to try to change the policy through legal and peaceful means. If the public policy proves to be unworkable or does not do the job it set out to do, then it will be re-examined and either discarded or reshaped.

Let's Think

1. How do issues develop?
2. What role do pressure groups play in the creation of public issues?
3. How do public opinion polls affect issues?
4. What should our role be after a public policy is created?

How to Get Involved

You may be interested in influencing a policy because it would have an impact on you and your life. Or you may want to right a wrong that has been done to others. What can you do to become involved?

Step One—Finding an Interest and Knowing Yourself

People express their opinions and get involved when something concerns them. The issue is generally one that directly affects the way they live or is a topic of great interest. It may be a local issue, for example, closing a garbage

CONCERNS	CHECK HERE, IF INTERESTED
Local environmental issues	
Traffic safety	
Creating safe places for young people to play	
Beautifying the neighborhood	
Tutoring other students	
Helping senior citizens	
Regulating teen behavior in public places	
Noise pollution	
Increasing the number of health facilities in the community	
Setting up single-gender high schools	
Creating all-year-round school programs	
Establishing English as the official language of the country	
Cutting or increasing state funding for the arts	
Spending state money for a superhighway that will cross the entire state	
Cutting or increasing federal military spending	
Developing criteria for sending U.S. troops to foreign countries in emergency situations	
Reforming the medical insurance system in the United States	
Decreasing or increasing government regulations aimed at the food and drug industries	
Increasing fees at national parks to help preserve them	
Changing the immigration policy of the United States	
Supporting a voucher plan to allow parents to send their children to private schools with government support	

dump. Or it might be a national issue such as raising taxes.

How do you decide if you want to get involved? The first step is self-discovery. Obviously, you can't be part of every issue that comes along. You have to pick and choose. First, you should make a list of your interests. The checklist above is designed to help you get started. Add your own ideas if you wish. Place a check next to the issues or activities that you care about. Remember that the standard you should use is interest, not whether you agree or disagree with a statement.

Look at the check marks you made. What types of issues and activities seem to interest you the most? What do they have in common: direct physical involvement or behind-the-scenes pressure actions?

Step Two—Listing Issues According to Priority

Obviously, you cannot involve yourself in every issue or activity you checked. You need to decide which are the most important to you. Look at the items and rank them according to what

◀REALITY CHECK▶
Creating Citizen Schools

We want to contribute to a worthwhile activity, but making the decision to volunteer can be difficult. You might say to yourself, "I'm not sure I have the time. My abilities probably aren't needed." One unique organization, Citizen Schools, has attracted the talents of a wide variety of volunteers.

The story begins in 1994 in Boston, Massachusetts. Education officials there were concerned about what they saw as a "downward spiral of youth crime, crumbling neighborhoods, and struggling public schools." Two individuals, Eric Schwartz and Ned Rimer, thought of an idea that they wanted to put in place. They volunteered to teach 30 fifth-grade students after school or in the summer. Since Schwartz was a former reporter, he taught the students journalism. Rimer had experience running an emergency response squad at the University of Vermont, so he decided to teach the youngsters first aid. The two men called themselves "Citizen Teachers."

By 1995, they had formed a nonprofit organization and launched a full program of activities. One idea behind Citizen Schools is that learning does not end once the last bell of the school day sounds. Consequently, Rimer and Schwartz developed after-school and summer programs to enrich the lives of the students. Another of their ideas is that learning is best done when young people engage in activities. The participants are known as apprentices. When some apprentices became part of the journalism program, they learned that they would publish a newspaper on their own. Students working with computers learned to design Web sites for their schools. Through such projects, apprentices gained new skills and developed new ideas while creating practical, hands-on projects. Students are involved in two apprenticeships a week and spend about 16 hours total on them.

The organization recruits Citizen Teachers from the private sector. The recruits learn methods that help them reach out to the young people who participate in the programs. Citizen Schools and its teachers are supported by many professional educators who believe that the programs are a great supplement to the educational experience of students in this age group.

After-school programs are designed to provide students with fun-filled, worthwhile educational experiences that extend beyond the classroom. As the organization's Web site states, "Explorations expose apprentices to the cultures, flavors and traditions of their city. Youth are challenged to test new ways of thinking about their world through experiences both in and out of the classroom. Off-campus explorations may take students to a local university, a distinctive neighborhood, a museum or a nature center. On-campus explorations teach students everything from new dances to hunger awareness, bringing the community into the classroom."

Over the years, the enrichment program has provided numerous students with a variety of learning activities that have improved their educational achievement and influenced their future careers.

From one small act of volunteering in an effort to make a difference, Schwartz and Rimer have extended their program to include volunteers in other states. According to Citizen Schools, it is working with 4,400 students and 3,200 volunteers in 7 states. Through this organization, many people have chosen to get involved and contribute to the life of their communities.

1. How did Citizen Schools begin?
2. Why did the city of Boston believe a program like this was needed?
3. How do students benefit from the apprenticeships?
4. How does this program appeal to adults who might want to get involved in making a contribution to their communities?

you believe is their order of importance to you. The ones that are most important should head the list.

Step Three—Deciding How to Participate

First of all, you should determine whether you need to join an organization to accomplish your goal or learn more about an issue. You'll need to find out what organizations in your area are concerned with the problems you want to help solve. If you want to influence policy, you'll need to do research to find out the facts and the arguments the various sides use to defend their points of view. It would be a good idea to find out who has the power to act on the issue you are promoting.

This 12th-grade student in Poughkeepsie, New York, has volunteered to help grade-school students with reading.

Step Four—Volunteering

Why does volunteering make you a better citizen? Good citizenship means participating in civic life. Helping others improves the quality of life in the community by making it a better place in which to live. We show we care about what happens to people in the community and to the community itself. We need to participate because

ORGANIZATION	PURPOSE
STRIVE, New York City (www.strivenewyork.org)	Trains young adults for entry-level jobs.
Focus: HOPE, Detroit (www.focushope.edu)	Offers the disadvantaged training in everything from repairing machinery to high-tech engineering.
Jobs for Youth, Chicago (www.jfychicago.org)	Tough-love training (technique for helping undisciplined young people).
Alternatives for Girls, Detroit (www.alternativesforgirls.org)	Fights teen pregnancy through a girls' club that promotes building self-respect; includes kindergartners through high schoolers.
MAD DADS, Jacksonville, Florida (www.maddads.com)	Recruits area men to patrol drug markets and report dealers to police. Volunteers serve as positive role models.
Keep Philadelphia Beautiful (http://keepphiladelphiabeautiful.org/aboutus.html)	Encourages individuals to take greater responsibility for improving their community environments by providing resources and education.
Volunteer.gov/gov (www.volunteer.gov/)	Provides an easy online portal to find ways to volunteer.
Good Shepherd Mediation Program, Philadelphia (www.phillymediators.org)	Educates young people about how to resolve conflicts without violence.
City Year, Boston (www.cityyear.org)	Offers one-year intensive community service for people 17 to 23 years old.

A selection of organizations that use volunteers.

For some 50 years, the Peace Corps has attracted volunteers to work in countries throughout the world. This volunteer is teaching villagers in Guatemala about good health practices.

government simply does not have the resources to do everything.

Once, *Newsweek*, a weekly newsmagazine, published a list of ways citizens can get involved in their communities. It named many organizations across the country that welcome volunteers. An updated list on page 263 shows the wide variety of opportunities available.

On a cold day in January 1961, John F. Kennedy stood before the Capitol to give his inaugural address. He presented an idea, a challenge that many Americans believe is at the heart of living in a democracy. He said: ". . . ask not what your country can do for you—ask what you can do for your country." Kennedy recognized that if a democracy is to be strong, citizens must take an active interest in civic life. They must contribute.

The Kennedy administration went on to create the Peace Corps. It trains volunteers age 21 and over to help carry out small-scale projects in developing countries. The volunteers serve for two years and receive a modest allowance and living expenses.

Recent presidents have followed Kennedy's lead in promoting service. In 1988, when George H.W. Bush accepted the nomination for president, he talked of the many volunteer organizations that serve people throughout the nation.

He referred to them as the thousand "Points of Light." Bush and his wife, Barbara, publicized many volunteer programs, particularly efforts to teach people to read.

After Bill Clinton became president, he too urged people to get involved in helping others. One program set up by Clinton in 1994 is Americorps, a national organization supported by the government. It recruits young people to work in a variety of public service projects. The volunteers get the minimum wage, some health coverage, child care, and a tuition grant for higher education. They can work for up to two years. By the time Americorps was in existence three years, over 25,000 members were serving in more than 430 programs across the country.

In 1989, Wendy Kopp, a Princeton University graduate, founded Teach for America. This organization places recent college graduates in public schools in many urban and rural areas around the country. In exchange for professional training and a modest salary, these people teach for two years. More than 4,000 have been placed in 13 different areas since the organization was founded.

In his 2002 State of the Union speech, President George W. Bush called for the creation of the USA Freedom Corps. According to its Web site,

P O W E R *of* ★ N E

Colleen Antas

Sometimes being a popular high school athlete and senior class president is not enough. This was the case for 17-year-old Colleen Antas in 2006 when she was a student

at Wheaton North High School in Wheaton, Illinois. It was during her senior year that Antas visited the Pediatric Outpatient Center at Central DuPage Hospital. There she saw many children receiving all kinds of treatments, including blood transfusions, chemotherapy, and other painful medical procedures.

She was impressed by how happy the children were when they received gifts at the end of their visits. Teen patients were thrilled with gift cards. Younger patients loved the toys they went home with. Colleen saw that the supply of toys and gift cards was beginning to run low. That concerned her, so she decided to do something about the problem. She went to her soccer team and talked to her teammates. The team also included students who attended a rival school, the Wheaton Warrenville South High School. The students de-

cided to set up a friendly competition between the schools to raise money to help the young patients at the hospital. Each school began a fund-raising drive.

"When Colleen called me, I was immediately impressed by her resolve to help the children in treatment. Here's a young person who saw a need and decided to take personal responsibility to make a positive difference in someone else's life," said Kurt Wolfbrink of the Central DuPage Health Foundation staff. "After seeing the results, I was impressed by the outpouring of support by the students at both schools."

Under Colleen's leadership, students at the two schools collected almost $6,000. The team members did not sell anything. They asked for donations. The money was used to buy toys and gift cards for the pediatric patients. The children would continue to have something to look forward to after undergoing painful procedures.

Colleen graduated from high school and went on to Northwestern University, where she studied education and Spanish and played on the women's soccer team. But she is still remembered in her hometown as a wonderful example of how one person can make a positive difference in the lives of others and in the life of the community in which they live.

1. Why did Colleen Antas decide to collect funds for the hospital?
2. Who helped raise the funds?
3. What difference did Colleen's effort make to the community?

---

the program's function was to build "a culture of service, citizenship, and responsibility in America. USAFC promotes and expands volunteer service in America by partnering with national service programs, . . . and helping to connect individuals with volunteer opportunities."

Schools around the country have incorpo-

rated community service programs into their educational requirements. For instance, Dade County, Florida, schools require a certain number of hours of community service as part of the requirements for graduation from high school. Some think it is a contradiction to "require volunteerism." Students, though, often seem to enjoy the experience and often volunteer for more than the minimum number of hours.

For those who say they can't commit themselves to a certain number of volunteer hours, an organization promoting flexibility of commitment was formed in 1986. Called City Cares of America, it made it easy for people who want to get involved. The program existed in 26 cities across the country and had a combined membership of over 75,000 people who signed up to be volunteers. Many of these communities' service activities are now coordinated through the Web sites for Points of Light and Hands On Network, which are the two largest clearinghouses for community service organizations.

Anytime a member wants to help out, he or she makes a phone call to find out where to go to work for a few hours. "If someone wakes up on a Saturday morning in a mood to help paint an elementary school, all he or she has to do is show up." One woman sorting cans of vegetables and soup at a food bank put it this way, "I travel a lot for work, and I don't want to make a commitment to be someplace the third Friday of every month. If I don't show up for a month, no one's going to think that I let them down."

Getting involved takes thought, time, and energy. An individual needs commitment to a cause and time to devote to that cause. But all talents can be used. Joining existing organizations is an easy way to participate. They offer support systems, provide individuals with information, and show you how you can make a contribution. A way to find information about organizations is through the Internet. Each day, new organizations add Web pages for you to consult. Once you get involved, you may wonder why you ever hesitated. Most people find that volunteering is very rewarding.

Let's Think

1. List the steps that an individual should take when deciding to participate in volunteer or community activities.
2. What organizations that you read about in this section sound most interesting to you? Why?
3. What are the pros and cons of volunteering?

Chapter Summary

A major task for all governments is creating and reshaping public policy. Citizens in a democracy participate in the making of public policy through letting leaders know their opinions. Being willing to compromise is essential to solving problems and developing public policies that will benefit the greatest number of people and win wide support.

Issues come to our attention and become important in a variety of ways. Events occur (terrorist acts). Knowledge is gained over the years (concern about the environment). Health issues arise (AIDS). Court cases are decided (abortion rights). Lobbies publicize issues (gun control). Public opinion polls highlight public concerns (crime).

Public policies can be modified if they do not work or have unfair consequences. Sometimes changing social conditions and needs require the modification of public policies.

To get involved in influencing policy, you need to take four basic steps. 1. Find an interest and know yourself. 2. List issues in order of their importance to you. 3. Decide the best way to participate. 4. Volunteer.

★ CHAPTER REVIEW ★

A. Matching

Match each term in Column A with its definition in Column B.

Column A

1. issue
2. opinion poll
3. public policy
4. event
5. *Roe* v. *Wade*
6. priority
7. volunteering
8. censorship
9. Peace Corps
10. Americorps

Column B

a. formal survey of views of a group of people
b. Supreme Court decision on abortions
c. a matter in dispute
d. position on an issue determined by government bodies
e. order of importance
f. an important happening
g. practice of supressing information based on official policy
h. participating without pay in a group that helps others
i. national organization set up in 1994 to promote public service in the United States
j. organization created in 1961 to recruit volunteers for service in developing countries

B. Multiple Choice

Select the statement or word that most correctly answers the question or completes the statement.

1. Political issues generally come to our attention through all of the following *except* (a) events (b) lobbyists and pressure groups (c) television gardening shows (d) public opinion polls.

2. An example of an issue that took time to gain the attention of the public is (a) the bombing of the federal building in Oklahoma City (b) pollution of the environment (c) the Supreme Court decision in *Roe* v. *Wade* (d) the crash of Flight 800.

3. Lobbying groups mainly publicize their positions on issues through (a) television interviews (b) printing their own position papers (c) articles in magazines (d) all of these ways.

4. An issue is settled in a way that satisfies most of the people on different sides of the argument. This is known as (a) minority rule (b) legislation by Congress (c) a compromise (d) none of the above.

5. Which of the following ideas is true of public policies? They (a) are set forever (b) can be changed by legal and peaceful means (c) are generally fully supported by everyone (d) are not important to most citizens.

6. The first step in "getting involved" is (a) finding an interest (b) deciding how to participate (c) volunteering (d) prioritizing interests.

7. President John Kennedy (a) never spoke about volunteering (b) inspired other presidents to promote volunteerism (c) said citizens should ask the country what it should do for them (d) only promoted military service.

8. All of the following are examples of participating in public life *except* (a) signing petitions (b) voting (c) volunteering at a homeless shelter (d) getting a paid job to support yourself.

9. President George H.W. Bush referred to the volunteer movement in the United States as (a) Americorps (b) Peace Corps (c) Points of Light (d) Teach for America.

10. The founder of Teach for America was (a) Wendy Kopp (b) Bill Clinton (c) George W. Bush (d) John F. Kennedy.

C. Essay

Write a paragraph about *one* of the following:

1. The art of bringing about compromises is an important skill to acquire.

2. Developing an interest inventory is an important way to determine how to get involved.

3. Volunteering helps our democracy to function better.

4. Polls can publicize issues as well as measure public opinion.

D. A Challenge for You

1. Prepare a cartoon strip or a poster that describes how an issue becomes a matter of concern to the American public.

2. Interview a local public official about an issue of concern in your community today. Find out during the interview what the possible solutions to the problem are. Report on the interview to the class or write an article for the school newspaper.

3. Find out how your school promotes volunteer activities. Report your findings to the class. Create a poster that informs students about the possibilities and, with permission, put it up in a public place.

4. Set up a clearinghouse for volunteer organizations and put fellow students in touch with suitable projects.

5. Select any *two* organizations discussed in the chapter. Contact them and get more information about how each operates. Explain why you think these organizations are successful.

6. Invite volunteers from a variety of projects to speak to the class about their positive and negative experiences.

Document-Based Question

State the main idea expressed in each document. Then use the information and your own knowledge to write an essay explaining how providing health care for all Americans is an important public policy issue.

Senator Takes Initiative on Health Care

Washington—Senator Max Baucus, the chairman of the Finance Committee, will unveil a detailed blueprint . . . to guarantee health insurance for all Americans by facilitating sales of private insurance, expanding Medicaid and Medicare, and requiring most employers to provide or pay for health benefits. . . .

Aides to [president-elect] Mr. Obama said they welcomed the congressional efforts, had encouraged Congress to take the lead and still considered health care a top priority, despite the urgent need to address huge problems afflicting the economy.

The plan proposed by Mr. Baucus, Democrat of Montana, would eventually require everyone to have health insurance coverage, with federal subsidies for those who could not otherwise afford it.

Other Democrats with deep experience in health care are also drafting proposals to expand coverage and slow the growth of health costs. These lawmakers include Senator Edward M. Kennedy of Massachusetts and Representatives John D. Dingell of Michigan and Pete Stark of California.

The proposals are all broadly compatible with Mr. Obama's campaign promises. But Mr. Baucus's 35,000-word plan would go further than Mr. Obama's in one respect, eventually requiring all people—not just children—to have coverage.

"Every American has a right to affordable, high-quality health care," Mr. Baucus said. "Americans cannot wait any longer." "Far from being a distraction from efforts to revive the economy," he said, "health reform is an essential part of restoring America's economy and maintaining our competitiveness."

Mr. Baucus would create a nationwide marketplace, a "health insurance exchange," where people could compare and buy insurance policies. The options would include private insurance policies and a new public plan similar to Medicare. Insurers could no long deny coverage to people who had been sick. Congress would also limit insurers' ability to charge higher premiums because of a person's age or prior illness.

People would have a duty to obtain coverage when affordable options were available to all through the insurance exchange. This obligation "would be enforced, possibly through the tax system," the plan says.

Health-Care Reform

The League of Women Voters believes that quality, affordable health care should be available to all U.S. residents. Other U.S. health-care policy goals should include the equitable distribution of services, efficient and economical delivery of care, advancement of medical research and technology, and a reasonable total national expenditure level for health care.

Furthermore, the League believes that all Americans should have access to a basic level of care that includes the prevention of disease, health promotion and education, primary care (including prenatal and reproductive health), acute care, long-term care, and mental health care.

Through decades of work in their communities, League members have learned that Americans believe that fairness and responsibility, as well as access, are important values for any health care system. We believe that health care reform can only succeed if it takes all these values into account.

From *Policy Position of the League of Women Voters of the United States*, 2008.

The Making of Foreign Policy

Look at the cartoon on page 271. Why is Uncle Sam greeting countries in the rest of the world? The countries of the world are our neighbors. Just as you would like to have a good relationship with your neighbors, countries generally want to have good relationships with one another. This is especially true as the world, through technological advances, has become smaller.

How a nation treats other nations is called its **foreign policy**. It is a kind of blueprint for the way a nation deals with other nations of the world. Foreign policy involves economic, political, and military issues. How foreign policy is conducted is of major importance to the domestic and international concerns of a nation.

The world is divided into many nations. Each one has its own special history and culture. Some nations, such as Russia, Japan, and Thailand, have been independent for hundreds of years. Others, such as the Czech Republic, Ukraine, and Eritrea, came into existence in the 1990s. The gov-

ernments of all nations want to maintain their independence and conduct their affairs as they see fit. They want to keep their sovereignty, their freedom from outside control. But nations must interact with each other for trade and travel and to settle disputes. They cannot escape having to develop a foreign policy.

Factors That Influence Foreign Policy

The United States is in a unique position as a country. It is large in area, and it has a large, well-educated, and productive population. The diverse population is made up of peoples from many different areas of the world. Our democratic way of government and free-enterprise economy have given us freedom and prosperity. The country has internal problems, but it does not

"Getting to Know You"

fear general civil unrest. Our neighbors to the north and the south (Canada and Mexico) are friendly.

Early in the 21st century, the United States is considered to be the most powerful nation in the world. Why then do we have to pay so much attention to our relations with other countries—our foreign policy? We need to have a plan to maintain good relations with other countries because it is in our best interest to do so. Given the capabilities of modern communication and weapons technology, unrest in any part of the world could affect us.

Goals of Foreign Policy

A major goal of foreign policy is to "win friends and influence people." We want to maintain peace in the world and to protect our own independence and security. Trade with other nations—buying goods from them and selling goods to them—is essential to our economic prosperity. We want to promote good relations in order to keep trade flowing smoothly. We need to be sure that we can freely obtain the natural resources that are vital to our economic and defense needs. The United States also seeks ways to strengthen democratic political systems in other countries and to promote human rights.

Good Trade Relations

A primary goal of any nation is to develop and maintain a strong economy. Foreign trade is a major factor in achieving this goal. The United States tries to negotiate trade agreements that will benefit American industries. Other countries want favorable terms to sell their products in the United States. Trade negotiations may also address nontrade questions such as human rights abuses and environmental problems. To gain a low tariff on exports to the United States, a country may promise to stop jailing journalists who disagree with the country's government.

An example of an attempt to lower trade barriers among nations is the North American Free

Trade Agreement (NAFTA), which went into effect in 1994. This agreement is designed to increase the flow of goods in North America among Canada, the United States, and Mexico. In 2005, Congress approved a free trade agreement between the United States and a number of Latin American countries. The Central American Free Trade Agreement (CAFTA–DR) includes Costa Rica, El Salvador, Guatemala, Honduras, and Nicaragua (in Central America) and the Dominican Republic (in the Caribbean).

During the presidential campaign of 2008, the candidates debated issues related to free trade agreements. Many Americans believe that free trade agreements have caused the United States to lose jobs to other countries where wages and benefits are lower and working conditions are poorer.

An older trade organization that tied together the major economic powers of the world, including the United States, was GATT, the General Agreement on Tariffs and Trade. It was started in the late 1940s to promote freer trade. In 1993, it changed its name to the World Trade Organization (WTO). The membership has grown to include 153 nations. The World Trade Organization meets periodically to update trade agreements, address new economic problems, and settle trade disputes.

The economic interests of the United States are increasingly centered on Asia. Four of our top ten trading partners are China, Japan, South Korea, and Taiwan—all in Asia. When the economies of several Asian countries had problems in 1997 and 1998, the United States was quick to offer help. It did not want economic problems to bring about unrest there or affect our foreign trade too severely.

National Security

National security is an important facet of foreign policy. It involves the safety, independence, and general well-being of the nation. Problems exist all over the world. Some are ongoing, and others are sudden events. Which should be considered threats to our national security? Which should the United States take action to stop or control?

The United States maintains a large military force for defense and to help maintain peace in other areas of the world. In 1996, we sent troops to Bosnia in order to end a civil war there. They acted with forces from countries in Europe to bring peace to this area. It was feared that unrest in Bosnia would spread to other areas of Europe if left unchecked.

In 1991, the United States, in cooperation with other nations, went to war against Iraq to preserve peace in the Middle East. Another aim was to protect oil supplies in that area. Oil from there is vital to the economies of many countries in Europe, the United States, and Japan. Even though Iraq was defeated in 1991, it continued to defy parts of the cease-fire agreement. The United States maintained armed forces in the area to keep Iraq from attacking its neighbors.

In response to the 2001 terrorist attacks on the World Trade Center, the United States sent troops to Afghanistan to overthrow the Taliban government which had supported the terrorist organization known as al Qaeda. This government, which was repressive, had denied rights to women and discriminated against anyone who was not Muslim. Elements of the Taliban have continued to fight against U.S. troops stationed in Afghanistan. International forces, along with Afghan forces, are trying to prevent a resurgence of the Taliban.

In 2003, President Bush, with the approval of Congress, sent troops to Iraq to overthrow the dictator Saddam Hussein. It was feared that he was stockpiling weapons of mass destruction. Unlike the previous war with Iraq, the UN did not support the United States. A coalition that included Great Britain was created.

The new action in Iraq did not uncover weapons of mass destruction. Many who supported Hussein mounted a strong military resistance against the coalition forces. Years later, in 2007, the United States increased the number of troops it assigned to Iraq. This action was known as the "Surge." As a result, resistance skirmishes and roadside bombings slowed down. As the United States turned over control to the Iraqi government, fighting lessened and a timetable for the withdrawal of U.S. troops was set. When Barack Obama became president, he was committed to an orderly withdrawal of U.S. troops by 2011. Some of the troops would be moved to Afghanistan, while others would come home.

The United States tries to protect its security through international agreements, such as the North Atlantic Treaty Organization (NATO). It also promotes peace through the United Nations and international disarmament agreements. Sometimes international cooperation is difficult to achieve.

Humanitarian Aid

Major tragedies in other parts of the world—such as earthquakes, floods, or famines—play a role in how we conduct foreign policy. The United States government often responds to these tragedies by sending medical supplies, food, water, and personnel to distribute the aid.

In December 2004, a devastating *tsunami* (large sea wave) struck several nations bordering the Indian Ocean. Indonesia, Thailand, Sri Lanka, and India were hit the hardest. Other nations in Asia and Africa were also affected. The disaster cost the lives of more than 200,000 people. The United States sent a massive amount of aid to the area, and many Americans volunteered to help the homeless and hungry.

Humanitarian aid may also take the form of monetary loans and expert advice. The giving of this type of aid is motivated by a genuine desire to help those in need. At the same time, such aid spreads goodwill, helps keep the peace, and may help develop markets for U.S. goods.

Human Rights

We want people all over the world to enjoy the same rights that we have in the United States. Not every leader in the world will agree with us. Many nations are not democratic, and the rights of their citizens may be restricted. The United States, in varying degrees, has made human rights a factor in dealing with other nations.

During the late 1970s, President Jimmy Carter made the issue of human rights a major component of his foreign policy. He refused to give foreign aid to countries in Asia, Africa, and Latin America that treated their people harshly. In 1975, the Helsinki Accords, an international agreement, was signed by many nations, including the United States. They agreed that all people should enjoy, among other rights, freedom of speech, a fair trial, and freedom of religion. Although strongly supported by the United States, the accords have been difficult to enforce because nations claim that human rights are domestic concerns.

During the administration of President George W. Bush (2001–2009), the stated U.S. policy was to support budding democracies around the world. At the same time, the Bush administration was criticized for not doing enough to prevent or stop human rights violations. Several human rights organizations criticized the way the United States treated its prisoners in Guantánamo, Cuba, who were being held as possible terrorists.

In the 1990s and early 2000s, the United States used a variety of pressures to persuade China to improve its human rights record. China has dealt harshly with domestic critics of the government and with members of nonapproved religious groups. One reason the United States sent troops to Bosnia was to end the persecution of Muslims by Christian Serbs.

Let's Think

1. Explain why a country needs a foreign policy.
2. List the major factors that influence American foreign policy.
3. Choose a factor that you think has the greatest influence on U.S. foreign policy. Give reasons for your choice.

Types of Policies

When two of your friends have an argument, what do you do? Do you get involved? If you do, what might happen? Would you lose your friends, or would they be grateful for your interference? Nations ask themselves similar questions when conflicts occur. What course of action will serve each nation's best interests? Over the years, the United States has answered this question in a variety of ways. The three primary responses have been neutrality, isolationism, and interventionism.

Neutrality

Sometimes a nation does not want to take sides in a dispute. It tries to stay out of an argument without favoring one side or the other. This is called **neutrality**. A nation might believe that taking sides in a dispute is morally wrong. Or intervention might disrupt trade with both parties in the dispute, thus bringing economic hardship to the third party. Another reason for remaining neutral might be that a nation is not prepared or is too weak to fight.

When World War I began in Europe in 1914, the United States officially remained neutral. It saw the war as a European problem that it did not need to get involved with. Over a period of time, it became apparent to the government and the public that it was not in the best interests of the United States to follow a neutral policy. The United States entered the war in 1917.

In 1939, war broke out again in Europe. Once again, the United States declared its official policy of neutrality. The natural sympathy of most American people was to support Great Britain and France in their fight against the dictatorships of Germany and Italy. All thoughts of staying neutral ended when Japan bombed Pearl Harbor, Hawaii, in December 1941. We declared war on Japan, and Germany, Japan's ally, declared war on us.

Isolationism

Do you think it is possible in this modern era for a nation to cut itself off from the rest of the world? In its early history, Japan found some success in following such a policy, and so did China. The United States attempted to adopt an isolationist policy at various times in its history. In his Farewell Address in 1796, George Washington urged the nation to stay away from alliances that would get the fledgling nation into wars that it was not ready to fight. But this policy was developed before the invention of the airplane and communications satellites. Today, it is increasingly difficult for a nation to follow a policy of **isolationism**.

During the period between World War I and World War II (1920s and 1930s), the United States turned inward. It did not join the League of Na-

tions, an international organization set up in 1919. The American people were tired of war and were determined not to get involved in one again. They soon learned, however, that wide oceans couldn't keep away the conflicts.

Interventionism

When there is a crisis in the world today, the United States is looked to for leadership in solving the problem. Because it is such a strong country, the United States is also sometimes seen as imposing its will on others.

The policy of getting involved in the affairs of other countries is called **interventionism**. The term is most often applied when one country sends troops to another country to end a civil war, replace a hostile government, or solve another type of political problem. The United States was accused of interventionism in 1994 when it sent troops to Haiti to restore elected President Jean-Bertrand Aristide to office. It seemed to be the right thing to do to help the Haitians improve their lives and rid themselves of a repressive government. The buildup to the Persian Gulf War in 1990 and the war itself in 1991 are other examples of U.S. interventionism to contain a conflict.

The recent policies toward Iraq and Afghanistan might be seen as a form of interventionism. The United States took military action in Afghanistan as a response to the attacks in September 2001. We knew that the al Qaeda terrorist organization, which planned and carried out the attacks, was hiding in Afghanistan with Taliban protection. The 2003 action in Iraq could more logically be seen as interventionism because the United States looked to topple a cruel dictator. The administration of President George W. Bush saw Hussein as a danger to the security of the United States and the Middle East.

In an 1823 pronouncement, President James Monroe put forth a policy of interventionism under certain circumstances. The Monroe Doctrine declared that the United States would no longer tolerate any further European colonization in North and South America. The United States promised not to get involved with the internal affairs of European nations. It wanted to protect the newly independent Latin American nations and its trade relations with them. The United States also stated that if European nations decided to try to regain their former colonies, the action would be considered a threat to the United States.

Containment

A policy related to interventionism that we followed during the cold war years (1947 to 1991) was called **containment**. The United States took action wherever necessary to prevent the spread of communism. The idea behind the policy was to confine Communist governments to the areas they controlled in the late 1940s. The United States gave military and economic aid to countries threatened by a Communist takeover. We even backed repressive leaders in Africa, South America, and Asia just because they claimed to be anti-Communist. We fought a three-year war in Korea and a ten-year war in Vietnam to contain communism.

Alliances

Until the end of World War II in 1945, the United States had not involved itself in any permanent alliances. During the war, U.S. President Franklin Roosevelt and British Prime Minister Winston Churchill urged their allies and other nations throughout the world to set up an organization to maintain peace. The United Nations came into being in October 1945 with 51 members, including the United States. (See pages 286–287 for a fuller discussion.)

In 1949, the United States committed itself to a regional military alliance called the North Atlantic Treaty Organization (NATO). Canada, the United States, and most Western European nations joined. Its original purpose was to defend Western Europe from invasion by the Communist countries of Eastern Europe and the Soviet Union. Since the Communist governments of the Soviet Union and the countries in Eastern Europe collapsed in the early 1990s, NATO has been reassessing its mission. NATO currently has 28 members. In recent years, it has admitted several former Communist countries in Eastern Europe.

Another long-standing alliance that the United States is part of is the Organization of American States (OAS). Its membership includes almost all of the countries of Central and South America and the Caribbean. Founded in 1948, OAS is mainly concerned with security matters and providing a forum for settling disputes between members.

The Changing Nature of Foreign Policy

An old saying observes that "today's enemies are tomorrow's friends." This is almost a true statement about the post–World War II period. The defeated nations in World War II, Japan and Germany, have since become our strong allies. We compete economically, but it is a peaceful competition.

During World War II, the United States and the Soviet Union were uneasy allies. We fought side by side to defeat a common enemy. With the end of the war, mistrust deepened between the two nations. This led to nearly 50 years of tension, a period called the cold war. The Communist group (the Soviet Union and its allies) and the Western pro-democracy group (the United States and Western Europe, primarily) competed for the loyalty of neutral countries. The nuclear capabilities of both sides contributed to the tension.

After the breakup of the Soviet Union and the toppling of the Communist governments in Eastern Europe in the early 1990s, the cold war ended. We no longer fear the spread of communism. There is now a greater spirit of cooperation between the United States and the countries that once made up the Soviet Union, especially Russia. We are working to shore up the democratic governments of the countries in Eastern Europe.

In the early 21st century, we are concerned about ethnic and religious disputes. Conflicts over differences have broken out in Bosnia, Serbia, Indonesia, and several African nations. We debate what we can and should do to bring an end to these types of conflicts and prevent future flare-ups.

The relationship between China and the

P O W E R *of* ★ N E

George C. Marshall

A career military officer who directed the strategy that won World War II for the allies contributed more to keeping the peace after 1945 than almost any other person. This individual was George Catlett Marshall.

Marshall was born on December 31, 1880, in Uniontown, Pennsylvania. Even as a boy Marshall knew that he would be a soldier. He graduated from the Virginia Military Institute (VMI) in 1901 and received his commission as a second lieutenant in the United States Army the following year. After serving a tour of duty in the Philippine Islands, he trained at the Infantry-Cavalry School and the Army Staff College at Fort Leavenworth, Kansas. Marshall excelled at planning and tactics and was known for his "quiet self-confidence" and "rigid self-discipline."

During World War I, he commanded troops in France. After the war, Marshall urged Congress to provide funds to maintain the fighting capability of the armed forces and to update military weapons. Congress refused, and U.S. war readiness deteriorated. As assistant commandant of training at the Infantry School at Fort Benning, Georgia, from 1927 to 1933, Marshall trained many officers who later became prominent in World War II.

Just as World War II broke out in Europe in 1939, Marshall was promoted to the rank of a four-star general and became the Army chief of staff. At that time, there were fewer than 200,000 soldiers in the Army and the Army Air Corps. During the next six years, the number of Army and Air Corps personnel expanded to 8.3 million. Marshall directed the strategy of the war. He also gained diplomatic skills as he accompanied President Franklin Roosevelt to meetings of the allied leaders.

After President Roosevelt's death in 1945, Marshall worked closely with the new president, Harry Truman. In November 1945, Marshall re-

---

United States is also undergoing change. As Communist China introduces its own brand of capitalism, trade has increased. But we are concerned about the suppression of human rights in China.

Let's Think

1. Define the following terms: neutrality, isolationism, interventionism, containment.
2. Which of these above policies is the United States following at the present time? Give examples to support your answer.
3. Describe how U.S. foreign policy has changed since 1945.

The President Makes Foreign Policy

One of the president's most visible jobs is that of director of foreign policy. Article II, Section 2, of the Constitution states: "He shall have power, by and with the advice and consent of the Senate, to make treaties, provided two-thirds of the senators present concur; and he shall nominate, and, by and with the advice and consent of the Senate, shall appoint ambassadors, other public ministers and consuls, . . ." The president and his or her foreign policy experts are the chief architects of treaties. Through the Cabinet position of secretary of state, the president acts to maintain good relations with the nations of the world.

tired as chief of staff and left the Army. Almost immediately, he was appointed a special envoy to China. There he used his diplomatic skills to try to end the civil war between the Communists and the Nationalists. He did not succeed. In 1947, Truman appointed Marshall to be secretary of state.

At the time, Communist groups were trying to take over the governments of Greece and Turkey. As a result, President Truman issued the Truman Doctrine. It called for sending aid to countries threatened by Communists. Marshall contributed to the formation of this policy and expanded the idea into what became known as the Marshall Plan. Officially called the European Recovery Plan, it provided for sending massive amounts of food, tools, and other items to the war-devastated countries of Europe. To receive the aid, the countries had to come up with a plan that detailed what they needed and how the materiel would be distributed. The program was a huge success. The democracies of Europe did not give in to the spreading threat of communism. They went on to develop strong and prosperous economies. (The Truman Doctrine and the Marshall Plan marked the beginning of the containment policy that the United States followed until the breakup of the Soviet Union in 1991.)

To strengthen the defenses of Europe, Marshall started the talks that led to the formation of the North Atlantic Treaty Organization (NATO) in 1949.

Marshall received the Nobel Prize for Peace in 1953 for his part in developing and promoting the Marshall Plan. His ideas and the manner in which he fulfilled his duties as a military officer and as secretary of state made Marshall a major shaper of American foreign policy in the years following World War II. These policies and actions established the United States as a world leader and kept Western Europe from being taken over by Communists. Marshall died in 1959.

1. Why do you think Marshall fought for an increase in the size of the military after World War I?
2. What do you think is the difference between being a good military leader and being a good diplomatic leader?
3. What was the Marshall Plan? Why is it considered to be one of the most successful aid programs ever created?
4. How did Marshall's accomplishments demonstrate great leadership abilities?

Secretary of State

George Washington created the Cabinet position of secretary of state early in his presidency. The secretary of state is the major adviser to the president about international relations. The Senate must "consent" to (approve of) the person appointed to be secretary.

As the person focusing on international relations, the secretary of state must be in constant contact with his or her counterparts in other countries. The secretary is a major player in the negotiation of treaties and other agreements. When there is disagreement between nations, the U.S. secretary of state may serve as a mediator in trying to settle the problem. The secretary travels frequently, carrying the president's message about foreign affairs to other leaders. Goodwill

trips are also included in the secretary's schedule. On such trips, the secretary can find out about conditions in other countries and show their people that the United States is concerned about their part of the world.

The secretary of state is in charge of the State Department and all the people who represent the United States overseas. Among these people are ambassadors and consuls. They are part of the Foreign Service.

Ambassadors are appointed by the president and approved by the Senate. There is one ambassador in each country with which the United States maintains official diplomatic relations. The U.S. ambassador has his or her office in the capital of the country in a building called the embassy. There the ambassador conducts the work

President Obama greeted his new National Security Adviser, General James Jones (right), with Secretary of State Hillary Clinton (center) looking on.

of representing the president's policies, entertains government officials, and aids American tourists, residents, and businesspeople. The embassy staff also handles the processing of requests for documents from people who want to travel to the United States or move here permanently. The embassy staff collects information to help U.S. officials understand political, economic, and social trends in each nation.

U.S. consulates are found in the major cities of the larger countries. Consuls are appointed by the president and approved by the Senate. The responsibilities of consuls are to promote trade, aid U.S. citizens, enforce U.S. customs regulations, and help people who want to settle in the United States.

Secretary of Defense

A second Cabinet official who is a major foreign policy adviser to the president is the secretary of defense. The main duty of this official is to make sure that the military is ready to meet any emergency or threat to our national security. If serious problems that the United States has an interest in cannot be solved by diplomatic efforts, the armed forces may be called in to keep the peace or preserve our interests.

The secretary of defense is always a civilian, as are the assistant secretaries. This reinforces the concept in the U.S. governmental system that the military is under civilian control.

Joint Chiefs of Staff

High-level military officers advise the secretary of defense. They assess the state of readiness of our armed forces and plan for future needs. They also evaluate the potential for conflict in trouble spots around the world. Their views are shared with the secretary of defense, who passes the information along to the president. The Joint Chiefs of Staff consists of the top officer in each of the armed services: the Army, Navy, Air Force, and Marines. In addition, the president appoints a fifth high-ranking officer as the chairman of the Joint Chiefs of Staff. This appointment is subject to approval by the Senate.

National Security Council

To make intelligent decisions about international issues and our national security needs, the president needs up-to-date information. The president also needs to hear a variety of points of view about any issue. To supply this information, the National Security Council was created in 1947. The council, headed by the president, includes the vice president, secretary of state, secretary of defense, the national security adviser, the director of national intelligence, and the Chair of the Joint Chiefs of Staff. The president may add others.

The Central Intelligence Agency

Intelligence agencies are another part of the foreign policy network. "Intelligence" in this sense means information about conditions and people in other countries. The U.S. government wants to know about potential hot spots and centers of terrorist activities. It also needs to know the strengths and weaknesses of the governments, economies, and leaders in the major (and some minor) countries of the world. The task of gathering this information has been given to the Central Intelligence Agency (CIA). The CIA was created in 1947 to coordinate intelligence gathering.

The director of the CIA is appointed by the president and confirmed by the Senate. The people employed by the CIA are usually Americans, but sometimes foreign agents are put on the payroll. The CIA chief reports to the president and congressional oversight committees.

Let's Think

1. How does the Constitution empower the president to conduct foreign policy?
2. List the people and groups who assist the president in the creation of foreign policy and explain their responsibilities.

Creating and Carrying Out Foreign Policy

A person who is elected president has ideas about what he or she would like to accomplish in international relations and how to bring about these goals. The general guidelines may have to be altered if a crisis occurs or if unusual circumstances develop. Suppose a group unfriendly to the United States takes over the government of a North African country. Or suppose a South American country decides to take over a Caribbean nation. Or suppose Russia wants expanded fishing rights off the North American coast. How should the president and our government react to these situations? The decision to take or not to take action is made in a systematic way. The procedure is designed to give the president the best, most current information that will allow him or her to make the response best suited to protect the interests of the United States in each situation.

Steps the President Can Take

Gathering information and consulting with advisers is the first step in creating policy. The president may also consult with our allies. The president relies on the National Security Council to gather and evaluate information. Other advisers are added to national security meetings as needed. A variety of possible actions and recommendations are prepared for the president. He or she chooses among them or comes up with an entirely different idea. The final policy is decided by the president. Sometimes a public statement of the U.S. view about an action will stop the action or allow it to continue.

Personal Diplomacy

Sometimes it is recommended that the president should get personally involved in negotiations with other nations. The president may have good personal relations with another leader and be able to persuade that individual to act in a particular way. Or disputing parties may feel that the U.S. president is the only one with the power and prestige to end a dangerous situation, so they turn to him or her. One example of personal diplomacy happened in 1978. President Jimmy Carter brought the leaders of Israel and Egypt together at the presidential country retreat at Camp David in Maryland. In this private setting, President Anwar Sadat of Egypt and Prime Minister Menachem Begin of Israel were able to bridge their differences and forge a peace agreement. This was accomplished, in large measure, because of the personal relationship the president had developed with each of the leaders. The Camp David Accords was the first formal peace agreement between Israel and one of its Arab neighbors.

An example of a failed attempt at personal diplomacy was President Woodrow Wilson's effort in 1919 to get the European allies to adopt his proposals for the peace treaty after World War I. European leaders rejected many of Wilson's Fourteen Points.

Today, the president engages in personal diplomacy only when there is reasonable assurance of success. This means that the groundwork for an agreement has been laid by presidential assistants before the president personally comes on the scene.

Another way the president engages in personal diplomacy is to host state visits of leaders

Egyptian President Anwar Sadat (left), U.S. President Jimmy Carter (center), and Israeli Prime Minister Menachem Begin in 1979 preparing to sign the peace treaty that resulted from the Camp David Accords. The flags of the three countries are behind the men. (From left: United States, Egypt, Israel.)

of other countries. The president also travels to other countries to meet with leaders and discuss issues and points of common interest. The secretaries of state and defense as well as other officials may undertake personal diplomacy missions on behalf of the president.

Negotiating Treaties

Many international disputes and problems can be resolved through treaties. Negotiations, however, can take weeks, even years. The president cannot personally devote enough time to work out the details of such agreements. A chief negotiator, along with advisers and experts, creates the provisions of treaties. When the agreement seems acceptable to all parties, the president may hold a special signing ceremony and personally attend.

Sometimes treaty negotiations do not go as planned. Then, the president may get involved at an earlier stage. The hope is that his or her personal powers of persuasion will help the parties reach an agreement. Even when the United States is not a direct party to the negotiations, the president may act as a mediator to help both sides reach an agreement. Such was the case in the Camp David Accords in 1978. A similar situation resulted in the Dayton Accords in 1995. President

Clinton insisted that the leaders of the opposing forces in Bosnia meet in Dayton, Ohio, to work out a peace agreement. They reluctantly did.

Tools the President Can Use

How does the president carry out foreign policy? What tools can be used to ensure that a policy has a reasonable chance of succeeding?

Trade

Foreign trade provides a tool to carry out foreign policy goals. The United States spends billions of dollars buying goods from other countries. We also sell billions of dollars' worth of items to other countries. We may try harder to get along with important trading partners than with countries that have little we want to buy. Of particular importance to us are countries that supply us with essential raw materials for manufacturing or national security needs.

Sometimes we use trade policies to influence a nation to change policies we think are wrong. For example, China was accused of violating international copyright laws by allowing Chinese manufacturers to copy CDs, DVDs, and computer software without permission or payment of royalty fees. The United States and other countries wanted China to stop doing this. We threatened to raise tariffs on goods China wanted to sell in the United States. China promised to change, and the tariffs were lowered.

Sanctions

A second tool is **sanctions**. These are official measures that attempt to force a government to do something or to stop an action. Sometimes sanctions take the form of trade restrictions. They are designed to hurt a nation in the "pocketbook" so that it will act in an accepted way.

Strict trade sanctions were placed on Iraq after the Persian Gulf War in 1991. That country was not allowed to sell its oil except to buy food and medical supplies. To have the ban lifted, Iraq had to agree to certain arms limitations and inspections. It kept violating that agreement, and the sanctions remained in place until the United States went to war with Iraq in 2003.

In 1986, the United States, most European countries, and former British colonies in the Commonwealth placed trade sanctions on the Republic of South Africa. They wanted to pressure South Africa to end its repressive apartheid system. (*Apartheid* laws strictly separated the races in South Africa and imposed severe restrictions on the rights of blacks and ethnic minorities.) Apartheid was legally ended in 1991, and the sanctions were removed.

When the Soviet Union invaded Afghanistan in 1979, the United States vehemently protested. The sale of wheat and high-technology equipment to the Soviet Union was halted, and fishing rights in U.S. waters were restricted.

In recent years, the United States has often persuaded other nations to cooperate in observing U.S. sanctions. We also work through the UN, if at all possible, in order to get as much support worldwide as we can.

Military Force

Sometimes a situation calls for more direct action than sanctions. The United States may feel the need to display a show of force. It may send an aircraft carrier to an area to protect U.S. interests.

Or U.S. troops may be used to maintain peace in a region where a government has requested such intervention. Troops were stationed in Saudi Arabia after the Persian Gulf War. Their mission was to monitor the cease-fire agreement with Iraq.

The United States sent troops into Iraq a second time in 2003. It believed that the Iraqi government had not complied with UN resolutions and was developing weapons of mass destruction. Although the weapons were never found, Iraqi dictator Saddam Hussein was removed, and the Iraqi people soon elected a new government. Military intervention had also taken place in Afghanistan, to root out terrorists after the attack on the World Trade Center in New York City in 2001. We continue to keep troops in South Korea to help the South Koreans repel a possible invasion from Communist North Korea.

The United States also uses the military to deliver food and medical supplies to countries, such as Somalia, that suffer from drought and civil war. Occasionally, troops are used to remove foreign leaders who threaten U.S. interests. This has occurred a few times in Latin American countries. In 1989, we sent troops to capture General Manuel Noriega, the leader of Panama, when it was believed that he was involved in drug trafficking.

Covert Action

Secret activities carried out by various intelligence agencies are another tool that can be used to achieve foreign policy goals. Through **covert action**, or secret missions, information about the movements and policies of international rivals is brought to the attention of officials in the highest levels of our government. In the United States, the CIA is the organization generally assigned to handle secret missions.

During the cold war years (1947 to 1991), covert missions tried to keep Communists from coming to power in various countries—one was Chile in the 1970s. Some missions arranged to give or sell weapons to the side we supported in an armed conflict, for example, Afghanistan in its battles with the Soviet Union in the 1980s.

Let's Think

1. What steps can the president take to carry out foreign policy?
2. Describe each of the following "tools" the president can use to carry out foreign policy aims: trade, sanctions, military action, covert action.
3. Which of the "tools" listed do you think is the most important to the president? Why?

When Colin Powell was secretary of state (2001–2005), he testified before the United States Senate Committee on Foreign Relations.

Congress, a Partner With the President

Although the president is looked on as the chief diplomat, Congress plays an important partnership role. The Constitution gives Congress a great deal to say about how foreign policy is carried out. Only Congress has the power to declare war. After the president appeared to take over this power in actions such as the Vietnam War, Congress passed the War Powers Act. It limits what the president can do. Even though the Constitution makes the president the commander-in-chief of the armed forces, it does not give the office the power to declare war. The Framers of the Constitution did not want one person to have that much power. Therefore, the president cannot exercise his or her authority as the chief of the military to conduct a war until after Congress passes a declaration of war.

Congress plays an important role in the treaty-making process. The Senate must ratify all treaties negotiated by the president. The Senate has been known to reject treaties, request changes in the terms, or just refuse to discuss the document.

With few exceptions, presidential appointments to various foreign policy posts are approved by the Senate. The Foreign Relations committee of the Senate holds hearings regarding the fitness of individuals nominated to the posts. Some win approval easily, while others, most often those nominated for highly visible positions, might be scrutinized more closely. In 1997, the chairman of the Senate Foreign Relations Committee refused to hold hearings on the person nominated to be the ambassador to Mexico. The proposed nominee held certain points of view that the chairman did not like. By having a say in the appointment of members of the upper ranks of the diplomatic corps, the Senate can shape the thinking of the president and policies that the president wants to carry out.

In 1996, the United States negotiated the Comprehensive Test-Ban Treaty (CTBT). It would limit all nuclear weapons tests and other nuclear explosions. It was to take effect as soon as 44 nations with a nuclear capability ratified it. By 2009, only 35 had done so. The U.S. Senate has not ratified the treaty. One reason for its unwillingness to do so is that it would be difficult to monitor all the nations involved to verify compliance with the treaty.

The House of Representatives affects foreign policy decisions through the power of the purse. All spending bills must start in the House, so the president must come to it to finance projects. If there is a need to send economic aid to a nation, the president must request such funds from Congress. If the president wants to send troops to another country for a special operation, Congress must vote to provide the funds needed to finance the mission.

Let's Think

1. What role does the Senate play in the treaty-making process? How did it get this power?

◀ REALITY CHECK ▶

U.S. Agency for International Development

How do we as individuals win friends and influence people? We do it by being nice to them and earning their respect. It is important to let our friends know that we care about them. The United States acts no differently when it deals with other countries around the world. Promoting peaceful relationships among countries is what foreign policy is about. We need allies, and we do have enemies. In a world that is smaller than ever because communication is instantaneous and transportation is so fast, no nation, big or small, weak or powerful, can stand alone.

One way the United States tries to "win" friends is through the work of an independent agency called the U.S. Agency for International Development (USAID). The type of work the agency does can be traced back to the period just after World War II, when the Marshall Plan was created in 1947. The agency became official in 1961 with the signing of the Foreign Assistance Act. USAID receives direction from the secretary of state, but it is an independent agency of the federal government. The overall purpose of the agency is to carry out American foreign policy by attempting to better the lives of people around the world. Its programs are of a nonmilitary nature.

The agency works with other countries in five regions around the world: Sub-Saharan Africa, Asia, Latin America and the Caribbean, Europe and Eurasia, and the Middle East.

In Senegal, a country in West Africa, the agency supports a program to help farmers grow enough food to feed their families by increasing agricultural productivity. To improve the health of the Senegalese people, a program for the prevention and treatment of HIV/AIDS is in place. As a result, there has been a drop in the mortality rate of infants and mothers in that country.

Senegal has a high rate of illiteracy. According to USAID, more than 50 percent of males in Senegal and 70 percent of females over 15 years old are illiterate. In 2008, USAID reported that it had built or renovated 58 schools that provide over 25,000 new students access to middle schools within walking distance of their homes. The program also provides training for more than 5,000 teachers, principals, and teacher-trainers. The program is designed to strengthen Senegal's democratic government and ensure its survival.

Nicaragua, a country in Central America, has also been pinpointed by the United States to receive assistance. Aid programs there attempt to support democracy, foster economic growth, and improve health and education. In the area of nutrition, USAID has provided free food and education about good eating habits to families in various communities in Nicaragua. The agency is also working on other fronts in Nicaragua to protect the rain forests, improve education, and develop the economy.

A fundamental mission of the United States Agency for International Development is to help maintain good relations with nations around the world. As you can see from the descriptions of the programs in Senegal and Nicaragua, it works in a variety of ways to create goodwill abroad. But some people believe that the agency does not do enough and that much of what it does depends on who the secretary of state and the president are. The programs and the way the funds have been spent do have critics. However, they also have many supporters. The agency is an arm of the government that is attempting to carry out a sound foreign policy for the United States that does not involve military action.

1. What is the main purpose of USAID?
2. How does the agency receive guidance in developing programs?
3. Describe the kinds of programs it operates.
4. Do you think the work of USAID is a good way for a nation to carry out foreign policy goals? Support your view with sound reasoning.

2. Explain why the following statement is true: Presidential appointments of foreign policy advisers can be influenced by the Senate.
3. What is the importance of the "power of the purse" to foreign policy programs?

Influences on Foreign Policy

What shapes your view of world events? Most likely, the major influence comes from television news programs. To a lesser extent, you receive information from radio, newspapers, magazines, and the Internet. How the media report an event or policy affects your reaction to the information. Is the story highlighted or played down? Are a variety of opinions of authorities presented? How much background information is given? Pictures and descriptions of events in foreign countries on television news programs have the ability to arouse emotions, stir debate, and shape the thoughts of the American public. We, in turn, try to persuade public officials to do something or come up with policies to support our point of view.

The Media

Pictures of starving children in Somalia pushed the United States into sending aid and troops to that country. Pictures of the horrifying conditions in refugee camps in Central Africa inspired the public to call for the United States to end the tribal conflicts there. (Aid was given, but we did not openly intervene.) Stories of "ethnic cleansing" during the civil war in Bosnia in the 1990s caused a public outcry in the United States. The government decided to become directly involved in a peacekeeping mission through NATO. Reports in the media affected government policy in all of these situations.

Television coverage of the war in Vietnam in the 1960s brought into millions of living rooms graphic pictures of the fighting. For the first time in American history, a viewer could see the action almost as it happened. The more pictures people saw of the war and the more they read in the print media, the more divided the nation became

over our policy in Vietnam. Eventually, public opinion turned against the war. It destroyed the popularity of President Lyndon Johnson, who decided not to run for reelection in 1968. Government leaders were urged to end the fighting and make peace. The Vietnam War had a deep and lasting effect on the military and the presidents who came after Johnson. They were reluctant to become involved in other conflicts that could not be convincingly won or that seemed to be civil wars affecting only limited areas.

Lessons learned from Vietnam became apparent during the Persian Gulf War in 1991. In this conflict, American troops were sent to the Middle East to end Iraqi occupation of Kuwait. During any war, the press is censored to protect the soldiers. But in the Persian Gulf War, the military managed more strictly than usual what the press could see and report back home. The military wanted the American public to support the war and to believe that advanced technology could keep the conflict short and the casualties to a minimum. Afterward, the public realized that the military had manipulated the reporting. The public had a generally positive attitude about how the war was conducted and gave high marks to President George H. W. Bush's leadership. Bush had used television to prepare the American people for the fighting and to get congressional backing for his actions.

A foreign policy that doesn't have the backing of the public will not last long. The president can only hope that the information people get from the media will persuade them to support his or her policies. Or if the policies are opposed, the opposition will be based on adequate and factual information.

Public Opinion

Citizens are concerned about U.S. relations with other nations. Our foreign policy affects our security as well as our pocketbooks. Trade is a major part of our foreign policy. Tense relations with other countries may bring about armed conflict or negatively affect trade in other ways.

Private citizens can affect foreign policy in the same way that they affect domestic policy. They can communicate with their elected officials to

Award-winnning photojournalist James Nachtwey was imbedded with U.S. troops fighting in Iraq in 2003. Here he rode on the top of a U.S. Humvee during a patrol in central Baghdad.

support or object to policies. People can write, call, and send e-mail messages to public officials to let the officials know how individuals feel about foreign policy issues or actions that touch them directly.

In the mid-1990s, the public became disturbed about the use of low-wage workers in foreign countries to produce well-known brands of clothing. Particularly offensive was the use of children in these factories. Many worked under very poor conditions. The American public called for government action to curb these policies. The president and others pressured the U.S. manufacturers to monitor their overseas plants and improve wages and working conditions. The other countries were urged to hold businesses to higher standards and protect workers' rights.

The attitudes and pressures of large voting blocs of ethnic citizens also affect policy decisions. For example, many Cuban Americans in Florida oppose improving relations with the Communist government of Cuba. Many Irish Americans took sides in the British-Irish dispute over Northern Ireland. Their actions often affected U.S.-British and U.S.-Irish relations.

Organizations

Private national and international organizations also have input into American foreign policy. Environmental groups call for attention to pollution problems and forest and animal destruction that affect nations throughout the world. Such organizations urge the government to ban certain practices or reach international agreements to reduce pollution.

The International Committee of the Red Cross (ICRC) works in conflict situations to provide protection and assistance to victims (including citizens), the sick and wounded, or those who have been detained in a conflict. This spreads goodwill and calls attention to trouble spots and how local governments respond to the needs of their citizens. Such publicity may shame nations into acting in a more responsible way toward their people. Its noninterference in government issues earns respect from almost every nation. The ICRC is a neutral, independent organization that maintains contact with all parties to a conflict and whose work is based solely on humanitarian priorities.

The goal of Amnesty International is to protect human rights around the world. Through the media and newsletters, it reports on and publicizes violations. In some countries, people are imprisoned without due process, and those with unpopular political ideas are put to death. Using torture on prisoners is common in many areas of the world. Once information of this sort is made public by organizations such as Amnesty International, the U.S. government can take steps to persuade other countries to stop such practices.

The Red Cross distributes food to refugees in Sudan and elsewhere when there are natural disasters and during conflicts.

The Foreign Policy Association is a national, nonprofit, nonpartisan, nongovernmental organization. By increasing public awareness of international matters, it hopes to foster citizen involvement in the issues. It publishes a magazine and conducts forums that provide background information by experts on foreign policy issues. Public officials pay attention to opinions expressed in Foreign Policy Association publications and forums.

The Roman Catholic Church has a presence all over the world through its one-billion-plus members. It urges individuals and political leaders alike to support policies and issues important to the Church. For instance, when the pope visited Communist Cuba in 1998, he called on the United States to lift trade sanctions against Cuba. He also urged Fidel Castro, Cuba's leader at that time, to stop violating the human rights of Cuban citizens. Pope John Paul II, whose home country was Poland, used his influence to bring an end to Communist rule in Poland and other countries in Eastern Europe.

The World Council of Churches is another organization that has influence on the foreign policy of many nations. Some 300 Protestant and Orthodox churches in more than 100 countries belong to this organization. The churches have about 400 million members. The council sponsors programs that work for the improvement of the human condition—aid to the sick, refugees,

the underprivileged. The council promotes world peace and interracial justice and studies how courts, prisons, and other social institutions can be improved. Governments throughout the world are urged to make changes based on the findings of these studies.

Let's Think

1. What role do the media and public opinion play in the development of U.S. foreign policy?
2. Organizations such as the International Red Cross, Amnesty International, and the Foreign Policy Association have an effect on U.S. foreign policy. Explain how.
3. How do religious organizations such as the Roman Catholic Church and the World Council of Churches affect the policies of nations around the world?

The United Nations and Its Role in U.S. Foreign Policy

During the peace conference after World War I, President Woodrow Wilson urged the creation of an international organization to promote world peace. The League of Nations was formed in 1919. It provided a place where the member nations could bring disputes and talk about problems. The hope was that differences would be settled through talk and not war. The League was unsuccessful for several reasons. A major one was the failure of the United States to become a formal member. Another was the lack of any way to enforce its decisions. It could not stop the arms buildups and disputes that led to another world war in 1939.

Early in World War II, world leaders again talked about forming an international peace-keeping organization. In 1941, U.S. President Franklin Roosevelt and Prime Minister Winston Churchill of Great Britain declared the need for such an organization in a statement called the Atlantic Charter. Four years later, in San Francisco, the United Nations charter was signed by 51 nations. This time, eager to see an international organization succeed, the United States ratified the charter and offered New York City as the site for the UN headquarters. From an attitude of isolationism that rejected the League of Nations, the United States had moved toward a strong spirit of internationalism with its support of the United Nations.

The Structure of the United Nations

General Assembly

The General Assembly is the main body of the UN and oversees all the other bodies of the UN. All 192 members of the UN send delegates to the General Assembly. Each nation has one vote. To pass resolutions or decide policy on what the UN calls ordinary matters, a simple majority is needed. Important questions require a two-thirds majority. Important matters might be sending a UN peacekeeping force to a member nation or admitting a new member. The members elect a president to preside over meetings. Although the General Assembly has only the power to make recommendations, its moral influence can be persuasive in settling disputes.

Security Council

The Security Council is the body of the UN that is responsible for maintaining peace. There are 15 members. Five are permanent members: the United States, France, Russia, the United Kingdom, and China. The remaining ten members are elected for two-year terms by the General Assembly. In order to reach a decision, the Council requires nine members to agree. If any one of the permanent members refuses to agree, the decision does not pass. Thus, each permanent member has a veto.

In case of a crisis between two member nations, the Security Council first tries to mediate the dispute and get the parties to negotiate an agreement. If that fails, economic sanctions or withdrawal of diplomatic recognition might be the next recommendation. If fighting breaks out, the Council can authorize troops to be sent to the area to keep the peace.

International Court of Justice (World Court)

The judicial branch of the UN is the International Court of Justice, or the World Court. Fifteen judges are chosen by the General Assembly and the Security Council from a variety of countries for a nine-year term. They hear cases in The Hague, Netherlands. Only member nations may bring cases before the Court. Once a decision is made, the parties are expected to obey it. If one party to the suit fails to go along with the Court's decision, the other party may bring the issue before the Security Council.

Secretariat

The Secretariat administers the everyday business of the UN. The head of the Secretariat is the secretary general. This person is nominated by the Security Council and appointed by the General Assembly to a five-year term. The secretary general uses the prestige of the office to call attention to world problems and to help solve these problems. The thousands of people who work in the Secretariat see that UN programs are carried out.

The Economic and Social Council

The Economic and Social Council is a major organ of the UN. Its 54 members are elected by the General Assembly. Each member serves for three years. The primary mission of the Economic and Social Council is to promote higher standards of living, better health, cultural and

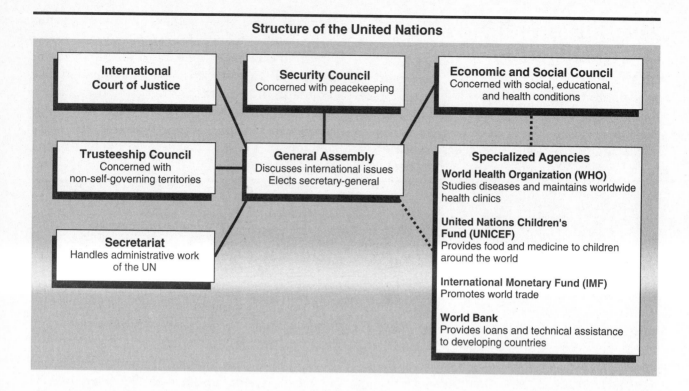

Structure of the United Nations

International Court of Justice

Security Council
Concerned with peacekeeping

Economic and Social Council
Concerned with social, educational, and health conditions

Trusteeship Council
Concerned with non-self-governing territories

General Assembly
Discusses international issues
Elects secretary-general

Specialized Agencies
World Health Organization (WHO)
Studies diseases and maintains worldwide health clinics

United Nations Children's Fund (UNICEF)
Provides food and medicine to children around the world

International Monetary Fund (IMF)
Promotes world trade

World Bank
Provides loans and technical assistance to developing countries

Secretariat
Handles administrative work of the UN

educational cooperation, and the observance of human rights. It works with international groups such as the Red Cross and with specialized agencies of the UN such as UNICEF.

The United States and the UN

Over the years, the United States has had an up-and-down relationship with the United Nations. A founder and developer of the UN, the United States has supported the overall aims of the organization. It has not, however, always agreed with the way the UN has acted to meet the aims. It also feels that the cost of running the UN is too high and that too little is being done to curb expenses. For this and other reasons, the United States has not always paid its full assessment to the UN. (Each member nation is asked to contribute a percentage of the UN budget based on the country's economic resources.)

The United States has been frustrated at times by votes against its proposals in the General Assembly. Smaller nations in Africa and Asia, in particular, have not always agreed with U.S. position on issues.

The UN peacekeeping missions have been supported by the United States. At times, the United States has urged the creation of such

forces. It does not normally send U.S. troops to be part of such forces. In order to gain wider support for actions it has wanted to take in other countries, the United States has gone to the UN for approval. As the most powerful nation in the world, the United States knows it might be seen as a bully if it always acts alone. It sought the cooperation of the UN in responding to the invasion of Kuwait by Iraq in 1990 and to Iraq's violations of the cease-fire agreement in 1997 and 1998.

In 2003, when the United States wanted to invade Iraq, it had trouble obtaining a supporting resolution from the United Nations. The other member nations did not agree that Saddam Hussein had persistently violated UN resolutions regarding disarmament.

Let's Think

1. What was the League of Nations?
2. Describe the responsibilities of the General Assembly and the Security Council.
3. Contrast the attitude of the United States toward the League of Nations and the United Nations.

The United States as World Leader

The primary foreign policy question of any era is how to keep the peace. The United States has answered the question by keeping militarily and economically strong. It also tries to stop armed flare-ups in other countries from spreading.

As a powerful and prosperous nation, the United States is looked to for help and guidance whenever a crisis occurs. But what are the responsibilities of the United States in these situations? Does it have the resources and political will to send troops to end every outbreak of fighting or send aid to every nation that is suffering through a drought or another natural disaster? (Sometimes local political leaders prevent the fair distribution of food for their own political reasons.)

The world is facing many problems today and will for a long time. The United States is trying to sort out what its responsibilities and limitations are in solving these problems. It needs to find answers to questions such as these:

How can ethnic or religious hatreds be kept from boiling over into armed conflict?

How can nuclear weapons or germ-spreading capabilities be kept out of the hands of irresponsible national leaders or terrorist groups?

What can be done to check terrorist activities?

How can environmental problems in one country that affect other countries be resolved?

How can the flow of illegal drugs into this country be stopped?

What can be done to curb illegal immigration?

Even with all of its power and wealth, the United States cannot dictate solutions to international problems. Every other nation wants to control its own interests and security and to be as prosperous as it can. As a democratic country, the United States must respect the rights of other nations.

Chapter Summary

Nations, like people, want to get along with each other. How a nation treats others is called foreign policy. Foreign policy involves economic, political, and military decisions. All nations want sovereignty—to be free from outside control.

Major goals of U.S. foreign policy are to make friends with other nations, maintain peace, protect our security, and have good trade relations with other countries. In order to keep the peace and help others, the United States sends humanitarian aid to nations in need. This also helps to spread goodwill.

Because the United States is a democracy, the preservation of human rights is important. We work to reduce human rights violations in other nations. Sometimes we tie beneficial trade agreements to progress in citizens' rights.

Throughout its history, the United States has engaged in several types of foreign policy. One is neutrality, not taking sides in a dispute. This was the official U.S. policy just before its involvement in World Wars I and II. Isolationism is another policy. It calls for not becoming involved in foreign affairs. Political and military alliances are to be avoided. A third policy is interventionism. This is almost the opposite of isolationism. If a country follows a policy of interventionism, it chooses to get involved in the affairs of others. Usually, the term refers to sending troops to a country to solve a problem.

During the cold war, in particular, the United States followed a policy called containment. It tried to prevent the spread of communism through military and economic aid to countries threatened by a Communist takeover. We fought wars to keep Communists out of South Korea and South Vietnam.

A way of ensuring a nation's national security is to create alliances. They are formal agreements with other nations to protect each other. The North Atlantic Treaty Organization (NATO) is one example of a regional military alliance.

Foreign policy is constantly changing because the world is constantly changing. During World War II, the United States and the Soviet Union were uneasy allies. After World War II, these two nations became bitter rivals. That rivalry led to the cold war.

The chief architect of U.S. foreign policy is the president. Constitutionally, the president can enter into treaties, negotiate agreements, and appoint ambassadors. The secretary of state is the person the president usually relies on most to help conduct foreign policy. The secretary of defense is another Cabinet official who plays a major role in the shaping of foreign policy.

Other members of the foreign policy team include the Joint Chiefs of Staff, the National Security Council, the national security adviser, the director of national intelligence, and the Central Intelligence Agency.

Sometimes the personal involvement of the president is necessary to achieve certain foreign policy aims. The president may speak directly to the leader of another country to solve a problem. Or two disputing parties may be brought together by the president to settle their differences. One example is the Camp David Accords in 1978. When formal agreements are about to be concluded, the president may personally negotiate the final details.

There are several tools the president can use to carry out foreign policy. They include trade, sanctions, military force, and covert action.

Congress is a major partner in the shaping of foreign policy. Presidential appointments to various foreign policy posts require the approval of the Senate. Treaties must also be approved by the Senate—by a two-thirds vote. When the president needs money for foreign aid or a special foreign policy project, the request must be approved by Congress.

Many unofficial factors shape foreign policy. The media, both broadcast and print, report about international issues and events. What is seen and heard influences public opinion. The media exerted much influence on the way Americans felt about the Vietnam and Persian Gulf wars and the recent war with Iraq.

Public opinion also influences foreign policy.

Elected officials, sensitive to the opinions of constituents, will consider their feelings before making foreign policy decisions.

Several national and international non-governmental organizations have an influence on U.S. foreign policy. Such organizations include the International Red Cross, Amnesty International, the World Council of Churches, the Roman Catholic Church, and the Foreign Policy Association.

Depending on the situation, the United Nations has exerted influence on U.S. foreign policy with varying success. The United Nations is a peacekeeping organization set up in 1945. Almost every nation in the world belongs. Member nations send delegates to the General Assembly, the main body of the UN. Each nation has one vote. The General Assembly makes recommendations and uses its moral influence to settle disputes. The Security Council is responsible for maintaining peace. It has 15 members, 5 permanent and 10 elected for two-year terms. Each of the permanent members—the United States, the United Kingdom, France, Russia, and China—has veto power over Security Council actions. Other bodies of the UN are the International Court of Justice, the Secretariat, and the Economic and Social Council. A secretary general heads the Secretariat.

The United States has had an up-and-down relationship with the UN. It supports the overall aims of the organization. But by withholding its assessment for UN expenses, the United States tries to make changes in the way the UN is run.

The United States is the acknowledged leader of the world. It is increasingly concerned with finding solutions to such international issues as conflicts between ethnic and religious groups, the spread of nuclear weapons and germ warfare technology, terrorism, environmental problems, and trade disputes.

★ CHAPTER REVIEW ★

A. Matching

Match each term in Column A with its definition in Column B.

Column A

1. GATT
2. North Atlantic Treaty Organization
3. free speech, fair trial
4. neutrality
5. Washington's Farewell Address
6. containment
7. secretary of state
8. Camp David Accords
9. treaty
10. sanction

Column B

a. a major regional military alliance
b. a policy of not taking sides in a dispute
c. promoted idea of not getting involved in foreign alliances
d. an earlier name for the World Trade Organization
e. an official measure to force a nation to stop or carry out an action
f. examples of human rights
g. U.S. policy followed during the cold war
h. a formal foreign policy agreement
i. an example of a president's personal diplomacy
j. principal foreign policy adviser to the president

B. Multiple Choice

Select the statement or word that most correctly answers the question or completes the statement.

1. The way one nation treats another is called (a) foreign policy (b) domestic policy (c) interventionism (d) isolationism.
2. A nation's independence and ability to control its own affairs is known as (a) neutrality (b) sovereignty (c) domestic relations (d) human rights.
3. The free trade agreement among Canada, Mexico, and the United States is called the (a) North Atlantic Treaty Organization (b) World Trade Organization (c) North American Free Trade Agreement (d) General Agreement on Tariffs and Trade.
4. The United States sends troops to Haiti to restore democracy. This is an example of (a) isolationism (b) neutrality (c) containment (d) interventionism.
5. This part of the government is constitutionally empowered to negotiate treaties: (a) Senate (b) House of Representatives (c) Supreme Court (d) president.
6. In order for a treaty to be ratified, it requires a two-thirds approval vote of the (a) Senate (b) House of Representatives (c) Supreme Court (d) National Security Council.
7. The person in charge of ambassadors and consuls is the (a) CIA chief (b) secretary of state (c) secretary of defense (d) vice president.
8. This arm of the United Nations has five permanent members that can exercise a veto: (a) Secretariat (b) Security Council (c) General Assembly (d) World Court.
9. The organization in charge of gathering foreign intelligence for the United States is the (a) CIA (b) UN (c) WTO (d) IRS.
10. An organization that distributes disaster relief around the world is the (a) World Court (b) International Red Cross (c) Foreign Policy Association (d) League of Nations.

C. Essay

Write a paragraph about *one* of the following:

1. Foreign policy is a major concern in any nation.
2. U.S. foreign policy has changed over time.
3. Many people help the president formulate foreign policy.
4. Congress and the president are partners in the creation of foreign policy.
5. The United Nations affects the foreign policy of its members.

D. A Challenge for You

1. Prepare a cartoon strip that describes how the president might decide how to handle an international issue.
2. Select a current international issue. Create a series of questions to ask your neighbors and friends to find out their opinions about the way the country should react to the issue. Poll

at least 15 people. Keep a record of your findings and share them with the class.

3. Cut out or photocopy newspaper and magazine articles or download information from the Internet about a current international issue. After collecting the articles, analyze them to determine how objective each is. Create a bulletin board display of the articles and your annotations. You could also include photos and your comments on the point of view you think they emphasize.

4. Select any two organizations mentioned in this chapter. Go to their Web sites to get information about how they operate and what their aims are. Explain to the class why you think the work that these organizations are doing is important.

5. Contact your local congressperson to find out his or her stand on a current foreign policy issue. Compare the congressperson's position on the issue with the way the issue is reported in newspapers, in magazines, and on television news.

Document-Based Question

State the main idea expressed in each document. Then use information in the documents and your own knowledge to write an essay about how U.S. foreign policy changed within a ten-year span.

The Neutrality Act of 1937

Whenever the President shall find that there exists a state of war between, or among, two or more foreign states, the President shall proclaim such fact, and it shall thereafter be unlawful to export, or attempt to export, or cause to be exported, arms, ammunition, or implements of war . . . to any belligerent state [nation at war] named in such proclamation, . . .

Whenever the President shall . . . find that the placing of restrictions on the shipment of certain articles or materials in addition to arms . . . is necessary to promote the security or preserve the peace of the United States . . . he shall so proclaim. . . .

[I]t shall . . . be unlawful . . . for any American vessel to carry arms, ammunition, or implements of war to any belligerent state, or to any state wherein civil strife [fighting] exists. . . .

Whenever the President shall have issued a proclamation . . . it shall thereafter be unlawful for any citizen of the United States to travel on any vessel of the [belligerent] state or states named. . . .

The Truman Doctrine, 1947

The United States has received from the Greek Government an urgent appeal for financial and economic assistance . . . that assistance is imperative [essential] if Greece is to survive as a free nation. . . . [Its] very existence . . . is today threatened by the terrorist activities of several thousand armed men, led by Communists. . . .

Greece's neighbor, Turkey, also deserves our attention. . . . As in the case of Greece, if Turkey is to have the assistance it needs, the United States must supply it. . . .

The seeds of totalitarian regimes are nurtured by misery and want. They spread and grow in the evil soil of poverty and strife. They reach their full growth when the hope of a people for a better life has died. We must keep that hope alive. The peoples of the world look to us for support in maintaining their freedoms.

If we falter in our leadership, we may endanger the peace of the world—and we shall surely endanger the welfare of this nation. . . .

Glossary

absentee ballot form for voting by mail in advance of election day

absolute monarch all-powerful king or queen

act law

amendment change added to a document

appellate jurisdiction authority of a court to review cases already decided in a lower court

apportionment process of redrawing election districts to make them nearly equal in population

arbitration process of settling a dispute by bringing in a third party to impose a solution

Australian ballot secret ballot

authoritarian government system under which there are no restraints on the ruling authority; dictatorship; unlimited government

bail money or property deposited with the court to guarantee that a defendant will appear in court when required

bait and switch illegal and deceptive sales practice in which only higher-priced items are offered for sale in place of an advertised lower-priced item

beneficiary person designated to receive money from a life insurance policy

bicameral legislature two-house lawmaking body

bill draft of a proposed law

bill of attainder law that convicts a person of a crime, sets the punishment, and denies the person a jury trial; not permitted by the U.S. Constitution

Bill of Rights first ten amendments to the U.S. Constitution

boycott refusal to buy from a company to force an action

budget financial plan for an individual or government that lists projected income and expenses

Cabinet group of advisers to the president

capitalism an economic system in which most of the resources of production are privately owned and most economic decisions are made by individuals and businesses

census official count of the population (in United States, every ten years)

certificate of deposit (CD) bank account that guarantees a certain interest rate for a set amount of money kept in the account for a specific period of time

change of venue moving a trial from one location to another

charter authorization to operate a business or govern a city or state

checks and balances system whereby each branch of government has the authority to curb the powers of the others

chief executive head of the executive department of government (president; governor)

citizen one considered a member of a country

city council legislature of a city

civic life activity related to public affairs, particularly government, education, and charity

civil law category of law concerned with disputes between individuals and between individuals and a government

civil liberties individual rights such as freedom of speech and press, right to vote

cloture process for stopping a filibuster by limiting debate

collective bargaining negotiations between a labor union and an employer to arrive at a contract

command economy system under which the government makes the major decisions about what goods and services to produce and owns and operates most businesses

commander in chief role of the president as head of the armed forces

commission governing body of a county

common law body of law based on common practices in a community and on past decision by judges

community area or place where people have shared interests and a sense of belonging

compromise give-and-take process of resolving an issue in which each side gives up something in order to reach an agreement all can live with

concurrent powers authority given by the Constitution that can be exercised by both the federal and state governments

concurring opinion statement by a Supreme Court justice in support of the majority decision of the Court

confederal system government in which states hold most of the power but delegate some authority to a central government

conference committee temporary, appointed group from both houses of a legislature that resolves differences in bills passed by both houses on the same subject to create one bill for the legislature to pass

Congress lawmaking body of U.S. government

constitution written rules and plan of government

consumer fraud illegal activities negatively affecting consumers

containment U.S. policy of keeping communism confined to certain areas

contract legal agreement

corporation business authorized to operate by a state-granted charter and owned by stockholders

council-manager form of city government in which the elected council hires a manager to handle day-to-day operations

court body in the judicial branch of governments that decides disputes and hold trials for criminal and civil offenses

covert action secret mission to find out information about the policies of another nation or to affect the policies of another nation

criminal law category of law concerned with offenses against public order

culture shared ideas, beliefs, and values of a particular group of people

custom one of many accepted practices that have existed for a long period of time in a culture

customs duty tariff; tax placed on goods imported into a country

delegated powers authority given specifically to the federal government by the Constitution

democracy rule by the people

democratic republic representative form of government in which the people hold the power

deregulate eliminating or reducing the number of government rules on the operation of businesses

dictatorship unlimited government by one person

direct democracy system of government in which the citizens themselves make the decisions and vote on laws

discrimination treatment of an individual or group in a way that denies them their basic rights as human beings

dissenting opinion written view of a Supreme Court justice who disagrees with the Court's majority opinion

divine right theory idea that a monarch's authority to rule was given by God

double jeopardy putting a person on trail twice for the same crime

due process legal and fair rules of procedure that must be followed by the government when attempting to take a person's life, freedom, or property

elastic clause section of the Constitution that allows Congress to pass laws it considers necessary to govern the country properly; necessary and proper clause

elector member of the Electoral College

Electoral College body set up by the Constitution to elect the president and vice president

eminent domain right of a government to take private property for a public purpose

enumerated powers those delegated to the federal government by the Constitution

estate tax one on the value of inherited gifts or property

ethnocentrism belief that one's own culture or ethnic group is superior to others

excise tax one placed on the manufacture or sale of certain goods and services

executive branch section of government responsible for carrying out the laws and supervising the day-to-day operation of government

executive privilege idea that the president must be able to communicate freely and in secrecy with advisers about key matters such as diplomatic or military strategies

ex post facto law rule that punishes a person for an action of the past that was legal at the time of the action

faction group formed within a larger body to promote a particular cause or point of view

federalism system of government that divides powers between national and state governments

federal system government in which power is shared between states and a national government

filibuster unlimited debate; tactic used in the U.S. Senate to prevent a vote on a bill

fiscal year financial accounting period of 12 months

flat tax one whose rate is the same for every income level

foreign policy plan for a nation's dealings with other nations

free enterprise system under which privately owned businesses compete for profits in the marketplace

general will rules people agree to live by

gerrymander process of redrawing election district lines to favor one political party

gift tax one on gifts worth over a set amount

governor chief executive in a state

grandfather clause law of several Southern states that restricted voting to those whose male ancestors had been qualified to vote in 1867

grand jury group of citizens called upon to decide if there is enough evidence to hold the accused for trial

Great Compromise agreement at the Constitutional Convention in 1787 that the national legislature (Congress) would have two houses and that membership in the House of Representatives would be based on population, while each state would have an equal number of senators

habeas corpus court order requiring that an arrested person be quickly brought before a judge to be charged with a crime or else released

holding company business that acquires enough stock in other companies to gain control of those companies

home rule independent authority given by states to a local government

House of Representatives lower house of U.S. Congress

identity theft using a person's name and personal information for illegal purposes

impeachment bringing of charges against a public official as a first step in removing the person from office

implied powers ones not specifically named in the Constitution but which Congress has taken on under the elastic clause

income tax government-imposed tax on money earned

incorporate to form as a legal unit, such as a city or business

indictment written document containing the charges against the accused

indirect tax hidden tax; one incorporated into the selling price

inheritance tax one placed on the value of gifts or property received after someone's death

initiative proposal by a group of citizens for a law, constitutional amendment, or regulation at the state or local level to be placed on the ballot for approval by the voters

injunction legal ruling that stops an action, such as a strike

insurance written agreement (policy) by a company to pay a certain amount on the death of a person, for a disability, or for damages to property or people

interest percentage fee paid for loans or earned on savings accounts, CDs, and bonds

interventionism policy of interfering in the affairs of other countries

isolationism policy of not taking part in world affairs

joint committee group made up of members of both houses of a legislature that is handling certain matters in both houses at the same time

judicial branch section of government responsible for interpreting laws and punishing lawbreakers; the courts

judicial review power of the highest court to declare unconstitutional laws passed by the legislature and actions of the executive branch

labor union organization of workers that attempts to improve working conditions, wages, and benefits

law bill that has gone through the lawmaking process, been approved, and been set forth as a binding rule

legislative branch lawmaking section of government

lieutenant governor elected official in a state who takes over the responsibilities of the governor if that person cannot perform the duties; usually presides over a state senate

limited government system under which the power of a government is restricted by laws or a constitution

literacy test reading test for qualifying to vote; is now against the law

lobby nongovernmental special interest group that acts to influence public policy

lobbyist person who works for a lobby to influence public policy

lockout closing of a business by the owner to keep workers from coming to work

loose interpretation idea that the federal government should be able to exercise powers not specifically mentioned in the Constitution in order to carry out authorized functions

majority decision document expressing ideas of a majority of the Supreme Court justices about a case

majority leader spokesperson for the political party holding the most seats in the House of Representatives or Senate

majority rule system whereby decisions are made by more than half of those involved

market economy system under which private citizens decide how goods and services are produced

mass media forms of communication that transmit information to great numbers of people, such as TV, radio, the Internet, magazines, newspapers, and books

mass production manufacturing of large numbers of goods quickly by machines

mayor chief executive of a city or village

mayor-council government structure for a city with an elected chief executive and elected legislative body

mediation process of resolving a dispute by calling in a third party to help reach an agreement

merger combination of two or more companies into a single company

minority leader spokesperson for the second-largest political party in the House of Representatives or Senate

mixed economy system under which both the government and private citizens make economic decisions

monarchy government headed by a king or queen

monopoly control of an entire industry by one company

mortgage loan agreement between a lending institution and an individual or group to obtain money to buy property

municipality urban center; city

mutual fund investment company that owns stocks and bonds of a variety of businesses; investors buy shares of the fund

nationalism strong sense of pride in and loyalty to a nation

naturalization process through which immigrants can become citizens

natural rights of man Locke's idea that people are born with rights such as life, liberty, and ownership of property—rights that they never give up to a ruler

neutrality not taking sides in a dispute

norms shared guidelines of behavior accepted by society

oligarchy government by a small group of people who exercise all of the power

original jurisdiction authority of a court to be the first to try the accused or listen to arguments in a dispute

parliamentary system form of government under which people elect representatives to a lawmaking body and the executive power is held by the leader of the political party that controls the majority of seats in the parliament

partnership business owned by two or more people

pigeonhole to set aside a proposed bill in committee with the intention of not acting on it

plaintiff person bringing a lawsuit

platform set of policies that a political party sets forth and promotes during an election year

pluralistic society community or nation in which live people of many different ethnic, racial, and religious backgrounds

pocket veto action by a state or national executive to kill a bill by not acting on it within a prescribed period of time

political action committee (PAC) special interest group for unions, business associations, or professional groups created to raise money to influence elections

political party organization created to win elections in order to control government and construct public policy

political process procedure followed to resolve important issues that concern a large number of people

polling place location where people go to vote

poll tax fee paid by voters in order to vote; no longer legal

population density number of people living in each square mile of land

power of the purse control over the finances and budget of government by Congress

prejudice prejudgment of others in a negative way

President Pro Tempore temporary President of the Senate; usually the most senior member of the majority party; presides when the vice president is absent

President of the Senate presiding officer of the Senate; duty given to the vice president

pressure group special interest group; lobby

primary election held to choose political party candidates to run for public office

privatization turning over governmental functions to privately owned organizations

progressive tax one whose rate increases as income rises

property tax one on the value of buildings and land

public opinion poll systematic or scientific survey to determine the population's views on particular issues

public policy governmental plan of action to solve problems and serve people

ratification process system set up to approve treaties, presidential appointments, and amendments to the Constitution

ratify to approve

recall citizen-initiated movement to remove a public official from office

referendum practice of allowing voters to approve or disapprove proposed laws

regressive tax one with a rate that does not rise with a rise of income

representative democracy system of government in which citizens elect representatives to make laws and decisions

reserved powers authority given specifically to the states by the Constitution

sales tax one on goods and services based on a fixed percentage of their prices

sanction government measure to force another government to do something or to stop an action

search warrant legal document issued by a judge giving permission to law enforcement officials to search a specific place

secret ballot practice of having voters cast their ballots in privacy

select committee temporary, appointed group of legislators that discusses and votes on bills of a certain category

Senate upper house of the U.S. Congress; also name of upper house in most state legislatures

seniority system method of selecting committee chairpersons based on their length of service

separation of powers division of government into three branches, each having specific, exclusive powers

small claims court body that hears lawsuits concerning small amounts of money without the involvement of lawyers

social contract idea put forth by Rousseau that people who live in society give up total freedom for protection

society community that has common interests, institutions, activities, and interests

sole proprietorship business owned by one person

Speaker of the House presiding officer of the U.S. House of Representatives

special court federal court that hears only certain types of cases

special district geographic division within a state formed to carry out specific tasks, such as running schools

special interest group organization that tries to influence public policy to benefit itself or bring about its goals

standing committee permanent, appointed group of legislators

statutory law written law put together in codes

stereotype sweeping generalization about a group of people based on little or no factual information

stockholder owner of one or more shares of a corporation

strict interpretation idea that the federal government should *not* exercise any powers that are not specifically mentioned in the Constitution

strike organized work stoppage

strikebreaker nonunion worker hired by a business to replace a union worker who is on strike

subpoena summons to testify in a legal case

suburb community or city close to a large city

suffrage right to vote

supremacy clause Article VI, Section 2, establishing the Constitution as the highest law in the nation

Supreme Court the highest court in the United States

symbol visible sign of an idea or ideal

tariff duty, or tax, placed on imported goods

third party minor political party that often focuses on a few issues of particular importance to its members

totalitarian government one that controls all aspects of its people's lives

town small community with its own elected government

town meeting form of direct democracy practiced in New England towns

township division of a county with its own elected government

tradition long-accepted pattern of behavior or way of doing something

treaty formal agreement between two or more nations

trust large business monopoly whose shareholders place control of the firm in the hands of trustees

truth-in-lending law government regulation that outlines the rights of consumers who take out a loan or receive credit

unicameral legislature one-house lawmaking body

unitary government highly centralized governmental system

unlimited government system under which the power of government has no restraints

unwritten constitution plan of government based on historical documents, statutory law, common law, and judicial decisions, not on a single written document

values ideas and principles that a society considers to be important, good, and desirable

veto refusal by a president or governor to sign a bill into law

village small community with its own elected government

warranty promise by a producer that a product will perform as expected for a specific time period

zoning officially designating areas in a community for specific purposes

The Declaration of Independence

Note: Capitalization, spelling, punctuation, and paragraphing have been modernized. In addition, the signers' names have been re-arranged and grouped alphabetically by state.

In Congress, July 4, 1776

The Unanimous Declaration of the Thirteen United States of America

When in the course of human events, it becomes necessary for one people to dissolve the political bands which have connected them with another, and to assume, among the powers of the earth, the separate and equal station to which the laws of nature and of nature's God entitle them, a decent respect to the opinions of mankind requires that they should declare the causes which impel them to the separation.

We hold these truths to be self-evident: that all men are created equal; that they are endowed by their Creator with certain unalienable rights; that among these are life, liberty, and the pursuit of happiness.

That to secure these rights, governments are instituted among men, deriving their just powers from the consent of the governed. That, whenever any form of government becomes destructive of these ends, it is the right of the people to alter or to abolish it, and to institute new government, laying its foundation on such principles, and organizing its powers in such form, as to them shall seem most likely to effect their safety and happiness. Prudence, indeed, will dictate that governments long established should not be changed for light and transient causes; and, accordingly, all experience hath shown that mankind are more disposed to suffer, while evils are sufferable, than to right themselves by abolishing the forms to which they are accustomed. But when a long train of abuses and usurpations, pursuing invariably the same object, evinces a design to reduce them under absolute despotism, it is their right, it is their duty, to throw off such government, and to provide new guards for their future security.

Such has been the patient sufferance of these colonies; and such is now the necessity which constrains them to alter their former systems of government. The history of the present King of Great Britain is a history of repeated injuries and usurpations, all having in direct object the establishment of an absolute tyranny over these states. To prove this, let facts be submitted to a candid world.

He has refused his assent to laws the most wholesome and necessary for the public good.

He has forbidden his governors to pass laws of immediate and pressing importance, unless suspended in their operation till his assent should be obtained; and, when so suspended, he has utterly neglected to attend to them.

He has refused to pass other laws for the accommodation of large districts of people, unless those people would relinquish the right of representation in the legislature—a right inestimable to them and formidable to tyrants only.

He has called together legislative bodies at places unusual, uncomfortable, and distant from the depository of their public records, for the sole purpose of fatiguing them into compliance with his measures.

He has dissolved representative houses repeatedly, for opposing, with manly firmness, his invasions on the rights of the people.

He has refused, for a long time after such dissolutions, to cause others to be elected; whereby the legislative powers, incapable of annihilation, have returned to the people at large for their exercise; the state remaining, in the meantime, exposed to all the dangers of invasion from without and convulsions within.

He has endeavored to prevent the population of these states; for that purpose obstructing the laws for naturalization of foreigners, refusing to pass others to encourage their migration hither, and raising the conditions of new appropriations of lands.

He has obstructed the administration of justice by refusing his assent to laws for establishing judiciary powers.

He has made judges dependent on his will alone for the tenure of their offices and the amount and payment of their salaries.

He has erected a multitude of new offices and sent hither swarms of officers to harass our people and eat out their substance.

He has kept among us, in times of peace, standing armies, without the consent of our legislatures.

He has affected to render the military independent of, and superior to, the civil power.

He has combined with others to subject us to a jurisdiction foreign to our constitution and unacknowledged by our laws, giving his assent to their acts of pretended legislation:

For quartering large bodies of armed troops among us;

For protecting them, by a mock trial, from punishment for any murders which they should commit on the inhabitants of these states;

For cutting off our trade with all parts of the world;

For imposing taxes on us without our consent;

For depriving us, in many cases, of the benefits of trial by jury;

For transporting us beyond seas to be tried for pretended offenses;

For abolishing the free system of English laws in a neighboring province, establishing therein an arbitrary government and enlarging its boundaries, so as to render it at once an example and fit instrument for introducing the same absolute rule into these colonies;

For taking away our charters, abolishing our most valuable laws, and altering fundamentally the forms of our governments;

For suspending our own legislatures, and declaring themselves invested with power to legislate for us in all cases whatsoever.

He has abdicated government here by declaring us out of his protection and waging war against us.

He has plundered our seas, ravaged our coasts, burned our towns, and destroyed the lives of our people.

He is, at this time, transporting large armies of foreign mercenaries to complete the works of death, desolation, and tyranny already begun with circumstances of cruelty and perfidy scarcely paralleled in the most barbarous ages, and totally unworthy the head of a civilized nation.

He has constrained our fellow citizens taken captive on the high seas to bear arms against their country, to become the executioners of their friends and brethren, or to fall themselves by their hands.

He has excited domestic insurrections among us, and has endeavored to bring on the inhabitants of our frontiers the merciless Indian savages, whose known rule of warfare is an undistinguished destruction of all ages, sexes, and conditions.

In every stage of these oppressions we have petitioned for redress in the most humble terms. Our repeated petitions have been answered only by repeated injury. A prince whose character is thus marked by every act which may define a tyrant is unfit to be the ruler of a free people.

Nor have we been wanting in attentions to our British brethren. We have warned them, from time to time, of attempts by their legislature to extend an unwarrantable jurisdiction over us. We have reminded them of the circumstances of our emigration and settlement here. We have appealed to their native justice and magnanimity; and we have conjured them, by the ties of our common kindred, to disavow these usurpations, which would inevitably interrupt our connections and correspondence. They, too, have been deaf to the voice of justice and consanguinity. We must, therefore, acquiesce in the necessity which denounces our separation, and hold them, as we hold the rest of mankind, enemies in war, in peace friends.

We, therefore, the representatives of the United States of America, in General Congress assembled, appealing to the Supreme Judge of the world for the rectitude of our intentions, do, in the name and by authority of the good people of these colonies, solemnly publish and declare: that these united colonies are, and of right ought to be, free and independent states; that they are absolved from all allegiance to the British crown, and that all political connection between them and the state of Great Britain is, and ought to be, totally dissolved; and that, as free and independent states, they have full power to levy war, conclude peace, contract alliances, establish commerce, and to do all other acts and things which independent states may of right do. And for the support of this declaration, with a firm reliance on the protection of Divine Providence, we mutually pledge to each other our lives, our fortunes, and our sacred honor.

[Signed by] John Hancock
[Massachusetts]

[Connecticut]
Samuel Huntington
Roger Sherman
William Williams
Oliver Wolcott

[Delaware]
Thomas McKean
George Read
Caesar Rodney

[Georgia]
Button Gwinnett
Lyman Hall
George Walton

[Maryland]
Charles Carroll
of Carrollton
Samuel Chase
William Paca
Thomas Stone

[Massachusetts]
John Adams
Samuel Adams
Elbridge Gerry
Robert Treat Paine

[New Hampshire]
Josiah Bartlett
Matthew Thornton
William Whipple

[New Jersey]
Abraham Clark
John Hart
Francis Hopkinson
Richard Stockton
John Witherspoon

[New York]
William Floyd
Francis Lewis
Philip Livingston
Lewis Morris

[North Carolina]
Joseph Hewes
William Hooper
John Penn

[Pennsylvania]
George Clymer
Benjamin Franklin
Robert Morris
John Morton

George Ross
Benjamin Rush
James Smith
George Taylor
James Wilson

[Rhode Island]
William Ellery
Stephen Hopkins

[South Carolina]
Thomas Heyward, Jr.
Thomas Lynch, Jr.
Arthur Middleton
Edward Rutledge

[Virginia]
Carter Braxton
Benjamin Harrison
Thomas Jefferson
Francis Lightfoot Lee
Richard Henry Lee
Thomas Nelson, Jr.
George Wythe

The Constitution of the United States of America

Note: Footnotes, headings, and explanations have been added to aid the reader. The explanations within the body of the text are enclosed in brackets [ ]. The parts of the Constitution that are no longer in effect are printed in *italic type*. Capitalization, spelling, and punctuation have been modernized.

PREAMBLE

We the people of the United States, in order to form a more perfect Union, establish justice, insure domestic tranquility,[1] provide for the common defense, promote the general welfare, and secure the blessings of liberty to ourselves and our posterity [descendants], do ordain [issue] and establish this Constitution for the United States of America.

ARTICLE I. CONGRESS

Section 1. Legislative Power All legislative powers herein granted shall be vested in a Congress of the United States, which shall consist of a Senate and House of Representatives.

Section 2. House of Representatives [1] The House of Representatives shall be composed of members chosen every second year by the people of the several states, and the electors [voters] in each state shall have the qualifications requisite [required] for electors of the most numerous branch of the state legislature.

[2] No person shall be a representative who shall not have attained to [reached] the age of twenty-five years and been seven years a citizen of the United States, and who shall not, when elected, be an inhabitant of that state in which he shall be chosen.

[3] Representatives and direct taxes[2] shall be apportioned [divided] among the several states which may be included within this Union according to their respective numbers [population], *which shall be determined by adding to the whole number of free persons, including those bound to service for a term of years* [indentured servants], *and excluding Indians not taxed, three-fifths of all other persons.*[3] The actual enumeration [census] shall be made within three years after the first meeting of the Congress of the United States, and within every subsequent term of ten years, in such manner as they shall by law direct. The number of representatives shall not exceed one for every thirty thousand, but each state shall have at least one representative; *and until such enumeration shall be made, the State of New Hampshire shall be entitled to choose three, Massachusetts eight, Rhode Island and Providence Plantations one, Connecticut five, New York six, New Jersey four, Pennsylvania eight, Delaware one, Maryland six, Virginia ten, North Carolina five, South Carolina five, and Georgia three.*[4]

[4] When vacancies happen in the representation from any state, the executive authority [governor] thereof shall issue writs of election[5] to fill such vacancies.

[5] The House of Representatives shall choose their Speaker and other officers; and shall have the sole power of impeachment.[6]

---

[1] "Insure domestic tranquility" means *assure peace within the nation.*

[2] Modified by Amendment XVI, which granted Congress the power to levy a direct tax on individual incomes rather than on the basis of state populations.

[3] "Other persons" refers to slaves. Amendment XIII abolished slavery; Amendment XIV specifically eliminated the three-fifths formula.

[4] Temporary provision.

[5] "Issue writs of election" means *call a special election.*

[6] "Power of impeachment" means *right to charge federal officials with misconduct.*

Section 3. Senate [1] The Senate of the United States shall be composed of two senators from each state, *chosen by the legislature thereof,*[1] for six years; and each senator shall have one vote.

[2] *Immediately after they shall be assembled in consequence of the first election, they shall be divided as equally as may be into three classes. The seats of the senators of the first class shall be vacated at the expiration of the second year, of the second class at the expiration of the fourth year, and of the third class at the expiration of the sixth year,*[2] so that one-third may be chosen every second year; *and if vacancies happen by resignation, or otherwise, during the recess of the legislature of any state, the executive* [governor] *thereof may make temporary appointments until the next meeting of the legislature, which shall then fill such vacancies.*[3]

[3] No person shall be a senator who shall not have attained to the age of thirty years and been nine years a citizen of the United States, and who shall not, when elected, be an inhabitant of that state for which he shall be chosen.

[4] The vice president of the United States shall be president of the Senate, but shall have no vote, unless they be equally divided [tied].

[5] The Senate shall choose their other officers, and also a president pro tempore [temporary presiding officer], in the absence of the vice president, or when he shall exercise the office of president of the United States.

[6] The Senate shall have sole power to try all impeachments.[4] When sitting for that purpose, they shall be on oath or affirmation.[5] When the president of the United States is tried, the chief justice [of the United States] shall preside; and no person shall be convicted without the concurrence [agreement] of two-thirds of the members present.

[7] Judgment in cases of impeachment shall not extend further than to removal from office, and disqualification to hold and enjoy any office of honor, trust, or profit under the United States; but the party convicted shall nevertheless be liable and subject to indictment, trial, judgment, and punishment, according to law.

Section 4. Elections and Meetings of Congress [1] The times, places, and manner of holding elections for senators and representatives shall be prescribed [designated] in each state by the legislature thereof; but the Congress may at any time by law make or alter such regulations, except as to the places of choosing senators.

[2] The Congress shall assemble at least once in every year, *and such meeting shall be on the first Monday in December,*[6] unless they shall by law appoint a different day.

Section 5. Rules and Procedures of the Two Houses [1] Each house shall be the judge of the elections, returns, and qualifications of its own members,[7] and a majority of each shall constitute a quorum[8] to do business; but a smaller number may adjourn from day to day, and may be authorized to compel the attendance of absent members, in such manner, and under such penalties, as each house may provide.

[2] Each house may determine the rules of its proceedings, punish its members for disorderly behavior, and with the concurrence of two-thirds, expel a member.

[3] Each house shall keep a journal [record] of its proceedings, and from time to time publish the same, excepting such parts as may in their judgment require secrecy; and the yeas [affirmative votes] and nays [negative votes] of the members of either house on any question shall, at the desire of one-fifth of those present, be entered on the journal.

[4] Neither house, during the session of Congress, shall, without the consent of the other, adjourn for more than three days, nor to any other place than that in which the two houses shall be sitting.

Section 6. Members' Privileges and Restrictions [1] The senators and representatives shall receive a compensation [salary] for their services, to be ascertained [fixed] by law and paid out of the treasury of the United States. They shall in all cases except treason, felony [serious crime], and breach of the peace [disorderly conduct], be privileged [immune] from arrest during their attendance at the session of their respective houses, and in going to and returning from the same; and for any speech or debate in either house, they shall not be questioned in any other place.[9]

---

[1] Replaced by Amendment XVII, which provided for popular election of senators.

[2] Temporary provision, designed to organize the first Senate in such a way that, thereafter, only one-third of its members would be subject to replacement at each successive election.

[3] Modified by Amendment XVII, which permits a governor to select a temporary replacement to fill the vacancy until the next election.

[4] "To try all impeachments" means *to conduct the trials of officials impeached by the House of Representatives.* When trying such cases, the Senate serves as a court.

[5] If taking an oath violates a member's religious principles, that person may "affirm" rather than "swear."

[6] Amendment XX changed this date to January 3.

[7] This provision empowers either house, by a majority vote, to refuse to seat a newly elected member.

[8] A "quorum" is the *number of members that must be present in order to conduct business.*

[9] "They shall not be questioned in any other place" means that *they may not be sued for slander or libel.* Freedom from arrest during congressional sessions and freedom of speech within the halls of Congress—two privileges granted to members of Congress—are known as *congressional immunity.*

[2] No senator or representative shall, during the time for which he was elected, be appointed to any civil office under the authority of the United States, which shall have been created, or the emoluments [salary] whereof shall have been increased, during such time; and no person holding any office under the United States shall be a member of either house during his continuance in office.

Section 7. Lawmaking Procedures [1] All bills for raising revenue shall originate [be introduced] in the House of Representatives; but the Senate may propose or concur with [approve] amendments as on other bills.

[2] Every bill which shall have passed the House of Representatives and the Senate shall, before it becomes a law, be presented to the president of the United States; if he approve, he shall sign it, but if not, he shall return it, with his objections, to that house in which it shall have originated, who shall enter the objections at large on their journal, and proceed to reconsider it. If after such reconsideration two-thirds of that house shall agree to pass the bill, it shall be sent, together with the objections, to the other house, by which it shall likewise be reconsidered, and, if approved by two-thirds of that house, it shall become a law. But in all such cases the votes of both houses shall be determined by yeas and nays, and the names of the persons voting for and against the bill shall be entered on the journal of each house respectively. If any bill shall not be returned by the president within ten days (Sundays excepted) after it shall have been presented to him, the same shall be a law, in like manner as if he had signed it, unless the Congress by their adjournment prevent its return, in which case it shall not be a law[1]

[3] Every order, resolution, or vote to which the concurrence of the Senate and House of Representatives may be necessary (except on a question of adjournment) shall be presented to the president of the United States; and before the same shall take effect, shall be approved by him, or, being disapproved by him, shall be repassed by two-thirds of the Senate and House of Representatives, according to the rules and limitations prescribed in the case of a bill.

Section 8. Powers of Congress The Congress shall have power:

[1] To lay and collect taxes, duties, imposts, and excises,[2] to pay the debts and provide for the common defense and general welfare of the United States; but all duties, imposts, and excises shall be uniform [the same] throughout the United States;

[2] To borrow money on the credit of the United States;

[3] To regulate commerce with foreign nations, and among the several states, and with the Indian tribes;

[4] To establish a uniform rule of naturalization [admitting to citizenship], and uniform laws on the subject of bankruptcies throughout the United States;

[5] To coin money, regulate the value thereof, and of foreign coin, and fix [set] the standard of weights and measures;

[6] To provide for the punishment of counterfeiting[3] the securities and current coin of the United States;

[7] To establish post offices and post roads;

[8] To promote the progress of science and useful arts by securing for limited times to authors and inventors the exclusive right to their respective writings and discoveries;[4]

[9] To constitute tribunals [establish courts] inferior to [lower than] the Supreme Court;

[10] To define and punish piracies and felonies committed on the high seas[5] and offenses against the law of nations [international law];

[11] To declare war, grant letters of marque and reprisal,[6] and make rules concerning captures on land and water;

[12] To raise and support armies, but no appropriation of money to that use shall be for a longer term than two years;

[13] To provide and maintain a navy;

[14] To make rules for the government and regulation of the land and naval forces;

[15] To provide for calling forth the militia[7] to execute [carry out] the laws of the Union, suppress [put down] insurrections [rebellions], and repel [drive back] invasions;

[16] To provide for organizing, arming, and disciplining [training] the militia, and for governing such part of them as may be employed in the service of the United States, reserving to the states respectively the appointment of the officers, and the authority of train-

---

[1] If Congress adjourns before the ten-day period is up, the president can kill a bill by ignoring it ("putting it in his pocket"). Therefore, this type of presidential rejection is called a *pocket veto*.

[2] "Duties, imposts, and excises" are forms of taxation. Duties and imposts are taxes on imports. Excises are taxes on goods produced or services performed within a country.

[3] Making an imitation with the intent of passing it as the genuine article.

[4] Copyright and patent laws, passed by Congress on the basis of this clause, protect the rights of authors and inventors.

[5] Open ocean; waters outside the territorial limits of a country.

[6] Letters of marque and reprisal are government licenses issued to private citizens in time of war authorizing them to fit out armed vessels (called *privateers*) for the purpose of capturing or destroying enemy ships.

[7] Citizen soldiers who are not in the regular armed forces but are subject to military duty in times of emergency; for example, the National Guard.

ing the militia according to the discipline [regulations] prescribed by Congress;

[17] To exercise exclusive legislation in all cases whatsoever, over such district[1] (not exceeding ten miles square) as may, by cession of particular states, and the acceptance of Congress, become the seat of government of the United States, and to exercise like authority over all places purchased by the consent of the legislature of the state in which the same shall be, for the erection of forts, magazines, arsenals, dockyards, and other needful buildings; and

[18] To make all laws which shall be necessary and proper for carrying into execution the foregoing powers and all other powers vested by this Constitution in the government of the United States, or in any department or officer thereof.[2]

Section 9. Powers Denied to the Federal Government

[1] *The migration or importation of such persons as any of the states now existing shall think proper to admit shall not be prohibited by the Congress prior to the year 1808; but a tax or duty may be imposed on such importation, not exceeding ten dollars for each person.*[3]

[2] The privilege of the writ of habeas corpus[4] shall not be suspended, unless when in cases of rebellion or invasion the public safety may require it.

[3] No bill of attainder[5] or ex post facto law[6] shall be passed.

[4] No capitation [head] or other direct tax shall be laid, unless in proportion to the census or enumeration herein before directed to be taken.[7]

[5] No tax or duty shall be laid on articles exported from any state.

[6] No preference shall be given by any regulation of commerce or revenue to the ports of one state over those of another; nor shall vessels bound to, or from, one state be obliged to enter, clear, or pay duties in another.

[7] No money shall be drawn from the treasury, but in consequence of appropriations made by law;

and a regular statement and account of the receipts and expenditures of all public money shall be published from time to time.

[8] No title of nobility shall be granted by the United States; and no person holding any office of profit or trust under them shall, without the consent of the Congress, accept of any present, emolument, office, or title, of any kind whatever, from any king, prince, or foreign state.

Section 10. Powers Denied to the States

[1] No state shall enter into any treaty, alliance, or confederation; grant letters of marque and reprisal; coin money; emit bills of credit;[8] make anything but gold and silver coin a tender [legal money] in payment of debts; pass any bill of attainder, ex post facto law, or law impairing the obligation of contracts,[9] or grant any title of nobility.

[2] No state shall, without the consent of the Congress, lay any imposts or duties on imports or exports, except what may be absolutely necessary for executing its inspection laws; and the net produce [income] of all duties and imposts, laid by any state on imports or exports, shall be for the use of the treasury of the United States; and all such laws shall be subject to the revision and control of the Congress.

[3] No state shall, without the consent of Congress, lay any duty of tonnage,[10] keep troops[11] or ships of war in time of peace, enter into any agreement or compact with another state or with a foreign power, or engage in war unless actually invaded or in such imminent [threatening] danger as will not admit of delay.

ARTICLE II. THE PRESIDENCY

Section 1. Executive Power [1] The executive power shall be vested in a president of the United States of America. He shall hold his office during the term of four years,[12] and, together with the vice president, chosen for the same term, be elected as follows:

[2] Each state shall appoint, in such manner as the legislature thereof may direct, a number of electors, equal to the whole number of senators and representatives to which the state may be entitled in the Congress; but no senator or representative, or person holding an office of trust or profit under the United States, shall be appointed an elector.

[3] *The electors shall meet in their respective states, and*

---

[1] "To exercise exclusive legislation ... over such district" means *to be solely responsible for making the laws for a designated area.*

[2] This is the so-called "elastic clause" of the Constitution, which allows Congress to carry out many actions not specifically listed.

[3] This temporary provision prohibited Congress from interfering with the importation of slaves ("such persons") before 1808.

[4] A "writ of habeas corpus" is a court order obtained by a person taken into custody, demanding to know the reasons for imprisonment. If the court rules that the reasons are insufficient, the prisoner is released.

[5] A law that deprives a person of civil rights without a trial.

[6] A law that punishes a person for a past action that was not unlawful at the time it was committed.

[7] Modified by Amendment XVI.

[8] "Emit bills of credit" means issue paper money.

[9] "Impairing the obligation of contracts" means *weakening the obligations persons assume when they enter into legal agreements.*

[10] "Duty of tonnage" means a tax based upon a vessel's cargo-carrying capacity.

[11] Other than militia.

[12] Amendment XXII limits a president to two terms.

vote by ballot for two persons, of whom one at least shall not be an inhabitant of the same state with themselves. And they shall make a list of all the persons voted for, and of the number of votes for each; which list they shall sign and certify, and transmit sealed to the seat of the government of the United States, directed to the president of the Senate. The president of the Senate shall, in the presence of the Senate and House of Representatives, open all the certificates, and the votes shall then be counted. The person having the greatest number of votes shall be the president, if such number be a majority of the whole number of electors appointed; and if there be more than one who have such majority, and have an equal number of votes, then the House of Representatives shall immediately choose by ballot one of them for president; and if no person have a majority, then from the five highest on the list the said House shall in like manner choose the president. But in choosing the president, the votes shall be taken by states, the representation from each state having one vote; a quorum for this purpose shall consist of a member or members from two-thirds of the states, and a majority of all the states shall be necessary to a choice. In every case, after the choice of the president, the person having the greatest number of votes of the electors shall be the vice president. But if there should remain two or more who have equal votes, the Senate shall choose from them by ballot the vice president.[1]

[4] The Congress may determine the time of choosing the electors, and the day on which they shall give their votes; which day shall be the same throughout the United States.

[5] No person except a natural-born citizen, *or a citizen of the United States at the time of the adoption of this Constitution,*[2] shall be eligible to the office of president; neither shall any person be eligible to that office who shall not have attained to the age of thirty-five years and been fourteen years a resident within the United States.

[6] In case of the removal of the president from office, or of his death, resignation, or inability to discharge the powers and duties of the said office, the same shall devolve on the vice president, and the Congress may by law provide for the case of removal, death, resignation, or inability, both of the president and vice president, declaring what officer shall then act as president, and such officer shall act accordingly, until the disability be removed, or a president shall be elected.[3]

[7] The president shall, at stated times, receive for his services a compensation, which shall neither be increased nor diminished [decreased] during the period for which he shall have been elected, and he shall not receive within that period any other emolument from the United States, or any of them.

[8] Before he enter on the execution of his office, he shall take the following oath or affirmation:

"I do solemnly swear (or affirm) that I will faithfully execute the office of President of the United States, and will, to the best of my ability, preserve, protect, and defend the Constitution of the United States."

Section 2. Powers of the President [1] The president shall be commander in chief of the army and navy [all the armed forces] of the United States, and of the militia of the several states, when called into the actual service of the United States; he may require the opinion in writing of the principal officer in each of the executive departments upon any subject relating to the duties of their respective offices; and he shall have power to grant reprieves[4] and pardons[5] for offenses against the United States except in cases of impeachment.

[2] He shall have power, by and with the advice and consent of the Senate, to make treaties, provided two-thirds of the senators present concur; and he shall nominate, and, by and with the advice and consent of the Senate, shall appoint ambassadors, other public ministers and consuls, judges of the Supreme Court, and all other officers of the United States whose appointments are not herein otherwise provided for and which shall be established by law; but the Congress may by law vest the appointment of such inferior officers as they think proper in the president alone, in the courts of law, or in the heads of departments.

[3] The president shall have power to fill up all vacancies that may happen during the recess of the Senate, by granting commissions which shall expire at the end of their next session.

Section 3. Duties and Responsibilities of the President He shall, from time to time, give to the Congress information of the state of the Union, and recommend to their consideration such measures as he shall judge necessary and expedient [advisable]; he may, on extraordinary [special] occasions, convene both houses, or either of them, and in case of disagreement between them with respect to the time of adjournment, he may adjourn them to such time as he shall think proper; he shall receive ambassadors and other public ministers; he shall take care that the laws be faithfully executed, and shall commission [appoint] all the officers of the United States.

Section 4. Impeachment The president, vice president, and all civil officers[6] of the United States, shall be removed from office on impeachment for, and conviction of, treason, bribery, or other high crimes and misdemeanors [offenses].

---

[1] Replaced by Amendment XII.

[2] Temporary provision.

[3] Modified by Amendments XX and XXV.

[4] A "reprieve" is a postponement of the execution of a sentence.

[5] A "pardon" is a release from penalty.

[6] "Civil officers" include executive and judicial officials, but not members of Congress or officers in the armed forces.

ARTICLE III. THE SUPREME COURT AND OTHER COURTS

Section 1. Federal Courts The judicial power of the United States shall be vested in one Supreme Court, and in such inferior [lower] courts as the Congress may from time to time ordain and establish. The judges, both of the Supreme and inferior courts, shall hold their offices during good behavior, and shall, at stated times, receive for their services a compensation, which shall not be diminished during their continuance in office.

Section 2. Jurisdiction of Federal Courts [1] The judicial power shall extend to all cases in law and equity[1] arising under this Constitution, the laws of the United States, and treaties made, or which shall be made, under their authority; to all cases affecting ambassadors, other public ministers, and consuls; to all cases of admiralty and maritime jurisdiction;[2] to controversies [disputes] to which the United States shall be a party; to controversies between two or more states, between a state and citizens of another state,[3] between citizens of different states, between citizens of the same state claiming lands under grants of different states, and between a state, or the citizens thereof, and foreign states, citizens, or subjects.[4]

[2] In all cases affecting ambassadors, other public ministers, and consuls, and those in which a state shall be a party, the Supreme Court shall have original jurisdiction.[5] In all the other cases before mentioned, the Supreme Court shall have appellate jurisdiction,[6] both as to law and fact, with such exceptions and under such regulations as the Congress shall make.

[3] The trial of all crimes, except in cases of impeachment, shall be by jury; and such trial shall be held in the state where the said crimes shall have been committed; but when not committed within any state, the trial shall be at such place or places as the Congress may by law have directed.

Section 3. Treason [1] Treason against the United States shall consist only in levying [carrying on] war against them, or in adhering to [assisting] their enemies, giving them aid and comfort. No person shall be convicted of treason unless on the testimony of two witnesses to the same overt [open; public] act, or on confession in open court.

[2] The Congress shall have power to declare the punishment of treason, but no attainder of treason shall work corruption of blood or forfeiture except during the life of the person attainted.[7]

ARTICLE IV. INTERSTATE RELATIONS

Section 1. Official Acts and Records Full faith and credit shall be given in each state to the public acts, records, and judicial proceedings of every other state.[8] And the Congress may, by general laws, prescribe the manner in which such acts, records, and proceedings shall be proved, and the effect thereof.

Section 2. Mutual Obligations of States [1] The citizens of each state shall be entitled to all privileges and immunities of citizens in the several states.

[2] A person charged in any state with treason, felony, or other crime, who shall flee from justice and be found in another state, shall, on demand of the executive authority of the state from which he fled, be delivered up, to be removed to the state having jurisdiction of the crime.[9]

[3] *No person held to service or labor in one state, under the laws thereof, escaping into another, shall, in consequence of any law or regulation therein, be discharged from such service or labor, but shall be delivered up on claim of the party to whom such service or labor may be due.*[10]

Section 3. New States and Territories [1] New states may be admitted by the Congress into this Union; but no new state shall be formed or erected within the jurisdiction of any other state; nor any state be formed by the junction [joining] of two or more states, or parts of states, without the consent of the legislatures of the states concerned as well as of the Congress.

[2] The Congress shall have power to dispose of and make all needful rules and regulations respecting the territory or other property belonging to the United States; and nothing in this Constitution shall be so

---

[1] "Cases in law" refers mainly to disputes that arise from the violation of, or the interpretation of, federal laws, treaties, or the Constitution. "Equity" is a branch of the law that deals more generally with the prevention of injustice.

[2] Legal disputes involving ships and shipping on the high seas, in territorial waters, and on the navigable waterways within the country.

[3] Modified by Amendment XI, which provides that a state may not be sued in the federal courts by a citizen of another state (or by a citizen of a foreign country). A state, however, retains the right to sue a citizen of another state (or a citizen of a foreign country) in the federal courts.

[4] Modified by Amendment XI.

[5] "Original jurisdiction" means the authority of a court to hear cases that have not previously been tried by lower courts.

[6] "Appellate jurisdiction" means the authority of a court to review cases that have previously been tried by lower courts.

[7] Punishment imposed on someone for treason may not be extended to that person's children or heirs.

[8] The official acts of each state must be accepted by the other states. The "full faith and credit" clause applies to court judgments, contracts, marriages, corporation charters, etc.

[9] The delivery by one state or government to another of fugitives from justice is called *extradition*.

[10] Since the phrase "person held to service or labor" refers to a slave, this clause was nullified by Amendment XIII.

construed [interpreted] as to prejudice [damage] any claims of the United States, or of any particular state.

Section 4. Federal Guarantees to the States The United States shall guarantee to every state in this Union a republican form of government, and shall protect each of them against invasion; and on application of the legislature, or of the executive (when the legislature cannot be convened), against domestic violence [riots].

ARTICLE V. AMENDING THE CONSTITUTION

The Congress, whenever two-thirds of both houses shall deem [think] it necessary, shall propose amendments to this Constitution, or, on the application of the legislatures of two-thirds of the several states, shall call a convention for proposing amendments, which, in either case, shall be valid, to all intents and purposes, as part of this Constitution when ratified by the legislatures of three-fourths of the several states, or by conventions in three-fourths thereof, as the one or the other mode [method] of ratification may be proposed by the Congress; provided *that no amendment which may be made prior to the year 1808 shall in any manner affect the first and fourth clauses in the ninth section of the first article; and*[1] that no state, without its consent, shall be deprived of its equal suffrage in the Senate.

ARTICLE VI. MISCELLANEOUS PROVISIONS

Section 1. Public Debts All debts contracted and engagements [agreements] entered into before the adoption of this Constitution shall be as valid [binding] against the United States under this Constitution as under the Confederation.

Section 2. Federal Supremacy This Constitution, and the laws of the United States which shall be made in pursuance thereof, and all treaties made, or which shall be made, under the authority of the United States, shall be the supreme law of the land; and the judges in every state shall be bound thereby, anything in the constitution or laws of any state to the contrary notwithstanding.[2]

Section 3. Oaths of Office The senators and representatives before mentioned, and the members of the several state legislatures, and all executive and judicial officers, both of the United States and of the several states, shall be bound by oath or affirmation to support this Constitution; but no religious test shall ever be required as a qualification to any office or public trust under the United States.

ARTICLE VII. RATIFICATION

The ratification of the conventions of nine states shall be sufficient for the establishment of this Constitution between the states so ratifying the same.

Done in convention, by the unanimous consent of the states present, the 17th day of September, in the year of our Lord 1787, and of the independence of the United States of America the twelfth. In witness whereof we have hereunto subscribed our names.

Signed by George Washington
[President and Deputy
from Virginia]
and 38 other delegates

---

[1] Temporary provision.
[2] This "supremacy clause" means that federal laws always override state legislation in cases of conflict.

Amendments to the Constitution

Note: The first ten amendments to the Constitution, adopted in 1791, make up the Bill of Rights. The year of adoption of later amendments (11 to 27) is given in parenthesis.

AMENDMENT I.

FREEDOM OF RELIGION, SPEECH, PRESS, ASSEMBLY, AND PETITION

Congress shall make no law respecting an establishment of religion, or prohibiting the free exercise thereof;[1] or abridging [reducing] the freedom of speech or of the press; or the right of the people peaceably to assemble, and to petition the government for a redress [correction] of grievances.

AMENDMENT II.

RIGHT TO BEAR ARMS

A well-regulated militia being necessary to the security of a free state, the right of the people to keep and bear arms shall not be infringed [weakened].

AMENDMENT III.

QUARTERING OF TROOPS

No soldier shall, in time of peace, be quartered [assigned to live] in any house without the consent of the owner, nor in time of war, but in a manner to be prescribed by law.

AMENDMENT IV.

SEARCHES AND SEIZURES

The right of the people to be secure [safe] in their persons, houses, papers, and effects [belongings] against unreasonable searches and seizures shall not be violated; and no [search] warrants shall issue but upon probable cause[2] supported by oath or affirmation, and particularly describing the place to be searched, and the persons or things to be seized.

[1] "The free exercise thereof" refers to freedom of worship.
[2] "Probable cause" means *a reasonable ground of suspicion.*

AMENDMENT V.

RIGHTS OF THE ACCUSED; PROPERTY RIGHTS

No person shall be held to answer for a capital or otherwise infamous crime unless on a presentment or indictment of a grand jury,[3] except in cases arising in the land or naval forces, or in the militia, when in actual service in time of war or public danger; nor shall any person be subject for the same offense to be twice put in jeopardy of life or limb;[4] nor shall be compelled in any criminal case to be a witness against himself; nor be deprived of life, liberty, or property without due process of law;[5] nor shall private property be taken for public use without just compensation.[6]

AMENDMENT VI.

OTHER RIGHTS OF THE ACCUSED

In all criminal prosecutions [trials], the accused shall enjoy the right to a speedy and public trial by an impartial [fair] jury of the state and district wherein the crime shall have been committed, which district shall have been previously ascertained by law; and to be informed of the nature and cause of the accusation; to be confronted with the witnesses against him; to have compulsory process for obtaining witnesses in his

[3] "A capital or otherwise infamous crime" refers to serious offenses punishable by death or by imprisonment. Before someone may be tried for such a crime, a grand jury must decide that sufficient evidence exists to bring that person to trial.

[4] A person may not be tried twice for the same offense (double jeopardy).

[5] "Due process of law" means proper legal procedure.

[6] The government has the power of eminent domain, or the right to take private property for public use. This provision requires the government to pay the owner a fair price for such property.

favor[1] and to have the assistance of counsel for his defense.

AMENDMENT VII.
CIVIL SUITS

In suits at common law[2] where the value in controversy shall exceed twenty dollars, the[1] right of trial by jury shall be preserved, and no fact tried by a jury shall be otherwise reexamined in any court of the United States, than according to the rules of the common law.

AMENDMENT VIII.
BAILS, FINES, AND PUNISHMENTS

Excessive bail shall not be required, nor excessive fines imposed, nor cruel and unusual punishments inflicted.

AMENDMENT IX.
RIGHTS NOT LISTED

The enumeration [listing] in the Constitution of certain rights shall not be construed to deny or disparage [weaken] others retained by the people.

AMENDMENT X.
POWERS RESERVED
TO THE STATES AND PEOPLE

The powers not delegated to the United States by the Constitution, nor prohibited by it to the states, are reserved to the states respectively, or to the people.

AMENDMENT XI.
SUITS AGAINST STATES (1798)

The judicial power of the United States shall not be construed to extend to any suit in law or equity, commenced or prosecuted against one of the United States by citizens of another state, or by citizens or subjects of any foreign state.

AMENDMENT XII.
ELECTION OF PRESIDENT
AND VICE PRESIDENT (1804)

[1] The electors shall meet in their respective states, and vote by ballot for president and vice president, one of whom at least shall not be an inhabitant of the same state with themselves; they shall name in their

ballots the person voted for as president, and in distinct [separate] ballots the person voted for as vice president; and they shall make distinct lists of all persons voted for as president, and of all persons voted for as vice president, and of the number of votes for each, which lists they shall sign and certify, and transmit sealed to the seat of the government of the United States, directed to the president of the Senate.

[2] The president of the Senate shall, in the presence of the Senate and House of Representatives, open all the certificates, and the votes shall then be counted; the person having the greatest number of votes for president shall be the president, if such number be a majority of the whole number of electors appointed; and if no person have such majority, then from the persons having the highest numbers not exceeding three on the list of those voted for as president, the House of Representatives shall choose immediately, by ballot, the president. But in choosing the president, the votes shall be taken by states, the representation from each state having one vote; a quorum for this purpose shall consist of a member or members from two-thirds of the states, and a majority of all the states shall be necessary to a choice. And if the House of Representatives shall not choose a president whenever the right of choice shall devolve upon them, *before the fourth day of March next following*,[3] then the vice president shall act as president, as in the case of the death or other constitutional disability of the president.

[3] The person having the greatest number of votes as vice president shall be the vice president, if such number be a majority of the whole number of electors appointed; and if no person have a majority, then, from the two highest numbers on the list, the Senate shall choose the vice president; a quorum for the purpose shall consist of two-thirds of the whole number of senators, and a majority of the whole number shall be necessary to a choice. But no person constitutionally ineligible to the office of president shall be eligible to that of vice president of the United States.

AMENDMENT XIII.
ABOLITION OF SLAVERY (1865)

Section 1. Slavery Forbidden Neither slavery nor involuntary servitude [compulsory service], except as a punishment for crime whereof the party shall have been duly convicted, shall exist within the United States, or any place subject to their jurisdiction.

Section 2. Enforcement Power Congress shall have power to enforce this article [amendment] by appropriate [suitable] legislation.

---

[1] The accused person has the right to request the court to issue an order, or subpoena, compelling a witness to appear in court.

[2] "Common law" is law based on custom and precedent (past decisions made in similar cases). Originating in England, it was brought to the English colonies by the early settlers and became the foundation of the American legal system.

[3] Changed to January 20 by Amendment XX.

AMENDMENT XIV.
CITIZENSHIP AND CIVIL RIGHTS (1868)

Section 1. Rights of Citizens All persons born or naturalized in the United States, and subject to the jurisdiction thereof, are citizens of the United States and of the state wherein they reside.[1] No state shall make or enforce any law which shall abridge the privileges or immunities of citizens of the United States; nor shall any state deprive any person of life, liberty, or property, without due process of law;[2] nor deny to any person within its jurisdiction the equal protection of the laws.[3]

Section 2. Apportionment of Representatives In Congress Representatives shall be apportioned among the several states according to their respective numbers, counting the whole number of persons in each state, excluding Indians not taxed.[4] But when the right to vote at any election for the choice of electors for president and vice president of the. United States, representatives in Congress, the executive and judicial officers of a state, or the members of the legislature thereof, is denied to any of the *male* inhabitants of such state, being *twenty-one* years of age and citizens of the United States, or in any way abridged, except for participation in rebellion or other crime, the basis of representation therein shall be reduced in the proportion which the number of such *male* citizens shall bear to the whole number of male citizens *twenty-one* years of age in such state.[5]

Section 3. Persons Disqualified From Public Office No person shall be a senator or representative in Congress, or elector of president and vice president, or hold any office, civil or military, under the United States, or under any state, who, having previously taken an oath, as a member of Congress, or as an officer of the United States, or as a member of any state legislature, or as an executive or judicial officer of any state, to support the Constitution of the United States, shall have engaged in insurrection or rebellion against the same, or given aid or comfort to the enemies thereof. But Congress may, by a vote of two-thirds of each house, remove such disability.

[1] This clause made the former slaves citizens.

[2] The primary purpose of this clause was to protect the civil rights of the former slaves. However, after the Supreme Court broadened the meaning of the word "person" to include "corporation," the clause began to be used to protect business interests as well.

[3] The "equal protection" clause has served as the legal basis for many civil rights cases.

[4] This clause nullifies the three-fifths formula of Article I, section 2.

[5] Italicized words in this section were invalidated by Amendments XIX and XXVI.

Section 4. Valid Public Debt Defined The validity [legality] of the public debt of the United States, authorized by law, including debts incurred for payment of pensions and bounties [extra allowances] for services in suppressing insurrection or rebellion, shall not be questioned. But neither the United States nor any state shall assume or pay any debt or obligation incurred in aid of insurrection or rebellion against the United States, or any claim for the loss or emancipation [liberation] of any slave; but all such debts, obligations, and claims shall be held illegal and void.

Section 5. Enforcement Power The Congress shall have power to enforce, by appropriate legislation, the provisions of this article.

AMENDMENT XV.
RIGHT OF SUFFRAGE (1870)

Section 1. African Americans Guaranteed the Vote The right of citizens of the United States to vote shall not be denied or abridged by the United States or by any state on account of race, color, or previous condition of servitude [slavery].

Section 2. Enforcement Power The Congress shall have power to enforce this article by appropriate legislation.

AMENDMENT XVI.
INCOME TAXES (1913)

The Congress shall have power to lay and collect taxes on incomes, from whatever source derived, without apportionment among the several states, and without regard to any census or enumeration.

AMENDMENT XVII.
POPULAR ELECTION OF SENATORS (1913)

[1] The Senate of the United States shall be composed of two senators from each state, elected by the people thereof, for six years; and each senator shall have one vote. The electors [voters] in each state shall have the qualifications requisite for electors of the most numerous branch of the state legislatures.[6]

[2] When vacancies happen in the representation of any state in the Senate, the executive authority of such state shall issue writs of election to fill such vacancies: Provided, that the legislature of any state may empower [authorize] the executive thereof to make temporary appointments until the people fill the vacancies by election as the legislature may direct.

[6] This amendment changed the method of electing senators as given in Article I, Section 3.

[3] *This amendment shall not be so construed as to affect the election or term of any senator chosen before it becomes valid as part of the Constitution.*[1]

AMENDMENT XVIII.
PROHIBITION (1919)[2]

Section 1. Intoxicating Liquors Prohibited *After one year from the ratification of this article, the manufacture, sale, or transportation of intoxicating liquors within, the importation thereof into, or the exportation thereof from the United States and all territory subject to the jurisdiction thereof, for beverage purposes, is hereby prohibited.*

Section 2. Enforcement Power *The Congress and the several states shall have concurrent power to enforce this article by appropriate legislation.*

Section 3. Conditions of Ratification *This article shall be inoperative unless it shall have been ratified as an amendment to the Constitution by the legislatures of the several states, as provided in the Constitution, within seven years from the date of the submission hereof to the states by the Congress.*

AMENDMENT XIX.
WOMEN'S SUFFRAGE (1920)

[1] The right of citizens of the United States to vote shall not be denied or abridged by the United States or by any state on account of sex.

[2] Congress shall have power to enforce this article by appropriate legislation.

AMENDMENT XX.
PRESIDENTIAL AND CONGRESSIONAL TERMS[3] (1933)

Section 1. Terms of Office The terms of the president and vice president shall end at noon on the 20th day of January, and the terms of senators and representatives at noon on the 3rd day of January, of the years in which such terms would have ended if this article had not been ratified; and the terms of their successors[4] shall then begin.

Section 2. Convening Congress The Congress shall assemble at least once in every year, and such meet-

ing shall begin at noon on the 3rd day of January, unless they shall by law appoint a different day.[5]

Section 3. Presidential Succession If, at the time fixed for the beginning of the term of the president, the president-elect[6] shall have died, the vice president-elect shall become president. If a president shall not have been chosen before the time fixed for the beginning of his term, or if the president-elect shall have failed to qualify, then the vice president-elect shall act as president until a president shall have qualified; and the Congresss may by law provide for the case wherein neither a president-elect nor a vice president-elect shall have qualified, declaring who shall then act as president, or the manner in which one who is to act shall be selected, and such person shall act accordingly until a president or vice president shall have qualified.

Section 4. Selection of President and Vice President The Congress may by law provide for the case of the death of any of the persons from whom the House of Representatives may choose a president whenever the right of choice shall have devolved upon them, and for the case of the death of any of the persons from whom the Senate may choose a vice president whenever the right of choice shall have devolved upon them.

Section 5. Effective Date *Sections 1 and 2 shall take effect on the 15th day of October following the ratification of this article.*[7]

Section 6. Conditions of Ratification *This article shall be inoperative unless it shall have been ratified as an amendment to the Constitution by the legislatures of three-fourths of the several states within seven years from the date of its submission.*[8]

AMENDMENT XXI.
REPEAL OF PROHIBITION (1933)

Section 1. Amendment XVIII Repealed The Eighteenth Article of amendment to the Constitution of the United States is hereby repealed.

Section 2. Shipment of Liquor Into "Dry" Areas The transportation or importation into any state, territory, or possession of the United States for delivery or use therein of intoxicating liquors in violation of the laws thereof is hereby prohibited.[9]

---

[1] Temporary provision designed to protect those elected under the system previously in effect.

[2] This entire amendment was repealed in 1933 by Amendment XXI.

[3] This amendment is often called the "Lame Duck" Amendment because it shortened the period (from four months to two) between the elections in November and the time when defeated officeholders or officeholders who do not run again (known as "lame ducks") leave office.

[4] A "successor" is a person who is elected or appointed to replace another in a public office.

[5] This section changed the date given in Article I, Section 4.

[6] A "president-elect" is a person who has been elected to the presidency but has not yet assumed office.

[7] Temporary provision.

[8] Temporary provision.

[9] This section allowed individual states to prohibit the use of intoxicating liquors if they wished to.

Section 3. Conditions of Ratification *This article shall be inoperative unless it shall have been ratified as an amendment to the Constitution by conventions in the several states,[1] as provided in the Constitution, within seven years from the date of the submission hereof to the states by the Congress.[2]*

AMENDMENT XXII.
LIMITING PRESIDENTIAL TERMS (1951)

Section 1. Limit Placed on Tenure No person shall be elected to the office of the president more than twice, and no person who has held the office of president, or acted as president, for more than two years of a term to which some other person was elected president shall be elected to the office of the president more than once. *But this article shall not apply to any person holding the office of president when this article was proposed by the Congress, and shall not prevent any person who may be holding the office of president, or acting as president, during the term within which this article becomes operative from holding the office of president or acting as president during the remainder of such term.[3]*

Section 2. Conditions of Ratification *This article shall be inoperative unless it shall have been ratified as an amendment to the Constitution by the legislatures of three-fourths of the several states within seven years from the date of its submission to the states by the Congress.[4]*

AMENDMENT XXIII.
SUFFRAGE FOR WASHINGTON, D.C. (1961)

Section 1. D.C. Presidential Electors The district constituting [making up] the seat of government of the United States shall appoint in such manner as the Congress may direct:

A number of electors of president and vice president equal to the whole number of senators and representatives in Congress to which the district would be entitled if it were a state, but in no event more than the least populous state;[5] they shall be in addition to those appointed by the states, but they shall be considered, for the purposes of the election of president and vice president, to be electors appointed by a state; and they shall meet in the district and perform such duties is provided by the Twelfth Article of amendment.[6]

Section 2. Enforcement Power The Congress shall have power to enforce this article by appropriate legislation.

AMENDMENT XXIV.
POLL TAXES (1964)

Section 1. Poll Tax Barred The right of citizens of the United States to vote in any primary or other election for president or vice president, for electors for president or vice president, or for senator or representative in Congress, shall not be denied or abridged by the United States or any state by reason of failure to pay any poll tax or other tax.

Section 2. Enforcement Power The Congress shall have the power to enforce this article by appropriate legislation.

AMENDMENT XXV.
PRESIDENTIAL SUCCESSION AND DISABILITY (1967)

Section 1. Elevation of Vice President In case of the removal of the president from office or his death or resignation, the vice president shall become president.

Section 2. Vice Presidential Vacancy Whenever there is a vacancy in the office of the vice president, the president shall nominate a vice president who shall take the office upon confirmation by a majority vote of both houses of Congress.

Section 3. Temporary Disability Whenever the president transmits to the president pro tempore of the Senate and the Speaker of the House of Representatives his written declaration that he is unable to discharge the powers and duties of his office, and until he transmits to them a written declaration to the contrary, such powers and duties shall be discharged by the vice president as acting president.

Section 4. Other Provisions for Presidential Disability [1] Whenever the vice president and a majority of either the principal officers of the executive departments, or of such other body as Congress may by law provide, transmit to the president pro tempore of the Senate and the Speaker of the House of Representatives their written declaration that the president is unable to discharge the powers and duties of his office, the vice president shall immediately assume the powers and duties of the office as acting president.

[2] Thereafter, when the president transmits to the president pro tempore of the Senate and the Speaker of the House of Representatives his written declaration that no inability exists, he shall resume

---

[1] This was the first amendment to be submitted by Congress for ratification by state conventions rather than state legislatures.

[2] Temporary provision.

[3] Temporary provision.

[4] Temporary provision.

[5] At the present time, the District of Columbia is entitled to three electors.

[6] By providing for electors, this amendment gave residents of Washington, D.C., the right to vote for president and vice president.

the powers and duties of his office unless the vice president and a majority of either the principal officers of the executive department, or of such other body as Congress may by law provide, transmit within four days to the president pro tempore of the Senate and the Speaker of the House of Representatives their written declaration that the president is unable to discharge the powers and duties of his office. Thereupon, Congress shall decide the issue, assembling within 48 hours for that purpose if not in session. If the Congress, within 21 days after receipt of the latter written declaration, or, if Congress is not in session, within 21 days after Congress is required to assemble, determines by two-thirds vote of both houses that the president is unable to discharge the powers and duties of his office, the vice president shall continue to discharge the same as acting president; otherwise, the president shall resume the powers and duties of his office.

AMENDMENT XXVI.
VOTE FOR 18-YEAR-OLDS (1971)

Section 1. Lowering the Voting Age The right of citizens of the United States, who are 18 years of age or older, to vote shall not be denied or abridged by the United States or by any state on account of age.

Section 2. Enforcement Power The Congress shall have power to enforce this article by appropriate legislation.

AMENDMENT XXVII.
CONGRESSIONAL PAY RAISES (1992)

No law varying the compensation for the services of the Senators and Representatives shall take effect until an election of Representatives shall have intervened.

Index

Acknowledgments

We gratefully acknowledge the permission of the following persons and organizations to reproduce the prints and photographs in this book. Each number refers to the page number where the image appears in this book.

Page